SHAKESPEARE IN PRODUCTION
AS YOU LIKE IT

As You Like It has sometimes seemed a subversive play that exposes the instability of gender roles and traditional values. In other eras it has been prized – or derided – as a reliable celebration of conventional social mores. The play's ability to encompass these extremes tells an interesting story about changing cultural and theatrical practices. This edition provides a detailed history of the play in production, both on stage and on screen. The introduction examines how changing conceptions of gender roles have affected the portrayal of Rosalind, one of Shakespeare's greatest comic heroines. The striking differences between the British tradition and the freer treatment the play has received abroad are discussed, as well as the politics of court versus country. The commentary, printed alongside the New Cambridge edition of the text, draws on primary sources to illuminate how costuming, stage business, design, and directorial choices have shaped the play in performance.

Cynthia Marshall is Professor of English at Rhodes College, Tennessee. She is the author of *The Shattering of the Self: Violence, Subjectivity, and Early Modern Texts* (2002).

SHAKESPEARE IN PRODUCTION

SERIES EDITORS: J. S. BRATTON AND JULIE HANKEY

This series offers students and researchers the fullest possible staging of individual Shakespearean texts. In each volume a substantial introduction presents a conceptual overview of the play, marking out the major stages of its representation and reception. The commentary, presented alongside the New Cambridge Shakespeare edition of the text itself, offers detailed, line-by-line evidence for the overview presented in the introduction, making the volume a flexible tool for further research. The editors have selected interesting and vivid evocations of settings, acting, and stage presentation, and range widely in time and space.

ALREADY PUBLISHED

A Midsummer Night's Dream, edited by Trevor R. Griffiths
Much Ado About Nothing, edited by John F. Cox
Antony and Cleopatra, edited by Richard Madelaine
Hamlet, edited by Robert Hapgood
The Tempest, edited by Christine Dymkowski
King Henry V, edited by Emma Smith
The Merchant of Venice, edited by Charles Edelman
Romeo and Juliet, edited by James N. Loehlin
Macbeth, edited by John Wilders
The Taming of the Shrew, edited by Elizabeth Schafer

FORTHCOMING VOLUMES

Troilus and Cressida, edited by Frances Shirley
Twelfth Night, edited by Elizabeth Schafer

AS YOU LIKE IT

EDITED BY
CYNTHIA MARSHALL

CAMBRIDGE
UNIVERSITY PRESS

PUBLISHED BY THE PRESS SYNDICATE OF THE UNIVERSITY OF CAMBRIDGE
The Pitt Building, Trumpington Street, Cambridge, United Kingdom

CAMBRIDGE UNIVERSITY PRESS
The Edinburgh Building, Cambridge, CB2 2RU, UK
40 West 20th Street, New York, NY 10011–4211, USA
477 Williamstown Road, Port Melbourne, VIC 3207, Australia
Ruiz de Alarcón 13, 28014 Madrid, Spain
Dock House, The Waterfront, Cape Town 8001, South Africa

http://www.cambridge.org

First published 2004

Printed in the United Kingdom at the University Press, Cambridge

Typefaces EhrhardtMT 10/12.5 pt. and FormataCond   *System* LaTeX 2ε [TB]

A catalogue record for this book is available from the British Library

Library of Congress Cataloguing in Publication data
Shakespeare, William, 1564–1616.
As You Like It / edited by Cynthia Marshall.
p. cm. – (Shakespeare in Production)
Includes bibliographical references and index.
ISBN 0 521 78137 X – ISBN 0 521 78649 5 (pb.)
1. Shakespeare, William, 1564–1616. As You Like It. 2. Shakespeare, William, 1564–1616 –
Stage history. 3. Fathers and daughters – Drama. 4. Exiles – Drama. 5. Comedy.
I. Marshall, Cynthia. II. Title.
PR2803.A2M37 2004
822.3'3 – dc22   2003055387

ISBN 0 521 78137 X (hardback)
ISBN 0 521 78649 5 (paperback)

CONTENTS

ILLUSTRATIONS

SERIES EDITORS' PREFACE

It is no longer necessary to stress that the text of a play is only its starting-point, and that only in production is its potential realised and capable of being appreciated fully. Since the coming-of-age of Theatre Studies as an academic discipline, we now understand that even Shakespeare is only one collaborator in the creation and infinite recreation of his play upon the stage. And just as we now agree that no play is complete until it is produced, so we have become interested in the way in which plays often produced – and pre-eminently the plays of the national Bard, William Shakespeare – acquire a life history of their own, after they leave the hands of their first maker.

Since the eighteenth century Shakespeare has become a cultural construct: sometimes the guarantor of nationhood, heritage, and the status quo, sometimes seized and transformed to be its critic and antidote. This latter role has been particularly evident in countries where Shakespeare has to be translated. The irony is that while his status as national icon grows in the English-speaking world, his language is both lost and renewed, so that for good or ill, Shakespeare can be made to seem more urgently 'relevant' than in England or America, and may become the one dissenting voice that the censors mistake as harmless.

'Shakespeare in Production' gives the reader, the student and the scholar a comprehensive dossier of materials – eye-witness accounts, contemporary criticism, promptbook marginalia, stage business, cuts, additions, and rewritings – from which to construct an understanding of the many meanings that the plays have carried down the ages and across the world. These materials are organised alongside the New Cambridge Shakespeare text of the play, line by line and scene by scene, while a substantial introduction in each volume offers a guide to their interpretation. One may trace an argument about, for example, the many ways of playing Queen Gertrude, or the political transmutations of the text of *Henry V*; or take a scene, an act, or a whole play, and work out how it has succeeded or failed in presentation over four hundred years.

For, despite our insistence that the plays are endlessly made and remade by history, Shakespeare is not a blank, scribbled upon by the age. Theatre history charts changes, but also registers something in spite of those changes. Some productions work and others do not. Two interpretations may be entirely different, and yet both will bring the play to life. Why? Without setting out to give absolute answers, the history of a play in the theatre can often show where the energy and shape of it lie, what has made it tick, through many permutations. In this way theatre history can find common ground with literary criticism. Both will find suggestive directions in the introductions to these volumes, while the commentaries provide raw material for readers to recreate the living experience of theatre, and become their own eye-witness.

J. S. Bratton
Julie Hankey

ACKNOWLEDGEMENTS

Preparing a book of this sort makes one keenly aware of the difficulty of capturing in words the ephemera of theatrical performance. Piecing together records such as cast lists, promptbooks, memoirs, photographs, and, where available, videotapes, one becomes especially grateful to those reviewers and commentators who succeed in making performance live for those beyond the immediate audience.

In the course of writing this book I have accrued many debts. My work was supported by a short-term fellowship from the Folger Shakespeare Library and by funds from the Connie Abston Chair of Literature at Rhodes College. Rhodes College also provided funds enabling the appearance of some of the illustrations; I am especially grateful to Brian Shaffer for his support of the project. The resourceful staff of the Folger Shakespeare Library provided a great deal of help; special thanks to Georgianna Ziegler. I am grateful as well to the staff of the Shakespeare Centre Library, especially Sylvia Morris; the Theatre Museum; the National Theatre Archive; the University of Bristol Theatre Collection; the British Library; and the Library of Congress. It was a privilege to build on Michael Hattaway's excellent New Cambridge text of the play. I would like to thank Andrew Gurr for sending me materials related to the production at Shakespeare's Globe and Mairi Macdonald for tracking down an important bit of information. I very much appreciate the fine work of Jessica Hoback, who served as my research assistant in 2001–2. John Ford, Shira Malkin, and Robert Meyer-Lee provided helpful information. Anna Traverse read the manuscript with an eagle's eye. John Traverse's intelligent commentary improved the book's arguments as well as my prose. I am grateful to the series editors, Jacky Bratton and Julie Hankey, for their extensive guidance, and to Sarah Stanton for her patience and efficiency.

ABBREVIATIONS

Arthur pbk	Julia Arthur, promptbook, 1898–9, Folger Shakespeare Library (Shattuck, *AYLI*, 72)
Asche pbk	Oscar Asche, promptbook, 1907, Shakespeare Centre Library (Shattuck, *AYLI*, 86)
ASF	American Shakespeare Festival
AYLI	*As You Like It*
Bell's edn	*As You Like It: a comedy, by Shakespeare, as performed at the Theatre Royal, Drury-Lane*, London: John Bell, 1774
Benson 1904 pbk	Frank Benson, promptbook, c. 1904, Shakespeare Centre Library (Shattuck, *AYLI*, 76)
Benson 1905 pbk	Frank Benson, promptbook, c. 1905, Shakespeare Centre Library (Shattuck, *AYLI*, 77)
Bridges–Adams pbk	W. Bridges–Adams, promptbook, 1933, Shakespeare Centre Library (Shattuck, *AYLI*, 97)
Daly pbk	Augustin Daly, promptbook, 1889, Folger Shakespeare Library (Daly's souvenir album) (Shattuck, *AYLI*, 60)
Dexter pbk	John Dexter, promptbook, 1979, National Theatre Archive (not in Shattuck)
edn(s)	edition(s)
Elliott pbk	Michael Elliott, promptbook, 1962, Shakespeare Centre Library (Shattuck, *AYLI*, 109)
Faucit pbk	Helena Faucit, rehearsal copy, 1839, Folger Shakespeare Library (Shattuck, *AYLI*, 15)
FRG	Federal Republic of Germany
FSL	Folger Shakespeare Library
GDR	German Democratic Republic
Goodbody pbk	Buzz Goodbody, promptbook, 1973, Shakespeare Centre Library (not in Shattuck)
Helpmann pbk	Robert Helpmann, promptbook, 1955, University of Bristol Theatre Collection (Shattuck, *AYLI*, 104)

Holloway pbk	Baliol Holloway, promptbook, 1942, Shakespeare Centre Library (Shattuck, *AYLI*, 99)
Jones pbk	David Jones, promptbook, 1968, Shakespeare Centre Library (not in Shattuck)
Kean pbk	Charles Kean, promptbook, 1851, Folger Shakespeare Library (Shattuck, *AYLI*, 31)
Kemble edn	*As You Like It: a comedy, revised by J. P. Kemble; and now first published as it is acted at The Theatre Royal in Covent Garden*, London, 1810
Kemble Promptbooks	*John Philip Kemble Promptbooks*, ed. Charles Shattuck, Charlottesville: University Press of Virginia for the Folger Shakespeare Library, 1974
Kemble partbook	John Philip Kemble, partbook,1799, 1805, Folger Shakespeare Library (Shattuck, *AYLI*, 8)
Macklin partbook	Charles Macklin, partbook, 1741, Folger Shakespeare Library (Shattuck, *AYLI*, 2)
Macready pbk	William Charles Macready, promptbook, 1842, Folger Shakespeare Library (Shattuck, *AYLI*, 18)
Modjeska pbk	Helena Modjeska, promptbook, 1882, Folger Shakespeare Library (Shattuck, *AYLI*, 54)
Moore pbk	John Moore, record of productions, 1855–76, Folger Shakespeare Library (Shattuck, *AYLI*, 37)
NY	New York
NYSF	New York Shakespeare Festival
Oxberry edn	Oxberry, W., ed., *As You Like It. A Comedy; by W. Shakspeare*, London, 1819.
Payne pbk	Ben Iden Payne, promptbook, 1935, Shakespeare Centre Library (Shattuck, *AYLI*, 98)
pbk(s)	promptbook(s)
Phelps pbk	Samuel Phelps, promptbook, 1847, Folger Shakespeare Library (Shattuck, *AYLI*, 26)
RSC	Royal Shakespeare Company
RST	Royal Shakespeare Theatre
SCL	Shakespeare Centre Library
sd	stage direction
1786 edn	*As You Like It: a comedy, by William Shakespeare, marked with the variations in the manager's book, at the Theatre-Royal in Covent-Garden*, London, 1786

Shattuck, *Macready*	Facsimile copy of William Charles Macready, promptbook (Shattuck, *AYLI*, 22), in Charles Shattuck, *Mr Macready Produces 'As You Like It,'* Urbana, IL: Beta Phi Mu, 1962.
Shaw pbk	Glen Byam Shaw, promptbook, 1952, Shakespeare Centre Library (Shattuck, *AYLI*, 102)
SMT	Shakespeare Memorial Theatre
Sothern–Marlowe pbk	E. H. Sothern and Julia Marlowe, promptbook, 1907, Folger Shakespeare Library (Shattuck, *AYLI*, 83)
SS	*Shakespeare Survey*
SQ	*Shakespeare Quarterly*
TM	Theatre Museum, London
Toye pbk	Wendy Toye, promptbook, 1959, University of Bristol Theatre Collection (Shattuck, *AYLI*, 107)
Williams pbk	Clifford Williams, promptbook, 1967, National Theatre Archive (not in Shattuck)

PRODUCTIONS

Location is London unless noted otherwise. Roles noted are Rosalind (R), Celia (C), Orlando (O), Jaques (J), Touchstone (T), Oliver (Ol), Phoebe (Ph), Duke Senior (S), Duke Frederick (F), Audrey (A), Amiens (Am), Charles (Ch).

Date(s)	Director/Producer/ Manager	Principal actors	Venue(s)
1600			Globe?
1603			Wilton House?
Jan. 1723	Charles Johnson (*Love in a Forest*)	Colley Cibber (J)	Drury Lane
20 Dec. 1740 (1740–53)	Charles Fleetwood	Hannah Pritchard (R) Kitty Clive (C) James Quin (J) Thomas Chapman (T)	Drury Lane, Covent Garden
15 Oct. 1741 (1741–57)	Charles Fleetwood	Peg Woffington (R) Theophilus Cibber (J) Charles Macklin (T)	Drury Lane, Covent Garden
19 Apr. 1742		Mr Page (R)	James Street
30 Apr. 1785	Richard Sheridan	Sarah Siddons (R)	Drury Lane
14 July 1786		Mrs Kenna (R)	John Street, NY
13 Apr. 1787 (1787–1805, 1813, 1814)	Richard Sheridan	Dorothy Jordan (R) John Philip Kemble (O)	Drury Lane, Covent Garden
14 Dec. 1796		Elizabeth Johnson (R) Lewis Hallam (T)	Argus Theatre NY
25 Oct. 1805	John Philip Kemble	John Philip Kemble (J) Charles Kemble (O) Miss Smith (R)	Covent Garden
1810		Mrs H. Johnson (R)	
10 Dec. 1824	Frederic Reynolds	Maria Tree (R)	Covent Garden

Date(s)	Director/Producer/ Manager	Principal actors	Venue(s)
1825		Mme Vestris (R)	Haymarket
Dec. 1827		Louisa Nisbett (R)	Stratford
2 Nov. 1833		Ellen Tree (R)	Drury Lane
12 Dec. 1836		Ellen Tree (R)	Park Theatre, NY
18 Mar. 1839	William Charles Macready	Helena Faucit (R)	Covent Garden
1 Oct. 1842	William Charles Macready	Louisa Nisbett (R)	Drury Lane
(1820–75)		William Charles Macready (J)	
		Robert Keeley (T)	
1847–60	Samuel Phelps	Samuel Phelps (J)	Sadler's Wells
		Hermann Vezin (O)	
		Mrs Charles Young (R)	
Feb. 1845		Charlotte Cushman (R)	Princess's
1849–57			NY
1850–1	Charles Kean	Charles Kean (J)	Princess's
		Ellen Tree (R)	
1855	Sille Beyer (trans.) (*Life in the Forest*)		Norwegian Theatre, Bergen
1855		Barry Sullivan (J)	Haymarket
		Helena Faucit (R)	
1856	George Sand (trans.) (*Comme il vous plaira*)		Comédie-Française, Paris
8 Apr. 1867	John Buckstone	Mary Scott-Siddons (R)	Haymarket
1868			NY
2 May 1871		Rose Evans (R)	Niblo's, NY
		E. L. Davenport (J)	
		James Mace (Ch)	
Summer 1874			Meininger Theatre Berlin
2 Dec. 1872		Adelaide Neilson (R)	Booth's, NY
1 Feb. 1876	John Buckstone		Haymarket
18 Nov. 1876	Augustin Daly	Fanny Davenport (R)	Fifth Avenue, NY
		Charles Coghlan (O)	
		Charles Fisher (J)	

Date(s)	Director/Producer/ Manager	Principal actors	Venue(s)
30 Apr. 1879	Barry Sullivan	Barry Sullivan (J)	Stratford
Mar. 1880	Miss Litton	Miss Litton (R)	Imperial
		Hermann Vezin (J)	
		Lionel Brough (T)	
30 Sept. 1880	Lester Wallack	Rose Coghlan (R)	Wallack's, NY
		Osmond Tearle (J)	
		William Elton (T)	
23 Sept. 1882		Lillie Langtry (R)	Imperial
13 Nov. 1882			Wallack's, NY
1890–1			London
1882–95		Helena Modjeska (R)	NY, then
		Maurice Barrymore (O)	touring
1 Nov. 1882		Mary Anderson (R)	Park Theatre, NY
		Maurice Barrymore (O)	
29 Apr. 1885	Henry Abbey	Mary Anderson (R)	Stratford
		Johnston Forbes-Robertson (O)	
24 Jan. 1885	John Hare, W. H. Kendal	John Hare (T)	St James's
		W. H. Kendal (O)	
		Mrs Kendal (R)	
		Hermann Vezin (J)	
1884, 1885	E. W. Godwin	Lady Archibald Campbell (O)	Coombe House, Kingston-upon-
		Eleanor Calhoun (R)	Thames
		Hermann Vezin (J)	
17 Dec. 1889	Augustin Daly	Ada Rehan (R)	Daly's, NY
1890		John Drew (O)	Lyceum
		Henrietta Crosman (C)	
		James Lewis (T)	
1897			Stratford, open-air
21 Nov. 1893		all-female cast	Palmer's, NY
1894		all-female cast and orchestra	Prince of Wales's
24 Apr. 1895		Ben Greet (T)	Stratford
1912		Stanley Drewitt (O)	Delafield Estate, Riverdale-on-Hudson

Date(s)	Director/Producer/ Manager	Principal actors	Venue(s)
27 Jan. 1889 (1889–1910)		Julia Marlowe (R) Eben Plympton (O) later, E. H. Sothern (J)	Fifth Avenue, NY
2 Dec. 1896	George Alexander	Julia Neilson (R) George Alexander (O)	St James's
28 Nov. 1898		Julia Arthur (R) John Malone (J)	Wallack's, NY
June 1901	Ben Greet	Edith Wynne Matthison (R)	Royal Botanic Gardens, Regent's Park
27 Feb. 1901		Henrietta Crosman (R)	Republic, NY
1894–1915	Frank Benson	Constance Benson (R) Frank Benson (O) Henry Ainley (O) G. R. Weir (T)	SMT, Stratford
7 Oct. 1907	Oscar Asche	Oscar Asche (J) Lily Brayton (R) Henry Ainley (O)	His Majesty's
1909–10			Australian tour
1908	Kalem Co. Kenean Buel		film, b/w, silent
1912	Vitagraph Charles Kent	Rose Coghlan (R) Maurice Costello (O)	film, b/w, silent
1916	London Film Co. (*Love in a Wood*)	Elizabeth Risdon (R)	film, b/w, silent
22 Apr. 1919	Nigel Playfair	Athene Seyler (R)	Stratford
24 Apr. 1920		Nigel Playfair (T) Ivan Samson (O) Herbert Marshall (J)	Lyric, Hammersmith
1920	Ben Greet	all-male cast	Central YMCA, London
21 July 1920	W. Bridges–Adams		Stratford
19 Apr. 1933	W. Bridges–Adams	Fabia Drake (R) John Wyse (O)	Stratford
1921	Nugent Monck		Maddermarket, Norwich

Date(s)	Director/Producer/ Manager	Principal actors	Venue(s)
1 Mar. 1926	Andrew Leigh	Edith Evans (R)	Old Vic
		Baliol Holloway (J)	
		Frank Vosper (O)	
		Duncan Yarrow (T)	
10 Feb. 1930	Harcourt Williams	John Gielgud (O)	Old Vic
		Martita Hunt (R)	
		Donald Wolfit (T)	
		Baliol Holloway (J)	
31 Oct. 1932	Harcourt Williams	Peggy Ashcroft (R)	Old Vic
		Alistair Sim (S)	
		William Fox (O)	
		Anthony Quayle (Ol)	
1934	Jacques Copeau	Jacques Copeau (J)	Théâtre de l'Atelier,
		Madeleine Lambert (R)	Paris
1938			Boboli Gardens,
			Florence
17 Apr. 1935	Ben Iden Payne		SMT, Stratford
1936	Inter-Allied	Laurence Olivier (O)	film, b/w
	Paul Czinner	Elisabeth Bergner (R)	
		Leon Quartermaine (J)	
1937	Sheppard Strudwick		Ritz, NY
5 Feb. 1937	BBC	Margaretta Scott (R)	TV, b/w
	Robert Atkins	Ion Swinley (O)	
10 Nov. 1937	Esmé Church	Edith Evans (R)	Old Vic
		Michael Redgrave (O)	
1936–7	Jirí Frejka		Prague
	Frontisek Tröster		
	(design)		
4 Apr. 1939	Baliol Holloway		SMT, Stratford
13 Apr. 1944	Robert Atkins		SMT, Stratford
1946	Robert Atkins		Regent's Park
14 July 1946	BBC		TV, b/w
	Robert Atkins (prod.)		
	Ian Atkins (dir.)		
26 Nov. 1948	Luchino Visconti (dir.)	Rina Morelli (R)	Teatro Eliseo,
	Salvador Dali (design)	Ruggero Ruggeri (J)	Rome
	(*Rosalinda, o Come vi piace*)	Paolo Stoppa (T)	

Date(s)	Director/Producer/ Manager	Principal actors	Venue(s)
26 Jan. 1950	Michael Benthall	Katharine Hepburn (R)	Cort Theatre, NY
		Ernest Thesiger (J)	
		Bill Owen (T)	
		Cloris Leachman (C)	
29 Apr. 1952	Glen Byam Shaw	Margaret Leighton (R)	SMT, Stratford
		Michael Hordern (J)	
		Michael Bates (T)	
15 Mar. 1953	BBC	Margaret Leighton (R)	TV, b/w
	Campbell Logan (prod.)	Laurence Harvey (O)	
	Peter Ebert (dir.)		
1954	Hans Schalla	Rosel Schäfer (R)	Schauspielhaus
		Hans Messmer (T)	Bochum, FRG
1955	Neville Coghill		Worcester College
			garden, Oxford
1955	Robert Helpmann	Virginia McKenna (R)	Old Vic
		John Neville (O)	
1956	Robert Atkins	Belinda Lee (R)	Regent's Park
2 Apr. 1957	Glen Byam Shaw	Peggy Ashcroft (R)	SMT, Stratford
		Richard Johnson (O)	
1958	Leslie French	Leslie French (T)	Regent's Park
1958	Stuart Vaughan	George C. Scott (J)	NYSF,
		Nancy Wickwire (R)	Heckscher Theatre
1958	Otto Falckenberg		Gelsenkirchen, FRG
1959	Peter Wood	Irene Worth (R)	Stratford, Ontario
3 Sept. 1959	Wendy Toye	Barbara Jefford (R)	Old Vic
		Alec McCowan (T)	
		Maggie Smith (C)	
		Judi Dench (Ph)	
1961	Word Baker	Kim Hunter (R)	ASF
			Stratford, CT
1961	Liviu Ciulei		Teatrul Bulandra,
			Bucharest
4 July 1961	Michael Elliott	Vanessa Redgrave (R)	RST, Stratford
1962			Aldwych
22 Mar. 1963	RSC/BBC	Vanessa Redgrave (R)	TV, b/w
	Richard Eyre (prod.)	David Buck (O)	
	Michael Elliott (dir.)		

Date(s)	Director/Producer/ Manager	Principal actors	Venue(s)
11 July 1963	Gerald Freedman (dir.)	Paula Prentiss (R) Frank Schofield (J)	NYSF, Delacorte Theatre
3 Oct. 1967	Clifford Williams	Ronald Pickup (R) Jeremy Brett (O) Derek Jacobi (T) Anthony Hopkins (A)	National Theatre / Old Vic
15 June 1967 1968	David Jones	Dorothy Tutin (R), then Janet Suzman (R) Roy Kinnear (T), then Patrick Stewart (T) Alan Howard (J)	RST, Aldwych
6 June 1972	William Hutt	Carole Shelley (R) William Needles (F)	Stratford, Ontario
12 June 1973	Buzz Goodbody	Eileen Atkins (R) Maureen Lipman (C) Richard Pasco (J)	RST, Stratford
1973	Joseph Papp	Kathleen Widdoes (R) Raul Julia (O) Frederick Coffin (J) Meat Loaf (Am)	NYSF, Delacorte Theater
27 May 1976	Petrica Ionescu		Bochum, FRG
20 Sept. 1977	Peter Stein (*Wie es euch gefällt*)	Jutta Lampe (R) Peter Fitz (J)	Berlin-Spandau, FRG
6 Sept. 1977	Trevor Nunn	Kate Nelligan (R) Peter McEnery (O)	RST, Stratford
17 Dec. 1978 (UK), 28 Feb. 1979 (US)	BBC/Time–Life TV Cedric Messina (prod.) Basil Coleman (dir.)	Helen Mirren (R) Brian Stirner (O) Richard Pasco (J)	TV, col.
19 July 1978	Peter James	Tikki Dayan (R)	Hayarkon Park, Tel Aviv
18 Aug. 1978	Robin Phillips	Maggie Smith (R) Brian Bedford (J)	Stratford, Ontario
1 Aug. 1979	John Dexter	Sara Kestelman (R) Simon Callow (O)	National Theatre
3 Apr. 1980	Terry Hands	Susan Fleetwoord (R)	RST, Stratford

Date(s)	Director/Producer/ Manager	Principal actors	Venue(s)
		Sinead Cusack (C)	
		Derek Godfrey (J)	
		John Bowe (O)	
1 Oct. 1980	Toshikiyo Masumi	Daishi Horikoshi (R)	Sunshine Gekijo,
		Kei Yamamoto (C)	Tokyo
24 Feb. 1982	Liviu Ciulei	Patti LuPone (R)	Guthrie,
		Roy Brocksmith (T)	Minneapolis
		David Warrilow (J)	
7 June 1983	John Hirsch	Roberta Maxwell (R)	Stratford, Ontario
		Andrew Gillies (O)	
		Nicholas Pennell (J)	
21 July 1983	John Bell and Anna Volska	Anna Volska (R)	Nimrod Theatre, Sydney
26 Aug. 1983	Kjetil Bang-Hansen	Lise Fjeldstad (R)	Bergen National
		Lothar Lindtner (T)	Theatre
		Per Sunderland (J)	
10 Nov. 1983	Lluis Pasqual (*Al vostre gust*)		Teatre Lliure, Barcelona
Jan. 1985	Nicholas Hytner	Janet McTeer (R)	Royal Exchange,
		Richard McCabe (T)	Manchester
23 Apr. 1985	Adrian Noble	Juliet Stevenson (R)	RST, Stratford
		Fiona Shaw (C)	
		Alan Rickman (J)	
1986	Estelle Parsons (dir.)		NYSF, Anspacher Theatre
1986	Peter Zadek		Hamburg
1988	Geraldine McEwan	Kenneth Branagh (T)	Renaissance Theatre Co., Phoenix Theatre
13 Sept. 1989	John Caird	Hugh Ross (J)	RST, Stratford
1990	Richard Monette	David Williams (J)	Stratford, Ontario
1990–1	ACTER (A Centre for Theatre, Education, and Research)	Clive Arrindell (O) Jane Arden (C) John Kane (T) Clifford Rose (J) Celia Bannerman (R)	touring

Date(s)	Director/Producer/ Manager	Principal actors	Venue(s)
2 Dec. 1991	Declan Donnellan Cheek by Jowl	Adrian Lester (R) Tom Hollander, then Simon Coates (C)	Lyric Hammersmith
23 Jan. 1995			Albery
1992	Christine Edzard	Emma Croft (R) Andrew Tiernan (O/Ol) James Fox (J) Griff Rhys Jones (T)	Sands Films
26 May 1992	Michael Kahn	Sabina Le Beauf (R) Mark Philpot (O)	Shakespeare Free For All, Washington DC
25 Apr. 1996	Steven Pimlott	Niamh Cusack (R) David Tennant (T)	RST, Stratford
May 1998	Lucy Bailey	Anastasia Hille (R) Paul Hilton (O)	Shakespeare's Globe
2000	Michael Grandage	Victoria Hamilton (R)	Sheffield Theatres
2000	Marianne Elliott	Claire Price (R) Peter Nicholas (J)	Royal Exchange, Manchester
23 Mar. 2000	Gregory Doran	Alexandra Gilbreath (R)	RST, Stratford

INTRODUCTION

'Of this play the fable is wild and pleasing', wrote Samuel Johnson of *As You Like It*.[1] The play in performance has sometimes veered towards the 'wild' side, appearing a dangerously subversive work that exposes the instability of traditional values. At other moments it has been simply 'pleasing', a stalwart demonstration of conventional social mores; this aspect prompted George Bernard Shaw to accuse Shakespeare of 'exploit[ing] the fondness of the British Public for sham moralizing and stage "philosophy".'[2] The play's ability to encompass these extremes tells an interesting story about changing cultural and theatrical practices. Tracing the history of *As You Like It* in the theatre and on film shows the extent to which a playscript is an evolving document that can be radically shaped in performance. Directors, actors, and venues are obviously central to this shaping process, and the current incarnation of *As You Like It* bears the imprint of various theatrical figures and general alterations in styles and playing places. Perhaps even more significant in following how the play has been evoked is a consideration of the wide and shifting context of social codes, gender norms, and attitudes towards the arts, especially theatre. The production history of *As You Like It* affords us a focused view of major social, political, and aesthetic changes over the past four centuries.

At the same time, the performance history of *As You Like It* testifies to the particular artistic poise of this comedy, written in 1600 when Shakespeare was at the height of his powers. A mode of refreshment and regeneration, Shakespearean comedy does not merely entertain by providing diversion, but seeks to accommodate viewers to the world in which they live. Towards this end, *As You Like It* addresses and seeks to manage a number of tensions of social life, and achieves success through its 'power to express conflict and order it in art'.[3] Its formal balance does not eradicate the importance of the play's historical context, however. Because *As You Like It* seeks to order specifically *social* ills, it draws on and develops changing conceptions of how people relate to one another, individually and in groups. In other words, the interrelation of diachronic (the chronological history of the play

---

1 Samuel Johnson, p. 264.
2 George Bernard Shaw, vol. 2, p. 267.   3 Barber, p. 238.

in performance) and synchronic (the form and attributes of the playscript) forces has produced the meaningful history of *As You Like It* on stage and screen.

Peculiarities of the play as a performance piece

As You Like It is not a heavily plotted play; indeed, its 'plot barely exists',[4] and most significant action occurs in the first act, with the subsequent four acts constructed primarily of encounters between paired characters.[5] Formally, the play balances court against country, underlining this structural comparison through the oscillation of settings in Acts 2 and 3. Within individual scenes, on stage spectators repeatedly add a layer of commentary to the observed action, mitigating the dominance of any particular perspective.

Prose heavily outweighs verse in this extremely conversational play, and one result is an emphasis on character rather than poetic structure. Although Jaques was a favourite part during the late eighteenth and early nineteenth centuries, Rosalind's character has usually dominated the play's stage history. Her romp in the Forest of Arden disguised as Ganymede is the play's best-known feature, and the cross-gendered disguise raises questions of dramatic style and intention. Since it is generally agreed that Rosalind's turn as Ganymede cannot be presented altogether realistically, the play does not enable or easily allow a mimetic style of performance. *As You Like It* offers a particularly striking example of a playscript that foregrounds its own fictional status, repeatedly undermining any sense of dramatic mimesis.

All of Shakespeare's comedies in which female characters don male disguise participate in the exploration of gender, but only in *As You Like It* does the girl masquerading as a youth take the further step of pretending to be a girl. This third level of performativity (actor as Rosalind as Ganymede as 'Rosalind') complicates the relationship between the actor's body and the presented character. As a result, not only do the particular signs of masculinity and femininity come into play, but the very nature of gender may be scrutinised.

In the eighteenth and nineteenth centuries, a further dimension of metatheatricality existed in relation to Rosalind, created in part by conventions of staging (the absence of dramatic mimesis) and in part by the theatrical culture. Much as spectators today go to the cinema to watch the latest vehicle of their favourite star, these earlier audiences went to the

4 Barton, p. 162.   5 Jenkins, pp. 41–2.

theatre to see Dora Jordan, or Helena Faucit, or Ada Rehan. The character portrayed – in this case, Rosalind – was largely the occasion for the famed actress's appearance. An observer of Dora Jordan wrote in 1791:

> there is more in her person and natural manners than in her acting. Her merit lies out of her part. The words set down by the author she does not repeat with greater propriety of tone, emphasis, or gesture, than others. But she has of these, certain peculiarities . . . such as take strong hold of the affections, at least of the male part of her audience.[6]

A century later, a critic made a similar comment about the crowd gathered at Stratford to see Mary Anderson as Rosalind:

> There was one question that preoccupied all minds: How would the prudish Mary manage with her legs? It was the prospect of seeing the new Rosalind's nether limbs that was responsible for the excited rush for seats on the part of the public. (*Bat*, 1 Sept. 1885)

When Shaw reported finding Ada Rehan 'irresistible', even though he was 'bound to insist that [she] has as yet created nothing but Ada Rehan', he was, in a sense, repeating an old line about the part.[7] Actresses created personae for themselves, so that the final link in the circuit whereby viewers watched the actor-as-Rosalind-as-Ganymede-as-Rosalind was invariably -as Dora Jordan, or -as Ada Rehan.

Within the play's fiction, connections between bodies, gender, and erotic desire are also explored. Among the questions raised by Rosalind's run as Ganymede is that of her lover Orlando's desire: whether he is attracted to the youth Ganymede, the girl Rosalind beneath the disguise, or both, is something every performance must decide. On the surface, Shakespeare has created in the courtship scenes of 3.3 and 4.1 the spectacle of two males flirting rather heavily with one another. In early modern theatres, the male–male surface attraction of Orlando and Ganymede corresponded to the male–male performance by two boy actors. The likelihood that viewers are meant to notice this homoerotic element in the play is increased by the inclusion of Phoebe's sudden attraction to Ganymede. For if Phoebe is judged to have fallen for the 'boy' Ganymede, it becomes much more difficult to suppose Orlando to have responded to the 'girl' beneath Ganymede's disguise. *As You Like It* thus acknowledges the mercurial nature of sexuality. Some productions have found this acknowledgment sophisticated and liberating, while others have sought to hide it behind a façade of conventional norms.

---

6 *Windham Diary*, 28 May 1791, p. 227, quoted in *London Stage*, pt 5, pp. 1357–8.
7 George Bernard Shaw, vol. 3, p. 210.

For modern readers, gender may be the most obvious of the play's inquiries into the status of 'reality', but it is by no means the only one. The cultural construction of violence is another of its preoccupations. The staged wrestling match of 1.2 and Duke Frederick's apparent cruelty to Oliver in 3.1 reverberate in Arden through Jaques's concern about hunting. Likewise, Jaques's melancholy may be presented as a pose or as a deep-seated emotional tendency; interpretive decisions on this point involve the issue of 'natural' emotion versus learned styles of affective behaviour and display. In the eighteenth and nineteenth centuries, Jaques's part was customarily shorn of its satiric edge, producing a benign, jaded, and sometimes pompous character. Hermann Vezin's Jaques prompted a reviewer to ask: 'Is Jacques a profound philosopher, as stage usage represents him, or is he, as the duke describes him, a libertine, who, satiated with excess of the world's enjoyments, has taken to decry and contemn them, and parades as stoicism what is but Epicureanism out-wearied?' (*Theatre*, 1 Apr. 1880). The extent to which Jaques functions as a counterpart to Touchstone also requires consideration.

The Forest of Arden itself challenges easy boundaries between reality and fantasy. In the broadest sense Arden is a version of pastoral simply by virtue of its rural setting.[8] The presence of contemplative and lovelorn shepherds and the featured debate on the relative merits of country and court life both indicate that Shakespeare is using pastoral in its more precisely literary form. Yet he works some complex changes on the tradition: rather than evoking on stage the idealised descriptions of classical pastoral, *As You Like It* offers down-to-earth country figures and treats them as if they were ideal. In the process, Shakespeare mocks the literary ideal as well as the rural folk. Through this process the pastoral convention is itself exposed as hollow, contributing to the play's multifaceted inquiry into the nature of reality. Corin's explanation of the economic realities of rural life – he does not own his sheepcote and cannot afford to buy it from the absentee landlord who has put it up for sale (2.4.73–82) – is scarcely Arcadian, and his plodding resistance to Touchstone's witty relativism in their debate on country and court manners threatens to undo the rhetorical form. Shakespeare is alert to class issues – exposing, for instance, the contrast between the jester–clown Touchstone and the rustic–clown William in 5.1 – whereas traditional pastoral would level or ignore such social distinctions. As Empson defined it, pastoral consists of making 'simple people express strong feelings (felt as the most universal subject, something fundamentally true about everybody) in learned and fashionable language'.[9] If *As You Like It* expresses supposedly universal truths, it also raises doubts about them.

8 Gifford, p. 2.   9 Empson, p. 11.

Furthermore, a play so concerned with property ownership has an inherently political edge, blunted through much of the English stage history by sentimental evocations of native scenery but often a factor in foreign productions. Over the years, productions of *As You Like It* have served as a kind of cultural barometer, indicating changing constructions of gender, romance, and social order.

Seventeenth century

There is a disappointing dearth of reliable records for the play's performance before 1740. A few indications about performance practice are embedded in the script: the absence of scenery, necessitating verbal establishment of place ('Well, this is the Forest of Arden' (2.4.11)), the easy delight in gender play produced by the dizzying layering of personae as the boy actor plays Rosalind-playing-Ganymede-playing-Rosalind, the ability of the theatrical space to accommodate a violent spectacle such as wrestling, and the liminal status of the actor delivering the Epilogue.

Through inference based on available information, we can fill in the picture a bit further, even if this chapter of the play's production history must remain less specific than later ones. First, the 'staying entry' in the Stationers' Register on 4 August 1600, together with the apparent reference to the new Globe theatre in Jaques's speech beginning 'All the world's a stage' (2.7.139), have been used to date the play's first performance soon after the Chamberlain's Men moved to the Globe in 1599. *As You Like It* may well have been Shakespeare's first play written for performance in the new venue.[10]

The part of Touchstone appears to have been written (or revised) to capitalise on the talents of Robert Armin, who joined the company in 1599. Armin's skill in mimicry and satire, his singing ability, and his diminutive physique suited a reserved and intellectual type of fool. The company's previous clown, Will Kemp, with his robust physical presence and talent for dancing, seems to be ridiculed in *As You Like It* in the character of William, whose name is repeated three times during Touchstone's encounter with him in 5.1, pointing out 'the contrast between the departed company clown . . . and the new fool/clown'.[11] As Gurr notes, Kemp often adopted 'the persona of the cunning country clown coming to town', whereas 'Touchstone is the reverse, a court jester who turns himself into a country clown.'[12]

10 Gurr, *Playing Companies*, p. 291.
11 Wiles, p. 146.   12 Gurr, *Playing Companies*, p. 291.

T.W. Baldwin speculates on the following assignment of parts, assuming that the Chamberlain's Men performed the play in 1600: Richard Burbage as Orlando, Henry Condell as Oliver, John Heminges as Duke Senior, Richard Cowley as William, Shakespeare as Adam, Thomas Pope as Jaques, and Armin as Touchstone.[13] The tradition that Shakespeare himself took the part of Adam seems to have originated in the eighteenth century and cannot be authenticated.[14]

Especially disappointing is the absence of information about the boy who played Rosalind. He was evidently an extremely skilled actor, for he played the female part given the most lines of any Shakespeare created – Rosalind's 668 lines outstrip even Cleopatra's.[15] Significantly, much of the time the actor was in the Ganymede persona. Rosalind's relatively restrained manner in Act 1 may give evidence that the part was written for an actor not entirely comfortable within a feminine role; the exuberance Rosalind shows upon adopting the Ganymede disguise registers the actor's relief at stepping out of drag.

The name 'Ganymede' was associated in early modern England with a catamite, a young male lover or prostitute.[16] By staging a flirtation between Ganymede and Orlando, *As You Like It* forces to the surface the element of the Renaissance theatre that most outraged anti-theatrical polemicists: titillating spectacles performed by men. For a male actor simply to put on woman's clothing as an assumed role was one thing; the series of disguises involved in Rosalind's part was quite another, because the resulting vertigo of performed roles undoes the stability of firm gender identity.[17] Stephen Gosson's warning in 1579 that theatre 'effeminates' the mind registers the erosion of inviolable masculinity effected by the subversive questioning of a play like *As You Like It*.[18]

In theatres lacking elaborate props and settings, and without controlled lighting, where the players were quite close to spectators, illusionism could only go so far. In both public and private venues, Andrew Gurr remarks, 'awareness of the illusion as illusion was . . . much closer to the surface all the time' than in theatres with proscenium stages.[19] If the actor's performance of

13 Baldwin, 1927, 1924, quoted in Knowles, p. 632.
14 Edward Capell reported hearing the story from a Stratford resident in 1774 (Chambers, *William Shakespeare*, vol. 2, p. 289).
15 Harbage, p. 31.
16 See Lisa Jardine's discussion of the play's 'erotic androgyny' on the Renaissance stage (pp. 9–36).
17 See Levine; Orgel.   18 Gosson, p. 19.
19 Gurr, *Shakespearean Stage*, p. 163.

Rosalind-as-Ganymede-as-Rosalind in one sense undermined the physical basis of sexual identity and suggested the performative aspect of gender, in another way it was simply a bravura display of layered theatrical roles. Although theatrical cross-dressing was risqué, it was also widely accepted as entertainment.

Still in the realm of inference and possibility is the tantalising tradition of a performance of *As You Like It* before King James at Wilton in December 1603. The established facts are these: an outbreak of plague had closed the theatres in the autumn of 1603, and the newly patented King's Men were on tour in the provinces; the court was installed at Wilton House during the late autumn, and payment is recorded to 'John Henyngs one of his Matie play- ers . . . for the paynes and expences of himselfe and the rest of his Companye' for coming from Mortelacke to court and 'there presentinge before his Matie one playe'.[20] Was the play *As You Like It*? And was Shakespeare touring with his company? Perhaps. In 1865 the historian William Cory wrote in his journal of seeing a letter at Wilton 'from Lady Pembroke to her son, telling him to bring James I from Salisbury to see *As You Like It*; "we have the man Shakespeare with us".'[21] Yet by the time Cory's account was first published (by F. W. Cornish in 1897), the letter could not be found nor its existence authenticated. Most scholars have remained interested but sceptical.[22] For our purposes, the tradition gives intriguing early provenance to the appeal of performing *As You Like It* in a setting that was literally a rural retreat. The play's celebration of the hunt would have made it an especially appropriate choice for performance at Wilton before King James, given his fondness for the sport.

Several even less substantiated rumours exist,[23] but no performances of *As You Like It* in the seventeenth century can be verified.

Charles Johnson's 'Love in a Forest'

When *As You Like It* returned to the theatre in the early eighteenth century, both the stage and the auditorium were strikingly changed. Unlike the thrust stage of early modern public playhouses, typical Restoration theatres fea- tured a proscenium arch that framed the stage and masked the machinery for sets along its sides. This framing, together with painted relief scenes, con- tributed to an illusion of depth. The apron or fore-stage extending beyond

20 Cunningham, p. xxxiv.
21 Chambers, *William Shakespeare*, vol. 2, p. 329.
22 Knowles summarises the debates, pp. 633–4. See also Lee, pp. 231–2, 411–12; Chambers, *Shakespearean Gleanings*, p. 128.
23 Knowles, pp. 632–5.

the proscenium arch supplied an additional, flexible playing space, where actors were in close proximity to viewers. In these intimate, candlelit theatres housing 500 to 800 people, interaction between the players and their typically responsive viewers was energetic.[24] The development of *As You Like It* as a vehicle for great actresses was directly related to these physical conditions.

Charles Johnson's 1723 adaptation at Drury Lane was the first recorded staging of *As You Like It*. *Love in a Forest* played six nights and was well received: 'there was as numerous an Audience as has for this great while been seen; not only the Boxes, Pit and Galleries, but the Stage too being crowded with Spectators'.[25] The adaptation may have been inspired by contemporary political issues involving hunting rights. George I had issued a proclamation in 1720 referring to the rebellious behaviour of a group known as the Blacks (because they disguised themselves by darkening their faces, as Celia does in *As You Like It*) who hid in the forest, traditionally the king's property, and hunted by night, challenging royal authority. Eventually their behaviour led to the Black Act of 1723, which 'made it a felony to enter a forest under disguise or with a blackened face and to hunt, wound, or steal deer'. Johnson, known to believe 'theatre should support the government', evidently found in Shakespeare's play's band of exiled forest-dwellers an opportunity for commentary on current events.[26] *As You Like It* associates freedom with the forest and tyranny with the court, and Johnson strives to break down this opposition, extending the Whig notion of liberty into the countryside to suggest that the establishment afforded freedoms of its own. He emphasises the legitimacy of the banished duke whom he renamed Alberto (lines about 'Mechanicks and Labourers in Handicraft' abandoning their occupations to follow 'their exil'd Sovereign' are inserted into Charles's account of Duke Senior's exiled court in Arden) and exaggerates the contrast between the virtuous Orlando and his treacherous brother Oliver (who kills himself, 'convicted of most foul Designs').[27] Of course, both Alberto and Orlando regain power at the end of the play. And Johnson added an invented Epilogue that contrasts the tedium experienced by 'dull Souls' in the country with the 'circulating Pleasures of the Town' where 'regular and virtuous Laws' prevail.[28] Johnson uses the play to 'justify the Hanoverian government's intervention in the forests' by disarming the opposition's affiliation with the countryside[29] and suggesting that government policies actually encourage freedom.

24 Powell, pp. 15–16.
25 *London Post*, 14 Jan. 1723, quoted in *London Stage*, pt 2, vol. 2, p. 704.
26 Scheil, pp. 51, 46.   27 Charles Johnson, pp. 5, 53.
28 Ibid., p. 70.   29 Scheil, p. 52.

The printed text also includes an enthusiastic dedication to the 'Worshipful Society of Free-Masons', begging their 'Protection' and allowing that 'your Society hath Enemies'.[30] Although the Freemasons had previously been associated with Jacobitism, they were at this juncture newly legitimised as a Whig institution,[31] so theirs was a cause Johnson wished to support. He may have been a member himself: the *Daily Courant* advertised the 15 January performance as 'For the Benefit of the Author, a Free Mason'.[32]

Johnson 'save[s] Shakespeare from vulgarity by excising virtually all its characters beneath the rank of courtier'.[33] In this streamlined version of *As You Like It*, Touchstone, Corin, Audrey, Phoebe, and Sir Oliver Martext have all vanished; Silvius has lost his erotomania and gained only a few of Corin's lines. Johnson also has corrected an offence against refined taste by making Charles 'the Duke's Fencer and Master of his Academy', rather than a rough wrestler. Orlando and Charles engage in a fencing match ('trial by rapier'), complete with lines lifted from *Richard II*. Touchstone's riff on the seven degrees of the lie is decorously replaced with the Pyramus and Thisbe play from *A Midsummer Night's Dream*. Some lines from *Twelfth Night* also creep in, and Jaques and Orlando joke about marriage in material borrowed from *Much Ado About Nothing*.

Jaques, in fact, has been pretty thoroughly overhauled, perhaps because Colley Cibber, a Whig like Johnson, took the part and 'padded' it for his own glorification.[34] He appropriates 1 Lord's speeches in 2.1 and replaces Oliver as Celia's lover. Her proximity inspires a 'Tingling' in his blood, and he quickly asks her to marry him. Why were these changes made? Just as Nahum Tate's improved version of *King Lear* reveals discordant elements in that play, so Johnson's revision points to tensions intrinsic to the design of *As You Like It*. Several of the alterations would be repeated: Jaques, rather than 1 Lord, describes his own melancholic behaviour through the eighteenth century and often in the nineteenth. A note in the 1774 Bell's acting edition explains that the lines are more properly assigned to Jaques because 'they afford an affecting useful lesson to human nature, and exhibit fine poetic painting'.[35] As an educated philosopher, Jaques demands a level of dignity that his melancholic excesses may jeopardise. Allowing him to speak for himself on first introduction alleviates, to some extent, his status as an object of our mirth and Duke Senior's interest, although it does risk turning him into a 'vain coxcomb'[36] who is too much in love with his own supposed sentiments. The romantic pairing of Jaques and Celia also would recur,

30 Charles Johnson, pp. v–vi.   31 Scheil, p. 55.   32 Holding, p. 43.
33 Dobson, p. 112.   34 Odell, *Betterton to Irving*, vol. 1, p. 246.
35 Bell's edition, 2.1.25–43 note.   36 Odell, *Betterton to Irving*, vol. 2, p. 22.

although far less frequently. Over a century later George Sand introduced the revision in her translated version of the play, *Comme il vous plaira*. Jaques's melancholic departure interrupts the comic conclusion of *As You Like It*; smoothing over this rough edge allows the play to accord more fully with a romantic design. *Love in a Forest* also handily dispenses with Oliver's unlikely conversion by having the second de Boys brother, renamed Robert, report the suicide of villainous Oliver.

These may seem shocking alterations by an author who 'presume[s] to weed the beautiful Parterre',[37] but it was an age of 'improved' Shakespeare, not one of textual accuracy. From our perspective, perhaps the most important thing about Johnson's adaptation was its fostering attention to one of Shakespeare's more complex and delicate comedies, long neglected in the theatre, or as Johnson put it in his Prologue, 'to give the Stage, from Shakespear one Play more'.[38] Although *Love in a Forest* leaves the impression more of pastiche than of political statement, it is significant that *As You Like It*, associated in the late twentieth century with liberal social values, would have so early a start in its conservative career. By affiliating Shakespeare's play with established rule, *Love in a Forest* anticipates the way that *As You Like It* served as a propaganda piece to display traditional social values in the nineteenth century.

Eighteenth century: romping actresses and the struggle for decorum

With the London theatre scene thriving in the first half of the eighteenth century, the two main houses, Covent Garden and Drury Lane, relied largely on revivals of familiar plays. Interest in Shakespeare was complicated by theatrical politics: the two patent houses held exclusive rights to perform 'legitimate', traditional drama, but faced with increased competition from new houses and other forms of entertainment such as pantomime and opera, they also wished to supplement their familiar offerings. Passage of the Licensing Act of 1737 re-established the patent houses' monopolies.

An unadapted version of *As You Like It* opened at Drury Lane on 20 December 1740. Met with 'extraordinary applause', the play was presented a total of twenty-eight times during the season.[39] The first of three long-dormant Shakespearean comedies to be revived at Drury Lane during the 1740–1 season (the others were *The Merchant of Venice* and *Twelfth Night*),

37 Charles Johnson, p. 70.   38 Ibid., p. 70.
39 *Daily Advertiser*, 22 Dec. 1740, quoted in *London Stage*, pt. 3, vol. 1, p. 875.

the success of the production helped to expand the repertory.[40] Indeed, some go so far as to attribute the entire mid-eighteenth-century 'Shakespearian revival with which Garrick alone has so often been credited' to Hannah Pritchard's success in *As You Like It*.[41] During this pivotal season (mid-December to the end of March), 'there were only six acting nights without a Shakespearean production at one of the three houses [Drury Lane, Covent Garden and Goodman's Fields, which opened in 1740]'.[42] *As You Like It* was itself catapulted into the position of a favourite piece on the London stage, with productions at one of the major theatres nearly every year for the next decade, and regularly thereafter.

Described in the playbill as 'not acted these forty years', this version was closer to Shakespeare's Folio text than Johnson's, although not altogether faithful. An edition based on the Drury Lane production, published in Dublin in 1741, includes a number of cuts that were continued in later acting editions: Sir Oliver Martext and Hymen disappear, Jaques's part is cleaned up, 'It was a lover and his lasse' is not sung. The strong cast for the initial staging featured Hannah Pritchard as Rosalind, her friend Kitty Clive as Celia, James Quin as Jaques, and Thomas Chapman as Touchstone. Charles Macklin, who took over the clown's role the following year and in several subsequent runs, may well have been a moving force behind the play's revival.[43] Thomas Arne composed settings for Amiens's songs 'Under the Greenwood Tree' and 'Blow, blow, thou Winter Wind', and for 'When daisies pied', interpolated from *Love's Labour's Lost* (sung here by Celia), which proved enduring in subsequent versions of the play. The playbill advertises dancing after Acts 1, 3, and 4, and the performance was followed by a pantomime of *Robin Goodfellow*. One of the earliest illustrations of Shakespearean drama was occasioned by the production: a painting by Francis Hayman of the wrestling scene, now in the Tate Gallery. Hayman's role as scene painter at Drury Lane, together with the resemblance of the represented Rosalind and Celia to Hannah Pritchard and Kitty Clive, indicate that the painting was based on the 1740 production.

Pritchard's triumph as Rosalind launched a major aspect of the play's theatrical life over several centuries: the succession of great actresses who played Rosalind. For Pritchard herself the role was a turning point: in the initial production she got off to a slow start, playing modestly and receiving little response from the audience until she reached 'Take the cork out of thy mouth that I may drink thy tidings' (3.3.168–9). Here her spirited delivery

40 Appleton, pp. 42–3. 41 Vaughan, p. 19.
42 *London Stage*, pt 3, vol. 1, p. cli.
43 Odell, *Betterton to Irving*, vol. 1, p. 228.

met with approval and inspired her own more enthusiastic performance. 'Every speech after this, convinc'd us more and more, that we had been long in possession of a jewel that we had scandalously neglected; till toward the end of the play, her raillery to her lover, who pretended to be dying for her, shew'd us fully what she was.'[44] That her success stemmed from a line that would regularly be cut for decorum's sake in more fastidious times tells us much about Pritchard's playing style: her Rosalind was a spirited hoyden. Indeed, she was thought by some to lack delicacy and was notoriously criticised by Samuel Johnson as a 'vulgar idiot'.[45] Others praised her natural acting style, her ability to convey various passions, and her eloquent and harmonious voice. A contemporary observed that Pritchard 'had an unaccountable method of charming the ear' and 'was a mistress of dramatic eloquence in familiar dialogue'.[46] The anonymous author of *A Letter of Compliment* (1749?) compared her to Garrick, opining that 'Her skill in acting seems to me universal . . . in "As You Like It" what words can paint her?'[47]

Pritchard soon had a rival in the part of Rosalind. When she was working at Covent Garden in 1741, Drury Lane brought out a version of the play featuring Charles Macklin as Touchstone and Margaret (Peg) Woffington as Rosalind.[48] Woffington's renowned beauty, racy love-life, and success in 'breeches' parts, made her a threat to Pritchard, who was acclaimed as a character actress but not for allure.[49] In John Hill's view, Pritchard had that 'ductility of mind' that enabled her to play the part of Rosalind 'with finesse, but it is all in character'.[50] Although no beauty, the young Pritchard was 'slim and handsome' enough to 'play "breeches" parts without looking ridiculous'.[51] Woffington, however, had 'the advantage of one of the finest persons that ever adorned a theatre', along with a 'great sensibility', yet her performances sometimes suffered from her vanity and the intrusive effects of 'her private passions'.[52] Francis Gentleman observed that 'her utterance and deportment were too strongly tinctured with affectation, especially for the rural swain; there is a peculiarity and embarrassment of expression in this part which requires good natural parts or able instruction, to hit it off happily'.[53]

Despite their different individual gifts, both Pritchard and Woffington played Rosalind in a frollicking style. It was primarily the good-looking Woffington who initiated what would become the dominant draw for stage

44 Hill, p. 113.   45 Boswell, *Life*, vol. 2, p. 485 quoted in Vaughan, p. 111.
46 Davies, vol. 2, p. 186.   47 Quoted in Vaughan, p. 124.
48 Both theatres opened *As You Like It* on 15 Oct. 1741.   49 Dunbar, p. 149.
50 Hill, pp. 61, 274.   51 Vaughan, p. 115.   52 Hill, pp. 104–5.
53 Gentleman, vol. 1, pp. 477–8.

Rosalinds: emphasising her seductive allure. A woman's exposing her ankles and calves was considered tantalisingly indecorous, and Woffington used her charms, and her legs, to attract the admiring gaze of male viewers. The physical exposure afforded by male costume fuelled the popularity of the cross-dressed actress, but evidently the 'playfully ambiguous sexual appeal' of gender crossing was also a factor,[54] a pleasurable stage commodity that would be threatening in real life.

Perhaps in parodic counter to the emergent norm of female display, the old tradition of male drag performance was briefly revived by a Mr Page, who took Rosalind's part in a benefit at James Street in 1742. The performance featured 'an new Epilogue spoken by Page', but beyond that, nothing is known about it, or him.[55] Other notable eighteenth-century Rosalinds included Ann Barry (Mrs Dancer), Maria Macklin, and Mary Ann Yates.

Sarah Siddons's failure in the role in 1785 gave ironic testimony to the crucial appeal of sexual display for eighteenth-century Rosalinds. Siddons, who had chosen the play for her benefit performance, brought her skills as an established tragic actress to bear on the part: a critic wrote that 'the mournful tone, the pathetic countenance, and the long-drawn expression pervaded the sprightly scenes of Rosalind . . .'[56] Perhaps Siddons agreed with those who judged Rosalind's 'colloquial wit' to be beneath 'the dignity of the Siddonian form and countenance'. Still, she was apparently charming and irresistible enough while as Rosalind she wore a dress; it was only when she appeared as Ganymede in an 'ambiguous vestment' dictated by 'the scrupulous prudery of decency' that her performance suffered (see commentary, 2.4.0sd).[57] Evidently the modest costume muffled her talents along with her limbs. Siddons's biographer quotes Mr Young, who observes: 'Her Rosalind wanted neither playfulness nor feminine softness; but it was totally without archness, – not because she did not properly conceive it; but how could such a countenance be arch?'[58] Archness, indeed, was to become the byword for Rosalinds of the nineteenth century. However, the greatest Rosalind of the late eighteenth century, Dorothy or Dora Jordan (Dorothy Bland), was anything but arch.

Dora Jordan: 'spirit of enjoyment'

Jordan arrived at Drury Lane from the northern circuits in 1785; she was the theatre's principal Rosalind for twenty years and regularly performed

54 Straub, p. 129.   55 *London Stage*, pt 3, vol. 2, p. 983.
56 *Public Advertiser*, 2 May 1784, quoted in *London Stage*, pt 5, vol. 2, p. 793.
57 Anna Seward, Letter to Miss Weston, 1786, quoted in Salgado, p. 163.
58 Campbell, p. 202.

the part on provincial stages as well. The established mistress of the Duke
of Clarence, later King William IV, Mrs Jordan bore him ten children and
endured celebrity and scandal throughout her long career. She was widely
admired, frequently propositioned, and generally considered a figure of sexual allure. Although our own age has rediscovered the erotic possibilities of
gender blending and the excitement of theatrical displays crossing boundaries of sexual identity, the image Mrs Jordan and other actresses presented
on stage differed from modern western notions of feminine appeal in one
respect: she was pregnant when she first played Rosalind at Drury Lane in
1787 and performed in a state of almost perpetual pregnancy throughout
her career.[59] (When Mrs Jordan's daughter, Fanny Alsop, briefly essayed the
part of Rosalind in 1814, she too was visibly pregnant)[60]. While it may well
have been that audiences were so accustomed to the pregnant shape that they
ceased to notice it, there surely was little chance of a pregnant Rosalind's
masquerade as Ganymede being even remotely convincing. This indicates
that the performance style was presentational rather than representational;
viewers came to the theatre to see feminine display, not convincing gender
transformation.

In the late eighteenth and early nineteenth centuries, observers invariably
comment on actresses' physical appearances. For instance, John Hill wrote
that it would be difficult to 'pardon' an actress's lack of beauty, 'personal
charms being more peculiarly the advantage of the other sex than of ours'.[61]
Rosalind's role was a favourite because of the enticing display of the performer's legs while she was in the Ganymede disguise. It was considered
exciting to see a woman personate a man, but cross-dressed actresses were
not expected to pass the line of successful gender illusion. In 1806, William
Cooke wrote:

> where a woman . . . personates a man *pro tempore*, as is the case in several of our
> stock comedies . . . the closer the imitation is made, the more we applaud the
> performer, but always in the knowledge that the object before us is *a woman
> assuming the character of a man;* but when this same woman totally usurps the
> male character, and we are left to try her merits merely as a man, without
> making the least allowance for the imbecilities of the other sex, we may safely
> pronounce, there is no woman, nor ever was a woman, who can fully supply this
> character. There is such a *reverse* in all the habits and modes of the two sexes,
> acquired from the very cradle upwards, that it is next to an impossibility for the
> one to resemble the other so as totally to escape detection.[62]

Similarly, Jordan's biographer James Boaden, writing of her performance
of a male part, maintained that 'the attraction after all is purely feminine,

59 Tomalin, p. 77 and passim.   60 Ibid., p. 291.
61 Hill, p. 57.   62 Cooke, p. 126.

and the display of female, not male perfections. Did the lady really look like a man, the coarse *androgynus* would be hooted from the stage.'[63] Boaden goes so far as to suggest that cross-dressed actresses could refine the crudeness of male characters. Certainly Henry Bunbury's painting of Mrs Jordan as Rosalind (later engraved by Charles Knight) shows her in a sexually provocative pose and attributes little that is masculine to her appearance (see figure 1). The painting represents the scene in which Phoebe falls for Rosalind/Ganymede's charms (3.6); although the episode acknowledges the erotic duality of a character who appeals to both men and women, few could doubt that the body beneath this costume was female.

Despite the part's evident eroticism, Mrs Jordan played a wholesome, if hoydenish, Rosalind. Her vivacious high spirits made her a great comic actress. Leigh Hunt wrote:

> though she was neither beautiful, nor handsome, nor even pretty, nor accomplished, nor 'a lady', nor anything conventional or *comme il faut* whatsoever, yet was so pleasant, so cordial, so natural, so full of spirits, so healthily constituted in mind and body, had such a shapely leg withal, so charming a voice, and such a happy and happy-making expression of countenance, that she appeared something superior to all those requirements of acceptability, and to hold a patent from nature herself for our delight and good opinion.[64]

Implying a parallel with Cleopatra, Hunt says Jordan 'made even Methodists love her'.[65] Macready saw in her 'a spirit of fun, that would have outlaughed Puck himself' and he particularly delighted in her laugh: 'so rich, so apparently irrepressible, so deliciously self-enjoying, as to be at all times irresistible'.[66]

Commentators repeatedly assert the naturalness of Dora Jordan's art. William Hazlitt claimed to see through her stage characters to the woman herself:

> It was not as an actress but as herself, that she charmed every one. Nature had formed her in her most prodigal humour . . . Mrs Jordan was the same in all her characters, and inimitable in all of them . . . She rioted in her fine animal spirits, and gave more pleasure than any other actress, because she had the greatest spirit of enjoyment in herself . . .[67]

Perhaps because she was understood to be presenting herself, rather than Rosalind (or Ganymede) to viewers, Mrs Jordan continued to perform the part past the age of fifty, with performances at Covent Garden in 1813 and 1814. Not that her age went unnoticed: even her friend Boaden admitted

63 Boaden, vol. 1, p. 46.   64 Hunt, vol. 1, pp. 148–9.
65 Ibid., p. 149.   66 Macready, p. 46.   67 Hazlitt, p. 169.

'that a time will arrive, when age, or perhaps, still more unluckily, figure, may somewhat clash with the performance of the *Romp*'.[68] When Crabb Robinson saw her on stage (not in *As You Like It*) in 1813, he remarked on 'the absurdity of an old woman aping the romping wantonness of a girl'.[69]

Not everyone approved of Jordan's interpretation of Rosalind. Boaden reported that her performance 'divided the town', with the 'lovers of the sentimental' lining up against those who favoured 'the humorous'. In Boaden's view, the part 'ought to excite laughter', because Rosalind exhibits a 'natural sprightliness', buoyancy, and wit for which Mrs Jordan's 'animal spirits' well fitted her.[70] Those who viewed such vivacity as vulgar endorsed instead a more sensitive, romantic interpretation of the part that anticipated the favoured style of the next centuries. Partly at issue was the performer's class status. William Oxberry attributed Mrs Jordan's fitness to play a romping Rosalind to her own ignobility: 'as she had not to unbend, she did not lose her dignity'.[71]

And yet, when Leigh Hunt, writing around 1850, recalled the playgoing scene of the late eighteenth and early nineteenth centuries, he noted the fluid social boundary between actors and audiences:

> people of all times of life were much greater playgoers than they are now . . .
> Everything was more concentrated, and the various classes of society felt a
> greater concern in the same amusements. Nobility, gentry, citizens, princes – all
> were frequenters of theatres, and even more or less acquainted personally with
> the performers. Nobility intermarried with them; gentry, and citizens too, wrote
> for them; princes conversed and lived with them.[72]

Hunt describes a casual and socially inclusive playgoing scene. As with cinema today, viewers may feel a sense of personal familiarity with stars whom they have watched many times and whose lives they have read and heard about; this effect was greatly heightened in Hunt's 'concentrated' theatre-going society, for high-status viewers would actually *be* 'more or less acquainted personally with the performers'. Clearly it was actresses

68 Boaden, vol. 1, p. 141.   69 Robinson, p. 53.
70 Boaden, vol. 1, pp. 139, 40, 41.   71 Oxberry, *Dramatic Mirror*, p. 81.
72 Hunt, vol. 1, p. 152.

Figure 1 Dorothy Jordan (1761–1816) as Rosalind, shown here in disguise as Ganymede in 3.5. Her coquettish pose as she observes Silvius and Phoebe suggests how feminine Jordan remained even while in the Ganymede disguise. The 1788 engraving by Charles Knight is dedicated 'To Mrs Jordan, In gratitude for the Pleasure receiv'd from her inimitable Performance of Rosalind'. Knight's engraving is after a painting by Henry Bunbury, presumably inspired by stage performance.

rather than actors with whom 'nobility intermarried' and 'princes . . . lived', contributing to the erotic attraction of these performers. To audiences witnessing performances of *As You Like It*, the sense of familiarity associated with Rosalind would be especially strong, given that the character has such a permeable fictional status, creating new identities at a moment's notice.

Throughout the eighteenth century and into the nineteenth, productions of *As You Like It* sought to balance the sometimes risqué humour of the play with a desire to maintain decorum. For instance, the 'Cuckoo song' ('When daisies pied') regularly interpolated from *Love's Labour's Lost* was a site of tension between pleasure and propriety. Obviously the song – inserted into the dialogue between Rosalind/Ganymede and Orlando in 4.1, when she speaks of unfaithful wives – was a drawing point, since playbills regularly advertised its inclusion, usually performed by Rosalind but sometimes by Celia (see commentary, 4.1.141). Dora Jordan taunted Orlando by holding two fingers 'saucily' behind his head while she sang.[73] Yet moralists objected and even a century later Augustin Daly worried about the song's indecency.

Whereas modern commentators often note the thematic and structural resemblance between Touchstone and Jaques, early acting editions show that an effort was made to differentiate the two. The clown Touchstone was pared of his more offensive lines, including much of the dialogue with Corin in 3.3. Charles Macklin's student John Hill wrote in 1750 of actors' difficulty in arousing more than tepid smiles from the audience with their performances of Touchstone; Hill recommended greater indulgence in mimicry. Macklin took the clown's part in numerous popular revivals with Hannah Pritchard and Kitty Clive, but Jaques was the role actor–managers would increasingly take for themselves.

To underline the propriety of the famously sagacious 'Seven Ages' speech, the mannered and educated Jaques needed to be accorded every dignity. Thus it was customary for Jaques to take over 1 Lord's description of his melancholic behaviour in 2.1. The transference works against a coherent characterisation of Jaques, because 1 Lord reports his remarks about the 'sequestered stag' (2.1.33) in heartfelt tones otherwise absent from the cynical moralist: 'as soon as Jaques is made responsible for expressions of sincere sentiment his individuality is destroyed' (*Academy*, 5 Sept. 1885). During the eighteenth and nineteenth centuries, Jaques also usually gave up his parody of Amiens's song in 2.5 (the 'ducdame' trick), his role in the Touchstone–Audrey nuptials in 3.4, and his self-diagnosis in 4.1.

---

73 Robson, p. 142.

TOUCHSTONE.

Figure 2 Comedian John Pritt Harley (1786–1858) played with Macready at Covent Garden in 1838, with Alfred Bunn at Drury Lane from 1841 to 1848, and became a permanent member of Charles Kean's company at the Princess's Theatre. Satirically known as Fat Jack because of his gaunt physique, Harley wears the parti-coloured costume and ass's ears of the fool. The lithograph by Richard James Lane carries a caption from 2.4: 'But all is mortal in nature, so is all nature in love mortal in folly.'

Into the nineteenth century: opera, spectacle, and a new Rosalind

The tripling of London's population in the first half of the nineteenth century affected the theatrical scene strikingly. The monopoly held by Drury Lane and Covent Garden was officially ended by the Theatres Act of 1843, which confirmed changes already initiated in practice. The number of venues increased (from ten to thirty London theatres between 1807 and 1870), while disorderly crowds, sometimes rioting over the price structures, discouraged the upper classes from attending. Theatre offerings changed in response to the demographic shift in audience: 'As the expensive seats emptied, it became more and more necessary to resort to spectacles of equestrianism, aquatics and performing menageries to keep the pit and the gallery full.'[74] Enlarged auditoriums accommodated the crowds eager for these spectacular events. Covent Garden had been restructured and enlarged in 1792, and two years later Drury Lane was rebuilt to house over 3,600 spectators – it was considered a huge space and disliked by actors. Covent Garden burned in 1808 and was reopened in 1809, the same year that Drury Lane was destroyed by fire. Throughout this period, both houses continued to seat over 3,000 people, democratising the drama by making it more widely available while also necessitating a broader, less subtle style of acting. The continued narrowing of the apron in front of the proscenium contributed to reduction of intimacy with the performers. The introduction of cantilevered balconies, replacing the old tiered galleries, meant that spectators were no longer in the actors' line of vision. Gas lights were introduced at Sadler's Wells in 1853; also, by mid-century, house lights were being lowered during the performance, contributing significantly to the visual emphasis on spectacular panoramas and elaborate scenes. By one estimate, 'only the grandiose and the artificial was possible' in the theatres at this time.[75]

Popular hunger for spectacular staging altered the way *As You Like It* was presented. In one way, *As You Like It* experienced an unusual fate for a popular Shakespearean play in the nineteenth century: the series of actresses playing Rosalind shaped its reception and interpretation, not the great actor–managers who produced and sometimes acted in the play but left little history or tradition of striking interpretations. From Kemble onwards, Jaques was played by actor–managers, most of whom were too old to play Orlando and too dignified to play Touchstone. The seriousness they accorded Jaques influenced conceptions of his character and, to some extent, contributed to the popular view of the play as a whole. Hazlitt, for instance, who calls *As You Like It* 'the most ideal' of Shakespeare's plays, revels in the way Arden 'seems to breathe a spirit of philosophical poetry . . . Never was there

74 Dobbs, p. 124.   75 Ibid.

such beautiful moralising.' Unsurprisingly, he particularly admires Jaques, 'the only purely contemplative character in Shakespear': 'he is the prince of philosophical idlers'.[76]

Hazlitt also reveals something important about how Shakespeare had come to be understood with his observation that *As You Like It* was heavily anthologised: 'There is hardly any of Shakespear's plays that contains a greater number of passages that have been quoted in books of extracts, or a greater number of phrases that have become in a manner proverbial. If we were to give all the striking passages, we should give half the play.'[77] As Shakespeare became part of the literate public's frame of reference, *As You Like It*, a play particularly well stocked with proverbial passages – thanks to all those philosophers, which Shaw was later to rue – took pride of place as a moralistic drama. Certain parts – notably Jaques, Duke Senior, and Adam – became vehicles for philosophical utterance rather than truly theatrical characters.

The Romantics' notion that the theatre was inadequate to Shakespeare's work was part of this view. Charles Lamb, like Hazlitt an inveterate playgoer who felt that Shakespeare's characters transcended the dramatic medium, wrote that one paid 'dearly' for the 'juvenile pleasure' of theatre: 'when the novelty is past, we find to our cost that instead of realizing an idea, we have only materialized and brought down a fine vision to the standard of flesh and blood', For Lamb, Shakespeare's characters are 'improper to be shewn to our bodily eye'.[78] Lamb and Hazlitt were hardly alone in imagining the characters existing independently of their theatrical realisation; Mary Cowden Clarke wrote of the girlhood of Shakespeare's heroines, and the pre-Raphaelites sometimes painted them in non-Shakespearean settings. The prefatory remarks in Oxberry's 1819 edition of *As You Like It* give a classic statement of this approach:

> There are no characters which are so easily spoiled on the stage as this author's . . . because there are none which are so completely made out to 'the mind's eye,' and in which consequently the smallest aberration from the distinct image we have formed to ourselves is so immediately detected and reprobated . . . Whoever plays Shakespeare, does it at his peril . . . but it is at the same time as gratifying as it is rare, to see any such part performed to the height of our wishes . . . [79]

Having thrown down this gauntlet to performers – challenging them to match the picture in his (and presumably in every other reader's) 'mind's eye' – Oxberry continues with his expectations for actors of the central characters of *As You Like It*:

---

76 Hazlitt, pp. 305, 306.   77 Ibid., p. 309.   78 Lamb, pp. 19, 33.
79 W. Oxberry, ed., Preface, *As You Like It*.

Who could pretend to act Jaques too well, or to speak the speech on the stages of human life with more genious than it is written; or to give additional interest to his melancholy or biterness to his sarcasm, or to combine an air of dignity and negligence to a greater degree than we suppose them united in his person? What actor could do more than echo the words of Touchstone, than assume the quaintness of his garb and of his sentiments, be as witty as malicious and provoking with his eye, as the poet has made him with his tongue, and make the accompaniment of smiles, of shrugs, and antic grimaces he must put on as significant and amusing as the text which they are meant to illustrate; or again, what could give us a finer idea of grace, of manliness, of generosity and youthful affection than Orlando perfectly well acted, or of voluble archness, of feigned indifference, and tender sensibility than his Rosalind; Audrey, too, should not play the fool in vain . . . and the shepherd, who had never wandered from the forest, should preach his humble philosophy with the efficacy of a hermit . . . but to see *As You Like It* as it is too often played, is altogether mortifying . . .[80]

A sense of intellectual ownership of Shakespeare's characters was coupled with hostility towards the theatrical norms of the day.

Tension between verbal and visual understandings of the play – which continues to the present day – contributed directly to the evolving idea of Rosalind. When Elizabeth Inchbald, who had played Celia, wrote in 1808 that *As You Like It* 'is never attractive, except when some actress of very superior skill performs the part of Rosalind', she identified the embodiment of her ideal: 'Mrs Jordan is the Rosalind of both art and nature.'[81] Lamb, on the other hand, claimed to 'despair' at the prospect of more actresses in Mrs Jordan's coquettish mould, who released 'their whole artillery of charms' upon 'the whole audience – a thousand gentlemen, perhaps'.[82] In fact, nostalgia for Mrs Jordan was slow to die, but emerging nineteenth-century ideals of femininity would require a heroine of a different sort.

Kemble's revisions

John Philip Kemble moved to Covent Garden in 1803, while Mrs Jordan remained at Drury Lane. In his youth Kemble had played Orlando, but with the death of John Palmer, the longtime Jaques of Drury Lane, Kemble switched to the more mature role, establishing a tradition other actor–managers would follow. He presented a moralising, sentimental philosopher and 'no one laughed at him'.[83] Mrs Inchbald wrote that Kemble's Jaques

---

80 Ibid.   81 Quoted in Furness, p. 394.
82 Lamb, p. 41.   83 *Kemble Promptbooks*, vol. 1, p. ii.

was 'one of those characters in which he gives certain bold testimonies of genius . . . yet the mimic art has very little share in this grand exhibition'.[84] Kemble moved Jaques's description of his melancholy from 4.1 to 2.5, with Amiens speaking Rosalind's part in the dialogue. The revision retained Jaques's diagnostic energy while avoiding a direct and potentially indecorous encounter between the eager Jaques and the unaccompanied Rosalind. Jaques's cynical outcry in 2.7 was omitted, as was standard at the time.

Kemble's acting edition, published in 1810, follows most of the 'decorum' cuts popularised by Bell's edition of 1774 although it includes the 'Cuckoo song' for Rosalind. Kemble called the two Lords who attend Duke Frederick in 2.2 Eustace and Louis, names that had a long career. Unlike the simple stagings of the eighteenth century, Kemble's productions featured sets of the wing-and-drop or wing-and-shutter variety, anticipating the visual grandeur which was shortly to evolve. To accommodate and reduce the number of scene changes, Kemble altered the order of scenes in Act 2, another standard practice in later nineteenth-century stagings.

Clearly Shakespearean drama was becoming a spectacular form of entertainment. Between 1817 and 1837, the imaginative Frederic Reynolds collaborated with the songwriter Henry R. Bishop to 'operatise' several Shakespearean comedies. The operatic *As You Like It* played at Covent Garden in 1824, featuring songs from other plays, a duet by Celia and Rosalind, and solos by Rosalind, Celia, Sylvius, and Touchstone, sprinkled with verses taken from the sonnets.[85]

Macready's restorations

William Charles Macready's production at Drury Lane in 1842 evidenced significant rethinking of the text as a performance piece and restored *As You Like It* to roughly Shakespearean form. Breaking with existing acting editions, Macready included the 'ducdame' parody in 2.5, returned Jaques and Sir Oliver Martext to 3.4, restored to its original place the dialogue between Rosalind and Jaques that opens 4.1, presented the hunting celebration (4.2) for the first time since Shakespeare's day, and included much of Hymen's part. He cut only passages he anticipated the audience would find offensive and rejected material – including the 'Cuckoo song' – not included in Shakespeare's text. He put the order of scenes in Act 2 back to almost Shakespearean order: 2, 3, 1, 4, 5, 6, 7. Macready was praised for

---

84 Quoted in Furness, p. 394.
85 Odell, *Betterton to Irving*, vol. 2, pp. 127, 142–3.

staging the play 'as the poet wrote it' and 'would have wished to see it represented – at least so far as the scenic accessories are concerned'. Macready's stage management had introduced 'completeness and finish in the various parts of the representation' and a unified presentation in which 'the integrity of the drama is preserved' (*Spectator*, 8 Oct. 1842).

Macready, known as a bitter character himself, took the role of Jaques and claimed it was 'a pleasure in representation to identify [him]self'.[86] Playing Jaques as 'a moody recluse' and 'severe moralist', he delivered the part with the sententiousness that would later blossom into full Victorian flower.[87] His Jaques was 'no misantrope, but a wilful man of melancholy mood, whose contempt for humanity is more nearly allied to pity than hate; his sarcasms are humorous not bitter, and his brusquerie anything but savage' (*Spectator*, 8 Oct. 1842). Queen Victoria approved, noting that Macready 'pronounced the famous speech about the Ages beautifully'.[88] Oxberry commented that, as an actor, Macready generally 'succeeds best where he has much to do, much to imply, little to enunciate; for, though a fine speaker, he ceases to act when he begins to declaim'.[89] By this standard, Macready must have disappointed, for if ever there were a passive, declamatory role, it is that of Jaques. He certainly disappointed Fanny Kemble, who called his production of *As You Like It* '*painfully* acted'. For her, the emphasis on spectacle over poetry was a bad bargain: 'though we had neither the caustic humor not the poetical melancholy of Jacques, nor the brilliant wit and despotical fancifulness of the princess shepherdboy duly given, we *had* the warbling of birds, and sheep-bells tinkling in the distance, to comfort us'.[90]

Tiny, red-haired Robert Keeley's Touchstone was 'a pleasant mixture of clown and courtier', although lacking 'the pompous fluency and oracular pedantry' deemed essential to the humour of the part (*Spectator*, 8 Oct. 1842; *Times*, 3 Oct. 1842). Mrs Keeley's Audrey 'was hardly wild enough in her rusticity', her eye showing 'far too much intelligence . . . for the dark, uncouth mind of the forest wench' (*Times*, 3 Oct. 1842).

Macready, more than Kemble, initiated spectacular nineteenth-century stagings of *As You Like It*. 'Every scene was a complete picturesque study' (*Times*, 3 Oct. 1842). Drury Lane's scenic artist Charles Marshall prepared ten settings – a matter of perspective paintings on canvas combined with 'cut flats' to produce the illusion of depth. Several scenes featured huge

86 Macready, *Reminiscences*, p. 148.   87 Pollock, *Macready*, p. 134.
88 Rowell, p. 41. Victoria visited the theatre on 12 June 1843.
89 *Oxberry's Dramatic Biography*, vol. 5, p. 49. Oxberry's comments were published by his wife after his death.
90 Frances Kemble, p. 362.

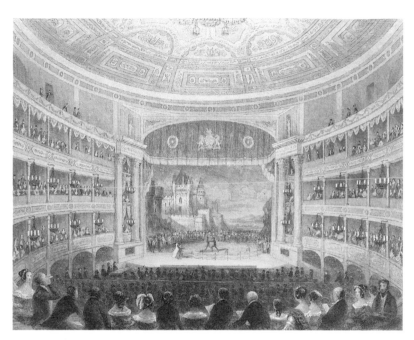

Figure 3 Thomas H. Shepherd's engraving of Drury Lane Theatre in 1842 shows the wrestling match in 1.2. The crowd of spectators on stage adds to the intense metatheatricality of the scene.

ensemble casts. For the wrestling match, Macready assembled seventy-four people on stage – guards, attendants, ladies, and courtiers. The Duke and some of the courtiers had live merlins on their wrists. 'The new effect was introduced of including the space where the wrestlers encounter with ropes and staves, round which the courtiers and spectators stand, pressing eagerly forward, watching every movement of the combatants' (*Times*, 3 Oct. 1842). The scenes at Duke Senior's forest court in exile were similarly splendid: against a background of old trees and a babbling brook, hunters played horns, attendants prepared weapons, falconers worked with birds, leashed hounds were led about, and sounds of sheep-bells and bird song were heard. Hymen's appearance occasioned a third crowded display, as dancing shepherds and shepherdesses constructed on stage a temple of flowers and garlands. The spectacle was praised as 'suggestive', useful in 'aiding the fancy in realizing the local and other characteristics of every scene', and with nothing 'overdone' (*Spectator*, 8 Oct. 1842). Macready's production initiated both the major trend in nineteenth-century stagings of *As You Like It* – visual spectacle – and the major problem with it – a lack of emphasis on the

Shakespearean verse. This was ironic, given Macready's restoration of the full play text, yet as Fanny Kemble noted, 'Macready's eye was as sensitive and cultivated as his ear was the reverse.'[91]

Macready's productions also contributed significantly to the evolution of Rosalind. Louisa Nisbett took the part in the famous 1842 production and was praised for her spirited performance in the hoyden tradition. Samuel Phelps remembered her Rosalind in ecstatic terms: 'Not having seen her, *ye* don't know what beauty is. Her voice was liquid music – her laugh – there never was such a laugh! – her eyes living crystals – lamps lit with the light divine! – her grace, her taste, her nameless but irresistible charm.'[92] But even the generally positive reviews hinted at something out of kilter in Nisbett's performance. One critic, while finding it 'impossible not to enjoy the merriment she provokes', complained that she 'does not sound the depths of the character' (*Athenaeum*, 8 Oct. 1842). The *Times* complained that her merriment was not that 'of the banished Duke's daughter' and detected 'an absence of that graceful sensibility which is the very soul of the character' (3 Oct. 1842). The *Spectator* similarly judged her performance 'utterly devoid of sentiment' (8 Oct. 1842). Nisbett had in fact replaced Macready's original choice for the part, Helena Faucit, who had appeared as Rosalind in an earlier production at Covent Garden. In casting Nisbett, Macready was in Charles Shattuck's words 'dreaming of Dora Jordan' and a Rosalind of the past.[93] Macready was not alone: Crabb Robinson in 1837 noted that 'Mrs Nisbett reminds me of Mrs Jordan but wants her delicacy', and John Cole wrote in 1860 that 'some have fancied' the revival of Jordan's 'irresistible' laugh 'in the ringing tones' of Nisbett.[94] But the cultural tide had turned, and as Faucit came to personify the new interpretation of Rosalind as a genteel, hyper-feminine aristocrat, even Macready would eventually regret having cast Nisbett in the part.[95]

Helena Faucit: Rosalind 'ethereally embodied'

If the two most salient characteristics of Faucit's Rosalind were her femininity and her emotionality, this was because tender feeling had come virtually to define the feminine in mid-century Britain. John Coleman, who played Orlando to Faucit's Rosalind, explained that 'it was reserved for my Rosalind to develop the poetic side of the character, and to present an impersonation of surpassing subtlety and grace – of dignity and delicacy, of truth and beauty . . . passion impermeated with love-breathing sighs, sunny smiles,

91 Ibid., p. 636.   92 Quoted in Mullin, p. 356.   93 Shattuck, *Mr Macready*.
94 Robinson, p. 154; Cole, vol. 1, p. 70.   95 Pollock, *Macready*, pp. 21–2.

and delicious tears'.[96] Coleman's rhetoric echoes that of George Fletcher, the influential *Athenaeum* essayist who believed Faucit 'infuse[d] into the part . . . all the tender though lively grace which the poet has made its principal attribute'. In Fletcher's view, *As You Like It* needed to be rescued from vulgar comic presentations by 'a true Shakespearian actress, in the highest and most peculiar sense of the term'.[97] Rosalind was 'ethereally embodied' in Faucit (*Athenaeum*, 8 Nov. 1845). As Julie Hankey has argued, Faucit was heavily indebted to Romantic conceptions of Shakespeare himself as an abstract, decorporealised genius in her creation of a 'pure' femininity appropriate for the stage. In doing so she advanced the Victorian conception of woman while claiming creative kinship with the bard.[98]

Clearly there were class issues at work: the *Edinburgh Observer* praised Faucit's Rosalind as 'never less than the high-born and high-bred gentlewoman'.[99] Rosalind, after all, is the daughter of a Duke, and for Faucit the character's high status conferred significant delicacy and refinement. Faucit's essay 'On Rosalind' gushes with sentimentality: 'at the core of all that Rosalind says and does, lies a passionate love as pure and all-absorbing as ever swayed a woman's heart . . .' Despite the interest of her 'pretty womanly waywardnesses playing like summer lightning over her throbbing tenderness of heart', readers are assured that 'never in the gayest sallies of her happiest moods' does Rosalind lose 'one grain of our respect'.[100] Faucit did not view Rosalind as 'a hoyden who loves to romp in a forest in boy's clothes', nor did she see 'humour [as] the leading feature of the character'; she emphasised instead the 'sentimental' plight of 'a high-spirited lady of deep feeling' (*Observer*, 12 Mar. 1865).

Faucit worked out a complex interpretation of Rosalind's character. She presented diverse emotions convincingly: the performance was 'remarkable for the variety and delicacy of its effects . . . a diamond with many facets' (*Pall Mall Gazette*, 10 Mar. 1865). Serious actors, George Henry Lewes observed, were often 'ineffective' or even 'vulgar' in comic roles because they resorted to adopting 'the 'business' and manner' of low comedy style. But Faucit, he recalled, possessed 'the gaiety of a serious nature' and could 'represent the joyous playfulness of young animal spirits, without once ceasing to be poetical'.[101] For George Taylor, Faucit's idealisation of Rosalind resulted in 'a portrait that was noted for sentiment rather than comedy'.[102]

---

96 John Coleman, vol. 1, p. 171.   97 Fletcher, pp. 237, 238.
98 Hankey, pp. 51–6.   99 Quoted in Fletcher, p. 239.
100 Faucit Martin, *On Rosalind*, p. 13.
101 Lewes, p. 178.   102 George Taylor, p. 184.

Whereas comic actresses of the eighteenth and later of the twentieth centuries exploited the ambiguity between the Rosalind and Ganymede personae, for Faucit, there was only Rosalind: she never allowed the woman to
effectively disappear behind the boy. Her Ganymede, as a result, was more
an awkward boy than a masculine youth.[103]

> She appeared sufficiently at home in her male attire to deceive Orlando, but
> always contrived by some slight movement, or tone, or look, to destroy such
> illusion to the audience. The way in which, in the passage of the mock marriage,
> she uttered her own share of the vows in an aside of solemn tone and deep
> feeling is an instance of this.   (*Observer*, 12 Mar. 1865)

> Her mannish disguise is just sufficient to warrant the illusion of her
> companions, yet never for an instant presents her as less womanly. It is like a
> cockade upon a woman's hat, a saucy symbol of the masculine type, which
> makes you the more conscious of the absent masculinity, for she never falls into
> the mistake so frequently committed by actresses who assume the male manner
> with the male attire.   (*Pall Mall Gazette*, 10 Mar. 1865)

The revising of Rosalind's part from hoyden to womanly woman evidences
the complex interplay of gender and class ideologies in the construction of
Shakespearean character. In 1855, Faucit's performance as Rosalind was
praised in these terms: 'nothing more delicate in conception or execution
was, perhaps, ever seen on the stage. The sentiment of it is as delicious as
the delineation is exquisite' (*Athenaeum*, 30 June 1855). Such delicacy, of
course, was as remote from the stages of early modern England as it was
from those of the supposedly vulgar eighteenth century against which many
Victorians defined themselves. Indeed, Faucit worried about playing the part
of Rosalind, reporting 'I had heard enough of what Mrs Jordan and others
had done with the character, to add fresh alarm to my misgivings.'[104] Faucit,
however, was confident that Shakespeare's intentions could be retained if
the trappings of an earlier age were removed. She explained that the play's
Epilogue 'was fit enough for the mouth of a boy-actor of women's parts in
Shakespeare's time, but it is altogether out of tone with the Lady Rosalind';
Faucit coped with the problem by omitting some words and altering others. In
her view, after all, 'through the guise of the brilliant-witted boy, Shakespeare
meant the charm of the high-hearted woman, strong, tender, delicate, to
make itself felt'.[105] With theatre audiences composed of those who had, or
aspired to have, refined sensibility, it would not do to offend against gender or

103 Carlisle, pp. 68–9.   104 Faucit Martin, *On Rosalind*, p. 4.
105 Ibid., pp. 74, 13.

class decorum, even within a pastoral fiction.[106] The moral burden attached to playgoing can be glimpsed in a reviewer's reflection on Faucit's Rosalind: 'the question is, does this play touch the spirit to finer issues, does it raise poetic suggestions, does it give delicate palates a more exquisite delight than sensation pieces and coat-and-waistcoat comedies? . . . It is certain that no one can read *As You Like It*, after seeing such a Rosalind as Helen Faucit, without reading it illuminated' (*Pall Mall Gazette*, 10 Mar. 1865).

Charles Kean and the growth of pictorial staging

In the summer of 1851, London was crowded with visitors to the Great Exhibition. Awed by the treasures on display in the Crystal Palace, visitors relished 'a scene of realized enchantment, an animated cosmorama . . . to think of for ever after'.[107] The Exhibition prompted London theatres to create competitively spectacular entertainments. As we have noted, Macready's 1842 production had been lauded for visual effects that required little imaginative work from its viewers. Extending this approach, Charles Kean mounted a production at the Princess's Theatre aiming at 'absolute historical accuracy'.[108] On stage were 'avenues of trees, rustic bridges, and running brooks' (*Athenaeum*, 8 Feb. 1851). In order to accommodate the 'weighty masses of scenery', the play itself was cut and scenes transposed and run together. Playgoers were becoming 'spectators in the theatre, rather than auditors',[109] to the dismay of some. Macready lamented Kean's lavish productions in which 'the poet is swallowed up in display', contrasting his own stagings, which 'enrich[ed]' Shakespeare's poetry. He even confessed to 'remorse' for his contribution to the growth of pictorial stagings.[110] George Ellis, Macready's assistant prompter, became Kean's stage manager and provided a copy of Macready's promptbook for the play, which Kean largely followed in his productions. Kean's rendition of Jaques was unexceptionable – he offered 'correct recitation and noble bearing' – while Mrs Kean (the former Ellen Tree)'s Rosalind was noted for 'buoyancy, vivacity, and sweetness' (*Athenaeum*, 8 Feb. 1851). Years later, Richard White remembered her as the only Rosalind he had ever seen to convey 'what the Rosalind of our imagination felt at the sight of the bloody handkerchief'.[111]

106 On the revision of Shakespeare's meaning for successive ages, see George Taylor; Dobson.
107 Cole, vol. 2, pp. 6, 4.   108 Odell, *Betterton to Irving*, vol. 2, p. 286.
109 Ibid., p. 287.   110 Pollock, *Macready*, p. 84.   111 White, p. 256.

Tree was the first great Rosalind to appear on the American stage (see figure 4). The play had been performed in the previous century, at New York's John Street Theatre in 1786, with Mrs Kenna playing Rosalind, but it was Tree's performance at the Park Theatre in 1836, and its subsequent revivals, that permanently established the play as a stockpiece of American as well as British theatres.

Charlotte Cushman: a Tiresian Ganymede

The unorthodox Charlotte Cushman, considered America's greatest actress of the nineteenth century and the only one to fully succeed abroad, presented a Rosalind who was quite decidedly not of the Faucit mould. As a tragic actress, Cushman was known for her emotional power and even masculine vigour; she had played Romeo to her sister Susan's Juliet. Despite a face like 'a feminine caricature of Mr Macready's physiognomy', 'ungraceful' movement, 'inelegant' manner, 'abrupt and angular movements', Cushman 'made a powerful impression . . . by the sheer force of passionate emotion, and *masculine* energy and determination of purpose' (*Spectator*, 15 Feb. 1845; emphasis in original). When she appeared as Ganymede, 'the transformation from woman to man had the same effect on her as on the famed Tiresias . . . Her mind became masculine as well as her outward semblance.' Not only did she '[look] in every inch a man' but 'a man she is in voice and manner also, and gesture, so long as she retains these outward and visible symbols of the stronger sex' (*Observer*, 2 Mar. 1845). Her 'hearty enjoyment' and 'downrightness' granted pleasure, but 'for an ideal Rosalind . . . she wanted not only personal qualifications, but that harmony and elevation of conception which Helen Faucit exhibited'.[112] Critics could enjoy the performance 'considered per se, and without reference to the performance of her predecessors in the part' (*Observer*, 2 Mar. 1845). Some, however, deemed her Rosalind superior even to Faucit's: her biographer quotes one reviewer who wrote 'Miss Cushman *was* Rosalind'.[113] Cushman, who never married and might today be considered a gender renegade, was one of only a few nineteenth-century performers to push *As You Like It* in a radical direction.

Samuel Phelps and the conventional Jaques

Sadler's Wells, the most successful of minor London theatres, was especially known for its spectacular stagings, having gained notoriety for aquatic melodramas. There Samuel Phelps mounted a production of *As You Like It*

112 Marston, vol. 2, p. 74.   113 Clement, p. 43.

Figure 4 Ellen Tree (1805–80), later Mrs Charles Kean, shown as Rosalind in October 1836. Several months later Tree was the first London artist to play Rosalind in America, at the Park Theatre in New York. Rather than doublet and hose, she wears tunic and cape, as was customary in the nineteenth century. The lithograph by Richard James Lane bears a caption from 2.4: 'Thou speak'st wiser than thou art ware of.'

in 1847 that introduced several new bits of pageantry. In 4.2, the huntsmen entered with a litter carrying a deer carcass. As the celebratory song was sung, a huntsman straddled the deer and was carried off in triumph – not a historically accurate staging of 'Let's present him to the Duke like a Roman conqueror' (4.2.3) but a vivid one. At the play's conclusion, Hymen's entry was presented as a rural ritual. Villagers drew on stage an ornamented 'temple', evidently a pageant wagon, from which Hymen emerged to speak and sing (Phelps pbk). Crabb Robinson found the staging so enjoyable that it made him question Romantic principles: 'The beauty of the poem made up for every defect in the getting up and this representation contradicts Lamb's doctrine that Shakespeare does not act as well as he reads. None of the chief characters very well played but still I had no ennuie'.[114]

As was traditional, Phelps himself took the part of Jaques. Although his performance was noted for 'taste, judgment, and effect' in 1847, by 1857 a reviewer found it tiresome, complaining that the set speeches had a 'conventional and familiar air' (*Athenaeum*, 4 Dec. 1847; 31 Oct. 1857). Clearly Jaques presented a problem for the nineteenth-century stage. The conventional interpretation of Jaques as a wise, kindly philosopher worked well enough in the study, and it had been satisfactorily staged when Jaques's part had been reduced by extensive cuts, as, for instance, when J. Wallack played him in 'the character of the chorus in the Greek tragedy' at the Princess's in 1845 (*Observer*, 2 Mar. 1845). Once the bulk of Jaques's lines had been restored, the evidence of cynical complexity worked against the notion of his gentle sagacity. In Phelps's production, for instance, the speeches of satirical denunciation (2.7.36–87) were eliminated and considerable effort was expended to rehabilitate Jaques as a friendly, nurturing fellow who appoints himself Old Adam's caretaker in the latter part of 2.7. But a leaden quality crept into the role. When Barry Sullivan played Jaques in Phelps's 1855 production, a reviewer damned him with faint praise: Sullivan 'appeared sedulously to avoid the sin of exaggeration with which he has hitherto been justly charged' (*Athenaeum*, 30 June 1855). Mr Anderson, playing with Helena Faucit at Drury Lane in 1865, conceived Jaques as 'a compound of the heavy tragedian and the serious Low Churchman . . . His mode of expressing melancholy was to keep his eyes thrown up to heaven' (*Pall Mall Gazette*, 10 Mar. 1865). Another commentator diagnosed the problem as simply that Anderson played Jaques 'as past middle age, when humour should come from contrast between his attitude and his situation' (*Observer*, 12 Mar. 1865).

114 Robinson, p. 184 (4 Dec. 1847).

Victorian excesses

In the second half of the nineteenth century, *As You Like It* became a favourite
performance piece in England and America, with productions proliferating
in major cities and the provincial circuits. By one estimate, the play has
appeared at least every five years in England since Macready's 1842 production.[115] Its popularity in America and on the continent grew apace. In
England, theatre once again became a respectable form of entertainment;
Kean's management of the Princess's Theatre from 1850 to 1859 had 'marked
the beginning of the end of a drama based upon the support of popular audiences'; he was able to 'rais[e] contemporary standards' and begin to attract
the socially respectable and intellectual classes back to the theatres.[116] Certainly the pictorial style continued, although it was balanced, in the case
of *As You Like It*, by emphasis on moralistic passages, delivered in the
favoured declamatory style. Developments in theatrical machinery, including the introduction of electrical lighting, contributed to the possibilities
of elaborate sets. If there were no bold new interpretations of *As You Like
It* during this period, previously established themes and approaches were
sometimes carried to surprising extremes. Notable elements of this Victorian heritage were the pictorial stage, the shaping of the play to accord with
conventional moral codes, and, most of all, the succession of great actresses
playing the part of Rosalind.

Scenic illusionism: Hare–Kendal's stage grass and
Sullivan's stuffed stag

Arden presented a terrific opportunity to the proponents of pictorial staging.
Rather than calling upon the audience to visualise the pastoral scene or
invoking it with symbolic props, designers sought to create on stage what
they thought the author had imagined. Fed with such a product since the
days of Macready's painted sets, audiences developed a taste for realistic
stage effects. By the 1860s, 'in the increased lighting, with the reduced fore-
stage, and the frequent entries in the scene', the idea of scenery providing
a 'complete illusion' – rather than a scenic accompaniment to the enacted
text – was in vogue.[117]

The growth of consumerism at this time contributed to playgoers' demand
for fresh spectacle and intriguing display, for plays that were as thoroughly
'done up' as the displays in shop windows. As a critic remarked, 'it is but
a due mark of respect to the work that the picture should be as complete
as possible in scenery and costume, having regard to the class of theatre

---

115 Child, p. 170.   116 Booth, p. 14.   117 Southern, p. 91.

and the audience appealed to . . .' (*Theatre*, 1 Apr. 1880). Increasingly, however, there were worries that spectacle had crowded out Shakespeare. As we have seen, Fanny Kemble felt that Macready's pictorial sets and stage effects were little consolation for the poverty of the acting in his production. Lady Pollock, writing around 1875, observed that Macready's legacy 'was hardly what he hoped when first he took the reins of management'. Despite Charles Kean's efforts, there were still complaints of 'a gradual decline of interest in the poetry of the stage', so that 'carpenters and scene-painters were more prized than authors; and extravaganzas which admitted every vagary of decoration and of costume finally became the fashion'.[118]

Perhaps the most notable manifestation of this trend was the revival staged at St James's Theatre in 1885 by John Hare and W. H. Kendal. Louis Wingfield designed a set with cascading water, ferns in a forested glade, 'sunlight effects' produced by electric lighting, and stage grass manufactured from dyed feathers sewn into mats (*Pall Mall Gazette*, 24 Jan. 1885). The first act was played on the terraced garden of a medieval chateau. Elaborate costumes by Froissart completed the picture of late medieval life, although critics objected to 'Celia's horribly ugly headdress' and to the inappropriately sumptuous cosumes worn by the banished Duke and his courtiers (*Referee*, 1 Feb. 1885). Did the play disappear beneath these layers of spectacular excess? Some judged that the production 'render[ed] easier the task of the imagination and enhanc[ed] the pleasure of the spectator' (*Athenaeum*, 31 Jan. 1885). Most, however, found the effect 'overdone' (*Punch*, 7 Feb. 1885); some went so far as to declare that 'Shakespeare nowadays is the hobby of stage decorators' (*Daily Telegraph*, 26 Jan. 1885). In the words of one contemporary:

> What at the outset was doubtless an earnest and reverent desire to emphasise the poet's meaning by stage arrangements which should bring the incidents and ideas home to ordinary spectators, has developed into a craze for millinery and archaeological details . . . *As You Like It* of all [Shakespeare's] plays is least calculated to bear overloading with decoration.
>
> (*Weekly Dispatch*, 1 Feb. 1885)

The replacement of Arne's musical settings with new music by Alfred Cellier, including some lyrics lifted from Christopher Marlowe and Ben Jonson, proved a further distraction. But the sure sign that overmuch attention had been paid to lavish effects was the disappointing level of the actors' performances. 'We had plenty of scenery, but very little Shakespeare', complained

118 Pollock, *Poet and the Stage*, p. 338.

one critic (*Illustrated London News*, 31 Jan. 1885); another commented 'more care is taken with the design of one headdress than in the proper delivery of one speech' (*Daily Telegraph*, 26 Jan. 1885). Its 'lavish expenditure' could appeal only to those 'devoid of imaginative and poetic ideas', because attention to 'bright dresses and gaudy apparel' surpassed that given to the way in which the lines were spoken. 'To the true lovers of Shakespeare . . . the play is the *first* thing to be considered; *secondarily*, the manner in which it is caparisoned and bedecked' (*Theatre*, 2 Mar. 1885).

Mrs Kendal's self-conscious, 'strangely lifeless' Rosalind set off debate about whether she was too old, at thirty-seven, to play the part. Although her elocution was good, she was 'physically unsuited for such a character' (*Theatre*, 2 Mar. 1885) and lacked 'that indefinable something which we designate as charm . . . her gaiety and badinage seem forced' (*Weekly Dispatch*, 1 Feb. 1885). Correspondingly, Mr Kendal's Orlando was awkward and unromantic: 'even his love for Rosalind scarcely rouses him to abandon his heavy, sententious manner' (*Weekly Dispatch*, 1 Feb. 1885). He was unconvincing in the match with Charles, somehow defeating the burly wrestler with a 'feeble push', 'merely patting him on the calf of the right leg' (*Theatre*, 2 Mar. 1885; *Referee*, 1 Feb. 1885). Mr Hare, 'quite paralysed' by nervousness, played Touchstone as 'a very dismal philosopher' who 'gives utterance to his wise sayings as if he were inoculated with nineteenth-century pessimism' (*Daily Telegraph*, 26 Jan. 1885; *Weekly Dispatch*, 1 Feb. 1885). One critic observed that 'the burden of responsibility for the entire production was . . . too much for the actor, who . . . all but merged his functions of clown in those of manager' (*Athenaeum*, 31 Jan. 1885). Hermann Vezin presented his already 'well known' version of Jaques: 'a sound, scholarly, intelligent reading of a character that might be desperately spoiled and misunderstood by a modern actor who cares little for the practice or study of elocution' (*Daily Telegraph*, 26 Jan. 1885). The positive response to Vezin, coupled with critics' general uneasiness about the excesses of the Hare–Kendal production, indicate that the appeal of scenic illusionism was not universally felt.

Nevertheless, the drive for realism led to the appearance on the Stratford stage at this time of 'real' Shakespearean artifacts. In 1879 Barry Sullivan's company presented *As You Like It* at the Shakespeare Festival. The production's most spectacular scene was the hunters' celebration in Act 4: 'the dead deer was no mere "property" animal, but had been shot for this representation in Charlecote Park', where Shakespeare himself supposedly poached a deer, by Sir Spencer Lucy. A local journalist prophetically claimed that the staging would 'long be remembered as an example of dramatic realism, the full significance of which it is hardly possible to over-estimate' (*Stratford-upon-Avon Herald*, 9 May 1879). In fact, the stag became an icon of Stratford productions of *As You Like It* – despite its moth-eaten condition, it continued to appear regularly until 1919 when Nigel Playfair revolted against tradition.[119] This was the same stuffed stag that Mary Anderson recalled as an authenticating prop of the production in which she appeared at Stratford in 1885:

> the stage was decorated with blossoms from Shakespeare's garden; the flowers used by Rosalind and Celia, as well as the turnip gnawed by Audrey, had been plucked near Ann Hathaway's cottage; the deer carried across the stage in the hunting chorus had been shot in Charlcote Park for the occasion – so I was told – by one of the Lucys.[120]

The related notions of a retrievable past and the collapse of fictive drama into spectacular display could hardly have been expected to go further, although with the developed vogue in outdoor settings, which I will discuss later, they did.

Moral entertainment

To understand the appeal of these illusionistic stagings of *As You Like It*, we need to remember the expectations of the theatre-going public. Whereas the rowdiness of audiences had been a cause of concern (and legislation) in the first half of the nineteenth century, in the latter half, it was their passivity that became noteworthy.[121] Refined playgoers did not visit the theatre to be challenged but to be edified and entertained, and their notions of what was edifying remained traditional. Although *As You Like It* has come to seem, by the early twenty-first century, a play whose attitudes towards social custom are potentially quite subversive, for the Victorians, it was a model of propriety, civility, and ethical virtue – just those moral lessons the growing middle class demanded from Shakespeare. We can glimpse these attitudes in a review of Augustin Daly's production, which praises the manager who brings it forward as 'a public benefactor. All the influences that flow out of it are gentle and noble. Its development of pure love kindles the heart. Its pastoral pictures tranquilize the mind . . .' (unidentified clipping, Moore pbk). Daly was masterful at influencing reviewers, but this is still an astonishing bit of salesmanship. How did the play manage to come across as such a paragon of moral demonstration?

For a romantic comedy, *As You Like It* is particularly well stocked with philosophers, of the sincere (Duke Senior), sentimental (Adam), down-to-earth (Corin), and cynical (Touchstone) varieties. Jaques, of course,

119 Beauman, p. 66.   120 Anderson, p. 199.   121 Booth, p. 24.

combines all these philosophical modes. Most nineteenth-century stagings emulated Duke Senior in attempting to find 'good in everything' (2.1.17) each philosopher presented. After all, a reviewer noted, the play offered a perfect balance:

> Where else shall we look for such happy harmonising of two moods of folly, like that of Jacques, the *blasé* sentimentalist and cynical Epicurean, with that of Touchstone, the sententious shooter of sharp bolts, the licensed whipper of affectations, the motley mocker of the time; such contrast of despotic injustice in the usurper, with philosophic use of adversity, and profitable study of nature, in the exile?   (*Theatre*, 1 Apr. 1880)

Each of these characters was accorded every possible dignity, and the result was a comedy so philosophical even Queen Victoria found it 'admirable' – while adding, 'still as a performance I thought it rather heavy'.[122]

Nineteenth-century stagings contain no hint that Duke Senior's exile might, like Prospero's, indicate his past mistakes. Dividing the moral poles evenly with his brother, the evil Duke Frederick, Duke Senior was presented as benevolent and genteel. Cowden Clarke described 'the exiled Duke' as 'a perfect exemplar of what should comprise a Christian's course – a cheerful gratitude for the benefits that have been showered upon him; a calm, yet firm endurance of adversity; a tolerance of unkindness; and a promptitude to forgive injuries'.[123] On stage, the Duke exercised authority by confidently greeting intruders (Orlando, Jaques de Boys), and his respectful band of forester–lords were carefully instructed to rise and sit as he did. The well-populated stagings of this period contributed in themselves to Duke Senior's rehabilitation: surrounded by so many well-armed followers, he was a force to be reckoned with (as the disappearing Duke Frederick evidently divined). An overly jolly Duke Senior would meet with disapproval – the fate of Henry Vernon, who 'looked and played like . . . Old King Cole' at Stratford in 1885 (*World*, 2 Sept. 1885).

Shaw denounced Adam as 'that servile apostle of working-class Thrift and Teetotalism', pointing out the intrusiveness of his sermon on the evils of alcohol (2.3.47–55), which bears scant relation to the action or themes of the play.[124] Adam had been established as a sentimental character early on: in 1750, John Hill wrote of the part as one in which 'sensibility alone will do . . . if the player have only feeling in himself, he will make every body else

---

122 Royal Archives, Queen Victoria's Journal, 31 Jan. 1851, quoted in Rowell,
     p. 55. During this period Charles Kean was Director of the Windsor
     Theatricals, and the production the Queen saw at Windsor was presented by
     his Princess's company.
123 Clarke, p. 36.   124 George Bernard Shaw, vol. 2, p. 270.

feel with him sufficiently', and described how the audience was moved to tears by Mr Berry's performance (see commentary, 2.3.38–53).[125] Easy as it is for Adam to come across as pathetic – and nineteenth-century reviewers regularly complained about lachrymose and overly antiquated renditions of the part – productions continued to allow him a bit of sentimental business when he departs from the de Boys household in 2.3 and to validate Orlando's, and often Jaques's, character by their displays of devotion to the sententious old servant.

Touchstone presented a different set of issues altogether. Cowden Clarke tried, unconvincingly, to make a case for the clown's 'good and gentlemanly feeling', as witnessed by his concern for women watching wrestling and his determination 'to act honourably by the trusting and doating Audrey'.[126] Even though Touchstone's part was carefully shorn of its more barbed passages (much of the dialogue with Corin in 3.3, the racier elements of his parody of Orlando's verses, and the lewder bits of his courtship of Audrey were all cut), he still sometimes offended nineteenth-century sensibilities. Reviewers complained that Lionel Brough's Touchstone showed a 'caressing familiarity' when he exited with Celia soon after their arrival in Arden: 'for all his devotion to her, and the familiarity allowed to the court-fool, he should never so far forget the distance that separates them as to lay her head on his shoulder, put his arm round her waist, and pat her cheek as he supports her off' (*Theatre*, 1 Apr. 1880). Another wrote that Brough as Touchstone betrayed 'complete . . . misconception of the relations possible under any circumstances between a jester and a princess of royal blood' (*Athenaeum*, 6 Mar. 1880). These comments remind us of the strict class decorum this age demanded of the play, in Arden as at court. Touchstone developed into a bizarre and sometimes grotesque character partly in order to protect the appearance of Rosalind's and Celia's virtue. Robert Keeley succeeded as the clown in Macready's production in part because his physical ugliness alleviated viewers' concerns about 'his presence with two beautiful ladies in a lonely wood'.[127] Arthur Cecil's Touchstone at the Opera Comique in 1875 was commended because he appeared 'familiar with courts, and may, perhaps, be supposed to bear himself with a fair amount of quietude and dignity',[128] which scarcely sounds amusing. All this helps us to appreciate the odd praise James Lewis garnered as 'the dryest, quaintest, cleanest-cut Touchstone that ever wore cap and bells'.[129] For the most part, Touchstones of the age were simply dull; Shaw wrote that 'an Eskimo would demand his

---

125 Hill, p. 43.   126 Clarke, pp. 54, 55.
127 *John Bull*, quoted in Shattuck, *Mr Macready*.   128 Mullin, p. 109.
129 Joseph Francis Daly, p. 486.

money back if a modern author offered him such fare'.[130] Since Touchstone appears bored with his own jokes, the character presents a challenge for any production. Interestingly, Ellen Terry writes that this is the part Henry Irving would have played had they produced *As You Like It*, as they 'ought to have done . . . in 1888'.[131]

Jaques occupied the moralising centre of nineteenth-century productions. Writing in 1898, Rev. H. N. Hudson called the melancholiac 'an universal favourite', considering it 'something uncertain whether Jaques or Rosalind be the greater attraction'.[132] Although reviewers wondered 'whether Shakespeare did not intend Jaques to be in part a comic character, a foil to Touchstone' (*Athenaeum*, 27 Feb. 1875), the dominant stage tradition continued to offer the sententious, respected melancholiac-as-philosopher. Hermann Vezin was the great Jaques of the day, and his presentation of the character in 'elderly makeup' became a stage tradition (*Times*, 27 Feb. 1875). Rather than offering the Seven Ages speech 'as an oration spoken for the purpose of edifying an appreciative body of hearers', Vezin seemed to forget his audience was present and 'reflectively pursue[d] his series of descriptions as if quite alone' (*Times*, 27 Feb. 1875). He understood, a critic wrote, that the speech 'has little bearing on the play', instancing only 'a melancholy man's discontented and misanthropic observation of life' (*Academy*, 6 Mar. 1880). Vezin was celebrated for his elocutionary abilities and his subtle understanding of Jaques's melancholia, although the more discriminating might lament, as did Henry James, the lack of 'colour and vivacity, humour and irony' in Vezin's Jaques.[133]

Others who took the role made a hash of it. At the Queen's Theatre in 1871, Mr Rignold offered 'a manly and impressive delivery' but marred the effect 'by trying to make points where no point is possible' (*Athenaeum*, 4 Mar. 1871). At Stratford in 1885, Mr Macklin, an 'ineffective substitute for Mr Hermann Vezin', 'maintained perfect rigidity of limb in a very inconvenient and unnatural attitude' (*Academy*, 5 Sept. 1885; *Birmingham Daily Post*, [1885], SCL). As Jonathan Trumbull acutely noted, the era had never seen a satisfactory Jaques, 'for the identity which Shakespeare gave to the character is completely wiped out': Shakespeare had given Jaques 211 lines, but available acting editions from the period give him only 156, 37 of which were pilfered from 1 Lord. Stage tradition dictated delivery of lines with 'almost uniform funereal solemnity' and turning the 'bit of woodland table talk' which the Seven Ages speech should be into a pronouncement from 'an arbiter of doom' ('The Jaques of the Modern Stage', *Shakespeariana*,

130 George Bernard Shaw, vol. 2, p. 268.   131 Terry, p. 328.
132 Hudson, pp. 343, 344.   133 Quoted in Mullin, p. 479.

n.d. [1889?], FSL small scrapbook). Cowden Clarke too found Jaques a
problem, not only for his affectations but because 'the fact is they all smoke
him for being a solemn pretender to a quality not natural to him'. Clarke
believed Jaques had been misinterpreted: 'Shakespeare certainly intended
the character of Jaques to be a satire upon your pretenders to wisdom'.[134] In
George Taylor's view, Jaques's 'melancholy cynicism was so out of tune with
Victorian romantic idealism', that actors warped the character, presenting
him 'as an affected, disagreeable and ugly grotesque' to contrast the young
lovers in the play.[135]

Shaw ridiculed Jaques as an 'ass' and railed against his most famous
speech:

> Nothing is more significant than the statement that 'all the world's a stage.' The
> whole world *is* ruled by theatrical illusion . . . And yet Shakespeare, with the
> rarest of opportunities of observing this, lets his pregnant metaphor slip, and,
> with his usual incapacity for pursuing any idea, wanders off into a
> grandmotherly Elizabethan edition of the advertisement of Cassell's Popular
> Educator. How anybody over the age of seven can take any interest in a literary
> toy so silly in its conceit and common in its ideas as the Seven Ages of Man
> passes my understanding . . .[136]

Shaw suggests that Shakespeare neglects an opportunity to extend the play's
metatheatricality, instead maintaining a relentless course through the trope.
Whether the problem is with Shakespeare or with interpretations of Jaques
seems an open question. In any case, the ponderous stage tradition prevailed,
and exploration of Jaques's cynicism towards established morality would not
take place until the next century.

The feminine ideal

The 'womanly' Rosalind aided the Victorian effort to create meliorising
versions of *As You Like It*. Helena Faucit, the ideal Rosalind of the age,
continued to appear in the part for decades: in 1875 she came out of re-
tirement to perform in *As You Like It* in a benefit at Drury Lane to aid
the Shakespeare Memorial Theatre fund (*Standard*, 24 Apr. 1875). In many
cultures women have been considered more emotional and closer to nature
than men, but Victorian gender ideology carried these associations to the
extreme and added an ethical component. Women's reproductive role, much

---

134 Clarke, pp. 41, 42.   135 George Taylor, p. 186.
136 George Bernard Shaw, vol. 2, pp. 270, 267–8.

emphasised in this era, indicated not only a physical capability but also a spiritual attribute of tenderness and nurturing emotions. In contrast to men's business role, women's function was that of domestic guardians – the 'angel of the house', as famously described by Coventry Patmore. And so, for at least one reviewer, Rosalind's femininity is confirmed not by her swoon over the bloody napkin but by her subsequent wish to be 'at home' (4.3.156) – the line revealing for him 'the deep-lying and permanent idiosyncrasy of the home-loving female heart' (*National Review*, Sept. 1884). That Rosalind – who is certainly not granted a nurturing role and who spends the majority of her time posing as a boy – could be regarded as an exemplar of this sort of 'womanliness' exposes the logical difficulties of the conception.

Despite the Victorian woman's alleged spirituality and ethical guardianship, she was valued by her male counterparts for a complex charm that included seductiveness. Rosalind's emotionalism and, as in earlier eras, the provocative display of her legs, brought this sort of charm before admiring viewers. The evolving myth of femininity associated with Rosalind depended on a delighted 'response felt most deeply by men', Mary Hamer observes.[137] We have seen how Dora Jordan was said to appeal particularly to 'the male part of her audience', and how Charlotte Cushman's masculine appearance limited her effectiveness in the role – Crabb Robinson wrote, 'Her face all but disgusting so that I could have no pleasure looking at her'.[138] Clearly 'pleasure looking at her' was part of what Rosalind was expected to provide, and one suspects that the emphasis on Faucit's ethereal 'womanliness' was at least in part rhetorical overkill. After all, the actor appeared on stage disguised as a boy in what was considered a revealing outfit, and enacted the part of a talkative and forward young woman – enough to provoke doubts about how 'womanly' she actually was. Samuel Johnson had wondered what the ladies would think of 'the facility with which both Rosalind and Celia give away their hearts', and not until the eristic Shaw did a critic overtly approve of Rosalind's forwardness in wooing Orlando.[139] Small wonder actresses had a formidable task to emphasise the character's upper-class bearing and moral scruples as the foundation of an emotional but restrained, alluring but loftily unavailable, playful but intelligent being. Rosalind was constantly called 'arch' in part because she needed to maintain some distance from those who were admiring her legs.

137 Hamer, p. 109.
138 Robinson, p. 176 (23 May 1845); Robinson had seen Cushman in Tobin's *Honeymoon*.
139 Samuel Johnson, p. 264; George Bernard Shaw, vol. 2, p. 269.

For the standard Ganymede costume was designed to accentuate the actress's legs. Richard Grant White wrote in 1885 that 'Rosalind, instead of wearing a tunic or short gown, cut up to the knees . . . should wear the very garments that she talks so much about, and in which I never saw a Rosalind appear upon the stage.' Instead of trunk hose, 'they go about with nothing but tight silk stockings upon their legs, amid the underwood and brambles of the Forest of Arden' (see commentary, 2.4.0sd). White notes acutely that the accurate costume 'would have concealed the womanliness of her figure'. He imagines a stage manager rebuking him for ignorance of what the public likes: 'they care more to see a pretty woman, with a pretty figure, prancing saucily about the stage in silk-tights, and behaving like neither man nor woman, than they would to see a booted, doubletted, felt-hatted Rosalind behaving now like a real man and now like a real woman'.[140]

Not everyone relished the Faucit ideal. Crabb Robinson thought her 'too sentimental for Rosalind'.[141] A reviewer was delighted when Miss M. Litton played Ganymede as 'a saucy, keen-witted, sharp-tongued lad', in a production at the Imperial Theatre in 1880, an interpretation that

> has not been the rule with previous Rosalinds of the day . . . all of whom, without exception, have made the woman so palpably apparent in look, bearing, even in dress, and still more in accentuation of every word to which womanly significance could be given that they not only rendered Orlando's blindness to Rosalind's disguise inconceivable, but deprived her dialogue with him of that charm of harmless high spirits and innocent love of fun which it is meant to convey. (*Theatre*, 1 Apr. 1880).

And Shaw equally panned Mary Anderson and the other actresses whom he observed as Rosalind (Dorothea Baird, Julia Neilson). He admitted to finding Ada Rehan 'irresistible' although she did nothing to shake his settled conviction that 'Rosalind is not a complete human being: she is simply an extension into five acts of the most affectionate, fortunate, delightful five minutes in the life of a charming woman'.[142] Puncturing the Romantic notion of transcendent character and the myth of an ideal, womanly Rosalind that derived from it, Shaw anticipated a modern (or even postmodern) understanding of dramatic character as the fleeting product of stage performance.

In keeping with these dissenting views, elements of the comic hoyden of earlier days would gradually creep back into stage portrayals. Interestingly, these stronger, more independent Rosalinds anticipated the New Woman of the turn of the century, even as they were, in another sense, throwbacks to

---

140 White, pp. 245, 243, 246.   141 Robinson, p. 163 (28 July 1840).
142 George Bernard Shaw, vol. 3, p. 210.

the less delicately behaved actresses of the late eighteenth century. Still, for the most part, Faucit's delicacy set the standard for Rosalinds of the era. Ganymede's image was never to obscure the feminine form or character of Rosalind; the turn as a boy was merely an interesting situation in which to observe the woman beneath – or in Victorian stylings, revealed by – masculine attire. Indeed, her gambit in male disguise was considered the test of Rosalind's true femininity, and Orlando's attraction the indication of how successfully Rosalind passed the test.

In the light of the fuss over Rosalind's character in the nineteenth century, it is interesting to notice the attention also given to Celia. Her second-class status is suggested by the critic who recalls, in 1896, the 'old days, when the Rosalind, being a star, would cut Celia to shreds and patches in order to aggravate the claims of Rosalind to major importance' (*Daily Telegraph*, 3 Dec. 1896). Celia was often conceived as Rosalind's sidekick (and played by her understudy); Celia's lofty position as the Duke's daughter was emphasised, and her character was accorded charm, sympathy, and a certain reserve. Because Celia always wears a dress, never talks too much, and chastises her cousin for sins against decorum – 'you have simply misused our sex in your love-prate' (4.1.162) – some found in her, not Rosalind, the feminine ideal. When Hazlitt, for instance, called Celia's 'silent and retired character' a 'relief' from 'the provoking loquacity of Rosalind',[143] he was implicitly critical of Rosalind. So too for Charles Cowden Clarke; Celia was one of 'inestimable worth', a character who 'would be a wit and heroine of the first water in any other play, and as a character by herself'. Only because her own modesty makes her 'yield the palm' to Rosalind does Celia tend to stand by silently, and for Clarke her modesty is a virtue. In his assessment, 'Celia is pre-eminently *womanly*. She has the best qualities of womanly nature. She is devoted, constant, femininely gentle, yet frank and firm in opinion'.[144] Alfred Austin similarly rhapsodised on 'the real, the active, the self-sacrificing love' that Celia shows towards Rosalind, and the 'silent power such a nature exercises over others'; she is, moreover, 'a true woman' because she 'remembers her jewels' when fleeing to Arden (*National Review*, Sept. 1884). When Celia, like Rosalind, was praised in theatre reviews, she was often called 'womanly' (*Athenaeum*, 31 Jan. 1885).

Other Rosalinds

On the American stage, one popular manifestation of the feminine ideal was Helena Modjeska, the Polish-born actress who for many years played

143 Hazlitt, p. 308.   144 Clarke, pp. 46, 48, 50.

Rosalind with charm and intelligence. Modjeska was a 'finished', accomplished artist at the time of her American début in 1882, and her exotic grace and skilful delivery of the verse were much admired, despite her failure ever to sound British.[145] Initially Modjeska played opposite Maurice Barrymore's athletic Orlando. A boxing champion as a youth, Barrymore recruited his friend William Muldoon, the 1880 Champion Wrestler of the World, to play Charles, and the two supposedly wrestled 'for real' in 1.2.[146] Modjeska maintained that her version of the character was 'closer to Lodge's idea' in *Rosalynde* than to Shakespeare's, because the playwright knew 'his feminine roles would be played by boys'. With this questionable analysis, Modjeska was making her best case for Rosalind's essential femininity. She also emphasised Rosalind's high-born nature, observing that 'although she assumes rude manners, her inborn gentleness and refinement must be visible from behind it'.[147] Her Rosalind was deemed 'arch, tender, elegant, intellectual, highly bred, and womanly, perfectly consistent, and executed with a technical perfection possible only to the complete artist'.[148] Less frenetic and more restrained than many Rosalinds, Modjeska in approaching Orlando after the wrestling match was 'mature, almost amusingly maternal'.[149] She succeeded in presenting the 'double identity' of Rosalind disguised as Ganymede, 'suggest[ing] to the audience the archness and coquetry of a woman, while to her lover she is nothing but a wayward and fanciful boy'.[150] Yet 'even in her "breeches", Modjeska maintained a dignified, courtly demeanor',[151] wearing a Ganymede costume of brocade and silk. In Modjeska's view, Ganymede had nothing of 'swagger or rudeness, but chivalry'.[152]

Lillie Langtry's qualified success in the role showed that something more than feminine attractiveness was demanded of the ideal Victorian Rosalind. Langtry's scandalous personal life included a well-known affair with the Prince of Wales. A latecomer to acting, she mastered the intricacies of Shakespearean language, but lacked the skill to present Rosalind's passion and 'womanliness'. If Langtry was praised for her beauty and 'tenderness' in the role, 'earnest and deep emotion' were judged beyond her reach

145 Odell, *New York Stage*, vol. 10, pp. 375–6.
146 Marion Coleman, pp. 273–4.   147 Ibid., pp. 417, 580.
148 John Rankin Towse, *Sixty Years of Theatre: An Old Critic's Memories* (1916), pp. 204–7, quoted in Mullin, p. 332.
149 Winter, *Shakespeare*, p. 292.
150 John Rankin Towse, *The Century Magazine*, XXVII (n.s. xxv), November 1883, 25; quoted in Marion Coleman, p. 287.
151 Derrick, p. 145.   152 Marion Coleman, p. 579.

(*Athenaeum*, 30 Sept. 1882). Her Rosalind was a 'merry, rather unrefined girl', and as Ganymede 'she wore the male attire with jaunty assurance', adding a 'pleasing swagger'.[153] Many critics disliked Langtry's tendency to emphasise the comic aspects of the character – a sin against the Faucit ideal of tender womanliness.

Adelaide Neilson played Rosalind at the Theatre Royal, Haymarket, in 1876, charming audiences with her high spirits but failing to bring out the character's 'higher and more refined beauties'. Her manner suggested 'a high-spirited school girl' and as Ganymede 'her boyish assumption lack[ed] delicacy' (unidentified clippings, TM). Several reviewers mention Neilson's exaggerated efforts to tug Ganymede's doublet into service as a more modest garment – efforts, one reviewer wrote, 'that smack too much of the burlesque lady of the French stage' (unidentified clipping, TM). Clearly Rosalind was expected in this era to call attention to her legs, but actresses had to walk a fine line between vaguely titillating display and accusations of vulgar exhibitionism.

A good example of a performer who trod this line and sometimes slipped over it was American Mary Anderson, who was enthusiastically received in England upon her visit in 1885. Anderson reported that Rosalind's 'sparkle' and 'wholesomeness' were so congenial to her 'that for a time I wished to act nothing else'.[154] Anderson's 'girlish rather than womanly' version of the part included a Ganymede who was the 'perfect embodiment of the "saucy lackey"'; whereas 'in most Rosalinds the woman obtrudes herself upon the physical as well as the mental eye', so that Orlando's failure to recognise her is inexplicable, Anderson made the transformation more convincing (William Archer, *Theatre*, 1 Oct. 1885). Not all were pleased by her departure from the Faucit standard of femininity: she was 'a little more of a hoyden than we care to see' (*Birmingham Daily Gazette*, 31 Aug. 1885). To convey aristocratic hauteur, Anderson adopted a declamatory style and tended to strike poses, both as Rosalind *and* as Ganymede.[155] For many in the audience 'it was the prospect of seeing the new Rosalind's nether limbs that was responsible for the excited rush for seats', and 'the success of the performance was determined in each man's mind according to the extent to which his ideal had been realised' (*Bat*, 1 Sept. 1885). Anderson called attention to her legs with 'little tricks' such as pulling her cloak about her legs: 'the device is well enough when in the first timidity of Orlando's presence in the forest her maiden modesty is shocked at the thought of being seen by him in her boy's clothes; but, being constantly repeated, it becomes wearisome, and invests

153 Winter, *Shakespeare*, p. 290.   154 Anderson, p. 199–200.
155 Derrick, pp. 149–50.

the character with an unnecessary suggestion of prudery' (*Birmingham Daily Post*, 31 Aug. 1885). Prudery bordering on prurience, one would guess; another critic observes 'again and again was repeated the gesture in which Rosalind strives to hide her lower limbs by turning her ample cloak into a petticoat' (*Observer*, 30 Aug. 1885).

Perhaps critics divined hints in Anderson's performance of a different model of Rosalind on the horizon: 'so swaggering and masculine a Rosalind we have not seen' (*Stage*, 4 Sept. 1885); 'the most masculine Rosalind of recent times' (*World*, 2 Sept. 1885). She embodied the 'saucy lackey' while managing to stay 'within the limits of womanly reserve' (*Academy*, 5 Sept. 1885), and depicted 'art within art' in the layered Ganymede scenes, where 'the real earnestness and the assumed cajolery were inimitable'. For instance, 'Anderson did not abandon the imported cuckoo song altogether, but instead of teasing Orlando with it, according to conventional usage, she came on to the stage singing it in an aimless and indifferent mood, her mind being apparently occupied by other thoughts' (*Birmingham Daily Post*, n.d., SCL). Certainly this was not a subtle performance; one reviewer wished for 'more contour', while another judged her 'broad' gestures as enabling Anderson 'to fill the stage' (*Bat*, 1 Sept. 1885; *Athenaeum*, 5 Sept. 1885).

Noted as a vehicle for feminine charms, *As You Like It* was staged several times in the 1890s by all-female troupes. At one such 'freak matinée' at Palmer's Theatre in New York in November 1893, some of the women in the cast wore false beards.[156] The performance was admired by Ellen Terry, who called Mme Janauschek's Jaques a 'remarkable bit of acting': 'I have never heard the speech beginning "All the world's a stage" delivered more finely, not even by Phelps, who was fine in the part'.[157] Soon after, a group of women put on the play at the Prince of Wales's Theatre in London, with the addition of an all-female orchestra.[158] Evidently their gender was both a challenge and a check to the play as traditionally staged: while some favourite passages were cut 'as a concession to feminine ideas of propriety', other portions of the text 'into which the coarser sense of men had read equivoke or innuendo, were restored' (*Athenaeum*, 3 Mar. 1894).

Although individual actresses won more or less renown for their performances as Rosalind, the part was so generally beloved in the Victorian period that some believed it virtually 'actress-proof'. 'Whoever failed, or could fail, as Rosalind?' Shaw remarked of Julia Neilson.[159] Another reviewer wrote 'out of a dozen Rosalinds with whom the memory can charge itself, some

156 Odell, *New York Stage*, vol. 15, p. 559.   157 Terry, p. 324.
158 Knowles, p. 641.   159 George Bernard Shaw, vol. 2, p. 270.

have been better than others, but none has been bad' (*Athenaeum*, 12 Dec. 1896).

The other female parts were often given scant attention during this period. The shepherdess Phoebe rarely wins mention, since by the standards of the day 'any young woman who has learnt how to hold herself on the stage may, if she be good-looking, hope to be delightful as Phoebe' (*Athenaeum*, 12 Dec. 1896). Audrey, by contrast, could sometimes offend with downright 'grotesqueness' (*Athenaeum*, 6 June 1885), as did Isabel Irving, whose Audrey 'was exaggerated, and certainly not funny' (*Daily Telegraph*, 16 July 1890). The ideal seemed to be an Audrey who was 'picturesquely uncouth without being ungraceful' (*Theatre*, 1 Apr. 1880). Mrs Keeley strayed from the mark because her 'blankest looks have more intelligence in them than Audrey's brightest perceptions' (*Athenaeum*, 8 Oct. 1842); she was not sufficiently 'stolid, unsophisticated, and ungainly' (*Spectator*, 8 Oct. 1842). 'Audrey's exertions' are largely physical, so an actress too old or too passive, as Mrs Billington was at Stratford in 1885, ruined the effect (*Academy*, 5 Sept. 1885). When the part of Hymen began to be restored in the latter half of the nineteenth century, it was frequently played by a woman. One critic asked: 'why is the god of marriage robed as a woman, and why also is he played by one?' (unidentified clipping, 6 Dec. 1896, TM).

Augustin Daly's triumph

Perhaps the greatest production of the late nineteenth century was Augustin Daly's, starring Ada Rehan as Rosalind. Daly's script was among the most faithful to the Folio text since Shakespeare's day. Like Macready, Daly restored the description of 'The melancholy "Jacques"' in 2.1 to 1 Lord and included in its original place the dialogue between Jaques and Rosalind that opens 4.1. Similarly, he allowed Jaques to witness Touchstone and Audrey's encounter with Martext and included most of the masque of Hymen as well as Rosalind's Epilogue, while excising passages likely to offend viewers, keeping a special eye out for lines that might sully Rosalind's purity.

However, Rehan's Rosalind recalled Peg Woffington and Dora Jordan more than the delicate Victorian renditions of the character.[160] Rehan presented 'a gleeful yet loving woman, and not a poetical conceit or a metaphysical abstraction'. This Rosalind conveyed emphatic 'relief' upon learning that Orlando returned her affection and was 'liberate[d] . . . into a gentle frenzy of pleasure'.[161] Deep emotion translated into physical activity for

160 Derrick, p. 153; Walkley, p. 33.   161 Winter, *Ada Rehan*, pp. 38, 72.

"Bear your body more seeming Audrey."
Mr. Lewis as Touchstone. Miss Irving as Audrey.
"As You Like It" at Daly's Theatre.

Figure 5 'Bear your body more seeming Audrey': in Augustin Daly's 1889 production, Isabel Irving's Audrey was considered by some 'exaggerated, and certainly not funny' (*Daily Telegraph*, 16 July 1890). Because the character was uncouth, it was easy for Audrey to offend nineteenth-century audiences, who also worried about Rosalind and Celia being alone in Arden with Touchstone. Daly's Touchstone, James Lewis, was praised as 'the dryest, quaintest, cleanest-cut Touchstone that ever wore cap and bells' (Joseph Francis Daly, p. 486).

Rehan's Rosalind. Some critics complained about her peripatetic style – Henry Clapp wrote of 'eye-fatiguing perambulations' or what Walkley referred to as 'steeple-chasing'.[162] Her restless movement registered a vigorous style of feminine behaviour – a precursor of the New Woman.

Daly conceived of the play as a 'piece [that] neither contains a sad person nor anywhere supplies a current of sad thought'. Even the timing of the music was 'quickened to harmonize with the abounding and rejuvenating spirit'.[163] Daly used the familiar settings by Arne and Bishop; Hymen's two verses, frequently cut in performance, were retained. However, the 'Cuckoo song' was not used, and Daly introduced orchestral background music during the Seven Ages speech.[164]

Many New York critics, including Daly's usual detractor Nym Crinkle, followed William Winter (who was under Daly's influence) in praising the production, although some criticised Rehan's exaggerated mannerisms and intonation, and objected to the light comic tone. After a healthy run in the 1889–90 season the production travelled to London's Lyceum in 1890, where it was even better received than it had been in New York. One commentator praised what he heard as an improvement over native performers: 'Occasionally a strong American accent startled the ear; but on our own stage it is rare to hear Shakespeare's lines spoken with such dignity, distinctness, and musical force. Here was just the happy mean between the modern familiar and flippant style and the frothy rhetoric of the old school' (*Daily Telegraph*, 16 July 1890). Daly was deemed to have 'preserved the play in all its purity' (*Daily Telegraph*, 16 July 1890). 'Miss Rehan simply took the house by storm', demonstrating appropriate 'dignity' in the opening scenes and memorable 'exuberance . . . so graceful, so eminently feminine' (*Theatre*, 1 Aug. 1890). Her 'voice [was] all music', 'her 'movements [were] all grace', so that Orlando could hardly help worshipping her (*Athenaeum*, 19 July 1890). This audience was delighted that Rehan's Rosalind 'never for one moment forgets, or allows her audience to forget, that she is a woman': 'Whatever "holiday mood" she may put on with Orlando, the very instant Rosalind is left alone with Celia she becomes a woman again to the very finger tips, kissing and clasping and embracing her sister for very reaction after all this pent-up excitement . . .' (*Daily Telegraph*, 16 July 1890). Walkley rhapsodically confessed himself 'hypnotised' by Rehan's performance: 'she realises for me, as no other actress can, the sex in Rosalind, the femineity [sic], the *odor di femmina*'.[165] Clearly Rosalind was still looked to as the feminine ideal,

162 Shattuck, *American Stage*, vol. 2, p. 79; Walkley, p. 32.
163 Winter, *Ada Rehan*, pp. 67, 69.   164 Winter, *Shakespeare*, p. 282.
165 Walkley, pp. 31, 33.

Figure 6 In early eras, Rosalind's swoon in 4.3 confirmed her 'womanly' nature. A reviewer described Ada Rehan's response to the bloody napkin as 'incomparably beautiful . . . in an instant the face alters – gaiety is dismissed for a look of horror . . . The masquerading boy has gone, and the veritable woman has come back again' (*Daily Telegraph*, 16 July 1890). Rehan appeared in Daly's production with Henrietta Crosman as Celia and Eugene Ormond as Oliver.

although the model of womanliness she represented had begun to change (see figure 6).

The person perhaps least pleased with Rehan's and Daly's triumph in 1890 was Henry Irving, who had contemplated staging *As You Like It*. He shelved his plans, so leading lady Ellen Terry, considered by many the pre-eminent actress of the age, never played Rosalind. Terry commented that Rehan 'understood, like all great comedians, that you must not pretend to be serious so sincerely that no one in the audience sees through it!'[166]

Daly's *As You Like It* was in many ways a culmination of nineteenth-century approaches to the play. The goal was to create a pleasing spectacle: picturesque qualities were emphasised; character complexity went unacknowledged; and Rosalind stole the show. Thus John Drew, who initially played Orlando against Rehan, tired of her pre-eminence and withdrew from the company.[167] The 'philosopher' parts continued to be acted somewhat drearily. George Clarke spoke too slowly as Jaques, and Adam was 'too feeble' (*Theatre*, 1 Aug. 1890). Shaw called this production *As You Like It* 'just as I don't like it . . . a spectacle to benumb the mind and obscure the passions'. He was dismayed not only by the pictorial emphasis but by the way the play did little more than fit established patterns. The characters were 'cognate impostures', who 'play each the same tune all through. This is not human nature or dramatic character; it is juvenile lead, first old man, heavy lead, heavy father, principal comedian, and leading lady, transfigured by magical word-music.'[168] As we have seen, Shaw was no fan of the play, but much of his weariness with it can be attributed to Victorian staging traditions.

Turn of the century: transition to a freer Arden

By the end of the nineteenth century, there was more widespread disgruntlement with the pictorial emphasis that had for so long been the hallmark of theatre in general and of *As You Like It* in particular. A production by Mr Lancaster at the Shaftesbury Theatre in 1888, for instance, featured a number of well-known performers, including Forbes Robertson as Orlando and Miss Wallis as Rosalind, but a reviewer complained that despite the 'pretty and poetical' scene and the money 'lavished upon costumes and decoration', 'no competent master mind directs the whole, the splendour is cumbrous, the reading of the play is wrong'. To the reviewer, Arden should be 'a better, higher fairy land', not a 'plain, prosaic land in which people

---

166 Terry, p. 318.   167 Shattuck, *American Stage*, vol. 2, p. 76.
168 George Bernard Shaw, vol. 3, pp. 208, 210.

more or less consciously make fools of themselves' (*Athenaeum*, 27 Oct. 1888). In striving for more realistic effects, the production had stymied the imagination.

George Alexander's 1896–7 production at the St James's Theatre provoked a similar response. The play was 'mounted handsomely, but by no means lavishly' (*Theatre*, 1 Jan. 1897). Alexander paid renewed attention to the script, presenting the masque of Hymen and the pages' song in 5.3, both frequently cut in earlier nineteenth-century stagings. Yet the play had become so familiar that its 'main lines . . . as presented on the stage, alike as regards interpretation of character and pictorial rendering, are so fixed and established by immemorial tradition and precedent as to leave no opportunity for any further development of originality in the production of the comedy' (unidentified clipping, 6 Dec. 1896, TM). This was all enough to remind Shaw of why he considered the wrestling match the chief attraction of any production: 'it is so much easier to find a man who knows how to wrestle than one who knows how to act'.[169] And if the settings were not lavish, the costumes were: the *Sketch* ran an article detailing the jewelled brocades worn by the production's central characters (9 Dec. 1896). The music included Arne's settings, plus ballet music, a march by Gounod, and specially composed incidental music by Edward German. Attention to textual accuracy did not prevent Julia Neilson's Rosalind from singing the 'Cuckoo song'.

Neilson's Rosalind was cut from familiar cloth, praised for her 'loveliness' and 'womanly feeling' (*Theatre*, 1 Jan. 1897), her 'refinement and charm' – she 'did not turn the pretty and graceful Epilogue into a coarse winking farce as many of our Rosalinds have done before her' (*Daily Telegraph*, 3 Dec. 1896). As these comments suggest, Faucit's Rosalind continued to prevail 'from the standpoint of imagination' (*Athenaeum*, 12 Dec. 1896), and Neilson received demerits because her Rosalind was 'vivacious rather than pensive' (unidentified clipping, 6 Dec. 1896, TM).

As Jaques, W. H. Vernon managed to 'extrac[t] every ounce of meaning from the author's words' without 'straining after effect' (*Theatre*, 1 Jan. 1897). Even the cynical Shaw found Vernon's Jaques 'more tolerable than I can remember'.[170] H. V. Edmond took an 'extraordinary' approach to Touchstone, playing the clown as 'a pantomime demon who had just popped up from a trap in a glow of redfire' (*Daily Telegraph*, 3 Dec. 1896). Avoiding sententiousness, this restless Mephistophelian Touchstone was 'delighted with human follies, not cynically depressed at having to keep others mirthful' (*Athenaeum*, 12 Dec. 1896). George Alexander's Orlando conveyed 'grace,

169 Ibid., vol. 2, pp. 267, 270.   170 Ibid., vol. 2, p. 270.

ease, and charm', although a 'tendency towards sedateness' sugested that 'Orlando never was, and never could be, a good part' (*Theatre*, 1 Jan. 1897; *Daily Telegraph*, 3 Dec. 1896). Mr Loraine played Adam 'about twenty years too old', in Shaw's view.[171]

At Stratford, meanwhile, things were slow to change; indeed, in the case of *As You Like It* Stratford productions entered a kind of time warp. A popular favourite, the play was staged sixteen times between 1894 and 1915, usually under the direction of Frank Benson. A local reviewer gushed that 'here are Rosalind for the humorous and Corin for the sentimental, Jaques for the melancholy and Touchstone for the merry, Orlando for the muscular Christians and Audrey or Phoebe for the pastorally inclined – all ages are engaged, all tempers met, all the keys of feeling touched' (*Stratford-upon-Avon Herald*, 27 Apr. 1894). Yet if the play's 'charm seem[ed] always new and fresh' (*Leamington Courier*, 29 Apr. 1904), the aging props, scenery, and stage business returned reliably. Benson's athletic, romantic Orlando, and his wife Constance's vivacious Rosalind were joined by a changing cast for the minor roles. As Jaques, Arthur Whitby 'tended to moroseness and discontent', and E. A. Warburton 'infused into [the part] a full measure of gloom and sadness' (*Stratford-upon-Avon Herald*, 12 May 1905; 8 May 1908). G. R. Weir conveyed Touchstone's 'quaintness and unctuousness' (*Stratford-upon-Avon Herald*, 12 May 1905).

Stratford audiences stoically applauded the familiar. The stuffed stag that first featured in Barry Sullivan's production in 1879 continued to appear annually, along with Audrey's ample supply of turnips and apples and Benson's hoary canvas flats, which quivered when Orlando nailed his verses to the painted tree trunks.[172] These stagings were so rigidly customary that the play became ritualistic in production. Benson's long association with the theatre lent continuity while maintaining a fundamentally conservative approach. As the play most emphatically linked to the Stratford area, *As You Like It* became especially encrusted with tradition, of which the stuffed stag was emblematic: it was not seen as an increasingly moth-eaten prop but as a relic linked to Shakespeare himself.

Still, if Benson's stagings were stilted, his cuts to the text were less prissy than earlier Victorian versions. Although he substituted 'marry' for 'enjoy' at 5.2.3, 7 and 'folk' for 'copulatives' at 5.4.52, Benson allowed most of Touchstone's bawdy parody at 3.3.77–89 (omitting only line 89 with its offensive 'prick'), permitted Rosalind to make reference to her 'child's father' (1.3.8), and had Celia speak of putting 'umber' (1.3.102) on her face as Aliena (1904 pbk). Similarly, Julia Arthur's promptbook (1898–9) shows

171 Ibid.   172 Beauman, p. 65.

the movement away from a Bowdlerised text. Here many decorum cuts and alterations have been changed back to the Folio version: references are made to 'God' not 'heaven', and Rosalind speaks of a weapon on her 'thigh' rather than at her side (1.3.107). She also says Oliver and Celia will 'climb incontinent' the stairs towards marriage (5.2.31). However, most of Touchstone's bawdier lines were cut, as usual, from this production, and Hymen was replaced by a priest who was accompanied by several monks-nés-shepherds.

Exemplifying the trends of turn-of-the-century stagings were the productions of E. H. Sothern and Julia Marlowe. Americans born of English parents, they were influential on both sides of the Atlantic. Arthur Symons praised their vocal technique – the 'power of using speech as one uses the notes of a musical instrument' – and their presentation of character depth, portraying characters 'in the round, whereas with our actors we see no more than profiles, picturesque glimpses'.[173] Sothern and Marlowe nudged *As You Like It* away from the sententiousness that had pleased Victorian moralists. Marlowe especially was dismayed by the theatrical practice of making 'points' – i.e. giving rhetorical emphasis to certain passages through increased volume and flamboyant gestures.[174] Marlowe was praised for her refined method, and for her Rosalind's 'lambent humor' and 'note of pathos'.[175] Still, some found her Rosalind sentimental and girlish: one 'could hardly believe that the merry, bewitching Rosalind of Miss Rehan and the Juliet-like Rosalind of Miss Marlowe could have come from the same text'.[176]

Critics accustomed to an oratorical Jaques were challenged by E. H. Sothern's more naturalistic version of the character.[177] For Sothern's Jaques, 'boredom was a pose' (*Christian Science Monitor*, 22 Nov. 1910). He chuckled merrily about Touchstone's words in 2.7, and even laughed along with Touchstone and Audrey at the end of 3.4 instead of pompously chiding their attempted forest coupling (pbk). A drive to defuse some of the play's troubling hostilities can be detected as Le Beau and the other courtiers join Celia and Rosalind in pleading with Duke Frederick in 1.3, reducing a sense of the court's dangers for the two girls. And Touchstone is accompanied by a child on his first entrance in 1.2, a precious addition for an acerbic clown. The 'scenes of proxy love were all the more human' because Marlowe could 'see the funny side of the tender emotion as well as its sweetness' (*Christian*

173 Symons, pp. 14, 15.   174 Russell, pp. 116–17.
175 George Rogers, *North American*, quoted in Russell, p. 154.
176 Odell, *New York Stage*, vol. 14, p. 255. He added 'neither was so poetically lovely as Modjeska's'.
177 Shattuck, *American Stage*, vol. 2, p. 283.

Science Monitor, 22 Nov. 1910). While observing Orlando in 3.3, she yelped for joy, jumped with delight, giggled, and clapped her hands (see commentary). In what Symons praised as Sothern and Marlowe's 'intelligent, unostentatious way of giving Shakespeare' lay the seeds of new approaches to the play.[178]

Oscar Asche's greenhouse

Ostentatious staging had one last hurrah with Oscar Asche's 1907 production at His Majesty's in London, featuring 'two thousand pots of ferns', 'large clumps of bamboos', 'cartloads of last autumn's leaves', and moss-covered logs.[179] 'The whole plantation was kept on the roof of the theatre during the day'.[180] The production prompted comment on the social and aesthetic value of scenic illusionism, with proponents arguing that: 'We need this sort of excursion in the playhouse – this stay by proxy under the greenwood tree, this transference to an ideal world . . . And the more lovely the surroundings, the more complete our emancipation' (*Illustrated London News*, 12 Oct. 1907). For others the verisimilitude was intrusive: Max Beerbohm, for instance, found Asche's Arden 'a very beautiful place', but not the 'enchanted place' Shakespeare intended.[181] The production included musical settings by Christopher Wilson, Harold Samuel, Henry Bishop, and Arne's setting for 'Blow, blow, thou winter wind.'

Asche's wife Lily Brayton played Rosalind in a more straightforward style than tradition had dictated. Her Rosalind was 'no self-conscious, mock-modest creature who conceals her limbs at the mention of Orlando's name. The actress, when in doublet and hose, does not force her sex upon the spectator's notice' (*Illustrated London News*, 12 Oct. 1907), prompting complaints of an 'underdone' performance (unidentified clipping by W. A., TM), while others found it 'refreshing' to be spared 'all the silly little femininities and oglings' of 'the average Rosalind'. As Ganymede, Brayton wore a shepherd's smock and 'frankly [tried] to look and act just as much like a boy as she possibly can' ('Beautiful Production at His Majesty's', TM).

Henry Ainley's 'manly', 'chivalrous' Orlando was taken by some as 'too bluff, too hard, too matter-of-fact' (*Illustrated London News*, 12 Oct. 1907; unidentified clipping by W. A., TM). This Orlando did 'not presume to see through Rosalind's disguise', furthering the sense that Ganymede was a convincing boy (*Illustrated London News*, 12 Oct. 1907). As was traditional,

---

178 Symons in Russell, p. 545.   179 Asche, *Oscar Asche*, p. 120.
180 Jackson, 'Perfect Types', p. 19.
181 Quoted in Mazer, *Shakespeare Refashioned*, p. 97.

Asche himself took the part of Jaques, 'emphasis[ing] the disillusionment of the man of the world' (*Illustrated London News*, 23 Nov. 1907); one critic called him 'a sort of cross between Socrates and Friar Tuck' (unidentified clipping by W. A., TM).

Nigel Playfair's break with scenic illusionism

War closed the Stratford Theatre from 1916 to 1919; it reopened in the spring of 1919 with a short festival that included Nigel Playfair's *As You Like It*, a revolutionary production in Stratford's history. Playfair made 'no attempt . . . to achieve an impossible realism' (1920 programme). Instead he challenged Stratford orthodoxy by reconceiving the play, discarding the tattered sets and introducing a look modelled on medieval tapestries and missals. With only five weeks to mount the show, Playfair had hired Claude Lovat Fraser to design the sets and costumes. The obviously artificial landscape was compared by one reviewer (who found the set effective) to 'penny plan outlines of the children's toy theatre of forty years ago, carefully coloured by hand' (*Birmingham Daily Post*, 23 Apr. 1919). The costumes, made of linen dyed in the Fraser bathtub, were of rich, jewel-like tones including scarlet, lime-green, saffron, and pink. Although medieval in style, the look was shockingly new for Stratford, and Playfair reported being treated like a 'national criminal', scorned by fellow guests at his lodging. In one encounter on the street, a woman 'shook her fist' in Lovat Fraser's face, challenging 'Young man, how dare you meddle with Our Shakespeare!'[182] The local newspaper reviewer lamented that 'All our appropriate scenery was discarded, and a lot of canvas, miserably painted and clumsily arranged, took its place . . . the environment of the play was altogether robbed of its picturesqueness . . .' (*Stratford-upon-Avon Herald*, 25 Apr. 1919). Although Frank and Constance Benson encouraged Playfair, Constance admitted she was unable to 'see the sylvan play in the very new and original setting'.[183]

Perhaps it was Athene Seyler's performance as Rosalind that troubled Constance Benson as much as the general look of the production. Deemed 'quite frankly a chatterbox', Seyler's Rosalind was freer, giggling, generally more 'hoydenish' than the womanly version that had for so long been the norm (*Manchester Guardian*, 23 Apr. 1919; *Stratford-upon-Avon Herald*, 25 Apr. 1919). Because Playfair used an uncut text, played speedily with only one interval, and because the cast was young overall, this *As You Like It* carried considerable energy. The style of delivery was offensive to some: one critic accused Playfair of 'robbing' Shakespeare of his 'beauty and rhythm,

182 Playfair, p. 55.   183 Constance Benson, p. 302.

his harmony, his overwhelming majesty', with actors who 'seemed to think they were walking down Bond Street'.[184] Herbert Marshall's bitter Jaques gave an 'almost sinister' quality to the speech on the Seven Ages, which, a reviewer notes, 'I thought had long ago been recited out of existence'.[185] It was an additional mark of iconoclasm that Playfair himself took the part of Touchstone, not Jaques. The production included Arne's settings for the songs by Amiens and Hymen, supplemented with instrumental versions of other 'popular tunes of the day' (1920 programme). Although derided by conservative critics, Playfair's production was remembered years later by Gordon Crosse as one that managed to be striking without being eccentric.[186]

Open-air Arden

Like *A Midsummer Night's Dream*, Shakespeare's other forest comedy, *As You Like It* has frequently been performed in outdoor settings, where the audience can feel themselves to be *in* the magical Forest of Arden. Oscar Wilde observed an early instance of *As You Like It* presented *en plein jour* at Coombe House, Kingston-upon-Thames, in June 1885 – one of several performances repeating a staging the previous year that had been attended by the kings of England and Sweden, among others. American actress Eleanor Calhoun, while playing Rosalind in London, conceived the idea with her friend Lady Archibald Campbell as they strolled in the grounds of the great house. Lady Campbell brought in E. W. Godwin as director and he understood his role: he 'did not place any great limitations on the actor's art, and increased tenfold the value of the play as a picture'.[187] 'All conventional stage business was set aside, and the whole representation thought out from an artist's stand-point.' Costumes were designed to 'blend picturesquely with the surrounding foliage' (*Theatre*, 1 Sept. 1884). The cast mixed professionals with amateurs; Hermann Vezin, the ubiquitous late nineteenth-century Jaques, presented him here; the cook was recruited to play Audrey; and tall Lady Campbell played Orlando (see figure 11). The court scenes were omitted.

To preserve the 'naturalism' of the setting, 'faggots of wood were heaped up to cover the exits', and a curtain was devised to work by means of ropes and pulleys attached to 'the two trees that formed the extreme ends of the proscenium'. A dead deer, live hounds, and live goats added to the realistic

---

184 Sydney Carroll, quoted in Playfair, pp. 43, 44.
185 *Spectator*, quoted in Playfair, pp. 46–7. 186 Crosse, p. 155.
187 Oscar Wilde, *Dramatic Review*, 6 June 1885, quoted in Salgado, p. 164.

effects (*Theatre*, 1 Sept. 1884). Viewers in the spirit of the thing found themselves 'in the Forest of Arden; not a painted semblance of the forest, not a dexterous picture befooling the eye for a moment, but Arden itself' (*National Review*, Sept. 1884). Yet the compounding of natural and theatrical effects was dismaying for some:

> Doublet and hose, blank verse, gestures never seen in real life, jokes and puns, intolerably dull, we endure in a theatre when we are accustomed to it. But when these are surrounded by the genuine accessories of nature, when a green doublet is shown up by a real tree, when Touchstone reclines on real grass, the absurdity of the whole thing is too evident. To carry out a play, to give it any semblance of nature, it must be as far away from nature as possible. (*Bat*, 2 June 1885)

These remarks diagnose a problem in the conception of outdoor performances of *As You Like It* and anticipate the advent in the theatre of non-illusionistic settings.

Ben Greet, 'the first actor–manager to begin a consistent policy of staging plays in the open air', presented the woodland scenes from *As You Like It* in a number of such venues.[188] He formed a young travelling company of 'Woodland Players' in 1886; the next year, when they appeared at a great house in Barnes, just outside London, the setting reportedly 'lent an air of reality to the performance', although perhaps there was an excess of good feeling: G. R. Foss's Jaques was inadequately cynical, and Greet's own Touchstone lacking in 'waggish drollery' (*Theatre*, 1 Sept. 1887). The following year brought a memorable performance in Stratford in the grounds of Clopton House. Greet also recreated the legendary performance that had supposedly been presented under Shakespeare's direction at Wilton House. At Ashridge in Herfordshire 'a herd of some hundreds of deer' were driven across the stage as a special feature (*Stratford-upon-Avon Herald*, 3 May 1895).

Greet, a doughty supporter of outdoor theatre, also established 'the first series of open air performances of Shakespeare's plays in the Royal Botanic Society's Gardens in Regent's Park, London'.[189] The opening season in 1901 included *As You Like It*, with Edith Wynne Matthison as Rosalind.

188 Isaac, p. 33.   189 Ibid., p. 216.

Figure 7 American actress Eleanor Calhoun persuaded her friend Lady Archibald Campbell to play Orlando to her Rosalind. The resulting open-air performance at Coombe House, Surrey, in 1884–5 enjoyed an audience of royalty, aristocrats, writers, and prominent people from the worlds of art and fashion. Calhoun wrote that at that time 'no play had ever been acted in the open forest, making scenes of nature, the scenes of the play', so that she and Lady Archie 'brought forth a new art form' (Lazarovich–Hrebelianovich, pp. 71, 72).

Several decades later, in 1933, Greet worked with Robert Atkins and Sidney Carroll to establish the current Open Air Theatre, once again staging *As You Like It* in the inaugural season. Gordon Crosse commented that the Regent's Park venue contributed to an understanding of 'how the plays appeared to the Elizabethan spectators', because the huge open space required a broad acting style, and entrances and exits were made in view of the spectators.[190] Certainly the gain in physical space is an advantage for suggesting the expanse of a forest, and since many scenes in *As You Like It* occur in unspecified forest locations, a spacious setting affords more opportunity for exits, entrances, chance meetings, and so forth. Neville Coghill produced a noted *As You Like It* in the romantic atmosphere of Oxford's Worcester College gardens, a famous inspiration for Lewis Carroll's *Alice's Adventures in Wonderland*. Viewers were 'confined to two blocks of tiered seats', while the players wandered throughout the 'unlimited sylvan space' (*Times*, 16 June 1955).

The tradition of open-air performances that supposedly 'democratise' Shakespearean drama for the masses has also been strong in America – more than 8,000 people watched Maude Adams as Rosalind in a performance at the Greek Theatre, Berkeley, California, in June 1909 (unidentified clipping, small scrapbook, FSL). Among the more memorable outdoor stagings in America were Joseph Papp's 1973 production at the Delacorte Theater in New York's Central Park, which featured pop singer Meat Loaf as Amiens and film star Raul Julia as Orlando. Semi-professional and amateur groups have consistently chosen *As You Like It* for outdoor Shakespeare festivals in many cities, to the general delight of their audiences. Oddly, while Rosalind's part is reputed to be a challenge for an actress, it is rare for one to fail in the execution – confirming Shaw's sense that the role is 'actress-proof'. Moreover, the reliable success of local park productions indicates that simple approaches and uncluttered stagings may work best, whereas the excrescences of realistic stagings have sometimes stifled the play.

The play settles in

Despite Playfair's iconoclastic gesture in 1919, the stuffed stag returned to the Stratford stage; Crosse reports seeing it in a 1925 production.[191] For several decades there were no striking interpretations of *As You Like It* in England. As political tensions increased throughout Europe in the 1920s and 30s, and during World War II and its aftermath, this pre-eminently

190 Crosse, p. 111.   191 Ibid., p. 74.

pastoral play served a reassuringly escapist purpose. In the mythic Arden, nothing changed; philosophers uttered their apolitical wisdom and youthful romance blossomed. Other Shakespearean plays were subject to modernist experimentation, so it is striking that *As You Like It* inspired no revisionary efforts. The most significant productions during this period were in the new medium of film and on the continent.

One check on free interpretation was the habit of recycling prompt-books, so that textual cuts and alterations, conceptions of character, and stage business remained consistent over the years. At Stratford, where the promptbook held almost the status of Shakespeare's script, *As You Like It* resumed the familiar status of the Benson years, appearing under William Bridges-Adams's direction seven times between 1920 and 1933. In the eyes of some, practice made perfect: in 1933 the tepid production was recognised as 'completely conventional', yet enjoyable because 'so well done' (*Birmingham Gazette*, 20 Apr. 1933); others were weary with 'scenery that was a shade too representational' (*Times*, 20 Apr. 1933). Under Ben Iden Payne's direction a few years later, *As You Like It* sank to being judged 'Shakespeare's dullest play on the stage' (*Birmingham Evening Despatch*, n.d., SCL). The malaise was general; another reviewer wrote that 'while it is difficult to say what was wrong with it, it would be much more difficult to say what was right' (*Birmingham Post*, 18 Apr. 1935). Matters scarcely improved under Baliol Holloway in 1939, who aimed for 'realism at the expense of pace', repeating an error of Victorian times (*Times*, 5 Apr. 1939). The production relied heavily on the dropped curtain to divide scenes (*Daily Telegraph and Morning Post*, 5 Apr. 1939). Some could appreciate the 'self-denying disci-pline' of Jay Laurier's Touchstone,[192] but others found a philosopher–clown who 'indulge[d] in pantomime business with a hayrake' inappropriate and even 'grotesque' (*Birmingham Post*, 5 Apr. 1939; *Times*, 5 Apr. 1939). The wrestling scene frequently won praise in productions of this era, lending credence to Shaw's point that it was the one reliable attraction of the play (*Birmingham Evening Despatch*, n.d., SCL; *Daily Telegraph and Morning Post*, 5 Apr. 1939).

At the Old Vic in 1932, Harcourt Williams experimented with an austere, fantasy staging in place of the usual 'dully realistic interpretation', but while the impulse was applauded, the result was not; reviewers were 'eye-starved', craving 'more grace of scene and less geometry' (*Times*, 1 Nov. 1932; *Sunday Times*, 3 Nov. 1932; n.p., by Ivor Brown, 6 Nov. 1932). Peggy Ashcroft as Rosalind was damned for lack of 'style', gabbling Rosalind's 'chop-logic . . . as though it bores her' (*Sunday Times*, 3 Nov. 1932; n.p. by Ivor Brown,

---

192 Kemp and Trewin, p. 198.

6 Nov. 1932). Malcolm Keen's Jaques, by contrast, seemed overly attached to his lines, 'marshalling them, as a defeated general would his beloved soldiers, with sad and exquisite perfection' (*Times*, 1 Nov. 1932). This Jaques was the first to light his pipe in the forest (*Daily Telegraph*, 1 Nov. 1932).

Many had considered Edith Evans too old to play Rosalind in 1926, when she was thirty-eight. So it was 'even more amazing . . . that she played her again eleven years later in a still more memorable performance', produced by Esmé Church at the Old Vic.[193] Evans was artist enough to take advantage of her age; rather than playing Rosalind in the romantic manner she further developed her earlier interpretation of an impudent Rosalind:

> she can move like an arrow, she can roll over on the ground in a delight of comedy, she can mock and glitter and play the fool with a marvellous ease and grace; and if the boyishness – or girlishness – is not there, it is because she has decided to reject it in favour of a feminine guile that is her own edge to the part – her deliberately implied and original criticism of it.
>
> (unidentified clipping, 2 Dec. 1937, TM)

Disappointing as this was to anyone who felt Rosalind was 'a girl in love' (ibid.), it gave a 'new and sparkling meaning' to the part (unidentified clipping, Clive McManus, TM). Evans 'began by looking like an intellectual but dowdy eighteenth-century German princess in exile at some elegant Frenchified court'. Her growing passion inspired Michael Redgrave, a 'manly, attractive and swaggeringly modest' Orlando (unidentified clipping, TM); and 'in all the teasing of Orlando one never lost sight for one moment of the reserves of feeling beneath'.[194] Evans avoided the 'danger' of archness, 'turning Rosalind, without pretence, into a Restoration belle'.[195] Leon Quartermaine, who took over the part of Jaques from Milton Rosmer in 1937, was familiarly ponderous, 'more mordant than melancholy', recalling 'both Dickens and Tennyson' (unidentified clipping, Clive McManus, TM). Molly McArthur's Watteau-esque scenery and costumes unified the production in a fresh way; the artificiality of Elizabethan pastoralism was rendered more available by 'transferring' it 'to the better-known eighteenth-century convention' (*SS* 2, 1949, p. 16). The rococo transference possibly bore the influence of Heinz Hilpert's 1934 production at the Deutsches Theater, in which Jaques 'in a powdered wig' recalled 'Molière's misanthrope'.[196]

There were no productions of *As You Like It* on the London stage between 1937 and 1955, although Stratford valiantly mounted several mostly dreary

---

193 Forbes, p. 113.   194 Williamson, p. 63.
195 Trewin, p. 145. He is describing Evans's delivery of the Epilogue in particular.
196 Hortmann, p. 126.

revivals. Certainly the time was out of joint for the opening of Robert Atkins's production in April 1944, two months before the Normandy landings – 'a slight depression' hung over the company – but the decision to 'retreat to behind the proscenium arch' also contributed to the dullness of the affair (*Birmingham Post*, 15 Apr. 1944).

By mid-century, the fore-stage of Stratford's Memorial Theatre had been extended, bringing the action closer to viewers and avoiding the deadly retreat into the recesses of the stage. Still, the theatre remained 'a structure designed for spectacular display and transformation', with 'the elaborateness of the stage-machinery' presenting a temptation to excessive pictorialism (*SQ* 3, 1952, pp. 355, 354). Yielding to this temptation, Glen Byam Shaw in 1952 introduced into the mise en scène a seasonal movement, with a wintry opening – in Arden, 'we find the Duke and his fellow exiles enjoying an alfresco meal of fruit in the snow' (*Times*, 30 Apr. 1952) – gradually yielding to spring, as the mood thawed in Arden. This was a pattern that would be repeated in many subsequent stagings. But Motley's elaborate décor in Louis XIII style did not enliven the fantasy of what was ultimately a 'conventional' production, and there were conflicting elements in the set, such as the peculiar literalism of the large palm tree, and the 'undulations of greenness' decorating the fore-stage during scenes in Duke Frederick's court (*SQ* 3, 1952, p. 353). The revival met with popular approval, although critics were challenged by the seasonal pattern, which might have been more convincing in a sylvan setting. Some thought the seasonal motif underlined a strongly enforced meliorism that denied the complex attitudes of Jaques and Touchstone. Michael Hordern missed the sardonic edge in Jaques, and Margaret Leighton was graceful but less commanding than the greatest Rosalinds (*New Statesman*, 10 May 1952; *Manchester Guardian*, 30 Apr. 1952).

Whatever depth and presence Peggy Ashcroft had lacked when she played Rosalind in 1932 she had gained by 1957, when she once more took the part, this time at Stratford. At fifty far from an ingenue, Ashcroft depended on her developed sense of language and its skilful delivery, 'the delicate crispness of her enunciation [setting] off finely the vigour and spirit of the boy Ganymede'. Glen Byam Shaw's staging repeated the seasonal motif of his 1952 production – Corin wore a sheepskin and muffler, and Touchstone shivered while wading into the icy brook. This time Shaw included Hymen, as a rustic on a farm cart, in the style of Macready (*SQ* 8, 1957, pp. 480, 482). The tone throughout was light-hearted, or as one critic put it, 'safe, sensible and good-natured'.[197] Evidently all facets of the play had not been explored.

197 Leiter, p. 51.

In contrast to Glen Byam Shaw's vaguely anthropological stagings, Robert Helpmann offered pictorial fantasy at the Old Vic in 1955, with court scenes played on the apron of the stage 'against a background suggesting a woodcut of some curious pantheon at the end of a colonnade'. The forest was a 'Breughel-like background of trees', their intertwining branches mildly threatening (*Times*, 2 Mar. 1955). Paul Rogers dealt with the problem of Touchstone's bad jokes by 'pawn[ing] off' the worst of them on his ventriloquist's doll (*Evening Standard*, 2 Mar. 1955); one critic compared him to 'a quietly demented Archbishop'.[198] Yet larger problems with the play, or the play's appeal to the era, remained. As Rosalind, Virginia McKenna came across as 'too sensible a body to have put up with all that stupid, lovesick dalliance in the woods' (*Financial Times*, 2 Mar. 1955). Orlando was never in much doubt about Ganymede's identity, largely collapsing the layering of sexual identities. With the central premise appearing 'fraudulent', the plot and the accompanying philosophising became a kind of 'nonsense which takes itself so seriously that it alienates the patience and becomes something of a bore' (*What's On In London*, 11 Mar. 1955). To pragmatic, modern sensibilities, *As You Like It* offered little substance; at best, it had become a vehicle from which accomplished actresses such as Ashcroft or Katharine Hepburn (who played Rosalind in New York in 1950) could still get considerable mileage.

Milton Shulman intuited the problem *As You Like It* presented for this era, as well as a route towards its solution, when he called it 'basically a woman's play' (*Evening Standard*, 4 Sept. 1959). At mid-century, gender was a 'woman's' issue, and gender is what *As You Like It* is largely about. Eighteenth-century audiences had been fascinated by the spectacle of a 'hoyden' Rosalind, and the nineteenth century had found delight in 'arch' displays of 'womanly' emotion. By the middle of the twentieth century, audiences were justifiably bored with realistic presentation of the play's central romance. As gender roles in society came under scrutiny, the more subversive potential of the play's fantastically conceived relationships could begin to be realised.

Shulman's comment was inspired by the 1959 Old Vic production with a female director, Wendy Toye, and three notable actresses in the cast – Barbara Jefford (Rosalind), Maggie Smith (Celia), and Judi Dench (Phoebe). Not a revolutionary production, Toye's *As You Like It* breathed some life into what had become a moribund play. The Regency setting called up Sheridan's ghost, and the formal costumes (as Ganymede, Jefford wore top coat and breeches) appeared incongruous in the woods: Toye's touch was mannered

---

198 Speaight, p. 270.

and whimsical, and definitely disdainful of realistic conventions. 'Charles, the Duke's wrestler, was portrayed amusingly as a sort of Gentleman Jim, attended by a pair of trainers' (*Daily Telegraph*, 4 Sept. 1959), and 'Duke Frederick, in the best Regency manner, ha[d] a mistress' (*Illustrated London News*, 3 Sept. 1959). Alec McCowan shaved years from Touchstone's age, presenting a 'red-headed, clown-faced fantastic whose claim to the status of courtier might well be true'. As a result, 'Touchstone revives', to the extent that McCowan 'seems to have rewritten the whole part without changing a word' (*Times*, 4 Sept. 1959; *Daily Mail*, 4 Sept. 1959). Donald Houston's Jaques was 'a difficult person to get into focus, almost as "humourous" in the phraseology of his period as melancholy' (*Times*, 4 Sept. 1959). Instead of the familiar 'pompous fool' or 'semonising bore, he is an intelligent man who has been through it' (*New Statesman & Nation*, 2 Sept. 1959). Even Adam was rescued from sentimentality, becoming 'an ancient stableman . . . never without his bottle' (*Theatre World*, Oct. 1959). Toye introduced a novel change by having Touchstone play the part of Hymen: after his speech on the virtues of 'If', the clown was dressed in festive garb to play the ceremonial role. This implicit recognition of the contingent quality of the couplings was a harbinger of coming interpretive changes.

Early film versions

Both Kalem (1908) and Vitagraph (1912) produced silent versions of *As You Like It*. Like other one-reelers in this line, Vitagraph's *As You Like It* features a simplified narrative, with emphasis on picturesque tableaux, and little exploration of the subtleties of the romance plot or pastoral. An enacted prologue shows the banishment of Duke Senior and the death of Sir Roland, and at the end Duke Frederick recalls his brother from banishment. None of the courtship scenes between Ganymede and Orlando are shown, but Orlando does fight briefly with a lion – extra business that becomes traditional in film versions. Rose Coghlan, originally an Irish burlesque star and sixty-one years old when the film was made, appears as an understandably sedate Rosalind.

Paul Czinner's 1936 film of *As You Like It* blends realism and fantasy in odd and charming ways, perhaps showing the influence of James Barrie, author of *Peter Pan*, who advised Czinner. Duke Frederick's turreted and terraced castle came straight from a medieval storybook, and Arden itself features a babbling brook, peasant huts, and fake trees, without seeming anything other than a studio set. Designer Lazare Meerson's generous addition of live animals – a cow and chickens outside Oliver's house, swans at court, and an Arden populated with rabbits, ducks, a sheepdog, and herds of sheep – 'shattered the fragile world of his imaginary barnyards and woods'.[199] Despite the scenic additions cinema allowed, the film retains strong conceptual links with theatrical tradition: the jovial Duke Senior (Henry Ainley, who had played Orlando in Asche's 1907 production), enjoying a hunting holiday rather than suffering exile; the elimination of Jaques's cynical speeches; the crowded wedding celebration from which most of Hymen's lines were cut. The staginess of the wrestling match – swarming crowds watching through the gates to the castle grounds, and six attendants required to lift Charles, who has nevertheless been thrown by the slender Orlando – derived from theatrical tradition, but Czinner took advantage of the cinematic medium by punctuating the fight with Touchstone's miming of its action and by including many reaction shots. William Walton's score performed by a full orchestra modulates the mood.

Elisabeth Bergner, Czinner's Polish-born wife, plays a Rosalind younger and less 'arch' than the familiar conception of the role. At court, she approaches Orlando shyly and responds with timidity to Duke Frederick's accusations. She and Sophie Stewart's Celia are 'intimate as two teenagers with a schoolgirl crush'[200] and maintain their closeness throughout the courtship scenes in Arden. When Rosalind, as Ganymede, first approaches Orlando, she skittishly moves towards him only to shy away, tugging at her tunic and retreating to the safety of Celia's embrace. The courtship game releases her spirit, however, and Bergner's Rosalind runs, whirls, giggles, embraces trees, and turns a somersault as she grows increasingly confident; she pokes at Touchstone with a rolled-up scroll, threatens Phoebe with a switch, and brandishes it before Orlando when she criticises his courtship techniques in 4.1.35–50. By thus 'indexing [Rosalind's] hidden need to dominate', Bergner pushed the role in a modern direction. Critics were distracted by her accent, and many criticised a performance Roger Manvell derided as 'kittenish'.[201] Laurence Olivier acquits himself gracefully as a handsomely indignant Orlando in the wrestling match, but becomes increasingly stolid in the courtship scenes, demonstrating the difficulties of the role, especially when Rosalind and Orlando are not well matched. 'Olivier was not even mentioned' when the film was advertised in August 1936 on BBC – 'the first Shakespeare film clip on television'.[202]

Much of the piquancy that makes *As You Like It* a serious comedy was cut from Czinner's script; the film runs a mere 97 minutes. Touchstone's pastoral debate with Corin is gone, as is his speech on the degrees of the lie and much of his early banter with the ladies. The contemplative but

---

199 Rothwell, p. 50.   200 Ibid.   201 Ibid. and p. 49.
202 Freedman, p. 54.

scarcely melancholy Jaques (Leon Quartermaine) is omitted from 2.5, 3.4, and 4.1. His departure from the final scene, which lends a significant note of contrast and perspective, is eliminated; instead the conclusion is one of unalloyed jollity, especially after a knight in shining armour, not identified as the Second Brother, arrives to announce the restoration of the dukedom to Rosalind's father.

The ambitiously conceived epilogue, in which Rosalind appears in her wedding dress, fades into the cross-dressed Ganymede for the lines addressed to women (9–10), only to dissolve back into the bride, suggests the film's limitations and achievements. Bergner did not succeed in exploring the ambiguities of Rosalind's dual identities or the complexities of her feelings for Orlando, and Czinner was not altogether confident of how to translate the subtleties of Shakespearean comedy into the cinematic medium. But the film has been influential as a document of early stage traditions and as a first look at Olivier's performance of Shakespeare, and despite the obviousness of its lavish studio sets, it evokes Arden at least as successfully as several later films have done.

Foreign productions

As I have suggested, traditional English conceptions of *As You Like It* have been securely tied to the native scenery, with a consequent conservatism in staging. By contrast, continental productions have experimented more freely, often in overtly political ways. Despite Shakespeare's universal status, use of a translated text often has a liberating effect. Although George Sand, whose translation of the play appeared at the Comédie-Française in 1856, understood it in romantic terms (explaining her decision to wed 'Jacques' to Celia as 'my own romance', 'not more improbable than the sudden conversion of the traitor Oliver'),[203] a woman's affiliation with the central Paris theatre was itself radical at the time. Later, Berlin's Meininger Theatre presented *As You Like It* 'in an entirely novel manner, altering the order and the arrangements of the scenes' and changing costumes and minor details to '[impart] a more decidedly realistic tone'. The changes 'raised a storm of angry discussion' and the controversy packed the house (*Academy*, 3 Oct. 1874).

Architectural décor and intellectual sophistication marked Jacques Copeau's 1934 staging at Paris's Théâtre de l'Atelier (see commentary, 1.1 and 2.1). According to Copeau, the heart of his enterprise was Shakespeare's characterisation:

203 Sand, p. 19.

All my efforts have been concentrated on that wonder of wonders – on Rosalind. A gigantic role beneath its fragile envelope. To discover the right note – throughout two acts – for this boy who is really a boy and this girl who is pretending to be one is certainly one of the most difficult problems that any director can set himself today.[204]

Copeau staged *As You Like It* again in 1938 in the Boboli gardens at Florence, fitting his design into the natural setting. Copeau emphasised the play's celebratory aspects; 'the hermit – an impressive figure in his Franciscan habit – who had been the instrument of Duke Frederick's conversion' appeared at the end, 'followed by a lion, a tiger, and a bear', all included in the 'highly mythological wedding'.[205] At Moscow's Maria Yermolova Theatre in 1940, pastoral received less emphasis than social critique. With a 'Robin Hood theme' as the 'leitmoif', the production presented Jaques as a 'skeptical commentator' in Swiftian mode.[206]

At Rome's Teatro Eliso in 1948, a lavish surrealistic version directed by Luchino Visconti featured costumes and sets by Salvador Dali. 'There were no trees or vegetation in the forest, except for a single large apple painted on the backdrop'.[207] The rococo costumes were transformed into 'a rich riot of colour and wild imagination' (*SS* 3, 1950, p. 118). The foresters in Dali's sketches, for instance, wear only animal pelts adorned with a stylised codpiece fashioned from a stag's antlers (FSL). 'On the stage were two elephants bearing obelisks like Bernini's sculptures and a Palladian temple'.[208] Emphasis on song and dance, rather than visual or psychological realism, heightened the surrealistic effect. 'Visconti's abandonment of his habitual *neorealismo* astonished some admirers', and some fellow Marxists privately berated him for 'working with a designer who had not denounced Franco'.[209] In another famously avant-garde production at Bucharest's Teatrul Bulandra in 1961, director Liviu Ciulei emphasised elements of fantasy and theatricality. Ciulei found ways to capture an awareness of tradition without allowing it to rule, 'by representing the Forest of Arden with live women dancers and by using mural paintings to represent the Elizabethan public as sitting alongside' the actual audience (*SQ* 31, 1980, p. 405). That 'dogmatic critics' derided the production for emphasising the love plot rather than Jaques's social critique gives a sense of how different the eastern European theatre scene was from that in England.[210]

Another dynamic encounter with the text occurred in Hans Schalla's production for the German Shakespeare Society in 1954, in which Touchstone was reconceived as a master of ceremonies:

204 Quoted in Speaight, p. 191.   205 Speaight, pp. 192, 193.
206 Lunacharsky, pp. 41–2; Morozov, p. 57.   207 Leiter, p. 46.
208 Jamieson, p. 636.   209 Ibid.   210 Blumenfeld, p. 244.

At the beginning of the play Touchstone, the jester, appears, wearing the costume of harlequin, and he opens the play by knocking thrice with a hammer. Then he shuffles in a tired way along to the side and cowers down in a chair near the edge of the scene. There he stays until he himself has to enter the stage, and between times he acts now and then as announcer. At the end he takes over the verses of Hymen.   (SQ 5, 1954, p. 321)

Such Brechtian displacement of the fiction was altogether remote from staid British productions of mid-century.

Continental stagings of *As You Like It* were especially influenced by Jan Kott's view that 'the Forest of Arden makes mockery of Arcadia . . . Love is escape from cruel history to an invented forest'.[211] Puncturing the idyllic myth, Kott revealed lust beneath the surface, prompting some productions to subvert the pastoral altogether. For instance, 'love could not operate, and was not meant to' in the coldly clinical staging by Roberto Ciulli in Cologne in 1974. Not only did Orlando cheat to win the wrestling match, but he 'robs Adam of his savings and while he feasts with the banished duke, his starved servant is hastily buried in the background'. Celia and Rosalind were locked in unresolved sexual tension while Orlando fought for 'sexual mastery' as he and Rosalind engaged in 'heartless taunting'.[212] Surpassing even Ciulli's production in its cynicism, Romanian director Petrica Ionescu presented the play at Bochum in 1976 on a set 'suggesting a vandalized slaughterhouse or a war-damaged factory, with burst pipes, torn-off tiles and heaps of rubble'. The all-male cast featured Celia and Rosalind as 'muscular fellows' given to 'crude physical jokes', and the wrestling match concluded with Charles 'hung up naked by his feet'. Neither love nor comedy made sense in this hellish post-atomic world, in a production that 'proclaimed the doom of a run-down civilization'.[213] Peter Stein's landmark production of 1977, discussed below, discovered a way to expose the pastoral's political charge without destroying the structure of fantasy.

In another part of the world, eucalyptus, gum trees, and carolling magpies evoked Arden at Sydney's Nimrod Theatre in 1983, in a novel production that capitalised on a prevailing 'vision of rural Australia as Arcadia' (*SQ* 135, 1984, p. 480). An aboriginal 'second' shadowed Charles in the wrestling match; 'topsyish-haired' Audrey too was 'part Negro or aboriginal or Islander'; and Jaques was a 'critical old world visitor–commentato[r] on the local scene'. The dispute within 'the House of Duke Senior' evoked the 'dynastic squabbles' and 'black sheep' known to 'certain Australian families' (*SQ* 135, 1984, p. 480).

---

211 Kott, p. 292.   212 Hortmann, pp. 191–2.   213 Ibid., pp. 190–1.

Vanessa Redgrave: 'a Rosalind to remember'

As Dora Jordan was to the late eighteenth century and Helena Faucit to the mid-nineteenth, so Vanessa Redgrave was to the latter half of the twentieth century: the benchmark Rosalind against whom all others would be compared. This was a function in part of sheer familiarity, for 'it is estimated that more people saw the Royal Shakespeare Company's television *As You Like It* in March 1963 during one showing than had previously seen the play during its whole earlier history on the stage'.[214] Redgrave's starring role in Michael Elliott's production, which opened at Stratford in July 1961, helped launch the fledgling RSC. Dispensing with the streams, bridges, and mossy logs of previous productions, Elliott opted for simplified staging: a single large spreading oak rising from a grassy mound that 'cover[ed] the stage like the cap of a huge green mushroom' (*Daily Herald*, 5 July 1961). Stage designer Richard Negri 'restored the old fashioned curtain', which 'seem[ed] an exciting experiment' at this point (*Financial Times*, 5 July 1961), and delicate lighting effects were achieved with the giant tree casting shadows on the stage.

Critics seemed helpless before Redgrave's charms: 'Can there ever be a better Rosalind?' asked Edmund Gardner. 'Any male who does not fall in love with Miss Redgrave for this performance alone must be as insensible as a plastic acorn' (*Stratford-upon-Avon Herald*, 7 July 1961). She overcame what had become to some an entrenched resistance to the play. Gerald Fay admitted that 'sometimes the heart sinks at the mere thought of *As You Like It* with its rustic slapstick and convoluted, courtly wit', but he was pleased with the absence of quaintness in Elliott's production and found Redgrave 'a Rosalind to remember' (*Manchester Guardian*, 6 July 1961). Redgrave's power to attract male attention did not mean that hers was a traditionally feminine Rosalind. She 'never [let] the woman peep out from under the jerkin and top boots' except when alone with Celia, thus avoiding the problem of 'reduc[ing] Orlando's blindness to the disguise to nonsense' (*Glasgow Herald*, 7 July 1961). 'Her particular achievement was to combine the coltishness and spontaneity of late adolescence with a growing sense of her power to attract. This gave her scenes with Orlando a special energy'.[215] Whereas other Rosalinds were either 'arch' and distant, or girlishly excited, Redgrave could be forward and emotional without sacrificing her poise. For instance, when she first approached Orlando in the forest, she kicked his foot as he lay recumbent on the stage, then strutted around him during the subsequent dialogue. She touched his 'beard neglected' (3.3.314) and thumped his chest, showing clear physical assertiveness, in contrast to those

214 John Russell Taylor, p. 13.   215 Leiter, p. 52.

Figure 8 In the twentieth century Jaques lost the gentle philosophical air that often rendered the character tedious in the previous century. In Michael Elliott's 1961 RSC production, Max Adrian's Jaques 'wore a mask at once voluptuous and melancholy, pale with sensual stings and unbitted lusts, as he wandered off at the end like Marcel Proust retiring to a monastery' (Speaight, p. 283).

demure Rosalinds who shrank from Orlando's glances, much less his touch (see commentary 3.3.250ff.).

Max Adrian's Jaques, more acerbic than the old-style philosophers, delivered the Seven Ages speech while seated, as though speaking actual thoughts prompted by the tabletalk, and did not mime the various declensions. When he approached the hunters celebrating their kill in 4.2, they seemed genuinely threatened by his disapproval. Still, many of the sentimental gestures remained. Negotiating Arden's rocky ground in a roaring wind, Orlando had to resort to crawling; the foresters roasted meat on a spit; and the exhausted Adam was fed bits of bread by hand. Corin took the part of Hymen for a wedding masque involving a chorus of foresters, with musical accompaniment. A dignified Jacques de Boys interrupted the festivities, presenting the Duke's crown on a pillow. The play concluded with an image of restored order and authority: everyone knelt to show respect for the Duke's renewed authority, and there was no Epilogue after the celebratory dance.

Enthusiastically received at the time of stage performance, Redgrave's Rosalind took on a legendary quality in subsequent years – aided, of course, by the ongoing availability of the BBC television version. The performance's long shadow was such that Clifford Williams's production with an all-male cast received a generally positive review from Milton Shulman, with one exception: 'the only thing missing is that touch of exquisite passion, that sense of romantic ecstasy, that someone like Vanessa Redgrave can provide when acting the part of Rosalind' (*Evening Standard*, 4 Oct. 1967).

Clifford Williams: sexless love

By the late 1960s, gender roles, along with many other aspects of social life, were questioned by feminists dubious of the naturalness of traditional domestic and work arrangements and by gay activists challenging the entrenched idea of homosexuality as a perversion. *As You Like It* had been played for two centuries as a 'straight' romantic comedy with disguise complications, but as gender was re-theorised in freer, more mutable terms, the play's implicit scrutiny of what is meant by 'masculine' and 'feminine' became more visible. A tendency that had been in the play all along came out of the closet with Clifford Williams's 1967 production at the National Theatre.

Although the production, with its all-male cast, was seen by some as an appropriation of Shakespeare's work for a gay agenda, the director claimed that his purpose was to discover the truth of love as something transcending both gender and sex:

> The examination of the infinite beauty of Man in love – which lies at the very heart of *As You Like It* – takes place in an atmosphere of spiritual purity which transcends sensuality in the search for poetic sexuality. It is for this reason that I employ a male cast; so that we shall not – entranced by the surface reality – miss the interior truth.   (programme, TM)

The picture was complicated by questions of Jan Kott's influence on the production. His essay 'Shakespeare's Bitter Arcadia' was about to be published in the United Kingdom in the second edition of *Shakespeare, Our Contemporary*. Kott reportedly attended rehearsals (*Sunday Times*, 1 Oct. 1967) and his views were quoted extensively in the programme notes, although these views were disavowed by Williams as an influence. Where continental productions influenced by Kott had demonstrated a tone of political cynicism, Williams's production adopted his rapturous notions of 'eroticism free from the limitations of the body . . . a dream of love free from the limitations of sex'. For Kott, the play imaged 'the unification of all opposites! In the Forest of Arden love is both earthly, and platonically sublimated'.[216]

Writing about the transcendence of gender and presenting transcendence on stage with human actors are two very different tasks. If the production achieved its goals – as by some accounts it did – it was because Williams's overall conception was so original, 'so visually and aurally hypnotic that the fact that all the girls are really men takes its place as merely one of the elements in a dream-like total experience, which you accept along with the rest' (*Daily Mail*, 4 Oct. 1967). Ralph Koltai's ultra-modern design was central to this disorienting effect: on a steeply raked stage of burnished steel, Arden was constructed of steel tubes and canopies, with Perspex shapes serving as abstract props and white lighting evocative of science-fiction films. Other departures from tradition were the musical effects of 'a lazy Latin-American rhythm, breaking into sour blues for the wicked duke and into amplified beat guitars for the songs' (*Daily Mail*, 4 Oct. 1967).

As Rosalind, Ronald Pickup looked 'like Twiggy' in a white yachting suit, 'a weedy, gauche creature, uncertain of what to do with her hands or when to cross her legs, that naturally comes into her/his own when she wears male clothes as Ganymede' (*Sunday Times*, 1 Oct. 1967; *Evening Standard*, 4 Oct. 1967). Pickup won praise for effecting something like the transcendence of gender (as others in the cast did not), leading one to suspect that the gender ambiguity built into the role was at least partly responsible.

> In his scenes with Orlando, Pickup plays simply an emotion, with no attempt to characterise. His eyes fasten, blazing, on the object of his love, with a passion to which sex and identity itself seem irrelevant. For a moment Orlando recoils, blinking uneasily, then surrenders to its current, a force as impossible to resist or suspect as light. This, presumably, is the Platonic height . . . on which sex and its warring differences are seen to be masquerade and play-acting.
>
> (*Observer*, 8 Oct. 1967)

216 Kott, pp. 221, 236.

Figure 9 Anthony Hopkins as Audrey was 'a bass-voiced Brunnhilde who sits expressionlessly through Touchstone's advances and then grasps him in a bear hug'. Derek Jacobi played Touchstone as 'a Frankie Howard gossip' who was oddly enough 'prettier than any of the girls' in Clifford Williams's 1967 production, featuring an all-male cast (Irving Wardle, *Times*, 4 Oct. 1967).

Jeremy Brett's strongly masculine Orlando helped to validate Pickup's performance and to offset Rosalind's gender.

Anthony Hopkins struggled with the part of Audrey and threatened to bolt, but the role came into focus when he first donned a practice skirt (*Sunday Times*, 1 Oct. 1967). Hopkins put his discomfort to work, creating a performance that seemed 'to have grown out of embarrassment' and became the 'funniest' of them all, his Audrey 'a bass-voiced Brunnhilde who sits expressionlessly through Touchstone's advances and then grasps him in a bear-hug' (*Times*, 4 Oct. 1967). At one point she thwacked him with a paddle. Derek Jacobi's Touchstone 'managed the incredible feat of making this clown actually very funny', also contributing to the visual disorientation by being 'prettier than any of the girls' (*Evening Standard*, 4 Oct. 1967; *Times*, 4 Oct. 1967) (see figure 9). Robert Stephens, carrying a plastic umbrella as a peevish and spinsterish Jaques, stared rudely at Touchstone and Audrey like 'some last of the Bloomsburians', clearly out of place in this world, wherever it was (*Guardian*, 4 Oct. 1967).

Although Pickup eschewed camp, elements of it crept into other performances. Adam was 'a silver-maned Dr Who', Duke Frederick 'a platinum-wigged parody of Dirk Bogarde in *Modesty Blaise*', and Richard Kay's Phoebe 'a nightclub female impersonation: a languorous, lipsticked sexpot with curiously hard muscles' (*Observer*, 8 Oct. 1967). Charles Kay's performance of Celia as 'a mini-skirted governess in owlish glasses' was called 'an exercise in suppressed camp' (*Times*, 4 Oct. 1967).

On the whole, conservative critics reported their initial resistance dissolved when watching the production, although they remained mystified about the larger point of Williams's experiment. 'It offers no grand design; and seems mainly concerned with discovering (no doubt to the wrath of the company's ladies) what happens when the women's parts are played by men' (*Times*, 4 Oct. 1967); if the encounters between Rosalind and Orlando were 'not embarrassing, they were somehow less effective than one has seen them' (*Guardian*, 4 Oct. 1967). Others, however, felt the production achieved the director's stated goals, returning the play to an elemental purity. 'The play is about love and here love was portrayed as sexless, or rather sexually ambiguous' wrote Peter Lewis (*Daily Mail*, 4 Oct. 1967). Harold Hobson thought that Pickup's performance 'divorces love from sex. So do the performances in the other transvestite parts. The result is that when one comes to the marvellous quartet on the ache and unfulfilled desire of love near the end of the play there is a purity . . . that has probably not been achieved in any professional performances in the last 300 years' (*Sunday Times*, 8 Oct. 1967). These remarks accord with contemporary feminist thinking, when androgyny was often considered a desirable and largely achievable solution to gender opposition and stereotyping. Clearly, the production broke decisively from the clichés of English pastoral and of womanly, or hoydenish, Rosalinds.

Experiments in the 1960s and 1970s

Compared with Williams's striking conception, David Jones's Stratford production opening in 1967 with Dorothy Tutin as Rosalind, continuing the next year with Janet Suzman moving into the female lead, was a relief to some because 'straightforwardly pleasant' (*Financial Times*, 16 June 1967), or perhaps, straightforwardly heterosexual – 'without nonsense about mirror-imagery and the complicated musings of Professor Jan Kott' (*Birmingham Post*, 22 May 1968). Performed on a spare, almost threatening set – 'two vast dead trees pivoted high up off-stage, whose roots come questing slowly out of the upstage gloom like the heads of two grazing dinosaurs' (*Financial Times*, 16 June 1967) – some of the play's bleaker elements were stressed. Roy Kinnear's Touchstone was 'a mean, wounded fatso, like W. C. Fields', and Alan Howard's Jaques, 'a diseased cynic', presented the 'ducdame' trick as 'an attack on the banished Duke, whose loyal courtiers have followed him into the wilderness' and transformed the Seven Ages speech 'from a mellow poetic recital into an expression of misanthropic disgust' (*Times*, 22 May 1968; *New Statesman*, 23 June 1967). In this production, 'when they kill a deer, they smear blood on their faces, leeringly' (*New Statesman*, 23 June 1967). Orlando did not just burst threateningly onto the scene in 2.7 but took a forester hostage, holding a knife to his throat (Jones pbk).

Productions increasingly emphasised elements of pain and violence. At Stratford, Ontario, in 1972, William Hutt created a 'vaguely sadistic' court, with a 'Dracula-like' Duke Frederick and a sense that Orlando was in real danger during the wrestling match.[217] As early as 1962, in Michael Elliott's production at Stratford, Oliver was not just questioned but tortured in 3.1, and Frederick's courtiers became thugs instead of the gentle fantasy creatures of Victorian times. In Buzz Goodbody's 1973 Stratford production, Frederick's court had 'the touchy atmosphere of Hitler's bunker', and while Duke Senior by contrast ruled over a place 'pretty cosy for a forest camp, with armchairs and the best wineglasses' (*Financial Times*, 13 June 1973), this Duke reached for a gun when he spoke of hunting, not a picturesque bow and arrow (pbk).

217 Leiter, p. 54; *SQ* 4, 1972, p. 392.

Buzz Goodbody had set out 'to win the play back for women', after Williams had shown how well it could work without any female cast members.[218] Eileen Atkins presented a 'deeply affecting' Rosalind, despite the 'minimal attempt to disguise her femininity' as Ganymede (*SQ* 24, 1973, 403; *Guardian*, 13 June 1973). She wore blue jeans and the production passed up the opportunity to explore the way an absence of feminine trappings might actually increase seductiveness (see figure 10). At the very least, David Suchet's Orlando was left looking foolish for his apparent failure to notice the shape inside the denim. Richard Pasco played Jaques as a 'Chekhovian eccentric', obsessive and cynical (*Coventry Evening Telegraph*, 13 June 1973.

Audiences did not warm to Trevor Nunn's 1977 'baroque pastoral opera' version at Stratford (*SS* 31, 1978, p. 146). The curtain rose on an allegorical prologue sung by Hymen, Fortune, and Nature. 'Blow, blow, thou winter wind', 'Under the greenwood tree', and 'It was a lover and his lass' were 'elaborate compositions of song and dance with music by Stephen Oliver in a kind of neo-Mendelssohn vein' (*Financial Times*, 9 Sept. 1977). Portions of the text were also sung, with 'backing of a small string and wind ensemble' (*Times*, 9 Sept. 1977). Occasionally the musical treatment worked: the lovers' chorus at the close of 5.2 was sung 'with the repetitions overlapping one another musically' (*SS* 31, 1978, p. 147). But overall the musical business got in the way of the play, reducing Shakespeare to 'an indifferent librettist' (*Guardian*, 9 Sept. 1977). Critics derided other elements of spectacle as well, especially Hymen's descent on a cloud, accompanied by winged cherubs. The artificiality of the music and the Restoration costumes ('laced breeches' and 'elaborate furbelows') conflicted with the purported naturalism of the snowy stage (*Daily Telegraph*, 9 Sept. 1977).

John Dexter's 'corn dolly' production at London's National Theatre in 1979 also featured natural settings in conjunction (or conflict) with traditional – in this case Renaissance – costumes, but the emphasis here came strongly to rest on anthropology *à la* Frazer's *Golden Bough*. The pastoral's established seasonal motif was given full throttle: not only did a white cloth signify winter in Arden and a green one the coming of spring in the second half, but pagan festivals and fertility rituals were introduced. Orlando's solidarity with the country folk was enacted in a harvest festival prologue, with Orlando binding sheaves of corn (pbk). A tree rose through a trap door in the stage as the second half began; then Silvius and Phoebe hung eggs on its lower branches (pbk). More shockingly, the celebration of the hunt in 4.2 included the gutting of the stag; the tree branches were festooned with its

218 Ibid., p. 55.

entrails. Eventually a maypole and flowers signalled the triumph of fertility (*Guardian*, 3 Aug. 1979). Although the cast, especially Sara Kestelman as a 'wild-eyed', 'hyper-energetic' Rosalind (*Listener*, 9 Aug. 1979; *Spectator*, 11 Aug. 1979), was praised for the clarity and intelligence of their performances, the production struck most as overworked, even bizarre, despite its academic interest.

BBC television

In 1937 the BBC transmitted a scene from *As You Like It*, directed by Robert Atkins and starring Margaretta Scott and Ion Swinley. A decade later when television sets were more widely available, the BBC presented an adaptation of a 1946 staging at the Open Air Theatre in Regent's Park. Director Ian Atkins was aware of the small screen's challenges: since the 'green foliage of a "realistic" set . . . would tend to appear dark' on television, he chose a 'stylised' forest. Atkins also worked to transfer the 'impression of gaiety and freedom' conveyed in the large space of Regent's Park to the confined area of the studio set (*Radio Times*, 12 July 1946). Another black and white version was broadcast by the BBC in 1953, starring Margaret Leighton and Laurence Harvey. Most influential at mid-century was the BBC broadcast of the RSC production starring Vanessa Redgrave, which is discussed above.

By the time the BBC, together with Time–Life, launched its Shakespeare series in 1976, television had become the dominant force in entertainment. The series was designed to reach a wide audience and to create a video archive for educational purposes. With regard to *As You Like It*, the BBC version may have done more harm than good, for it confirmed the suspicion of some viewers 'that Shakespeare is a bore' (*SQ* 30, 1979, p. 411). In deciding to film on location at Glamis Castle in Scotland, producer Cedric Messina was like others before him in succumbing to rural enchantments. Unhappily, the effort to naturalise Arden within the confines of the small screen alienated viewers. Despite the fresh scenery, a 'bias towards realism' overwhelmed

Figure 10 Eileen Atkins wore blue jeans as Ganymede in Goodbody's 1973 production. 'One has to assume that Orlando is either extremely short-sighted or very naïve about the facts of life to mistake the very feminine Miss Atkins as being anything remotely resembling a boy' (*Evening Standard*, 13 June 1973). Each programme contained a free souvenir poster, featuring Atkins in jeans, seen from behind, with a quotation from Martin Luther: 'women . . . have broad hips and a wide fundament to sit upon, keep house and bear and raise children' (SCL). The juxtaposition of essentialising text and liberated image made a point about the production's (and perhaps the play's) feminist agenda. Richard Pasco appeared as a Chekhovian Jaques.

the theatricality of Shakespearean pastoral so that this 'very nearly became a production more about Mother Nature than about Rosalind, Orlando, or the dukes'.[219] The exiled court wades through ferns in their supposedly wintry camp site in Arden, and viewers may be forgiven for being distracted by the fly caught buzzing around Helen Mirren's face and by her efforts to swat it away while, as Ganymede, she attempts to interest Orlando in the love-cure. J. C. Bulman argues that director Basil Coleman 'made a virtue of necessity', emphasising the play's elements of satire to mock the pastoral ethos – for instance, Touchstone steps in sheep dung during his debate with Corin about country life in 3.3. Likewise, 'Coleman strains our belief in pastoral most comically in the appearance of Hymen . . . a fey figure dressed in gossamer'.[220] But for most viewers these efforts fell flat, primarily because the performances were uninspired.

Helen Mirren's intelligent Rosalind conveys clear relief at shedding her brocade gown and piped headdress. This Rosalind puts a friendly arm around Phoebe's shoulder to tell her that she is 'not for all markets' (3.6.60), then self-consciously crosses her arms over her chest and deepens her voice upon sensing Phoebe's attraction to her. The camera repeatedly catches her smiling responses to Orlando's speeches when she has turned her back to him, as when she chides him for being late in 4.1. Yet there is no chemistry between Rosalind and Orlando, or Rosalind and Celia, or any other couple. Even Touchstone is static, pleading with Audrey rather than taking advantage of her. When the two young pages show up to sing 'It was a lover and his lass', they stand like statues on either side of Touchstone until the final verse, when each deals the clown a stagey shove, and he responds by rolling them down the hillside as if they were bowling pins.

The reaction of Richard Pasco's morosely hollow-eyed and bibulous Jaques to this enervating Arden becomes understandable. He stumbles drunkenly towards the merry group around the campfire, giddily reporting his meeting with Touchstone. Duke Senior, a concerned patron, chides the melancholiac harshly for being a 'libertine' (2.7.65) and is startled to be interrupted by 'All the world's a stage' (2.7.139). Jaques delivers the speech in acid tones as he walks among the men, gesturing with his cup, and then looks on in disgust as Adam is fed by hand.

Peter Stein's journey to Arden

In the urbanised 1970s, the notion of pastoral offering an unambiguous retreat from the cares of civilisation had come to seem overly simple. *As You Like It* took on new interest as a text allowing for exploration of the definitions

---

219 Willis, pp. 187, 188.   220 Bulman, pp. 176, 177.

of 'nature' and 'civilisation'. The space-age set of Williams's production, Nunn's retreat into artifice, and Dexter's anthropological experiment exemplified three very different explorations of the play as a meditation on these issues.[221] The most compelling investigation of the utopian dream of escape from politics into a world of nature was Peter Stein's 1977 production in Berlin.

Even attending the play required audiences to venture outside the city, lending peculiar resonance for a Berlin audience surrounded by the GDR. After the hour-long bus journey to the CCC Film Studio at Berlin-Spandau, viewers were 'herded' into a 'glaring white vestibule' where they stood in a cramped space evocative of the 'suffocating effect of the courtly world' to watch the opening part of the play performed on 'balustrades and pedestals'.[222] The scenes near Oliver's house and at Frederick's court (all of Act 1, also 2.2, 2.3, and 3.1) were 'cross-cut in a cinematic style of juxtaposition . . . one actor or group would speak a few lines and freeze into a tableau while a passage from another scene was interposed . . . elsewhere in the hall'.[223] The opening act culminated in a stylised version of the wrestling match featuring a professional wrestler. Then the audience was invited to share the journey to Arden – actually hounded from the hall by the sound of barking dogs playing over the sound system.

The fifteen-minute walk to Arden passed through a dark, gusty maze, with dangling vines, dripping water, and occasional surprises such as a wild bear. 'The conception was brilliant: to pass from the formality and brutality of the court through an underground labyrinth to the freedom and innocence of the forest was like being born anew'.[224] In the vast space of Arden, the scene was 'equipped with every detail of the traditional *locus amoenus* (rustling trees, stream, pond, wavy cornfield, chirping noises, singing shepherds)' (*SQ* 29, 1978, p. 299). Here the audience was seated for the rest of a production that lasted four and a half hours, while a variety of activities – extra business involving Robin Hood, Robinson Crusoe, modern hikers, a witch, and a hermit – evoked the forest's complexity. The Forest activity presented a decided contrast to the sterility of the court setting, although this Arden was hardly idyllic. The banished court shivered miserably, and Rosalind, Celia, and Touchstone, bundled in coats and scarves, 'arrived as a group of refugees pushing and pulling a small cart that contained their belongings, a cart that tilted over on the uneven ground' (*SQ* 29, 1978, p. 299). In the hunting scene (4.2), the hart was skinned, and one lord wore its hide and another its horns for a primitive dance.

221 Kennedy, p. 257.   222 Patterson, p. 134; *SQ* 29, 1978, p. 298.
223 Patterson, p. 134.   224 Ibid., pp. 137–8.

Stein was not especially interested in exploring the subtleties of the love story. The style of the forest scenes 'possessed Brechtian elements: a beguiling informality, a cheekily irreverent tone and the emphasis on situation rather than on individual psychology'. Jaques delivered the Seven Ages speech as if reciting 'a familiar piece of folk wisdom' and the mock wedding of 4.1 'was performed like a children's game'.[225] Similarly, the pastoral scenes between Silvius and Phoebe were 'rendered alien by being performed as a play-within-the-play on a movable stage mounted over the pond' (*SQ* 29, 1978, p. 299). Eventually 'Hymen entered all in gold' and 'the forest-dwellers threw off their rough cloaks to reveal their Elizabethan garments underneath, as if they had been playing at exile all along'. The ending was equivocal: a door was left open 'so that the audience saw again that cold blue light' of the court, 'beckoning in the distance'. But the wagon carrying the wedding party jolted into the door, the actors tumbled off and 'stumbled back on foot to the world of politics and intrigue'.[226] Stein replaced Rosalind's epilogue with a prose poem by Francis Ponge, read by Frederick, emphasising nature's 'inflexible laws' and thus puncturing the dream of escape into the freedom of an idyllic nature. 'By using an environmental setting that required the spectator's participation, Stein made the spectator part of the court, part of the forest, and part of the journey between them'.[227] Together with designer Karl-Ernst Herrmann, Stein pushed the conception of *As You Like It* far beyond the pastoral tradition by deconstructing the terms of nature and escape.

Five years later in Munich, Ernst Wendt directed a bleakly 'pessimistic twentieth-century view of the play': differences between court and forest were mostly obliterated; when the lovers were finally reunited, Orlando 'lost all interest in Rosalind and merely clutched a bottle of liquor'; Celia was driven near madness by 'lesbian jealousy' (*SQ* 34, 1983, p. 238). Working overtime to make the play speak to the modern world, Wendt's production showed how intrinsic the oscillating movement between court and forest is to the comic conclusion.

Adrian Noble and gender-bending in the 1980s

Adrian Noble and designer Bob Crowley sought to cleanse the play of the clichés of rural romp that Peter Brook had compared to an advertisement for beer (*Guardian*, 26 April 1985). Where Stein's production in a divided Germany exposed the workings of geographical politics, Noble was

---

225 Ibid., pp. 142, 140, 144.   226 Kennedy, pp. 262, 265.
227 Patterson, p. 149; Kennedy, p. 265.

concerned with psychological effects, in particular a liberal feminist notion of gender fluidity. Each production was, in its way, political, but they reflected the difference between continental conceptions of theatre as a potent force in power relations writ large and a native tradition that rarely extended beyond liberal questioning of established social arrangements.

Noble's Arden was a dream-like version of the ducal court, with dust-sheets covering the furniture, a large stopped clock, and mirrors contributing to the sense of psychological exploration. An enormous white silk cloth trailed behind the exiles as they arrived in Arden, obliterating the court furniture and providing 'possibilities for transformation into a hiding-place, a wedding-canopy or anything else that the scenes required'.[228] Touchstone pulled it up about himself and Audrey to suggest bed clothes; she arranged it like a wedding dress; and when Rosalind encouraged Orlando to 'woo me, woo me', she likewise fabricated a dress from the stage cloth. This Arden was a 'realm in which you make of life what you want to make of it; it's a realm where you can dress up and change your gender, change your way of life' (*Plays and Players*, May 1986). Joseph O'Conor played both Duke Frederick and Duke Senior 'without any change of costume or make-up', simply stepping through a magical mirror to emerge as an altered personality (*SQ* 37, 1986, p. 116). Likewise, the usurper's court was transformed into the court of the exiled duke by the actors wrapping draperies around their evening dress.

Interestingly, this strongly conceptual Arden was to some extent constricting rather than liberating. Fiona Shaw and Juliet Stevenson, who played Celia and Rosalind, note that 'one cannot *act* with a metaphor', and the production was simplified when it moved from Stratford to London. Whereas Stein's elaborate and enormous settings were key to the production's intent, for Noble the set was meant to release the actors so that characters might be explored in new ways. Not only was Arden 'a realm of the imagination', but the production's emphasis shifted increasingly from stage effects 'towards making its characters' inner lives more visible'.[229]

In particular, gender roles were 'turned on their heads'.[230] Stevenson's Rosalind and Hilton McRae's Orlando 'embod[ied] the Jungian animus and anima . . . each having something of the other's sexual nature. Ms Stevenson's Rosalind [became] an almost Chaplinesque figure in bowler, scarlet braces and baggy white pants; Mr McRae's Orlando [was] rather like an androgynous Scottish Mick Jagger' (*Guardian*, 26 Apr. 1985). McRae's Orlando several times knelt to cool his fevered head in the pool; he seemed on the

228 Shaw and Stevenson, p. 64.   229 Ibid., p. 63; Rickman, p. 73.
230 Rutter, p. 105.

verge of tears when he announced he could 'live no longer by thinking' (5.2.40). He was not averse to physical display, as most memorably when he wrestled in a thong bikini, throwing Charles off his game by planting a kiss on his lips. As for Stevenson, with her 'contemporary unisex hairstyle', she was 'equally convincing as boy and girl. Her baggy trousers followed the latest fashion but also suggested that she was in part a clown: she used a bowler hat and cane like a cabaret artiste to illustrate the "divers paces" of Time' (*SQ* 37, 1986, p. 116). And this Ganymede 'did not simply replace Rosalind in Arden: he ran parallel with her. The two would sometimes collude, sometimes collide and even sometimes betray each other.' Despite, or perhaps because of, the fluidity of gender definitions, the dialogues between Orlando and Rosalind conveyed a significant erotic charge (*Times*, 24 Apr. 1985; *Daily Telegraph*, 25 Apr. 1985). Celia hid her face in a book while the two rolled around on the stage during the 4.1 love-talk, and the kneeling Rosalind fell towards Orlando at the climax of the mock marriage. The production contained much swooning, erotic passion: Rosalind's pretend faint at 'come, Death' (4.1.149) anticipated her collapse in 4.3 when handed the bloody napkin and echoed Phoebe's swooning response to Ganymede's attractions in 3.6. Phoebe removed her bodice and washed it in the stream in an effort to cool her passion (see figure 11). Stevenson described *As You Like It* as 'dangerous' and 'subversive', a play that 'challenges notions of gender'.[231]

In keeping with the wish to explore all facets of the play's central characters, Alan Rickman sought to convey 'Jaques's story', suggesting a former libertine at once arrogant and vulnerable, savage in his criticisms yet deeply dependent on others. Rickman saw the Seven Ages speech as one in which 'Jaques might be in real danger of losing control'.[232] Some commentators thought it was the *actor* who lost control in a 'horrible attack of over acting', 'needlessly characterizing every figure' in the speech (*Stratford-upon-Avon Herald*, 3 May 1985; *Times*, 24 Apr. 1985). Yet others thought that Rickman's 'intelligent, sardonic – even faintly threatening – Jaques's added to the imaginative scope of the production (*Financial Times*, 25 Apr. 1985).

---

231 Ibid., p. 97. 232 Rickman, pp. 75, 78.

←—————————————————————————————

Figure 11 Many productions since the mid-nineteenth century have featured on-stage streams. Although Bob Crowley's design for Adrian Noble's 1985 production was non-illusionistic and did not represent the forest, 'after the interval Arden had greened' and 'a natural mirror, a stream, crossed the stage' (Rutter, p. 105). Touchstone, predictably, took several dunkings, and the overheated lovers Orlando and Phoebe used it to cool their passion. Lesley Manville exaggerated Phoebe's 'vamping' of Ganymede; Roger Hyams as Silvius was 'more a Petticoat Lane spiv than a rustic' (Martin Hoyle, *Financial Times*, 5 Apr. 1985).

Christine Edzard's dystopic Arden

Acutely aware of the problems of filming pastoral illusion as a realistically green and pleasant land, Christine Edzard sought to evoke the spirit of Arden in a different place: the urban wasteland of London's docksides. Edzard's brilliant reconception was faithful to the play's central contrast between the court's luxurious corruption and the social freedom of the more perilous forest, updated for an era in which 'a leafy glade' seems recreational rather than 'savage'.[233] 'On the wind-chilled wharf, Duke Senior's banishment has a poignancy that no shaded green forest could ever convey; his becomes the plight of an older set of values displaced by the money-grabbing forces of development'.[234] Academics have lauded the film for ferreting out the social commentary within a play that native theatrical tradition has rendered sedately bourgeois. Setting the communalism of Arden against an invidious capitalism, Edzard's *As You Like It* was seen as offering an alternative to Thatcherite politics: 'in the wasteland, an audience experiences a move beyond individualism, encountering a place where a sense of communal feeling is generated'.[235]

Sacrificing, in Derek Elley's words, 'sylvan whimsy for social edge',[236] the film aims for an educated, even avant-garde audience. Although Edzard includes touches such as the single sheep led about by Corin to indicate an intention to comment on pastoral myth rather than to reject it outright, the puddly grey expanses of an Arden where the Duke and his men huddle around a campfire built in a trash bin and drink from recycled plastic soda bottles offended some viewers. 'The contemporary social focus [was] hopelessly vague', noted Russell Jackson. Moreover, production values were low and the film was derided for a puritanical denial of visual pleasure. In Jackson's words, 'it takes pains to avoid wooing us with entertainment' – 'refus[ing] to show the wrestling match', for instance, and eliminating Hymen – and paradoxically misses the play's capacity for social critique while also suppressing some of its 'joyousness'.[237]

Certainly the film succeeds in highlighting the difference between the opulent pleasures of court – where Rosalind licks an éclair from the lavish spread at the 1.2 cocktail party, and Celia scatters clothing around a room-sized wardrobe as she packs for her journey – and the drably monochromatic spaces of Arden. The disjunction between the Shakespearean language and the modern setting creates more strain than the rejection of pastoral convention. There are witty moments, such as Duke Senior's

233 Edzard, quoted in Marriette, p. 77.
234 Lennox, p. 54.   235 Marriette, p. 80.   236 Quoted in Rothwell, p. 216.
237 Jackson, 'Shakespeare's Comedies on Film', p. 102.

Figure 12 In her jeans, parka, and stocking cap, Emma Croft was a convincingly boyish Ganymede in Christine Edzard's 1992 film. Orlando's love poems were graffiti scrawled in the urban wasteland that was Arden.

man slicing open a cellophane packet of meat at 'shall we go and kill us venison?' (2.1.21) and the footage of prowling thieves attacking the sleeping Oliver that accompanies his narrative about the assault of the 'gilded snake' and hungry 'lioness' (4.3.103, 109). But Celia Bannerman's mature, confident, and obviously wealthy Celia has so many resources at her command that the flight to an underworld Arden (rather than, say, Antigua) challenges credulity. The clash between the layering of theatrical language and a filmic style recalling 'social documentaries' compounds the problem: many of Touchstone's lines fall flat because they '[depend] upon direct collusion with an audience comprised of spectators and not cinematic "overhearers".'[238]

Rosalind's references to curtal axe and to doublet and hose also sound odd, although for a different reason: in androgynous jeans and jersey, the lanky Emma Croft makes a convincing boy, so the accustomed note of gender-bending flirtatiousness is absent (see figure 12). This Rosalind as Ganymede flirts – she struts and whirls and stalks about Orlando – but in her relationship with the camera she remains a sincere character; that is, Croft does not flirt with *us*. More than in most versions, Rosalind and Orlando come across

238 Hattaway, 'Comedies on Film', p. 95.

as soul-mates, in part because the hardships of their exile are so visible. Orlando camps out in a tent of plastic sheeting, while Rosalind and Celia make do in a workman's hut. The lovers, in their jeans and sneakers, 'become mirror images of one another', as do Touchstone and Jaques in their dark overcoats.[239] Edzard follows theatrical convention in doubling the parts of the two Dukes and those of Le Beau and Corin, but she creates a new set of doubles in casting Andrew Tiernan as both Orlando and Oliver – a feat the film medium makes possible, although still subject to certain limitations (in the wrestling match, for instance). The emphasis on doubling, which would also have been a factor in the early modern theatre, allows Edzard to further her inquiry into the play's political structure.

Cheek by Jowl

Although not explicitly a politically activist company, Cheek by Jowl, founded by Declan Donellan and Nick Ormerod in 1981, responded to conservative theatre traditions 'by refusing to accept the "star" system, performing in non-theatrical spaces, and showing a lively irreverence for the letter of the text that can usually be traced back to a close study of it'.[240] The most striking feature of the company's *As You Like It* – its all-male cast – recalled the production directed by Clifford Williams in 1967. Williams had pitched his production somewhere between platonic love and camp, suggesting that gender might be constructed rather than natural but eschewing overt inquiry into sexual identity with the claim that the play was about 'sexless' love. By 1991, when the Cheek by Jowl production opened, progressive audiences could be expected to view gender and sexuality as social constructions; this opened the way for a production that seriously explored the layering of performed identities in the play's characters, instead of manipulating gender roles in a coy manner.

While recalling Elizabethan practice in terms of the male acting company, the production was modern in its use of 'colour blind' casting: Rosalind was played by the black actor Adrian Lester. Graceful, sensuous, and funny, Lester 'manage[d] to evoke femininity without resorting to any of the cheap mannerisms of female impersonation' (*Independent*, 6 Dec. 1991). 'When he played the female Rosalind playing at being the male Ganymede he seemed more like a woman playing a man than a man playing a woman. And when he played at Rosalind playing Ganymede playing Rosalind, one simply gave up trying to work out in one's mind' where the lines of gender and performance intersected.[241] When Rosalind as Ganymede first presented herself

---

239 Marriette, p. 84.   240 Bate and Jackson, p. 220.   241 Ibid., p. 6.

to Orlando in Arden, she clearly expected him to recognise her, but he did not, despite her prompting, giggling, and even her fingering of the necklace she had given him after the wrestling match. Where most actresses playing Rosalind use this moment to display a convincingly masculine disguise as Ganymede, Lester instead conveyed the girl hiding, embarrassed, under the male disguise (see commentary, 3.3.251). Similarly, 'when Orlando playfully punched Ganymede's arm and Rosalind awkwardly and tentatively returned the male gesture, though the actor could clearly have made the gesture with ease', one glimpsed the 'gaps of gender action' (*SS* 45, 1992, p. 128). There was nothing arch about this Rosalind: initially 'shy and bookish', she became more 'impulsive' with her attraction to Orlando, but never lost a tendency to be 'tongue-tied and hesitant' (*Financial Times*, 27 Jan. 1995).

Donnellan's goal was not discernibly sociological. He used the actors 'to polymorphously perverse and liberating effect: every tug of affection, in any direction, is unloosed to be played explicitly' (*City Limits*, 12 Dec. 1991). Part of the pleasure was 'the sense that something very racy was being staged'. It was precisely the willingness to open up questions of desire and identity that brought an erotic charge. For instance, Wayne Cater offered a 'preposterously oversexed' Phoebe who '[fell] into a reverie while describing Rosalind . . . but simultaneously sliding her hands and legs all over a stunned Silvius'.[242] The complex tension between Orlando and Rosalind was far from being 'glibly homosexual' because the desire of each was distinctly unclear. When Rosalind revealed herself in a wedding dress in the final scene, Orlando alarmingly stalked away: he seemed at once troubled by the return of feminine Rosalind (when he really loved Ganymede), upset to recognise the male Ganymede in drag, and 'shamed at his failure to have recognized her' (*SS* 45, 1992, p. 130) (see commentary, 5.4.101–2). In short, it 'frightens the life out of Orlando', and viewers may feel something akin to this mixture of titillation and confusion when Orlando and Rosalind finally share 'a long searching kiss, joltingly reminding us that we are watching two men' (*Time Out*, 18 Jan. 1995).

Some less than progressive critics took issue with what was seen as a gay agenda. Jaques, 'with his cashmere overcoat, bow-tie and effete supercilious manner', was 'a would be sugar-daddy' to Ganymede and Orlando (*Times*, 5 Dec. 1991), who propositioned most of the male characters. Eventually he hooked up with Hymen/Amiens and stuck around for the final dance, a tango. In Michael Hattaway's words, this was 'in some ways' an 'appropriation of the play for a homosexual perspective', and Orlando rejected

242 Ko, p. 17.

Figure 13 In the 1994–5 revival of Cheek by Jowl's celebrated production, Celia (Simon Coates) stroked a melancholy Rosalind (Adrian Lester). The affectionate intimacy between the two included a ritual of spitting at the word 'man'.

Rosalind because 'he was straight'.[243] Yet Adrian Lester commented, 'what can be more heterosexual than four weddings at the end of a play?' (*Time Out*, 4 Dec. 1991). Some feminists viewed the production as misogynistic in its rejection of female actors, its picture of homosocial male bonding, and its reliance 'on the mannerisms of men in drag'.[244] Given the affection with which Rosalind and Celia stroked one another in the first act and their custom of spitting when the word 'man' was uttered, Rosalind's attachment to Orlando seemed even more of a defection from previous loyalties than usual (see figure 13).

The staging was 'almost ostentatiously simple' (*Times*, 5 Dec. 1991), again recalling conditions of the early modern theatre: a bare stage for the court scenes; later, dangling strips of green paper to evoke Arden. In the opening moments, the entire company appeared on stage: with the words 'All the world's a stage And all the men and women merely players', those taking female parts separated themselves from those playing men. 'Dress was modern, but more colourful and larger than life than that of everyday – as it would have been in the 1590s'.[245] Rosalind and Celia wore sumptuous gowns for the opening scenes, but otherwise there were no drag accoutrements: no wigs, no makeup, no prostheses.

Rather than trying to make Touchstone amusing, the joke here was precisely that he was *not* funny. It was Jaques who wore, and circulated among others, the stock red nose of a clown. As Touchstone, Peter Needham was 'a jobbing variety hack' and the 'now-conventional tiredness' of his routines was so obvious that he could release pressure because expectations were punctured (*City Limits*, 12 Dec. 1991). In its way, this performance was emblematic of the production overall: rather than seeking to cover over the difficulties of the script, Cheek by Jowl explored them as theatrical possibilities. Donnellan claimed that the 'all-male cast forces the audience to tread a tightrope of willed belief, a quintessentially theatrical act of faith' (*Independent*, 4 Jan. 1995).

Shakespeare's Globe

Like other early productions at Shakespeare's Globe in London, Lucy Bailey's 1998 *As You Like It* was very much concerned with working out the best uses of the amphitheatre's physical space. In addition to the obvious issues – the challenges of being heard in the multi-level, open-air space; the difficulty of maintaining viewers' attention amid competing interests;

243 Michael Hattaway, ed., Introduction, *As You Like It*, p. 59.
244 Dusinberre, p. 9; Ko, p. 17.   245 Bate and Jackson, p. 5.

ongoing experimentation with the large stage and its controversial pillars – there was a requirement of historical 'authenticity', which meant that costumes for the production were 'authentically made' Elizabethan clothing and that the stage was 'minimally decorated with hangings' in keeping with early modern usage.[246] More troublingly for Bailey, her decision to use the yard extensively – she added steps from the fore-stage into the pit, staged many exits and entrances through the yard, and, most spectacularly, brought the wrestling match down to this level – met with considerable resistance from historical purists. Some of the actors as well found the wrestling risky, 'to themselves and the audience members'. Bailey valued the ground-level wrestling for the excitement it created; it accorded with her sense of the original Globe's connection to street theatre.[247] She attempted to use the extent of the Globe's stage schematically, by limiting the court scenes to the narrow fringe beyond the square area marked off by the pillars.

An invented prologue lent narrative coherence: a ballad singer recounted the story of Sir Roland de Boys's death, while his three sons presented the action in dumbshow. Elements of ritual action also appeared, notably the bloody hunting scene, in which Amiens, wearing horns, played the part of the deer. Most of the male cast members appeared wearing Morris bells, while Jaques 'watched from the balcony'; the victorious hunter smeared blood on his own forehead.[248]

While most characters were played to familiar type, Anastasia Hille, as Rosalind, reached for a 'more complex, more female-oriented' interpretation than the production generally allowed. Hers was 'a thoroughly feminine Ganymede' who had given up 'all pretence of disguise' by Act 4, except for the doublet and hose that she had attempted to shed in 'a buttock-flashing panic' when first informed of Orlando's proximity (*SQ* 50, 1999, p. 77; *SS* 52, 1999, pp. 223–4). Hille reported that she 'would have liked to actually physically take something off on stage, but it was too complicated'. The Cheek by Jowl production had strongly influenced Hille, although she felt that in the Globe production 'the heterosexuality created a bond between us (Rosalind and Orlando) that is not possible between two heterosexual men playing a man and a woman'.[249] Her conception of the character, and of the play, thus recalled the Victorian doctrine of true womanhood, defining personality in terms of an essentialised body and sexual desire.

As the twentieth century ended, several of the old complaints about *As You Like It* resurfaced in new contexts. Bailey's production at Shakespeare's

246 Miller-Schütz, 'Interview', p. 5.   247 Miller-Schütz, 'Findings'.
248 Ibid.   249 Miller-Schütz, 'Interview', p. 12.

Globe exemplified the spectacular, crowd-pleasing style that venue was quickly establishing as its own – a style not altogether dissimilar from the nineteenth-century vogue of elaborate sets and costumes. Gregory Doran's Stratford production in 2000 was ridiculed for its plush furnishings of traditional English decor – a late capitalist manifestation of the turnip and flowers from Anne Hathaway's garden and the stuffed stag from Charlecote Park, earlier used to authenticate the play's local ties. Although the notable success of non-illusionistic stagings by Clifford Williams, Adrian Noble, Peter Stein, and Declan Donnellan showed how well the play works without a tether to local place, *As You Like It* continued to demonstrate an ineradicable 'Englishness' as far as many directors were concerned. And yet, as Michael Dobson suggests, 'with sheep farming in deep crisis, the relations between the country and the city making regular front-page news, and even the ethics of deer-hunting a topic of national debate, the play suddenly looked more topical than at almost any time since the 1590s' (*SS* 54, 2001, p. 267). Indeed, the capacity of *As You Like It* to interpret social experience remains unexhausted.

AS YOU LIKE IT

LIST OF CHARACTERS

The de Boys household
OLIVER, *oldest son of Sir Roland de Boys*
JACQUES DE BOYS, *second son of Sir Roland*
ORLANDO, *third son of Sir Roland*
ADAM, *servant to the de Boys household*
DENIS, *servant to Oliver*

The court of the usurping Duke
DUKE FREDERICK, *younger brother to Duke Senior*
CELIA, *his daughter*
ROSALIND, *daughter to Duke Senior*
LE BEAU, *a courtier*
CHARLES, *a wrestler*
CLOWN (TOUCHSTONE)

The court in exile
DUKE SENIOR, *older brother to Duke Frederick*
AMIENS, *a lord attendant*
JAQUES, *a melancholic traveller*

The greenwood
CORIN, *a shepherd*
PHOEBE, *a shepherdess*
SILVIUS, *a shepherd*
WILLIAM, *a countryman*
AUDREY, *a country girl*
SIR OLIVER MARTEXT, *a vicar*
HYMEN, *god of marriage*
LORDS, PAGES, FORESTERS, *Attendants*

Invented prologues began some twentieth-century productions. Trevor Nunn's Restoration setting featured 'a toy proscenium . . . within the proscenium proper', and the action was preceded by a musical prologue featuring Hymen, Fortune, and Nature (*Financial Times,* 9 Sept. 1977). John Dexter's anthropological production at the National opened with a 'procession of country fellows . . . bearing and twisting the last sheaves of corn'; Orlando, in a straw crown, was 'helping the yokels' tie the sheaves; in the background a haystack glowed in autumnal light (*The Month,* Oct. 1979; *New Statesman,* 10 Aug. 1979; *Guardian,* 3 Aug. 1979). The countryfolk remained on stage, responding chorus-like, through the first scene (pbk). At the start of Liviu Ciulei's 1982 production, a 'wooden horse on wheeled cart stood at the front of the stage'. Adam, Orlando, and other servants entered to dress the horse in bronze and black trappings. Later, 'Oliver swaggered in, with riding crop, in lavish red and black, and mounted the horse from the back of a kneeling servant' (*SQ* 34, 1983, p. 231). John Hirsch's production at Stratford, Ontario, in 1983 opened with 'a Dickensian street scene in the snow, where a ragged urchin sang "Under the greenwood tree" in a cracked voice' (*SS* 39, 1986, p. 181); Oliver's harsh regime was evidenced as 'soldiers tramped across the stage, escorting some wretch in chains to a nameless fate' (*SQ* 34, 1983, p. 464). Michael Kahn's 1992 production began with the three de Boys brothers placing 'a memorial wreath on what was obviously their father's funeral monument' (*SQ* 43, 1992, p. 469). Christine Edzard's film opens with Jaques reciting the Seven Ages speech as he wanders through a marble-columned hall replete with mirrors (later one of the central settings). Cheek by Jowl's production began by dividing the cast into male and female characters, as the words 'All the world's a stage / And all the men and women merely players' were spoken. At Shakespeare's Globe in 1998, a 'ballad singer supplied . . . background material found in Lodge's *Rosalynde* while the characters mimed Old Sir Rowland and his three sons, establish[ing] the atmosphere of a lighthearted adventure story' (*SQ* 50, 1999, p. 76). Director Lucy Bailey thought the prologue would help viewers 'to identify Jacques de Boys immediately when he appears at the end' (Miller-Schütz, 'Findings').

ACT I, SCENE I

Enter ORLANDO *and* ADAM

From the eighteenth century onwards, the scene has usually been set outside a house within an orchard (Bell's edn, Macready pbk). Nineteenth-century sets featured painted backdrops representing Oliver's house and Frederick's court. In Czinner's film, peasants eat a meal at a long table within a courtyard filled with chickens and horses. For his 1934 production, Jacques Copeau 'built a false proscenium and included the stage boxes in the area of play. Two curtains, appropriately painted, indicated the dwellings of Duke Frederick and Oliver. These were raised for the wrestling match and, later, for the forest' (Speaight, p. 191). The 1978 BBC version, shot on location at Glamis Castle in Scotland, locates the scene in a walled garden, where Oliver practises swordplay in the background as Orlando shovels manure. Trevor Nunn's production opened on a painted-cloth backdrop of Oliver's house that evoked 'a nineteenth-century print of an eighteenth-century chateau' (*SS* 31, 1978, p. 146). At Bergen National Theatre in 1983, 'the court scenes were played out in front of a Medieval backcloth, inspired by . . . *Les Très Riches Heures du Duc de Berry*, whose illuminated "pages" formed a frozen tableau. The court gradually woke up, out of a Sleeping Beauty sleep, to act out its sinister intrigue against Orlando and Rosalind' (*SQ* 35, 1984, p. 95). Edzard filmed this and the 'court' scenes in what appears to be a bank lobby, replete with marble columns and mirrors.

A seasonal motif, in which the action opens in winter and gradually yields to spring, was introduced by Glen Byam Shaw and frequently recurs. Farrah added a textural element at Stratford in 1980: 'white fur surfaces . . . suggest[ed] luxury at court and snow in the country' in the play's wintry first half, then 'moss-covered trees' and 'a profusion of daffodils' marked the coming of spring (*SS* 34, 1981, p. 149).

Sets became more stylised or conceptual in the latter half of the twentieth century. For Clifford Williams's 1967 production, Ralph Koltai 'created a space out of a white raked stage, Perspex shapes and screens and white light' (*Daily Mail*, 4 Oct. 1967). Hans Peter Schubert's set for Ionesco's 1976 production at Bochum 'suggest[ed] a vandalized slaughter-house or a war-damaged factory, with burst pipes, torn-off tiles and heaps of rubble' (Hortmann, p. 249). Karl-Ernst Hermann's design for Peter Stein's 1977 production required the audience to stand in a narrow, brightly lit hallway while the court scenes were played upon balconies and balustrades. Then the viewers literally followed the exiles to Arden, squeezing

ORLANDO As I remember, Adam, it was upon this fashion bequeathed
me by will but poor a thousand crowns and, as thou say'st, charged
my brother, on his blessing, to breed me well: and there begins my
sadness. My brother Jacques he keeps at school, and report speaks

through a dim, meandering passageway to emerge into the huge space of a film studio
(Kennedy, pp. 261–2). John Dexter's production was 'set on a rectangular, raked platform of
wooden planks, with huge sheets of white or green to suggest the forest' (*Guardian*, 3 Aug.
1979). For Noble's 1985 production, Bob Crowley designed a dream-like ducal palace,
where the clock was stopped, the furniture covered with sheets, and the mirror one the
characters could step through. At the Comédie-Française in 1989, Lluis Pasqual presented
the Duke's palace as 'just a narrow, red-carpeted passage placed before an immense mirror
reflecting the auditorium'. The escape to the forest was a flight from the modern society
thus imaged on stage, although Arden itself was 'only a piece of cloth before a wall covered
with tags bearing the name of Rosalind' (Boquet, p. 202). John Caird's 1989 production at
Stratford sought to erase 'boundaries between playing areas and auditorium': the audience
arrived to find most of the cast dancing down stage, and actors – some of them wearing the
uniforms of ushers – 'entered the stage from the auditorium'. Orlando's opening speech
was presented as a prologue (*SQ* 41, 1989–90, p. 491). The stage itself was 'dominated in
the middle of the back wall with a large clock working in real time . . . an easy way for those
who were bored to calculate exactly how long the play had been running' (*SS* 44, 1991,
p. 162). At Shakespeare's Globe, Lucy Bailey differentiated the forest and court scenes by
playing the former on the square space created by the pillars (an area covered by a rough
white cloth) while the 'court scenes were played on the bare boards of the margin that runs
around the edge of the stage' (Miller-Schütz, 'Findings').

0 SD   Orlando is often discovered working at some menial chore: nailing ivy, digging with a spade,
chopping wood (Benson 1904, Bridges-Adams, Helpmann pbks). Oscar Asche seems to
have introduced the wheelbarrow, on which his Orlando (Henry Ainley) sat after wheeling it
in (pbk). Toye's production opened with a pantomime in which a stable boy and a cook
delivered a bucket of slops to a pigsty. Orlando left off sawing wood to give the cook a 'mock
bow', then took up the bucket and poured the slops into the sty (Toye pbk). In Noble's
production, the scene was played on the lip of the stage, before the curtain, and sounds of
an approaching storm could be heard. Edzard's Orlando, in jeans and parka, leans against a
marble column as he bitterly complains, then crouches to tell Adam, a cardiganed custodian,
of his misery. In Donnellan's production, Orlando and Adam stepped forward from the rest
of the cast; Orlando's mud-splattered forearms were washed clean by Adam. Most
Orlandos have been furiously indignant. Olivier plays him as resigned in Czinner's film.

1   Williams inserted 'my father' after 'fashion' (pbk).
4   'Roland' for 'Jacques' (Helpmann pbk).

goldenly of his profit. For my part, he keeps me rustically at home   5
or, to speak more properly, stays me here at home unkept – for call
you that 'keeping' for a gentleman of my birth, that differs not from
the stalling of an ox? His horses are bred better for, besides that they
are fair with their feeding, they are taught their manège, and to that
end riders dearly hired. But I, his brother, gain nothing under him   10
but growth – for the which his animals on his dunghills are as much
bound to him as I. Besides this nothing that he so plentifully gives
me, the something that Nature gave me his countenance seems to
take from me: he lets me feed with his hinds, bars me the place of a
brother, and, as much as in him lies, mines my gentility with my   15
education. This is it, Adam, that grieves me, and the spirit of my
father, which I think is within me, begins to mutiny against this
servitude. I will no longer endure it, though yet I know no wise
remedy how to avoid it.

Enter OLIVER

ADAM Yonder comes my master, your brother.   20
ORLANDO Go apart, Adam, and thou shalt hear how he will shake me
up.
[Adam withdraws]
OLIVER Now, sir, what make you here?
ORLANDO Nothing: I am not taught to make anything.
OLIVER What mar you then, sir?   25
ORLANDO Marry, sir, I am helping you to mar that which God made, a
poor unworthy brother of yours, with idleness.
OLIVER Marry, sir, be better employed, and be naught awhile.

19 SD Oliver laughs off stage (Asche pbk). In traditional stagings, Oliver carried a whip or riding
crop (Bridges-Adams, Toye pbks). He was 'a strutting Elizabethan gallant dressed in stiffly
elaborate court splendour, complete with starched ruff and single ear-ring' in Dexter's
production (*SS* 33, 1980, p. 179). Playing Oliver and Orlando in Edzard's film, Andrew
Tiernan wears the 'stockbroker "uniform" of a bold striped shirt, double-breasted suit and
slick-backed hair' (Marriette, p. 79), in contrast to his unkempt younger brother. Asche had
two courtiers enter with Oliver, then quickly exit (pbk).
21 The line 'suggests that Adam should hide'; at Shakespeare's Globe in 1998 he retreated to
the discovery space (Miller-Schütz, 'Findings').
23 In Donnellan's production, Oliver was reclining on stage, reading a book, when he was
approached by Orlando.
26 In early productions, 'God' is regularly replaced with 'Heaven,' here as throughout the script.
26–30 Frequently cut (1786 edn, Macready pbk).

ORLANDO Shall I keep your hogs and eat husks with them? What
  prodigal portion have I spent that I should come to such penury?   30
OLIVER Know you where you are, sir?
ORLANDO O, sir, very well: here in your orchard.
OLIVER Know you before whom, sir?
ORLANDO Aye, better than him I am before knows me: I know you are
  my eldest brother, and in the gentle condition of blood you should   35
  so know me. The courtesy of nations allows you my better in that
  you are the first-born, but the same tradition takes not away my
  blood, were there twenty brothers betwixt us. I have as much of my
  father in me as you, albeit I confess your coming before me is nearer
  to his reverence.   40
OLIVER [*Raising his hand*] What, boy!
ORLANDO [*Seizing his brother*] Come, come, elder brother, you are too
  young in this.
OLIVER Wilt thou lay hands on me, villain?
ORLANDO I am no villein: I am the youngest son of Sir Roland de Boys;   45
  he was my father, and he is thrice a villain that says such a father
  begot villeins. Wert thou not my brother, I would not take this hand
  from thy throat till this other had pulled out thy tongue for saying
  so: thou hast railed on thyself.

41–5 Most directors have assigned the first show of aggression to Oliver. Daly has Oliver advance
at 41 to seize Orlando, who 'throws him off' at 43 (pbk). Benson as Orlando pinioned Oliver
at 45 (1904 pbk). In Sothern and Marlowe's production, when Oliver raised his fist, Orlando
caught it in his hand (pbk). Bridges-Adams had Oliver threaten his brother with his whip
(pbk). Toye's Oliver carried a riding crop, which he lost during the scuffle; Orlando returned
it (pbk). Macready went against tradition by making Orlando the first to act, with 'seizes
him' at 42 (pbk); the promptbook examined by Charles Shattuck indicates that Orlando
'lays hold of Oliver, as he passes him' (Shattuck, *Macready*). Whoever initiates the violence,
Orlando invariably prevails, dominating the dialogue until 60. Often on stage he keeps
Oliver pinioned to the ground. Henry Ainley as Orlando lifted Oliver, swung him around,
and placed him on the wheelbarrow (Asche pbk). In the 1963 RSC/BBC version, Orlando
casts him into the straw emptied from his farm cart. In Noble's production, Orlando sat on
Oliver's chest, choked him, and shook him by the lapels. In the 1978 BBC version, a
confident Oliver turns to leave after striking his brother, only to be grabbed from behind
and choked. In Edzard's film, in which the same actor played both brothers, the fight
consists of intercut head shots of the combatants.
  In Czinner's film, the peasants look on during the fight, highlighting the parallel with the
wrestling match to follow.

ADAM [*Coming forward*] Sweet masters, be patient, for your father's   50
remembrance, be at accord.
OLIVER Let me go, I say.
ORLANDO I will not till I please. You shall hear me. My father charged
you in his will to give me good education: you have trained me like
a peasant, obscuring and hiding from me all gentleman-like quali-   55
ties. The spirit of my father grows strong in me – and I will no
longer endure it. Therefore allow me such exercises as may become
a gentleman or give me the poor allottery my father left me by
testament: with that I will go buy my fortunes.
[*He releases Oliver*]
OLIVER And what wilt thou do? Beg when that is spent? Well, sir, get   60
you in. I will not long be troubled with you: you shall have some
part of your 'will'; I pray you leave me.
ORLANDO I will no further offend you than becomes me for my good.
OLIVER [*To Adam*] Get you with him, you old dog.
ADAM Is 'old dog' my reward? Most true, I have lost my teeth in your   65
service. God be with my old master: he would not have spoke such
a word.

Exeunt Orlando [*and*] *Adam*

53   In Macready's production, Orlando held Oliver until this line (pbk). Phelps specified that
Adam wrings his hands (pbk). Benson had Oliver draw his sword as soon as he was released
from Orlando's grip; Adam came between the two fighting brothers, his intervention
convincing Oliver to sheathe his sword (1904 pbk). Henry Ainley as Orlando maintained
control over Oliver even when the elder brother rose by wresting his whip and breaking it
across his knee. Oliver later picked the pieces up just as he spotted Charles (Asche pbk).
58   Donnellan had Oliver laugh sarcastically at 'gentleman'.
61–2   Edzard's Oliver hands Orlando folded bills of money, which the latter indignantly crumples
and tosses aside.
62   'Fiercely point to gate' (Sothern–Marlowe pbk). Donnellan had Oliver offer his hand to
Orlando with the offer of his 'will'; after a long pause, Orlando accepted the hand.
63   'Orlando exits into cottage' (Asche pbk).
64   In Czinner's film, Adam attempts to help the vanquished Oliver to his feet but is rewarded
with a kick and abrupt dismissal. Oliver kicks the hoe from Adam's hands in the 1978 BBC
version.
65–7   Edzard's Adam mumbles the words to himself.
66   Although the Samuel French edition used as the basis for the Julia Arthur promptbook prints
'Heaven' for 'God', the Folio reading is restored by hand.
67   Oliver stands at the gate glaring as Orlando and Adam exit (Sothern–Marlowe pbk).

OLIVER Is it even so, begin you to grow upon me? I will physic your
rankness, and yet give no thousand crowns neither. – Holla, Denis.
Enter DENIS

DENIS Calls your worship?   70
OLIVER Was not Charles, the Duke's wrestler, here to speak with me?
DENIS So please you, he is here at the door, and importunes access to
you.
OLIVER Call him in.
[*Exit Denis*]
'Twill be a good way, and tomorrow the wrestling is.   75

Enter CHARLES

CHARLES Good morrow to your worship.
OLIVER Good Monsieur Charles, what's the new news at the new
court?

69 SD Macready had Denis 'passing hastily' across the stage, unaware of Oliver's presence, until
he was summoned (pbk). Holloway directed Oliver to call off stage to summon Denis (pbk).
Many productions, including Benson's, Asche's, and Toye's, have eliminated Denis (pbks).

70 Denis removes his hat (Kean pbk), touches his cap (Bridges-Adams pbk).

72 Macready substituted 'gate' for 'door'. Shattuck suggests that 'door' is a remnant of
'stagedoor' in the Elizabethan theatre (Shattuck, *Macready*). Whatever its provenance, the
term occasioned the stage tradition of moving the action indoors at this point. In Czinner's
film Oliver meets Charles in a dark, wood-panelled hall. The 1963 RSC/BBC production
places the action in a low-ceilinged farm building; through the window glimpses of Orlando
pitching hay are seen. Edzard's Oliver, followed by several businessmen in suits, enters an
office.

74 SD Holloway had Denis remove the wheelbarrow (pbk).

75 SD Charles is typically a large man, somewhat rough in his mannerisms. In Czinner's film,
Lionel Braham wears the black-and-white striped tights of his wrestling costume beneath his
tunic. In the 1978 BBC version, Charles wears a leather tunic and metal-studded belt.
Edzard's Charles is a black man, the only dark-skinned member of the cast, wearing a
well-cut grey suit. Noble had Oliver light a cigarette while waiting for Charles.

76–126 In Stein's production, 'two lords appeared and, exchanging the information ascribed to
Charles and Oliver . . . , moved amongst the audience like two nobles conversing in a busy
London street. Because "overheard", the lines made a much greater impact than is
normally the case when actors, framed by a proscenium arch, try to impart information in a
natural manner' (Patterson, p. 135).

77–95 Sometimes cut (Benson 1904, Sothern–Marlowe pbks).

CHARLES There's no news at the court, sir, but the old news: that is,
the old Duke is banished by his younger brother, the new Duke,   80
and three or four loving lords have put themselves into voluntary
exile with him, whose lands and revenues enrich the new Duke;
therefore he gives them good leave to wander.

OLIVER Can you tell if Rosalind, the Duke's daughter, be banished
with her father?   85

CHARLES O no; for the Duke's daughter, her cousin, so loves her, being
ever from their cradles bred together, that she would have followed
her exile or have died to stay behind her; she is at the court and no
less beloved of her uncle than his own daughter, and never two
ladies loved as they do.   90

OLIVER Where will the old Duke live?

CHARLES They say he is already in the Forest of Arden, and a many
merry men with him; and there they live like the old Robin Hood of
England. They say many young gentlemen flock to him every day,
and fleet the time carelessly as they did in the golden world.   95

OLIVER What, you wrestle tomorrow before the new Duke?

CHARLES Marry, do I, sir; and I came to acquaint you with a matter. I
am given, sir, secretly to understand that your younger brother
Orlando hath a disposition to come in, disguised, against me to try
a fall. Tomorrow, sir, I wrestle for my credit, and he that escapes me   100
without some broken limb shall acquit him well. Your brother is but
young and tender and, for your love, I would be loath to foil him, as
I must for my own honour, if he come in; therefore, out of my love
to you, I came hither to acquaint you withal, that either you might
stay him from his intendment, or brook such disgrace well as he   105
shall run into, in that it is a thing of his own search and altogether
against my will.

OLIVER Charles, I thank thee for thy love to me, which thou shalt find
I will most kindly requite. I had myself notice of my brother's
purpose herein, and have by underhand means laboured to dissuade   110
him from it – but he is resolute. I'll tell thee, Charles, it is the

83   Edzard cut here to 2.1, the insertion replacing 84–95.

84   Charles 'shadow punching' (Toye pbk).

86–90   Cheek by Jowl's Celia and Rosalind mimed the events as Charles narrated. Charles gave a
'cheap little smirk' in Pimlott's production (*SS* 50, 1997, p. 205).

92–107   Throughout this dialogue, the two trainers accompanying Charles massage and exercise
him (Toye pbk). Williams had Denis return to serve drinks to Oliver and Charles (pbk).

103b–7   Sometimes cut (1786 edn, Sothern–Marlowe, Williams, Jones pbks). Macready also cut
115–19 and 121b–23 (pbk).

stubbornest young fellow of France, full of ambition, an envious
emulator of every man's good parts, a secret and villainous contriver
against me, his natural brother. Therefore use thy discretion: I had
as lief thou didst break his neck as his finger. And thou wert best   115
look to't – for if thou dost him any slight disgrace or if he do
not mightily grace himself on thee, he will practise against thee by
poison, entrap thee by some treacherous device, and never leave
thee till he hath ta'en thy life by some indirect means or other. For
I assure thee – and almost with tears I speak it – there is not one so   120
young and so villainous this day living. I speak but brotherly of him,
but should I anatomise him to thee as he is, I must blush and weep,
and thou must look pale and wonder.

CHARLES I am heartily glad I came hither to you. If he come tomorrow,
I'll give him his payment; if ever he go alone again, I'll never wrestle 125
for prize more – and so God keep your worship.   *Exit*

OLIVER Farewell, good Charles. – Now will I stir this gamester. I hope
I shall see an end of him, for my soul – yet I know not why – hates
nothing more than he. Yet he's gentle, never schooled and yet
learned, full of noble device, of all sorts enchantingly beloved, and   130
indeed so much in the heart of the world, and especially of my own
people who best know him, that I am altogether misprized. But it
shall not be so long this wrestler shall clear all: nothing remains but
that I kindle the boy thither, which now I'll go about.   *Exit*

---

115   Benson had Oliver give a purse to Charles (1904 pbk).

122   David Buck's Oliver feigned weeping, with his face in his hands, in the 1963 RSC/BBC version.

126   'Charles shakes hands with Oliver' (Asche pbk).

127–34 Oliver anxiously chews on his lip in the 1978 BBC version. He was 'vulnerable and
        bewildered' at Shakespeare's Globe, 'obviously ripe for conversion' (*SQ* 50, 1999, p. 7).

ACT I, SCENE 2

Enter ROSALIND *and* CELIA

Traditionally set before a turreted palace, with steps leading to a terrace or balcony. Lewis Wingfield created 'a feudal castle after the Chateau d'Amboise' with 'a dais for the Duke in place of a garden bench' at St James's (*Pall Mall Gazette*, 24 Jan. 1885). For Asche's production, Joseph Harker designed a palace lawn enclosed in a semi-circular stone bench, with marble terraces leading to a dark grove (unidentified clippings, TM). Modjeska's promptbook indicates a small raised platform with a 'throne chair', occupied by Duke Frederick during the wrestling match and by Celia during part of this scene's opening dialogue. In Benson's Stratford productions, flourishes and shouts were heard from off stage throughout the first half of the scene, growing louder as the Duke and the wrestling party approached (1904 pbk). A painted back-cloth 'suggested Versailles' in Nunn's production. Courtiers and ladies in silks and satins danced before Rosalind and Celia drew aside to talk (*SS* 31, 1978, p. 146; *Financial Times*, 9 Sept. 1977). The faux medieval palace in Czinner's film features swimming swans in the courtyard. Edzard places the scene at a bustling cocktail party, featuring a heavily laden buffet table.

0 SD Sumptuous costumes for the ladies have been traditional. In the early nineteenth century Rosalind might wear a 'white dress, drapery spangled with gold', Celia a 'white dress spangled with silver' (Oxberry edn). Julia Neilson's Rosalind wore a blue brocade robe with 'high waistband of gold tissue, embroidered with a leaf design in brilliant green and gold sequins', a 'quaint head-dress' with a long veil, and 'strings of pearls' and 'festoons of sapphires'. Fay Davis's Celia had a gold brocade gown featuring brown velvet sleeves, the head-dress 'rolled up at either side in high, tapering points', and finished with a 'veil of gold tinsel' (*Sketch*, 9 Dec. 1896). In Czinner's film, Elisabeth Bergner and Sophie Stewart look tiny beneath their tall crespines. Reviewers thought the Elizabethan costumes of Dexter's production clashed with its anthropological emphasis; Sara Kestelman resembled 'Glenda Jackson dressed up as Queen Elizabeth' (*Spectator*, 11 Aug. 1979). At Stratford in 1980, 'everyone at court wore uniform black and silver, even Rosalind and Celia, whose severe black velvet dresses were edged with . . . white fur' (*SS* 34, 1981, p. 149). The richly authentic dresses with hooped petticoats created challenges at Shakespeare's Globe: since it was 'difficult for the two women to play very close to each other', they were forced to 'find a

CELIA I pray thee, Rosalind, sweet my coz, be merry.

ROSALIND Dear Celia, I show more mirth than I am mistress of, and
would you yet were merrier: unless you could teach me to forget a
banished father, you must not learn me how to remember any
extraordinary pleasure. 5

CELIA Herein, I see, thou lov'st me not with the full weight that I love
thee; if my uncle, thy banished father, had banished thy uncle, the
Duke my father, so thou hadst been still with me, I could have
taught my love to take thy father for mine; so wouldst thou, if the
truth of thy love to me were so righteously tempered as mine is to 10
thee.

ROSALIND Well, I will forget the condition of my estate to rejoice in
yours.

CELIA You know my father hath no child but I, nor none is like to have;
and, truly, when he dies thou shalt be his heir: for what he hath 15

compromise between intimacy and the etiquette imposed by the clothing' (Miller-Schütz,
'Findings').

Ada Rehan dashed on stage 'with a face all smiles, followed, after an interval sufficient to
give the audience time to applaud, by Celia coming on in much the same manner, as if the
two ladies were playing at a game of hide-and-seek' (*Blackwood's*, Sept. 1890, cited in
Sprague, p. 32). Bridges-Adams had Celia enter with a basket of flowers and discover
Rosalind 'in deep thought' (pbk). In Toye's production, Rosalind and Celia admired the
artistry of a painter working down stage (pbk). Elliott had them sit on a rug, looking at a
book (pbk). The tedium of these quiet occupations is conveyed in the 1963 RSC/BBC version
through the sounds of a clock chiming and another ticking loudly. In the 1978 BBC version,
the ladies play badminton, active in spite of their constricting golden gowns and veiled
head-dresses. Juliet Stevenson's Rosalind 'entered running, then stopped, as if hit by a wave
of pain. Ludicrously out of place in an evening gown, she wandered among the packing
crates and suitcases. She tugged on a dust-sheet. It fell away. Underneath was a mirror.
Slowly, she wound herself in the cloth, watching her reflection in the mirror . . . Then Celia
entered. She was clutching a champagne bottle by the scruff of its neck, stalking her cousin.
Having run her to the ground, she finally spoke the first words of the scene, growling them:
"I pray thee, Rosalind, sweet my coz, *be merry!*"' (Rutter, p. 99).

Cheek by Jowl played the scene on a bare stage with a spotlight in the centre on
Rosalind and Celia, seated cosily together on a cloth, recording their 'sports' in a small
book.

12–13 Rehan's Rosalind put an arm around her cousin's waist with this line (Daly pbk). Helen
Mirren delivered it sharply in the 1978 BBC version.

taken away from thy father perforce I will render thee again in
affection. By mine honour, I will, and when I break that oath, let me
turn monster. Therefore, my sweet Rose, my dear Rose, be merry.

ROSALIND From henceforth I will, coz, and devise sports. Let me see,
what think you of falling in love?   20

CELIA Marry, I prithee do, to make sport withal: but love no man in
good earnest – nor no further in sport neither – than with safety of
a pure blush thou mayst in honour come off again.

ROSALIND What shall be our sport then?

CELIA Let us sit and mock the good housewife Fortune from her wheel,   25
that her gifts may henceforth be bestowed equally.

ROSALIND I would we could do so: for her benefits are mightily mis-
placed, and the bountiful blindwoman doth most mistake in her
gifts to women.

CELIA 'Tis true, for those that she makes fair she scarce makes honest,   30
and those that she makes honest she makes very ill-favouredly.

ROSALIND Nay, now thou goest from Fortune's office to Nature's:
Fortune reigns in gifts of the world, not in the lineaments of
Nature.

Enter [TOUCHSTONE *the*] *clown*

17a Celia bent over to 'kiss' Rosalind's rear in Cheek by Jowl, and then bit her ankle.

20   Rosalind fans herself (Dexter pbk). In the 1978 BBC version, Rosalind scampers up a set of
     stairs and strikes a dramatic pose, as if on stage.

21b In Cheek by Jowl's production, the ladies together spat ritualistically after saying 'man'.

21–34 Doris Westwood on a 1923 production at the Old Vic with Florence Saunders as Rosalind
       and Jane Bacon as Celia: 'like the lily and the rose they sit together on the same garden
       seat, playing with their lines as if they were coloured toys' (Westwood, p. 90). In Edzard's
       film, the girls talk as they sit at a cocktail table; another guest sleeps on an adjacent chair.
       Rosalind licks an éclair; Celia pushes her plate aside and smokes a cigarette.

25–45 Dexter's ladies 'paced gravely backwards and forwards, as if this was all the movement their
       imprisoning dresses and (especially) constricting ruffs allowed them' (SS 33, 1980, p. 179).
       Donnellan had the ladies in intimate posture: Rosalind brushed Celia's hair, as she lay with
       her head in Rosalind's lap.

32–7a Cut in Benson's production (1904 pbk). Bridges-Adams and Toye cut to 44a (pbks).

34 SD Touchstone's early nineteenth-century costume: 'tri-colour doublet, trunks, and cloak', with
       corresponding cap and stockings (Oxberry edn). Paul Rogers had a ventriloquist's doll for
       his partner (*Evening Standard*, 2 Mar. 1955). 'With a child' (Sothern–Marlowe pbk). Alec
       McCowan was a 'red-wigged, chalk-faced, patchwork-suited' fantastic in Toye's production

CELIA No? When Nature hath made a fair creature, may she not by   35
Fortune fall into the fire? Though Nature hath given us wit to flout
at Fortune, hath not Fortune sent in this fool to cut off the
argument?

ROSALIND Indeed there is Fortune too hard for Nature, when Fortune
makes Nature's natural the cutter-off of Nature's wit.   40

CELIA Peradventure this is not Fortune's work neither but Nature's
who, perceiving our natural wits too dull to reason of such god-
desses, hath sent this natural for our whetstone: for always the
dullness of the fool is the whetstone of the wits. – How now, Wit,
whither wander you?   45

TOUCHSTONE Mistress, you must come away to your father.

CELIA Were you made the messenger?

(*Daily Mail*, 4 Sept. 1959). At Stratford in 1973, tuxedo-clad Derek Smith gave the
impression of vulgar sophistication or 'the dregs of music hall', his cheeks brilliantly red (*SQ*
24, 1973, p. 403; *Daily Telegraph*, 13 June 1973). In Stein's production, 'Werner Rehm played
Touchstone as a pathetic, fleshy, and infantile clown: his voice squeaked, he sucked his
thumb, he adopted sulky attitudes. Occasionally he was disturbingly grotesque, as when he
entertained Rosalind and Celia by producing a dead mouse from his mouth' (Patterson,
p. 137). In Noble's production, Touchstone emerged from under the dust-cloth, having first
opened his umbrella. Kenneth Branagh played an 'ebulliently vulgar and cockney bookie of
a Touchstone, with hair sleeked back and in Archie Rice costume – a broad bow tie and
red-and-orange check suit' in McEwan's production. This Touchstone 'roll[ed] around on his
heels with self-conscious enjoyment of his own waggishness' (*SS* 42, 1989, p. 130). In
Edzard's film, Griff Rhys Jones plays Touchstone as a nervous spiv in a dark business suit,
repeatedly glancing over his shoulder. Cheek by Jowl's Touchstone was self-consciously *not*
funny; on this entrance, he wore a clown mask. David Fielder played Touchstone as
'ill-humoured' in Bailey's production; he wore 'a formal scarlet court suit' with 'a very
high-cut doublet' that 'looked a bit like a nappy', featuring a cod-piece and coxcomb
(Miller-Schütz, 'Findings'; 'Interviews', p. 16).

Czinner cut Touchstone and his banter with the ladies; the clown appears only later in the
scene at the wrestling match.

36   Nineteenth-century acting editions retained Kemble's inserted stage direction, 'Without,
Touchstone sings.' Moore's promptbook specifies that Touchstone sings: 'Hey Robin! Jolly
Robin, Tell me where my lady is.' He sang 'Frank adillo! Frank adillo!' at Wallack's theatre in
1898–9 (Arthur pbk). Touchstone put his hands over Celia's eyes (Goodbody pbk).

39b–40 Cutting the second part of this speech rendered Rosalind less prolix (1786 edn). Macready
cut to 44b; so did Benson, Asche, Williams, and Jones.

46   In Cheek by Jowl, the ladies sprang from one another at the word 'father'.

TOUCHSTONE No, by mine honour, but I was bid to come for you.

ROSALIND Where learned you that oath, fool?

TOUCHSTONE Of a certain knight that swore, by his honour, they were   50
good pancakes, and swore, by his honour, the mustard was naught.
Now, I'll stand to it, the pancakes were naught and the mustard was
good – and yet was not the knight forsworn.

CELIA How prove you that in the great heap of your knowledge?

ROSALIND Aye, marry, now unmuzzle your wisdom.   55

TOUCHSTONE Stand you both forth now. Stroke your chins and swear,
by your beards, that I am a knave.

CELIA By our beards – if we had them – thou art.

TOUCHSTONE By my knavery – if I had it – then I were. But if you
swear by that that is not you are not forsworn: no more was this   60
knight swearing by his honour, for he never had any; or if he had,
he had sworn it away before ever he saw those pancakes or that
mustard.

CELIA Prithee, who is't that thou mean'st?

TOUCHSTONE One that old Frederick, your father, loves.   65

CELIA My father's love is enough to honour him. Enough! Speak no
more of him; you'll be whipped for taxation one of these days.

TOUCHSTONE The more pity that fools may not speak wisely what wise
men do foolishly.

CELIA By my troth, thou say'st true: for, since the little wit that fools   70
have was silenced, the little foolery that wise men have makes a
great show. – Here comes 'Monsieur the Beau'.

Enter LE BEAU

49–72   Some or all of this dialogue was cut in early productions, presumably to protect the dignity
of Celia and Rosalind (Macklin partbook; 1786 edn); Macready cut from 64 (pbk).

50–4   In Asche's production, Courtice Pounds 'set the scene, as it were, with the pancakes on the
right, and the mustard left' and pointed to each 'with a great deal of wrist- and leg-play,
every time that it is mentioned' (unidentified clipping by W.A., TM).

58   Benson distributed the line between Celia, who spoke 'By our beards', and Rosalind, who
followed with 'if we had them'; the ladies spoke the final two words together (1905 pbk).

66   Touchstone kneels (Bridges-Adams pbk). Celia hits Touchstone's arm (Jones pbk).

72 SD   Oxberry describes Le Beau's white costume decorated with blue satin flowers, silver trim,
and feathers. At St James's in 1885, Le Beau sported 'a live falcon on his wrist', which
distractingly flapped its wings as he spoke (*Dramatic Review*, 1 Feb. 1885, cited in Sprague,
p. 32). Muriel St Clare Byrne found Peter Cellier's Le Beau at Stratford in 1957 a familiar

ROSALIND With his mouth full of news.

CELIA Which he will put on us as pigeons feed their young.

ROSALIND Then shall we be news-crammed. 75

CELIA All the better: we shall be the more marketable. – *Bonjour*,
Monsieur Le Beau, what's the news?

LE BEAU Fair princess, you have lost much good sport.

CELIA 'Sport': of what colour?

LE BEAU 'What colour', madam? How shall I answer you? 80

ROSALIND As wit and fortune will.

TOUCHSTONE [*Imitating Le Beau*] Or as the destinies decrees.

CELIA Well said: that was laid on with a trowel.

TOUCHSTONE Nay, if I keep not my rank –

ROSALIND Thou loosest thy old smell. 85

LE BEAU You amaze me, ladies! I would have told you of good wrestling
which you have lost the sight of.

---

bore: 'I have met him at cocktail parties, particularly stage cocktail parties. I tend to forget his name; but he is always there, and *he* never forgets anyone' (*SQ* 8, 1957, p. 481). In Papp's production, Le Beau was 'a perfumed queen in pink and green alternately emitting matronly laughter and excited by the spectacle of male wrestling' (*SQ* 24, 1973, p. 424). In Caird's production, Hugh Ross doubled as a 'toupéed and distinctly camp Le Beau' and later as Jaques (*SQ* 41, 1989–90, p. 491). In Cheek by Jowl, Le Beau carried ropes; to mark off the wrestling ring, he arranged them around the ladies and Touchstone. In Edzard's film, Roger Hammond's fat and effeminate Le Beau so offends Touchstone that he picks up his chair, repositioning it with his back towards the ladies and their new companion.

73–84 Ian McEwan described Dexter's Rosalind and Celia 'wheeling about each other like automated chess pieces while the preposterous Le Beau spins dizzily between them' (*New Statesman*, 10 Aug. 1979). Susan Fleetwood's less-than-melancholy Rosalind 'grab[bed] Le Beau's hat and strut[ted] about with it' (*Financial Times*, 5 Apr. 1980).

74 On spotting Le Beau, the ladies and Touchstone walked away in an attempt to avoid him in the 1978 BBC version.

74–6 Sothern and Marlowe cut these lines; Touchstone along with his child companion greeted Le Beau upon his entrance (pbk).

76 'Both curtsey' (Asche pbk).

78 Le Beau kisses Celia's hand; Touchstone and Rosalind imitate (Jones pbk).

84–5 Cut for decorum's sake from the eighteenth century (Bell's edn) through Daly and Bridges-Adams (pbks).

86 Le Beau waves his glove in Touchstone's face before speaking in the 1978 BBC version. At Shakespeare's Globe, Jonathan Cecil's Le Beau had 'a very slight French accent, carrying the

ROSALIND   Yet tell us the manner of the wrestling.
LE BEAU   I will tell you the beginning and, if it please your ladyships,
    you may see the end, for the best is yet to do; and here where you   90
    are they are coming to perform it.
CELIA   Well, the beginning that is dead and buried.
LE BEAU   There comes an old man and his three sons –
CELIA   I could match this beginning with an old tale.
LE BEAU   Three proper young men, of excellent growth and presence –   95
ROSALIND   With bills on their necks: 'Be it known unto all men by these
    presents'.
LE BEAU   The eldest of the three wrestled with Charles, the Duke's
    wrestler, which Charles in a moment threw him and broke three of
    his ribs that there is little hope of life in him. So he served the   100
    second and so the third: yonder they lie, the poor old man, their
    father, making such pitiful dole over them that all the beholders
    take his part with weeping.
ROSALIND   Alas!
TOUCHSTONE   But what is the sport, monsieur, that the ladies have   105
    lost?
LE BEAU   Why, this that I speak of.
TOUCHSTONE   Thus men may grow wiser every day. It is the first time
    that ever I heard breaking of ribs was sport for ladies.
CELIA   Or I, I promise thee.   110
ROSALIND   But is there any else longs to see this broken music in his
    sides? Is there yet another dotes upon rib-breaking? Shall we see
    this wrestling, cousin?
LE BEAU   You must if you stay here, for here is the place appointed for
    the wrestling and they are ready to perform it.   115

First Folio spelling of wrestling as "wrastling" over to "sport" and making it into a language
tic' (Miller-Schütz, 'Findings').

93–110   Toye remedied the tedium of Le Beau's narration by staging the action he described: a
    gallery cloth was removed, revealing the wrestling up stage. When the second brother was
    thrown and carried out on a stretcher, a fight broke out, resulting in injury to the third
    wrestling brother, who was also removed on a stretcher (pbk). This sight of Charles's
    victims added to Rosalind's distress over Orlando's challenge later in the scene (*Daily
    Telegraph*, 4 Sept. 1959). In the 1978 BBC version, Le Beau revelled in his own description,
    giggling at the mention of the young men's ribs.

96   In Daly's production, Le Beau spoke the first half of line 96. Touchstone chanted 'oh' as
    Rosalind laughed in Asche's version (pbk).

CELIA Yonder, sure, they are coming. Let us now stay and see it.

Flourish. Enter DUKE [FREDERICK], *Lords,* ORLANDO,
CHARLES, *and Attendants*

116 SD   Frederick has often been richly attired. Oxberry dictates a 'black velvet jacket and trunks' with a 'crimson velvet robe lined with white satin', embroidered and decorated with roses. In Czinner's film he wears a plumed hat and ducal medallion with his long black robe. Frederick became more menacing as the twentieth century progressed. In Shaw's 1957 production, Mark Dignam was 'the living image of . . . the dark, sinister, leering François I himself . . . resplendent in white satin and black and gold' (*SQ* 8, 1957, p. 482). At Stratford, Ontario, in 1972, William Needles was a 'Dracula-like tyrant in basic black whose taste in accoutrements included a mauve cummerbund, a whip, a perpetual frown, and a hawk that mechanically waggled its wings and turned its head' (*SQ* 4, 1972, p. 392). In David Thacker's 1992 Stratford production, a 'Mephistophelean Duke Frederick, shaved head shimmering in the red glow, acutely pointed beard jutting in front of him . . . fetishistically fondl[ed] the hair of Orlando, of Oliver, of Hisperia . . . as he cross-examined them' (*SQ* 44, 1993, p. 347).

Macready staged the scene as a grand pageant, with 74 people on the stage. As attendants placed chairs and set up the ring with ropes and pillars, groups of courtiers and ladies chatted, congratulated Charles, and sneered at Orlando. The Duke, Le Beau, and several other courtiers had merlins on their wrists (Shattuck, *Macready*). 'The new effect was introduced of enclosing the space where the wrestlers encounter with ropes and staves, round which the courtiers and spectators stand, pressing eagerly forward, watching every movement of the combatants.' The scene was 'most vivid, and the natural manner of the two wrestlers through every vicissitude of the struggle elicited shouts of applause' (*Times*, 3 Oct. 1842). The on-stage crowd created a meta-theatrical effect, since 'the eager spectators pressing round the roped ring and cheering the wrestlers showed as much excitement as the larger arena of the audience' (*Spectator*, 8 Oct. 1842). Mr G. Bennett, Macready's 'superfluously brutal and coarse' Frederick, '[broke] sentences into bits with the hammer of [his] emphasis' (*Spectator*, 8 Oct. 1842).

Traditionally the Duke and his attendants have entered in a formal procession. In Modjeska's production, Rosalind dropped her bouquet of roses as the court party approached (pbk). In Daly's production, four guards with garlanded spears and ropes placed themselves in a square, stretching the ropes between them to form the wrestling ring (pbk). Asche choreographed a meeting of Rosalind and Celia with Orlando, as they crossed up stage and he crossed down; he paused to stare at them, inclining his head. The processional entry was punctuated by much bowing to both Celia and the Duke. Touchstone

DUKE FREDERICK Come on; since the youth will not be entreated, his
    own peril on his forwardness.

sat on the dais at the Duke's feet (pbk.). Asche's courtiers were 'beings of strange phantasy
and splendour, pacing proudly hither and thither, in their scarlet plumes and golden chains
and parti-coloured hose . . . [the] ladies, sweeping over the grass in their long silken robes,
jewelled and gorgeous after an almost Oriental fashion, some with turbans on their heads
and some with gilded horns and some with crowns – and all pure phantasy, a true court of
dreamland' ('Beautiful Production at His Majesty's', unidentified clipping, TM).

Playfair admired Lovat Fraser's set for the scene in his 1919 production: 'In front of the
stage was a cloister, forming a sort of false or second proscenium. Under it, in shadow,
stood the Court. Beyond was a brilliant sunlit triangle of grass, where they wrestled; behind,
a high wall, over which the villagers watched. Thus the wrestlers were half out of sight,
continually appearing and disappearing behind the spectators' (Playfair, p. 51). But a
realistic-minded critic ridiculed the decision to stage the scene 'in the corner of the courtyard
of a palace', a site which would only make sense if Oliver and Charles 'had been left to make
all the arrangements, and had chosen a spot where Orlando, when thrown, must dash out
his brains against some bit of masonry, or, failing that, the pavement' (*Morning Post*, 23 Apr.
1919). In Coleman's BBC version, the camera moves to another garden, featuring 'medieval'
tents and a ring surrounded by a wooden fence. The scene became a sadomasochistic
fantasy in a production by the Berkeley Repertory Theatre in 1981, where 'white-faced
courtiers clad in black leather whipped androgynous, chained figures'; Duke Frederick gave
orders 'either from a wheelchair or as a man barely able to support himself on canes' (*SQ*
33, 1982, p. 399). Hytner's Duke Frederick was a 'bony-headed, wire-spectacled Bolshevik
tyrant', issuing 'orders with mechanical impersonality' to his accompanying band of 'grim
commissars in grey uniforms' (*SS* 40, 1987, p. 174). Noble's Duke 'in military evening dress,
carried a brandy snifter and briefly kissed his daughter; his courtiers brought in the
atmosphere of a gentlemen's club. The women seemed suddenly out of place, uneasy'
(Rutter, p. 101). Noble's courtiers marked off the wrestling ring with burning braziers. In
Edzard's film, Frederick enters with his entourage of business people, one of whom lights
his cigarette for him. Cheek by Jowl's previously ebullient ladies became subdued in
the presence of Frederick, who carried a glass of brandy and smoked a cigar. His
rough-mannered, tuxedoed courtiers aggressively turned on Le Beau and debagged him.

As Charles, Judo expert Joe Robinson was accompanied by two trainers in Toye's
production (*Daily Telegraph*, 4 Sept. 1959). In Stein's production, Charles was preceded by
a Lord who shouted 'Make way for Charles, the Duke's wrestler' and so created a path
through the middle of the audience' (Patterson, p. 135).

Jones indicates laughter at Orlando's entrance (pbk).

ROSALIND Is yonder the man?

LE BEAU Even he, madam.　　　　　　　　　　　　　　　　　　　　120

CELIA Alas, he is too young; yet he looks successfully.

DUKE FREDERICK How now, daughter – and cousin: are you crept
　　hither to see the wrestling?

ROSALIND Aye, my liege, so please you give us leave.

DUKE FREDERICK You will take little delight in it, I can tell you: there　　125
　　is such odds in the man. In pity of the challenger's youth, I would
　　fain dissuade him, but he will not be entreated. Speak to him, ladies:
　　see if you can move him.

CELIA Call him hither, good Monsieur Le Beau.

DUKE FREDERICK Do so; I'll not be by.　　　　　　　　　　　　　130

　　　　　　　　　　[The Duke stands aside]

LE BEAU Monsieur the challenger, the princess calls for you.

ORLANDO I attend them with all respect and duty.

ROSALIND Young man, have you challenged Charles the wrestler?

ORLANDO No, fair princess, he is the general challenger. I come but in
　　as others do to try with him the strength of my youth.　　　135

CELIA Young gentleman, your spirits are too bold for your years: you
　　have seen cruel proof of this man's strength. If you saw yourself
　　with your eyes or knew yourself with your judgement, the fear of
　　your adventure would counsel you to a more equal enterprise. We
　　pray you, for your own sake, to embrace your own safety and give　　140
　　over this attempt.

ROSALIND Do, young sir: your reputation shall not therefore be
　　misprized. We will make it our suit to the Duke that the wrestling
　　might not go forward.

ORLANDO I beseech you, punish me not with your hard thoughts,　　145
　　wherein I confess me much guilty to deny so fair and excellent
　　ladies anything. But let your fair eyes and gentle wishes go with me

---

122　Celia kisses Frederick (Elliott pbk).

125　The Duke motions Touchstone out of the seat he has taken (Arthur pbk).

131　Le Beau strikes his staff on the ground. As Orlando moves towards Rosalind, Le Beau blocks
　　the way and indicates with his head for Orlando to approach Celia; he does, dropping to his
　　knee (Dexter pbk). In Hands's production, the two ladies 'competed for Orlando's attention'
　　(*SS* 34, 1981, p. 149).

136–41　Celia spoke the lines gigglingly as she looked at Rosalind in Cheek by Jowl. Edzard's
　　commanding Celia lectures Orlando; he politely removes his blue stocking cap.

144　Moore indicates that Rosalind should turn 'as if to speak to the Duke', but stop when
　　Orlando speaks (pbk).

to my trial, wherein if I be foiled, there is but one shamed that was
never gracious; if killed, but one dead that is willing to be so. I shall
do my friends no wrong, for I have none to lament me; the world no   150
injury, for in it I have nothing; only in the world I fill up a place,
which may be better supplied when I have made it empty.

ROSALIND The little strength that I have, I would it were with you.

CELIA And mine to eke out hers.

ROSALIND Fare you well: pray heaven I be deceived in you.   155

CELIA Your heart's desires be with you.

CHARLES Come, where is this young gallant that is so desirous to lie
with his mother earth?

ORLANDO Ready, sir, but his will hath in it a more modest working.

DUKE FREDERICK You shall try but one fall.   160

CHARLES No, I warrant your grace you shall not entreat him to a
second, that have so mightily persuaded him from a first.

ORLANDO You mean to mock me after: you should not have mocked me
before. But come your ways.

ROSALIND Now Hercules be thy speed, young man.   165

CELIA I would I were invisible, to catch the strong fellow by the leg.

[*They*] *wrestle*

148b–52 Cut by Toye, Williams (pbks).

155 Helen Mirren appeared about to cry as she put her hand to her mouth and fled.

157 Charles stands in the middle of the ring, challenging Orlando to enter (Phelps pbk). 'Several laugh and murmur' (Holloway pbk). In Cheek by Jowl, Charles ran around the ring preening.

159 Orlando prepares to fight by removing his cloak and giving it to Denis (Shattuck, *Macready*). More boldly, Orlando throws his cap into the ring; then jumps into it himself (Benson 1904 pbk). Henry Ainley removed his cap, headdress, and doublet, which an attendant took up stage (Asche pbk).

164 Olivier demonstrated his athleticism by leaping over the crowd to enter the ring in Czinner's film.

165 Kean moved Rosalind's line back to follow Celia's at 156 and cut 167–70 (pbk). The tension was heightened in Modjeska's production by a long flourish of trumpets and drums that continued until Charles was thrown (pbk).

167 SD The nineteenth-century vogue for pictorial realism extended to the person of Charles. When James Mace, 'the champion athlete of the world', took the part at Niblo's in 1871, the audience admired his 'brawny limbs and Herculean build' and feared for an Orlando (Walter Montgomery) who appeared 'shapely but fragile' by comparison. At the match,

Mace surveyed 'the orchestra, the parquet, and the first circle, as though he were trying to make up his mind into which of the three he should throw' his adversary (unidentified clippings, Moore pbk). Frank Benson 'in his earlier days . . . would lift Oscar Asche, even then no light weight, and throw him clear over his head' (Crosse, *Fifty Years of Shakespearean Playgoing*, p. 31, cited in Sprague, p. 33). Doris Westwood on the 1923 Old Vic production: Ion Swinley's Orlando 'pitches Robert Glennie over his shoulder head first. To watch it is both thrilling and startling, for yesterday it looked remarkably as though Glennie would have his neck broken' (Westwood, p. 90).

Later productions too have featured 'real' wrestlers. Toye cast Joe Robinson, 'world and European champion in 1951–2–3' as Charles (*Evening News*, 4 Sept. 1959). Goodbody's production featured professional wrestler Brian Glover, who was quickly recognised by the audience 'in the finger-stretching gestures which accompanied his dialogue, and the wicked relish with which he punched a fist into the palm of his other hand'. The match occurred 'improbably, in the plush casino that Duke Frederick's court had become', with Touchstone as 'a bookie' (*SS* 27, 1974, p. 149). Because Stein's production featured a professional wrestler as Charles, his lines were reassigned, most of them to Le Beau, and the match was elaborately choreographed: 'Orlando, played by the strikingly beautiful Michael König stripped to a loin-cloth, matched himself against this forbidding heavyweight. After a sequence of carefully rehearsed holds and throws, Orlando found himself almost to his own surprise lifting Charles upside-down off the ground to dash him to unconsciousness at the Duke's feet. The whole thing was so polished and the moves so premeditated that it failed to convince as a spontaneous conflict. In retrospect, however, this was no doubt precisely what Stein intended; for later . . . Orlando wrestled for his very life with a wild beast. This early contest was not allowed to develop too much tension; it was a public display of strength, whereas the later fight was to the death' (Patterson, p. 135).

The promptbook for Bridges-Adams's production includes choreography notes: 'Round 1. Engage and break. Engage, circle, break. Round 2. Engage. Throw. Orlando recover. Round 3. Leg. Break. Final Throw. Flourish between each round.' Czinner highlighted the match by featuring Touchstone's mimicry of the various moves and positions, panning to reaction shots of the assembled crowd and the ladies, and playing up the symphonic score by William Walton. In the 1978 BBC version, Orlando offers Charles his hand just before the match begins, but Charles bats it away. After prevailing in a one-sided contest, a shocked Charles is jumped from behind and thrown from the ring by Orlando. Dexter's courtiers broke formal order in their excitement to watch the fight (pbk). At Stratford in 1980, Terry Wood was 'so huge' and fought 'so dirty that Sinead Cusack's Celia [was] provoked into assisting his opponent with some fierce maidenly pummelling' (*Observer*, 13 Apr. 1980). Ian McKay, fight director, said the wrestling mixed 'free style and Cumberland', and included 'drop kicks, flying mares and half nelsons'. John Bowe (Orlando) said 'there's

ROSALIND O excellent young man.
CELIA If I had a thunderbolt in mine eye, I can tell who should down.
          [*Charles is thrown to the ground.*] *Shout*
DUKE FREDERICK No more, no more!
ORLANDO Yes, I beseech your grace, I am not yet well breathed.   170
DUKE FREDERICK How dost thou, Charles?

always a gasp from the audience when I get slung off the stage and land among them. The knack is to make it appear spontaneous' (*Birmingham Evening Mail*, 9 May 1980). In Hirsch's 1983 production, 'Charles's shoulders hit the boards with a series of thuds that left the audience as emotionally exhausted as he was physically' (*SQ* 34, 1983, p. 464). In Noble's production, ruthless Charles contended with a playfully burlesque Orlando who at one point kissed his opponent on the lips.

    In 1991, ACTER's Clive Arrindell played both Orlando and Charles, 'lock[ing] himself into a sequence of choke holds before throwing himself to the ground' (Mazer, 'As You Like It', p. 23). At Stratford in 1989, 'some of the cast joined the audience in the stalls and shouted encouraging suggestions'; 'afterwards, Orlando signed autographs, posed for photographs and received a huge trophy' (*SS* 44, 1991, p. 161). In Donnellan's production, six courtiers held the encircling rope above their heads, then lowered it to waist-level to begin the fight. They stamped rhythmically during the wrestling, and taunted the contenders, whose sport broke the rules of fair play, including, for instance, kicks to the crotch. At Shakespeare's Globe, the match occurred in the yard: 'the wicked Duke's followers strong-armed [viewers] out of the way to make room for the wrestling match at ground level' (*SQ* 50, 1999, p. 76). Edzard does not show the wrestling at all. The camera tracks the responses of party-goers milling about with champagne flutes in hand as the wrestling takes place. Rosalind chews her fingers. Based on the looks of the crowd, the fight continues well past Frederick's call of 'no more' (169), and Orlando afterwards is quite winded (though still dressed in jeans and jersey).

    As Rosalind, Helena Faucit's 'face and every movement eloquently expressed her growing interest in the contest' (*Belfast Daily Mercury*, 6 June 1856; *Manchester Examiner and Times*, 3 Oct. 1879, cited in Carlisle, p. 76). Helen Mirren watched the match through parted fingers.

169–8   Cut in the eighteenth century (Bell's edn). Daly followed Kemble in cutting 167 and reassigning 168 to Rosalind.

170   Maggie Smith as Celia 'ease[d] in' with this line, causing Charles to 'look around and [be] thrown off' (Toye pbk).

170   Macready's crowd of onlookers crowded around Orlando to congratulate him on his victory (Shattuck, *Macready*).

LE BEAU He cannot speak, my lord.
DUKE FREDERICK Bear him away.

[Charles is carried out]

What is thy name, young man?
ORLANDO Orlando, my liege, the youngest son of Sir Roland de Boys.   175
DUKE FREDERICK I would thou hadst been son to some man else;
        The world esteemed thy father honourable
        But I did find him still mine enemy.
        Thou shouldst have better pleased me with this deed
        Hadst thou descended from another house.   180
        But fare thee well. Thou art a gallant youth:

---

172   Touchstone began to steal Le Beau's line in the eighteenth century and has frequently done
       so since (Bell's edn). Moore's Touchstone punctuated the line by 'kneeling behind Charles
       with his hand on his breast' (pbk). Arthur's promptbook indicates that Touchstone steps
       over Charles's body. Macready restored the line to Le Beau, but had Touchstone precede
       the guards as they carried out Charles (Shattuck, *Macready*). With the same actor playing
       both Orlando and Charles, ACTER's Le Beau answered Duke Frederick's question as he
       stood 'between an erect, out-of-breath Orlando and the empty space on the floor where
       [viewers] were to imagine the body of the defeated Charles'. He 'look[ed] intently at the
       empty space', and his line here 'brought down the house' (*SQ* 42, 1991, p. 218).

173 SD Touchstone often struts in this exit (Moore, Daly pbks). In Benson's production, Touchstone
       took charge by motioning to the soldiers who raised Charles and carried him out (1904
       pbk). Czinner makes much of the comic opportunity, as increasing numbers of courtiers fail
       to lift the portly Charles; finally six are required.

175   Celia glances warily at Rosalind and the Duke glares in Coleman's BBC version. In Dexter's
       production, the court 'froze into attitudes of obsequious horror' (*SS* 33, 1980, p. 179).
       In Caird's production, there was 'a comic mass panic and the sudden appearance of
       bodyguards drawing pistols, putting on sunglasses and effectively turning Ferdinand into a
       comic mafioso surrrounded by a gang of protective clichéd thugs' (*SS* 44, 1991, p. 162).
       Orlando was still winded as he knelt in Cheek by Jowl's production; Frederick presented him
       with a medal to wear around his neck, but took it away on learning Orlando's name.

176–81 In Macready's version, the party was over at this point; the courtiers cast timid, doubtful
       glances at the Duke and Orlando, then exited diversely (Shattuck, *Macready*). Czinner,
       apparently eager to neutralise the disturbing chords, had the Duke sound genuinely
       regretful upon learning Orlando's lineage.

181   'Gives Orlando his hand to kiss' (Asche pbk). Edzard's Frederick takes out his handkerchief
       and attempts to wipe Orlando's face in insultingly condescending manner; Orlando swipes
       his hand away.

I would thou hadst told me of another father.
[*Exeunt Duke Frederick, Le Beau, Touchstone, Lords, and Attendants*]
CELIA Were I my father, coz, would I do this?
ORLANDO I am more proud to be Sir Roland's son –
　　　　　His youngest son – and would not change that calling   185
　　　　　To be adopted heir to Frederick.
ROSALIND My father loved Sir Roland as his soul
　　　　　And all the world was of my father's mind;
　　　　　Had I before known this young man his son,
　　　　　I should have given him tears unto entreaties   190
　　　　　Ere he should thus have ventured.
CELIA　　　　　　　　　　　　　Gentle cousin,
　　　　　Let us go thank him and encourage him;
　　　　　My father's rough and envious disposition
　　　　　Sticks me at heart. – Sir, you have well deserved:
　　　　　If you do keep your promises in love   195
　　　　　But justly, as you have exceeded all promise,
　　　　　Your mistress shall be happy.
ROSALIND [*Giving him a chain from her neck*] Gentleman,
　　　　　Wear this for me: one out of suits with Fortune,
　　　　　That could give more, but that her hand lacks means. –
　　　　　Shall we go, coz?

183–97　A reviewer on Mr Rousby at Queen's Theatre: 'after the wrestling-bout, while the ladies are discussing his merits, [Orlando] stretches himself out at the foot of the throne lately occupied by the Duke. This . . . has the effect of rendering the character loutish' (*Athenaeum*, 4 Mar. 1871).

194　After Orlando finishes dressing and is about to depart, Celia calls out for him (Asche pbk).

198 SD　In blocking that became traditional, Macready's Orlando knelt to accept the chain around his neck (Shattuck, *Macready*; Daly, Benson 1904 pbks). Helena Faucit gave the chain after 'stealthily kissing' it (*Blackwood's*, Dec. 1885, cited in Carlisle, p. 76). Mary Anderson poured it slowly from her hand to his, indicating a wish to caress that receiving hand (Shattuck, *American Stage*, p. 108). Patrick Allen's Orlando does not kneel before Vanessa Redgrave's Rosalind in the 1963 RSC/BBC version; instead, they lock eyes and hold each other's gaze throughout the exchange. In Donnellan's production, the chain Rosalind presented replaced the ornament Frederick had taken away; Celia smirked as Rosalind gave it to Orlando.

199–208　In Asche's production, Rosalind and Celia gradually ascended the steps to the top platform, Rosalind stopping once to lean over the balustrade, then dropping her bouquet of roses from on high as the music stopped (pbk).

CELIA   Aye. – Fare you well, fair gentleman.   200
                                    [*They turn to go*]
ORLANDO [*Aside*] Can I not say, 'I thank you'? My better parts
                  Are all thrown down, and that which here stands up
                  Is but a quintain, a mere lifeless block.
ROSALIND [*To Celia*] He calls us back. My pride fell with my fortunes,
                  I'll ask him what he would. – Did you call, sir?   205
                  Sir, you have wrestled well and overthrown
                  More than your enemies.
                                    [*They gaze upon each other*]
CELIA   Will you go, coz?
ROSALIND Have with you. – Fare you well.
                                    Exeunt [*Rosalind and Celia*]
ORLANDO What passion hangs these weights upon my tongue?
                  I cannot speak to her, yet she urged conference.   210

                                    Enter LE BEAU

                  O poor Orlando! thou art overthrown:
                  Or Charles or something weaker masters thee.
LE BEAU Good sir, I do in friendship counsel you
                  To leave this place. Albeit you have deserved
                  High commendation, true applause, and love,   215

---

203   The archaic word 'quintain' needed modification by 1723, when Johnson substituted 'a
      statue' (*Love in a Forest*). The word has also simply been dropped, resulting in a short line
      (Bell's edn). Macready cut the speech after 'thank you' (Shattuck, *Macready*).

204   Maggie Smith's 'elbows [went] one way, the wrists another, and the audience [was]
      convulsed' (*SS* 29, 1978, p. 226).

207   Celia taps Rosalind's elbow (Phelps pbk). In Pimlott's production, Celia was 'as interested in
      Orlando on first meeting as her cousin, but beaten in the race for his attention by the need
      to maintain a princess's dignity' (*SS* 50, 1997, p. 206).

208 SD The ladies look back at Orlando as they exit (Moore pbk). Helen Mirren seemed to be on
      the verge of tears.

211   Benson's Orlando gazed after the ladies, sat on the stone bench they had vacated, and
      picked up the flowers Rosalind had left behind (1904 pbk).

211 SD Le Beau enters with some urgency, shouting 'Sir! Sir!' from off stage (Sothern–Marlowe
      pbk).

213–37 Le Beau speaks very swiftly in the 1978 BBC version. Le Beau's words to Orlando 'were
      noted down by a sinister figure in dark glasses and a greatcoat, attended by armed guards'
      in Hirsch's production (*SS* 39, 1986, p. 181).

Yet such is now the Duke's condition
That he misconsters all that you have done.
The Duke is humorous: what he is indeed
More suits you to conceive than I to speak of.
ORLANDO I thank you, sir; and pray you tell me this: 220
Which of the two was daughter of the Duke,
That here was at the wrestling?
LE BEAU Neither his daughter, if we judge by manners,
But yet indeed the taller is his daughter;
The other is daughter to the banished Duke   225
And here detained by her usurping uncle
To keep his daughter company, whose loves
Are dearer than the natural bond of sisters.
But I can tell you that of late this Duke
Hath ta'en displeasure 'gainst his gentle niece,   230
Grounded upon no other argument
But that the people praise her for her virtues
And pity her for her good father's sake;
And, on my life, his malice 'gainst the lady
Will suddenly break forth. Sir, fare you well,   235
Hereafter, in a better world than this,
I shall desire more love and knowledge of you.
ORLANDO I rest much bounden to you: fare you well.
                              [*Exit Le Beau*]
Thus must I from the smoke into the smother,

217   Le Beau glances off left, presumably indicating nervousness (Bridges-Adams pbk).

224   'Shorter' has regularly replaced 'taller' where casting renders the change necessary (Bell's
       edn). Benson's 1905 promptbook has 'fairer', 'darker', and 'smaller' written as possible
       alternatives. Fiona Shaw's Celia was two inches taller than Juliet Stevenson's Rosalind,
       'forcing the audience to abandon any preconceptions about "the tall skinny one and the
       little dumpy one"' (Shaw and Stevenson, p. 57).

225–35 These lines are frequently cut, either for speed or, as the eighteenth-century editor thought,
       'because Le Beau is generally given to a wretched actor' (Bell's edn).

234–5 Edzard's Le Beau is on the verge of terrified tears.

237   'Bow elaborately' (Sothern–Marlowe pbk).

238   In Papp's 1973 production, 'Orlando kissed Le Beau's hand, sending him giggling and
       flustered off the stage' (*SQ* 24, 1973, p. 424).

From tyrant duke unto a tyrant brother.   240
But heavenly Rosalind!   *Exit*

240   In Asche's version, Orlando here crossed to pick up the roses dropped by Rosalind; he kissed them, looking up to where she had exited (pbk).

241 SD   Daly specifies how this scene should be played continuously with the next: 'After he has gone away, Rosalind comes upon the terrace and looks after him; then goes forward, looking after him, and sinks on a seat, gazing in the direction which he took. Celia enters and creeps behind her' (pbk).

ACT I, SCENE 3

Enter CELIA *and* ROSALIND

CELIA Why, cousin; why, Rosalind – Cupid have mercy, not a word?

ROSALIND Not one to throw at a dog.

CELIA No, thy words are too precious to be cast away upon curs: throw
some of them at me. Come, lame me with reasons.

ROSALIND Then there were two cousins laid up, when the one should   5
be lamed with reasons, and the other mad without any.

CELIA But is all this for your father?

ROSALIND No, some of it is for my child's father – O how full of briars

---

0 SD   Usually set in a domestic interior. Asche had two ladies seated up stage reading; they rose
as Celia entered, bowed to her, and exited (pbk). Celia carried her embroidery work in
Bridges-Adams's production (pbk). Toye specified a bedroom complete with bed, dressing
table, chair, and bench (pbk). The ladies wore dressing gowns in the 1963 RSC/BBC version.
Czinner's Celia runs through the corridors of the castle searching for Rosalind, whom she
finds gazing out of a window. In Donnellan's continuous staging, the two ladies approached
and seated themselves on stage as the previous scene was ending. Edzard divides the scene
into action in three settings, suggesting passage of time: first the girls talk in a lamp-lit room
(1–28); 29–30 is cut, and the encounter with Frederick (31–79) is in the office foyer; the final
segment occurs in a huge closet, with the girls tossing clothing about.

4   Rosalind sighs; Celia mocks her (Moore pbk). Rosalind removed a necklace from Celia's
neck in Toye's production (pbk).

7   'Archly' (Phelps pbk).

8   Rosalind's reference to her 'child's father' was considered indecorous to refined sensibilities;
Nicholas Rowe's amendment 'my father's child' was substituted from the eighteenth century
through Daly and Asche. William Winter, supporting Daly's substitution of the 'foolish and
vulgar' Folio reading, observed that 'even if you think it right to make Rosalind talk like a
prurient wanton, you have no warrant to make her talk like a fool' (W.W., 'A Brief
Shakespearian Commentary', hand identified as *The New York Tribune*, Dec. 1898, Daly
pbk). Arthur's promptbook restores 'child's father' as does Benson's. Cheek by Jowl's Celia
frowned and rolled her eyes.

is this working-day world!

CELIA They are but burs, cousin, thrown upon thee in holy-day foolery: 10
    if we walk not in the trodden paths, our very petticoats will
    catch them.

ROSALIND I could shake them off my coat: these burs are in my heart.

CELIA Hem them away.

ROSALIND I would try, if I could cry 'hem' and have him.   15

CELIA Come, come, wrestle with thy affections.

ROSALIND O they take the part of a better wrestler than myself.

CELIA O, a good wish upon you: you will try in time in despite of a fall.
    But turning these jests out of service, let us talk in good earnest. Is
    it possible, on such a sudden, you should fall into so strong a liking   20
    with old Sir Roland's youngest son?

ROSALIND The Duke my father loved his father dearly.

CELIA Doth it therefore ensue that you should love his son dearly? By
    this kind of chase I should hate him for my father hated his father
    dearly; yet I hate not Orlando.   25

ROSALIND No, faith, hate him not, for my sake.

CELIA Why should I not? Doth he not deserve well?

Enter DUKE [FREDERICK] *with Lords*

---

9   Edzard's Emma Croft becomes extremely agitated, shouting and punching the sofa on which
      she lies.

16   Celia kneels at Rosalind's feet (Benson 1904 pbk).

23   Moore indicates that Celia playfully pushes Rosalind (Moore pbk). She slapped Rosalind's
      back in Cheek by Jowl.

25   In Czinner's film, Rosalind's petulance gives way to giggling at the mention of Orlando's
      name.

27 SD   Trumpets announced the Duke's entry in the 1978 BBC version. In Modjeska's production,
      the Duke's Lords served as Guards, lending an ominous air (pbk). Asche's Duke entered
      leaning on the arm of a gentleman; upon seeing Rosalind, he turned and gestured to
      dismiss the gentlemen (pbk). In the 1963 RSC/BBC version, the Duke appears loomingly at
      the top of the stairs leading down to the ladies' chamber. William Hutt's Lords were
      'pseudo-Cossacks in black leather that jumped about at [Frederick's] command' (*SQ* 4, 1972,
      p. 392). Le Beau has sometimes replaced the Lords, as in Williams (pbk). In the Cheek by
      Jowl production, Celia, angry with Rosalind, moved to the Duke's side of the stage, leaving
      Rosalind alone to face him. But she hid her head on Le Beau's shoulder, unable to watch
      the confrontation. David Rintoul, who played both Dukes in Bailey's production,
      threatened the audience by 'distinctly curl[ing] my lip at them' (Miller-Schütz, 'Interview',
      p. 18).

ROSALIND Let me love him for that, and do you love him because I do.
      Look, here comes the Duke.
CELIA With his eyes full of anger.   30
DUKE FREDERICK Mistress, dispatch you with your safest haste
      And get you from our court.

ROSALIND   Me, uncle?
DUKE FREDERICK   You, cousin.
      Within these ten days if that thou be'st found
      So near our public court as twenty miles,
      Thou diest for it.
ROSALIND   I do beseech your grace   35
      Let me the knowledge of my fault bear with me:
      If with myself I hold intelligence,
      Or have acquaintance with mine own desires,
      If that I do not dream or be not frantic
      (As I do trust I am not) then, dear uncle,   40
      Never so much as in a thought unborn,
      Did I offend your highness.
DUKE FREDERICK   Thus do all traitors:
      If their purgation did consist in words,
      They are as innocent as grace itself.
      Let it suffice thee that I trust thee not.   45
ROSALIND Yet your mistrust cannot make me a traitor;
      Tell me whereon the likelihoods depends?
DUKE FREDERICK Thou art thy father's daughter, there's enough.
ROSALIND So was I when your highness took his dukedom,
      So was I when your highness banished him;   50

35   Rosalind often kneels here (Phelps, Daly, Benson 1904 pbks).
35–42 Juliet Stevenson observed that Rosalind 'demonstrates such control', maintaining 'a
       perfectly regular metre through those lines, holding on to a rhythm which is fluid, rational
       and calm . . . It is empowering her' (Rutter, p. 102).
42b–44 Spoken to the Lords (Payne pbk).
48   Frederick threw Rosalind to the floor in Noble's production.
49   Phelps had Rosalind rise from her knees with this line (pbk). Rosalind begins 'with dignified
       sorrow' but becomes more pathetic as the speech progresses and bursts into tears at its end
       (Moore pbk).
49–55 William Archer objected to Mary Anderson's 'unpolished' delivery of this speech: 'it lacked
       nobility and loftiness. Its indignation was too loud. It was invective rather than
       self-restrained and scathing sarcasm' (*Theatre*, 1 Oct. 1885). George Odell, however,
       recalled her 'tragic, eloquent outburst' against Frederick (quoted in Derrick, p. 149); and

Treason is not inherited, my lord,
Or if we did derive it from our friends,
What's that to me? My father was no traitor.
Then, good my liege, mistake me not so much
To think my poverty is treacherous.   55
CELIA Dear sovereign, hear me speak.
DUKE FREDERICK Aye, Celia, we stayed her for your sake,
Else had she with her father ranged along.
CELIA I did not then entreat to have her stay,
It was your pleasure – and your own remorse.   60
I was too young that time to value her,
But now I know her: if she be a traitor,
Why so am I. We still have slept together,
Rose at an instant, learned, played, eat together,
And wheresoe'er we went, like Juno's swans,   65
Still we went coupled and inseparable.
DUKE FREDERICK She is too subtle for thee, and her smoothness,
Her very silence, and her patience
Speak to the people and they pity her.

Sidney Lee thought 'the proud scorn with which she replied to Duke Frederick's accusation of treason was the only speech in the first act which she delivered with any approach to real feeling' (*Academy*, 5 Sept. 1885).

53 In Doran's production, Rosalind showed the Duke a photograph of her father, which she had mournfully examined at the start of the previous scene.

55 Ada Rehan burst into tears and retreated up centre (Daly pbk). Constance Benson first approached the Duke, then retreated as Celia came forward to kneel before her father (Benson 1904 pbk).

56 Celia kneels and grasps her father's hand as Rosalind sits, head bowed, weeping (Sothern–Marlowe pbk).

59–63 William Winter on Mary Anderson: 'her stately figure towering in affluent power, and her fiery spirit blazing forth in vehement indignation, – created a perfect illusion and for one electrical moment set forth the consummate image of tragic majesty' (Derrick, p. 150).

60 In Coleman's BBC version, Frederick looks away as if acknowledging his guilt at Celia's accusation. Frederick slapped Celia in Cheek by Jowl.

66 Celia throws her left arm around Rosalind's neck (Phelps pbk), 'entwines her arms around Rosalind' (Arthur pbk).

67 Anxious to make amends, Cheek by Jowl's Frederick caressed Celia.

67–74 Coleman's Duke takes Celia aside to speak these lines out of Rosalind's hearing. Edzard's assertive Celia draws Frederick aside.

Thou art a fool: she robs thee of thy name   70
And thou wilt show more bright and seem more virtuous
When she is gone.
                    [*Celia starts to speak*]
                    Then open not thy lips!
Firm and irrevocable is my doom
Which I have passed upon her: she is banished.
CELIA Pronounce that sentence then on me, my liege,   75
    I cannot live out of her company.
DUKE FREDERICK You are a fool. – You, niece, provide yourself:
    If you outstay the time, upon mine honour
    And in the greatness of my word, you die.
                                    Exeunt Duke and Lords
CELIA O my poor Rosalind, whither wilt thou go?   80

70   In Dexter's production, Frederick made the unusual attempt 'to convey love for his daughter as well as hatred for his niece' (*Observer*, 5 Aug. 1979); here he tried to touch Celia's face in an imploring gesture (Dexter pbk).
70–2 Sometimes cut in early productions (1786 edn; Shattuck, *Macready*).
75   Celia knelt before her father in Daly's production (pbk). He pushed her to the ground in Cheek by Jowl.
77   James Fagan, in Benson's production, delivered the line 'with the following emphasis, "You *are* a fool!"' (Constance Benson, pp. 136–7).
79 SD In Hare–Kendal's production in 1885, Frederick was a 'blustering, lolloping, restless sort of under-bred person, the uneasy state of whose conscience is expressed by the hurried manner in which he makes his exits, as though he were perpetually hearing the dread whisper, "Here's a policeman coming!"' (*Punch*, 7 Feb. 1885). Julia Marlowe's histrionic Rosalind sobbed 'lying prostrate . . . after the tyrannical Duke's stumping exit up the terrace-steps' (*Poet-Lore* 1 [1889], p. 142, cited in Sprague, p. 33). Sothern and Marlowe sought to defuse some of the scene's animosity by having Le Beau and the Lords take the girls' part in pleading with the Duke, although he disregarded their efforts, sternly waving them aside and stomping out angrily (pbk). Maggie Smith's spirited Celia ran to the door after her father; when Barbara Jefford as Rosalind sank to her knees, Smith returned to kneel briefly beside her before rising to pace (Toye pbk). Vanessa Redgrave did not kneel or crouch while the Duke was present, but her valour vanished once he exited; she shrank back, terrified (1963 RSC/BBC). In Bailey's production, 'the lords left making an obscene gesture' towards Rosalind, signalling her vulnerability once the Duke withdrew his protection of her (Miller-Schütz, 'Findings').

Wilt thou change fathers? I will give thee mine!
I charge thee be not thou more grievèd than I am.
ROSALIND I have more cause.
CELIA   Thou hast not, cousin:
Prithee be cheerful. Know'st thou not the Duke
Hath banished me, his daughter?
ROSALIND   That he hath not.   85
CELIA No? 'Hath not'? Rosalind lacks then the love
Which teacheth thee that thou and I am one;
Shall we be sundered, shall we part, sweet girl?
No, let my father seek another heir!
Therefore devise with me how we may fly,   90
Whither to go, and what to bear with us;
And do not seek to take your change upon you,
To bear your griefs yourself and leave me out:
For, by this heaven, now at our sorrows pale,
Say what thou canst, I'll go along with thee.   95
ROSALIND Why, whither shall we go?
CELIA To seek my uncle in the Forest of Arden.
ROSALIND Alas, what danger will it be to us
(Maids as we are) to travel forth so far?
Beauty provoketh thieves sooner than gold.   100
CELIA I'll put myself in poor and mean attire
And with a kind of umber smirch my face;
The like do you. So shall we pass along
And never stir assailants.
ROSALIND   Were it not better,

86–95 Adrian Lester's Rosalind furiously gathered books and letters into her satchel.

97 In Czinner's film, the scene dissolves to the Forest of Arden. As the camera pans through the trees, the hunters' chorus from 4.2 is sung, followed by the first twenty lines of 2.1, and Amiens's performance of 'Blow, blow, thou winter wind' from 2.7. In this comfortable forest glen, the exiled lords roast meat on a spit and Duke Senior drinks from a silver goblet. The action at Frederick's court resumes after the vision of Arden. In Edzard's film, Celia drags out a huge suitcase.

98–9 In Noble's production, Rosalind shook her skirt to indicate their gender identity as 'maids'.

101 Sinead Cusack's Celia, 'heroic but horrified', delivered the line 'like a duchess contemplating a visit to an Oxfam shop' (*SS* 39, 1986, p. 200).

102 The line about umber, with its implied stage direction, was often cut early on (1786, Kemble edns; Daly, Sothern–Marlowe pbks).

> Because that I am more than common tall,   105
> That I did suit me all points like a man,
> A gallant curtal-axe upon my thigh,
> A boar-spear in my hand, and in my heart
> Lie there what hidden woman's fear there will.
> We'll have a swashing and a martial outside   110
> As many other mannish cowards have
> That do outface it with their semblances.
> CELIA What shall I call thee when thou art a man?
> ROSALIND I'll have no worse a name than Jove's own page,
> And therefore look you call me 'Ganymede'.   115
> But what will you be called?
> CELIA Something that hath a reference to my state:
> No longer 'Celia' but 'Aliena'.
> ROSALIND But, cousin, what if we assayed to steal
> The clownish fool out of your father's court: 120
> Would he not be a comfort to our travail?
> CELIA He'll go along o'er the wide world with me:
> Leave me alone to woo him. Let's away
> And get our jewels and our wealth together,
> Devise the fittest time and safest way   125
> To hide us from pursuit that will be made

105   Cut for Rosalinds who were not tall (Phelps pbk, Czinner film). The line became a joke at Sheffield in 2000, with tiny Victoria Hamilton 'standing on tiptoes and then jumping to reach the hand she held up at what ought to have been head height for the line to match the reality' (*SS* 54, 2001, p. 268)

107   The line was cut early on (Bell's edn), restored by Macready, cut again by Kean, who substituted 'by my side' for the indelicate reference to a thigh. Arthur restored 'upon my thigh', but Julia Marlowe said 'upon my side' while slapping her thigh (Arthur, Sothern–Marlowe pbks). As the dithering suggests, the line was a focus for anxieties about the Ganymede costume.

109   Celia seems shocked by Rosalind's suggestion in Czinner's film.

110   Rosalind imitates a man's stride, and Celia claps her approval (Bridges-Adams pbk). Rosalind stands and swishes her skirts about in the 1978 BBC version.

115   The ladies tittered at the name in Cheek by Jowl.

119   Touchstone's entry here in Modjeska's production prompted Rosalind's proposal to take the fool along to Arden (pbk). James Lewis sang out off stage in Daly's production, then entered in the closing lines of the scene to exit, hand in hand, with the two ladies (Daly pbk).

After my flight. Now go in we content,
To liberty, and not to banishment.

Exeunt

128 In Benson's production, the curtain fell as Touchstone sat on the steps with Rosalind and
Celia, who busily explained their plans (1904 pbk). Czinner shows the ladies and
Touchstone fleeing by night through the courtyard, with a whispered cry of 'To liberty!'

ACT 2

The order of scenes in Act 2 has often been altered, to increase cohesiveness, to avoid rushed changes of setting, and to accommodate elaborate sets. Kemble ordered the scenes 3, 1, 2, 5, 4, 6, 7. Macready's sequence was closer to Shakespeare's – 2, 3, 1, 4, 5, 6, 7 – while allowing the palace scenes to be completed before the move to the forest. Phelps presented the scenes in Shakespearean order. Scene 2 has sometimes been cut, as in Modjeska's production, where the order was 3, 1, 4, 5, 6, 7, and in Daly's, where it was 3, 5, 1, 4, 6, 7. In Julia Arthur's promptbook, 2.3 appears after 1.2, and 2.2 and 2.5 are cut, creating a tidy second act. Benson interpolated 3.1 into this act, producing the following sequence: 3, 1, [3.1], 5, 4, 6, 7 (1904 pbk). Sothern and Marlowe introduced perhaps the most radical reorganisation by moving scene 3 to Act 1, cutting scene 2, and ordering the remaining scenes 6, 4, 5, 1, 7. Czinner's film inserts part of 2.1, embellished with songs, into 1.3, and cuts 2.5 and 2.6. Edzard freely rearranges the material, inserting 2.1 within 1.1, 2.5 before 1.3, then 2.4, 2.2, 2.3, 2.6, and 2.7.

ACT 2, SCENE I

Enter DUKE SENIOR, AMIENS, *and two or three* LORDS *dressed as foresters*

On the nineteenth-century stage, the first act was merely a prelude for the spectacular move to Arden. A contemporary described Macready's production: 'the sylvan scenes have a wild and primitive aspect, denoting the remoteness and seclusion of that "desert inaccessible" the Forest of Arden: old trees of giant growth spread their gnarled and knotted arms, forming a "shade of melancholy boughs" for the banished Duke and his sylvan court; the swift brook brawls along its pebbly bed' (*Spectator*, 8 Oct. 1842). Lewis Wingfield's set for John Hare and W. H. Kendal included a trickling brook, live vegetation, convincing-looking grass made of dyed feathers, and perspective sets offering flower-strewn banks. Modjeska's production featured a raked platform to represent a bank, a downed tree, and stumps of various sizes (pbk).

For Nigel Playfair's production, Claude Lovat Fraser designed forest scenery that critics called 'cubist', although 'the looped curves by which he represented the foliage were copied exactly from a fourteenth-century missal' (Playfair, p. 49). Owen P. Smyth's scenery for the 1932 Old Vic production made Arden 'a bare, wind-swept plateau without hint of vegetation' (*Sunday Times*, 3 Nov. 1932). The 'ingenious device' of Copeau's 1934 production was 'to open an immense sunshade, behind which the exiled Duke's picnic was prepared, while Adam and Orlando were playing their scene in front of it. When they had left, it was removed to disclose the Duke and his courtiers at table. The revolve, decorated with a half-circle of greenery, was used only once to allow Corin to go in search of Rosalind and Celia; when it had completed its round Silvius and Phoebe were discovered with the others peeping through the branches' (Speaight, pp. 191–2). Malcolm Pride's settings for Toye's production recalled 'a petrified forest', with 'few trees, and twigless – their grey trunks are more like the antlers on some Scottish baronial wall than anything else' (*Observer*, 6 Sept. 1959). The foresters were engaged in target practice with bows and arrows (pbk). Richard Negri's set for Elliott's 1961 Stratford production featured a single huge oak tree atop a grassy mound. 'At the end of Part One the Duke was seen blotting himself in despair against the same bark upon which, at the beginning of Part Two, Orlando would hang his verses' (Speaight, p. 282). Negri's design was anticipated by the 'hyperbolic realism' of Frantisek Tröster's scenography twenty-five years before at the Czech National, where the forest was evoked by 'giant stylized maple and alder leaves and their projections on a cyclorama'

(Stríbrny, pp. 92–3). Timothy O'Brien's set for the 1968 RSC production consisted of a tangle of large logs, vaguely evocative of a lumberyard disaster. Christopher Morley designed 'a forest of vertical organ pipes', some 400 of them 'lowered from the flies', 'representing but by no means suggesting the Forest of Arden' for Goodbody's production (*Daily Express*, 13 June 1973; *Financial Times*, 13 June 1973; *Nottingham Evening Post*, 13 June 1973). Among the bleaker Ardens were those inspired by Jan Kott's cynical view of the play, including two Eastern European productions of the 1970s. At Cologne in 1974, 'the set (designed by Bert Kistner) was dominated by a huge felled tree on whose leafless and ice-glazed branches the banished Duke and his listless companions in heavy greatcoats perched like owls in winter' (Hortmann, p. 191). Ionescu's 1976 Bochum production featured 'a few sickly plants under plastic covers, watered hopefully but without success by the shepherds' (Hortmann, p. 190).

In Stein's production, viewers 'did not merely observe characters moving into the green innocence of Nature', they made the journey themselves:

> The first part ended with Frederick issuing orders to Oliver to pursue Orlando . . . Over loudspeakers the barking of hounds resounded around the hall, and Oliver and his servants exited by a door in one of the walls. The audience were invited to follow, and left the hall in single file, each one like Alice at the door into Wonderland garden.
>
> We found ourselves in a dimly lit, green labyrinth, artificial creepers hanging from above, water dripping down the walls. As we followed the twists and turns of this passage, we passed curious collages pasted on the walls, small booth-like openings containing, for example, an Elizabethan workshop or, more strikingly, [an] androgynous man . . . , a life-size plaster statue with fully formed breasts and a penis bulging from his/her breeches. As the sound of the barking dogs grew distant, we began to hear the hunting-horns of Arden beckoning us forwards. The conception was brilliant: to pass from the formality and brutality of the court through an underground labyrinth to the freedom and innocence of the forest was like being born anew . . .
>
> (Patterson, pp. 137–8)

In the vast space of the CCC Film Studios' Arden, 'a complete woodland enrivonment' had been created, featuring a cornfield, a pool, and tall trees. Extra business, including appearances by Robin Hood, Robinson Crusoe, a witch, and hikers, interrupted any static sense of pastoral illusion (Patterson, pp. 138–9).

Realistic in a different sense, the 1978 BBC version opens on Arden with an establishing shot of the brook panning out to show Duke Senior washing his face in the water. He then returns to the hunting camp where the lords are busy cooking and mending. In Noble's production, 'Arden looked just like the Court, for Arden was through the looking glass' (Rutter, p. 103). Pastoral was 'a country of the mind' and the 'usurping court doubled as the forest court, simply wrapping white dust sheets around their evening dress', and huddling around braziers to indicate the wintry weather (*SQ* 37, 1986, p. 116). At the Guthrie Theater in 1982, Liviu Ciulei created a forest of 'anthropomorphic trees', thus 'literalizing the "tongues in trees"' of Duke Senior's first speech. The trees 'respectfully boughed, as natural courtiers' to the Duke (*SQ* 34, 1983, p. 230). Kjetil Bang-Hansen's 1983 production in Bergen featured a great central tree that changed colour with the passing seasons; 'the pastoral idyll was gently mocked by the presence of toy sheep on wheels' (*SQ* 35, 1984, p. 95). The grey, repressive setting of Hytner's production evoked 'Russia in the years after the revolution'; the 'exiled court' was 'a band of Czarist counter-revolutionaries huddled around a Siberian camp-fire' (*SS* 40, 1987, p. 174). In Caird's production, 'Duke Senior and his followers made their appearance through the floor of the stage, pulling up floor boards after them to reveal a forest floor of tawny brown' (*SQ* 41, 1989–90, p. 492). In Cheek by Jowl's continuous staging, 'while Celia and Rosalind, still at court but preparing for exile, speak of the Forest of Arden, in rushes the banished Duke, in a circle round them and flings himself rapturously to the floor. He is bare-chested, and in seconds that simple act of running and falling has taken us into the Forest – and prepares us for the speech in its praise he is about to make. And yet Celia and Rosalind are still speaking, and we are also still at court with them. At such a moment, being in two places at once *and* feeling the connection and contrast between them, yet having no scenery to support us, we sense just how magical theatre can be' (*Financial Times*, 27 Jan. 1995). The Duke's concerned followers, armed with coats and scarves, ran after him. Edzard, who inserts this scene into Charles's dialogue with Oliver in 1.1, puts Arden in the wastes of London's docklands.

0 SD Multitudes assembled on stage in nineteenth-century productions. Macready's staging included forty actors, diversely occupied: attendants preparing weapons; falconers working with hoops of birds; hunters playing airs on horns, leading leashed hounds, or lounging in conversation (Macready pbk). At St James's in 1885, the banished Duke and his courtiers were attired in rich silks and satins; the designer Lewis Wingfield argued that it was inappropriate for those of high rank to appear in simple clothing (*Pall Mall Gazette*, 24 Jan. 1885). More usually, they have appeared here in rustic dress (Oxberry edn). Daly, who combined this scene with 2.5, offered particularly well-armed foresters: they were discovered 'preparing for the chase – arranging their cross-bows, examining their spears, sharpening the points; some lying on the ground, and firing at a target off the stage' (pbk). Benson's more sedate staging opened with the foresters in chorus; at the end of their song the Duke entered (1904 pbk). Arthur's promptbook indicates that the foresters were armed with boar-spears, short swords, bows, quivers, and arrows, but the Duke and Jaques were without weapons; the scene opened with the song 'What is to the sound the cheerful horn'. Asche's well-mannered forest gentlemen rose at the Duke's entrance (pbk). Goodbody's exiles enjoyed a 'cosy . . . forest camp, with armchairs and the best wineglasses' (*Financial Times*, 13 June 1973). In Dexter's production, Duke Senior was revealed while the forest folk removed the corn dolly remaining from the earlier festivities (pbk). The Berkeley Repertory Theatre presented the exiled court as 'a Hollywood version of *guerillistas* in their mountain hideaway' (*SQ* 33, 1982, p. 399). In Edzard's film, Duke Senior stands near an oil drum

DUKE SENIOR Now, my co-mates and brothers in exile,
    Hath not old custom made this life more sweet
    Than that of painted pomp? Are not these woods
    More free from peril than the envious court?
    Here feel we not the penalty of Adam,   5
    The seasons' difference, as the icy fang
    And churlish chiding of the winter's wind –
    Which when it bites and blows upon my body
    Even till I shrink with cold, I smile and say,
    'This is no flattery' – these are counsellors   10
    That feelingly persuade me what I am.
    Sweet are the uses of adversity
    Which like the toad, ugly and venomous,
    Wears yet a precious jewel in his head,
    And this our life exempt from public haunt   15
    Finds tongues in trees, books in the running brooks,

brazier, surrounded by an expanse of damp concrete; his followers collect packing crates and boxes, only occasionally glancing at him as he philosophises. At Stratford in 1996, the Duke 'kicked off his boots to prove his fortitude' in Arden's 'howling snowstorm' – then promptly 'clicked his fingers to order one of the underlings to put the boots back on again' (*SS* 50, 1997, p. 204).

    Frequently the parts of Duke Senior and Duke Frederick have been played by the same actor, as in Noble and Cheek by Jowl. The two Dukes' attendants were also doubled at Shakespeare's Globe in 1998, where 'the rapidity with which one group followed another onto the stage focused attention on their quick-change virtuosity rather than, say, the totalitarian nature of the court' (*SQ* 50, 1999, p. 77).

1–17 Hare–Kendal's Duke was ridiculed as 'the Banished cheesemonger, so stolid and unobtrusive is the bearing of this Nobleman in reduced circumstances' (*Punch*, 7 Feb. 1885). In Stein's production, courtiers 'shiveringly drew a tarpaulin closer round their master as he attempted to persuade them' of adversity's usefulness (Patterson, pp. 139–40). Cheek by Jowl's 'almost demented' Duke was 'in anguish at being exiled'; his '"sermons in stones" were not merely stout moralizing, but pebbles he takes from his pocket and flings in the air' (*Times Literary Supplement*, 20 Dec. 1991).

3–5 Jones introduced the novelty of scuffling foresters: one dropped the load of wood he was hauling, causing another to trip; he lunged at the first and a fight ensued; the Duke broke it up (pbk).

5 Benson (1904 pbk) follows the Folio reading; so does Williams (pbk). Asche follows Theobald's emendation (pbk).

Sermons in stones, and good in everything.
AMIENS I would not change it; happy is your grace
    That can translate the stubbornness of Fortune
    Into so quiet and so sweet a style.   20
DUKE SENIOR Come, shall we go and kill us venison?
    And yet it irks me the poor dappled fools,
    Being native burghers of this desert city,
    Should, in their own confines, with forkèd heads
    Have their round haunches gored.
I LORD   Indeed, my lord.   25
    The melancholy 'Jacques' grieves at that,
    And in that kind swears you do more usurp
    Than doth your brother that hath banished you.
    Today my lord of Amiens and myself
    Did steal behind him as he lay along   30

18a   Many productions have assigned this line to the Duke (Kean, Sothern–Marlowe, Bridges-Adams pbks).

18–20   Asche has 1 Lord speak Amiens's lines (pbk).

21   In 1898–9 at Wallack's, the Duke took a spear from Amiens, provoking a movement of disgust from Jaques (Arthur pbk). Asche's Duke, by contrast, gave a gentleman his spear at this point (pbk). Goodbody's Duke got a gun and Coleman's a bow (pbks). In Edzard's film, one of the Duke's men rips the cellophane cover from a packet of meat.

21–68   Cut in Czinner's film.

25–43   Many early productions followed *Love in a Forest* in assigning this speech, and the following one by 1 Lord, to Jaques. Henry Morley objected in 1866 'if Shakespeare were stage-manager he never would permit it' (p. 295). Macready restored the lines to 1 Lord (pbk). Playing Jaques at Stratford, 'Mr Macklin's task was rendered the more difficult by the transference to Jaques of the First Lord's famous speech . . . as soon as Jaques is made responsible for expressions of sincere sentiment his individuality is destroyed' (*Academy*, 5 Sept. 1885). Occasionally on the modern stage Jaques has been introduced here to describe himself, as in the 1982 production at Oslo's National Theatre (*SQ* 34, 1983, p. 243). In Edzard's film, 1 Lord is female.

26   In a letter to Augustin Daly, dated 5 Nov. 1889, Horace Howard Furness suggests that 'the true pronunciation is Jakes' yet he begs that it be pronounced Ja-ques because 'Jakes is such a disagreeable name, indissolubly associated, especially to New Yorkers, with Bowery boys' (Daly pbk). Confusion about the pronunciation of the name has often been turned to comic effect. In Caird's Stratford production, 'Amiens managed to offer a French Jacques, jakwez and jakes' (*SS* 44, 1991, p. 162).

Under an oak, whose antique root peeps out
Upon the brook that brawls along this wood,
To the which place a poor sequestered stag,
That from the hunter's aim had ta'en a hurt,
Did come to languish; and indeed, my lord,   35
The wretched animal heaved forth such groans
That their discharge did stretch his leathern coat
Almost to bursting, and the big round tears
Coursed one another down his innocent nose
In piteous chase; and thus the hairy fool,   40
Much markèd of the melancholy Jaques,
Stood on th'extremest verge of the swift brook,
Augmenting it with tears.
DUKE SENIOR   But what said Jaques?
Did he not moralise this spectacle?
I LORD O yes, into a thousand similes.   45
First, for his weeping in the needless stream:
'Poor deer', quoth he, 'thou mak'st a testament
As worldlings do, giving thy sum of more
To that which hath too much.' Then, being there alone,
Left and abandoned of his velvet friend: 50
''Tis right', quoth he, 'thus misery doth part
The flux of company.' Anon a careless herd,
Full of the pasture, jumps along by him
And never stays to greet him. 'Aye', quoth Jaques,
'Sweep on you fat and greasy citizens,   55
'Tis just the fashion. Wherefore do you look
Upon that poor and broken bankrupt there?'
Thus most invectively he pierceth through
The body of country, city, court,
Yea, and of this our life, swearing that we   60
Are mere usurpers, tyrants, and what's worse,
To fright the animals and to kill them up
In their assigned and native dwelling-place.
DUKE SENIOR And did you leave him in this contemplation?
2 LORD We did, my lord, weeping and commenting   65
Upon the sobbing deer.
DUKE SENIOR   Show me the place;

45–63 Asche directed that pages serve food and wine during 1 Lord's speech (pbk).
64–6 These lines were cut when Jaques himself explained his malaise (Bell's, Kemble edns), and
sometimes when he did not (Macready, Daly, Benson 1904 pbks).

> I love to cope him in these sullen fits,
> For then he's full of matter.

I LORD   I'll bring you to him straight.

Exeunt

67–8   At Wallack's in 1898–9, the song which had opened the scene was repeated here, continuing until Rosalind, Celia, and Touchstone were on stage for 2.4, which directly followed (Arthur pbk).

ACT 2, SCENE 2

Enter DUKE [FREDERICK] *with* LORDS

DUKE FREDERICK Can it be possible that no man saw them?
        It cannot be: some villeins of my court
        Are of consent and sufferance in this.
1 LORD I cannot hear of any that did see her;
        The ladies, her attendants of her chamber,   5
        Saw her abed and, in the morning early,
        They found the bed untreasured of their mistress.
2 LORD My lord, the roinish clown, at whom so oft
        Your grace was wont to laugh, is also missing.
        Hisperia, the princess' gentlewoman,   10
        Confesses that she secretly o'erheard
        Your daughter and her cousin much commend

Frequently cut in production, making the removal to Arden's freedom and happiness more complete. Darker productions highlight the scene's threatening aspects. Toye included the Duke's mistress, stomping angrily through the bedroom (pbk). The 1978 BBC version shows an irate Frederick delivering orders in the torchlit courtyard of the castle. Caird had Frederick's bodyguards search for the runaways 'through the auditorium, flashlights beaming in all directions' (*SQ* 41, 1989–90, p. 492). Richard Monette had 'the duke cross-examin[e] a long row of servants' at Stratford, Ontario, in 1990 (*SQ* 42, 1991, p. 215).

0 SD   Kemble gave the names Eustace and Louis to 1 and 2 Lords. Phelps had two Lords and four attendants accompanying Frederick, but assigned the speaking parts of both 1 and 2 Lords to Le Beau (pbk). In Ciulei's 1982 production, Frederick was in his bathtub throughout the scene (*SQ* 34, 1983, p. 233). Noble's exiled courtiers threw off their cloaking sheets and were transformed into their previous court personae. John Kane played both Oliver and Duke Frederick in ACTER's 1991 touring production, 'holding a flashlight to his face at different angles, alternately the accuser and the accused' (Mazer, '*As You Like It*', p. 23).

4–7   Cut in many productions (Bell's, 1786 edns).

10   Hisperia has sometimes appeared. In Czinner's film she is brought in weeping. In Ciulei's 1982 production, she 'either glanced into the tub' in which Frederick was bathing 'or was "groped"' by him. Earlier, in 1.3, she had urged Rosalind and Celia to go to bed (*SQ* 34, 1983, p. 233).

The parts and graces of the wrestler
That did but lately foil the sinewy Charles;
And she believes, wherever they are gone, 15
That youth is surely in their company.
DUKE FREDERICK Send to his brother: 'Fetch that gallant hither.'
If he be absent, bring his brother to me –
I'll make him find him. Do this suddenly,
And let not search and inquisition quail 20
To bring again these foolish runaways.

Exeunt

ACT 2, SCENE 3

Enter ORLANDO

ORLANDO Who's there?

[*Enter* ADAM]

ADAM What, my young master! O my gentle master,
        O my sweet master, O you memory
        Of old Sir Roland, why, what make you here?
        Why are you virtuous? Why do people love you?   5
        And wherefore are you gentle, strong, and valiant?
        Why would you be so fond to overcome
        The bonny prizer of the humorous Duke?
        Your praise is come too swiftly home before you.
        Know you not, master, to some kind of men   10
        Their graces serve them but as enemies?
        No more do yours: your virtues, gentle master,
        Are sanctified and holy traitors to you.
        O what a world is this when what is comely
        Envenoms him that bears it!   15

Sometimes this scene has been moved back to follow 1.2 (Arthur, Sothern–Marlowe, Asche pbks). Francis Gentleman placed the scene at Oliver's house, where 'Orlando appears knocking at the door' (Gentleman, vol. 1, 465). In Edzard's film, Adam repairs small hardware at a lamp-lit workbench.

0 SD   In Czinner's film, Orlando carves 'R' on a bench in the farmyard, as a peasant leads a cow past. Adam sits at a candlelit table, his head down as if sleeping, in the 1963 RSC/BBC version; Orlando approaches outside.

1 SD   Asche's Adam carried gold and a stick with a bundle on the end (pbk). He wore mittens and huddled beneath a comforter in Shaw's 1957 production (SQ 8, 1957, p. 480). Toye's Adam 'like an ancient stableman, was never without his bottle. Such a tippler would never have saved five hundred crowns' (*Theatre World*, Oct. 1959).

2   'Taking both his hands' (Asche pbk).

10–21   Cut in the Sothern–Marlowe promptbook, presumably to reduce sentimentality. Toye cut 10–15 (pbk), Williams cut 10–15 and 19b–21 (pbk).

ORLANDO Why, what's the matter?
ADAM   O unhappy youth,
    Come not within these doors: within this roof
    The enemy of all your graces lives
    Your brother – no, no brother – yet the son –
    Yet not the son, I will not call him son   20
    Of him I was about to call his father –
    Hath heard your praises, and this night he means
    To burn the lodging where you use to lie
    And you within it. If he fail of that,
    He will have other means to cut you off: 25
    I overheard him and his practices.
    This is no place, this house is but a butchery:
    Abhor it, fear it, do not enter it.
ORLANDO Why whither, Adam, wouldst thou have me go?
ADAM No matter whither, so you come not here.   30
ORLANDO What, wouldst thou have me go and beg my food,
    Or with a base and boisterous sword enforce
    A thievish living on the common road?
    This I must do or know not what to do;
    Yet this I will not do, do how I can.   35
    I rather will subject me to the malice
    Of a diverted blood and bloody brother.
ADAM But do not so: I have five hundred crowns,
    The thrifty hire I saved under your father,
    Which I did store to be my foster-nurse   40
    When service should in my old limbs lie lame
    And unregarded age in corners thrown;
    Take that, and He that doth the ravens feed,
    Yea providently caters for the sparrow,
    Be comfort to my age. Here is the gold: 45
    All this I give you; let me be your servant –

30   Adam pushes Orlando back a little (Elliott pbk).
37   Frank Benson as Orlando moved towards his brother's house, but Adam blocked his way
     (1904 pbk). Goodbody had Adam grab Orlando's leg (pbk).
38–53 John Hill described an early performance by Mr Berry: 'The unfeigned tears that trickled
     down the player's cheeks, as he delivered this generous and noble speech, were
     accompany'd with those of every spectator; and the applause that succeeded these, shew'd
     sufficiently the sense of the audience, and spoke in the strongest terms the praises of that
     sensibility, that feeling, which we are so earnestly recommending to every other player'
     (Hill, p. 45).

Though I look old, yet I am strong and lusty;
For in my youth I never did apply
Hot and rebellious liquors in my blood,
Nor did not with unbashful forehead woo   50
The means of weakness and debility;
Therefore my age is as a lusty winter,
Frosty but kindly. Let me go with you:
I'll do the service of a younger man
In all your business and necessities.   55
ORLANDO   O good old man, how well in thee appears
The constant service of the antique world,
When service sweat for duty not for meed.
Thou art not for the fashion of these times
Where none will sweat but for promotion   60
And, having that, do choke their service up
Even with the having. It is not so with thee;
But, poor old man, thou prun'st a rotten tree
That cannot so much as a blossom yield,
In lieu of all thy pains and husbandry.   65
But come thy ways: we'll go along together
And, ere we have thy youthful wages spent,
We'll light upon some settled low content.
ADAM   Master, go on, and I will follow thee
To the last gasp with truth and loyalty.   70
From seventeen years till now almost fourscore
Here lived I, but now live here no more.

48–53   Cut in the Sothern–Marlowe promptbook, and sometimes later, as in Coleman's BBC version. Toye's Orlando initially turned away from the proffered gold, but assented when Adam implored him (pbk).

53–5   Adam typically makes a gesture of supplication, 'throw[ing] himself upon Orlando's neck' (Phelps pbk), or kneeling (Benson 1904 pbk).

69–70   The traditional staging has Adam go into the house, then re-enter with a wallet or bag of gold, and often (as in Benson 1904 pbk) with a cloak and staff as well.

72   As Adam is about to leave the house, he 'pauses at foot of steps, looks back, pulls a twig from bush near door, kisses it and puts it into his bosom' (Moore pbk). George Bernard Shaw praised Mr Loraine's Adam, who 'made a charming point by bidding farewell to the old home with a smile instead of the conventional tear' (Shaw, vol. 2, p. 270). Toye's bibulous Adam, who had been tippling throughout the scene, had his bottle confiscated by Orlando (pbk).

At seventeen years many their fortunes seek,
But at fourscore it is too late a week;
Yet Fortune cannot recompense me better   75
Than to die well and not my master's debtor.

Exeunt

76   Asche's Orlando departed alone, but promptly returned to take Adam's bundle from him.
     After a brief tussle over it, the two exited, laughing (pbk).

ACT 2, SCENE 4

Enter ROSALIND [*in man's attire as*] GANYMEDE, CELIA [*as a shepherdess*]
ALIENA, *and* [*the*] *clown* TOUCHSTONE [*in the costume of a retainer*]

In Czinner's film, the opening shot shows a waterfall in the forest. The forested hillside in
the 1978 BBC film is covered with ferns. At Shakespeare's Globe, the forest's 'sense of
spookiness . . . was created by bird-calls and sounds' (Miller-Schütz, 'Findings').

0 SD Eighteenth-century actresses played Ganymede in form-fitting trousers designed to exhibit
the legs. Sarah Siddons was considered a failure in the role, partially because her modesty
dictated an 'ambiguous vestment' of hussar boots, gardener's apron, and petticoat
(Salgado, p. 163; Kelly, p. 53). For early nineteenth-century productions, Rosalind wore a
green, fur-trimmed tunic and pantaloons, with russet boots (Oxberry edn). In the Victorian
period, the competing 'demands of historical consistency and feminine modesty' required
careful compromises. Some Rosalinds wore skirt-length tunics over silk tights, impractical as
they would be in a forest. Some wore gaiters (Mrs Kendal, Helena Modjeska). Eventually
the established Ganymede costume consisted of doublet, trunk-hose, and thigh-high leather
boots (Jackson, 'Perfect Types', p. 24). Helena Faucit wore 'a page's dress of lavender
cashmere, edged with emerald green velvet . . . her hair falling in natural loose curls upon
her shoulders, from under a broad felt hat, with a hawthorn spray or some stray wild flower
twined into its band' (*Blackwood's*, Dec. 1885, cited in Carlisle, p. 79). Fanny Davenport was
praised as 'one of those who can safely make the experiment' of wearing boy's clothes,
appearing in a 'neat and modest' costume as Ganymede (*The World*, May 25, 1876).
Photographs show the curvaceous Davenport's version of boy's clothes to be a tunic
reaching to just above her knee. Helena Modjeska's brocade doublet established a
Ganymede who was more court page than forester, and her over-the-knee boots ensured
that her modesty remained intact (Derrick, p. 145). In 1876, Adelaide Neilson's Ganymede
looked 'as if she were Diana in a burlesque' (unidentified clipping, TM). Mrs Kendal wore 'a
skirt of rich green brocade which reaches down to the knees, long boots of grey leather, a
leather jerkin as a bodice, rhubarb-coloured sleeves, and a hat of grey' (*Pall Mall Gazette*,
24 Jan. 1885). Mary Anderson wore a russet doublet and hose, a belted brown leather

jerkin, and high leather boots that forestalled the admiring glances less modest Rosalinds had sometimes invited (Shattuck, *American Stage*, p. 108). Ada Rehan's 'drab-coloured male attire', accentuated by a 'ruby-coloured cloak' and 'brown hose' were much admired (*Theatre*, 1 Aug. 1890), except by Henry Irving, who muttered 'How long d'you suppose those silk tights would last in the forest?' (Shattuck, *American Stage*, p. 80). Because Rehan's tights were 'unmated by boots or leggings' (*New York Times*, 18 Dec. 1889) her costume was considered more daring than those of her recent predecessors in the role. Henry P. Goddard reported a 'ludicrous incident' occurring at New Haven, when Mary Scott-Siddons played Rosalind in silk stockings with long buttoned gaiters atop 'high and narrow French heels, on account of which, during one of her scenes in the forest of Arden, she tripped on some obstacle so that she fell prone on her back. Before recovering herself she cried out, "D—n it, ring down that curtain"' (unidentified clipping, small scrapbook, FSL). Of Julia Neilson's costume, a reviewer quibbled that 'despite the fact of special reference being again and again made to her doublet and trunk hose, she wears neither, her disguise consisting of tunic worn without "trunks"'. (unidentified clipping, 6 Dec. 1896, TM). The tights Julia Marlowe wore as Rosalind were sold at auction for $1 in 1916. They were 'very, very pink' and 'worn to an appalling degree of thinness' (unidentified clipping, 4 Feb. 1916, small scrapbook, FSL). Photographs of Marlowe in the Ganymede disguise suggest that the tights were little seen, however, for her boots and jerkin nearly met. In Playfair's production, Athene Seyler wore a tunic to mid-thigh, with close pants beneath tucked into boots; a hood around her head was topped with a cap (photograph, TM). Barbara Jefford 'looked splendid in top coat and breeches' (*Daily Telegraph*, 4 Sept. 1959).

At Stratford in 1973, every programme contained a free souvenir poster, featuring a rear view image of the slim Eileen Atkins in jeans and a quotation from Martin Luther: 'women . . . have broad hips and a wide fundament to sit upon, keep house and bear and raise children' (SCL). The juxtaposition of essentialising text and liberated image indicated the production's (and perhaps the play's) feminist agenda. Sara Kestelmann played Ganymede in 'a fey, elegant costume, based on the portrait by Nicholas Hilliard of an unknown youth' (*Evening Standard*, 2 Aug. 1979).

In Stein's production, the exiles, pulling a cart loaded with suitcases, wore Victorian-style overcoats. Later, when the weather warmed a bit, Rosalind wore a 'loose-fitting shirt and white cotton trousers which reached to her calves, with a floppy hat on her head and moustache painted on her upper lip' (Patterson, pp. 140, 142). Roberta Maxwell offended critics by sporting a moustache in the early runs of Hirsch's production at Stratford, Ontario, in 1983 (Berry, p. 464). The moustache is a rare feature of Rosalinds in disguise.

In Noble's production, as the exiles arrived in Arden, they trailed the white silk sheet behind them, obliterating the furniture of the ducal palace still on stage. Juliet Stevenson as Rosalind wore a white suit with baggy pants, looking both stylish and Chaplinesque – a bowler hat and cane completed the effect. Emma Croft, in jeans, parka, work boots, and stocking cap, makes a convincingly androgynous Ganymede in Edzard's film. Adrian Lester as Ganymede wore a sweater, scarf, and jacket over trousers in Cheek by Jowl, looking like a 1920s schoolboy but standing with legs together like a woman. Anastasia Hille was a decidedly feminine Ganymede, whose 'breeches needed endless adapting' because 'the buttons kept falling off' (Miller-Schütz, 'Interview', p. 11). Her 'sheepskin cap . . . had a habit of falling off, to reveal shoulder-length fair hair' (*SS* 52, 1999, p. 223). In summary, we might note Lindsay Duguid's remark, inspired by Samantha Bond's Rosalind at Stratford in 1992: 'The English actress playing Rosalind is a gender all her own' (*Times Literary Supplement*, 8 May 1992).

In a 1991 production in Bangkok, actors wore papier mâché breastplates as markers of gender – female plates creating full breasts and slim waists, the male versions dark and muscular. When Rosalind became Ganymede, she 'doffed her female breast plate for a muscular, male one – only it was pink' (Wayne, p. 200).

Rosalind's weapons: Daly had Rosalind carry a 'boar-spear' and Celia a shepherd's crook (pbk). At the Haymarket in 1876, Adelaide Neilson also carried a boar-spear; a reviewer complained that she used it 'very much as a clown uses a hot poker' (unidentified clipping, TM). Vanessa Redgrave carried a sword in her belt. Helen Mirren did too, and fingered it anxiously while speaking to Corin.

Oxberry describes Celia's costume as a blue, flower-trimmed dress with a muslin petticoat. Fay Davis's Celia wore a serge gown of 'forget-me-not blue' over a dark blue petticoat with 'the bodice . . . turned back with white from a little chemisette of drawn white muslin' and 'tight sleeves just below the elbow' (*Sketch*, 9 Dec. 1896). Edzard had Celia don 'sensible walking-shoes and a headscarf – the characteristic garb of a middle-class urbanite planning a trip to the country' (Marriette, p. 75).

The Folio stage direction 'Clowne alias Touchstone' indicates that he is in disguise, but whereas Jaques mentions Touchstone's motley (and calls him 'fool' [2.7.12–19]), the rustics take the clown to be a courtier. Touchstone's costume cannot, therefore, be the traditional fool's garb, which they would presumably recognise. Wiles, observing that Touchstone is reported to draw a dial from a 'poke' (a bagged sleeve), deduces that he 'wear[s] a coat that is motley in colour, is marked as a fool's coat by hanging elbows, and yet in certain respects is of a wholly unfamiliar design . . . [perhaps of] the woven, chequered type of motley' (p. 186). Most Touchstones have worn some version of motley throughout the forest adventures. At Shakespeare's Globe, the 'costume gradually fell apart, until Touchstone appeared for the final scene in his shirt and crowned with twigs, having (temporarily) lost all the suits and trappings of court life for the love of Audrey' (Miller-Schütz, 'Findings'). Robert Keeley was so unattractive that 'his presence with two beautiful ladies in a lonely wood' did not offend nineteenth-century sensibilities (*John Bull*, cited in Shattuck, *Macready*).

In Macready's production, Touchstone bore several heavy packets. The two girls typically lean heavily on Touchstone, and often all three collapse onto the ground. In the 1963

ROSALIND O Jupiter, how merry are my spirits!

TOUCHSTONE I care not for my spirits, if my legs were not weary.

ROSALIND [*Aside*] I could find in my heart to disgrace my man's apparel
and to cry like a woman; but I must comfort the weaker vessel, as
doublet and hose ought to show itself courageous to petticoat;   5
therefore – courage, good Aliena!

CELIA I pray you bear with me, I cannot go no further.

TOUCHSTONE For my part, I had rather bear with you than bear you;
yet I should bear no cross if I did bear you, for I think you have no
money in your purse.   10

ROSALIND Well, this is the Forest of Arden.

TOUCHSTONE Aye, now am I in Arden, the more fool I! When I was at
home I was in a better place; but travellers must be content.

Enter CORIN *and* SILVIUS

RSC/BBC version, the travellers rest on barren rocks. In the urban wasteland of Edzard's
Arden, they rest on an overturned barrel. In the 2000 Stratford production, Celia was carted
in in the wheelbarrow Orlando had used in the opening scene.

1   Czinner's film followed Theobald's emendation of 'weary' for 'merry', as did Coleman's BBC
version.

8   Daly had Touchstone throw himself on the ground, repeating Ganymede's action a few lines
earlier and initiating a pattern that was repeated through the forest scenes of the production
(pbk).

8–10 Lionel Brough's Touchstone was criticised for showing 'over-familiarity' with 'the disguised
princess . . . supporting his mistress, [he] places her head on his shoulder and pats her
cheek or "chucks her chin"', exhibiting 'complete . . . misconception of the relations possible
under any circumstances between a jester and a princess of royal blood' (*Athenaeum*, 6
Mar. 1880).

9–10 Cut by Benson, presumably as obscure (1904 pbk).

10   In Dexter's production, Rosalind removed her cloak and spread it on the ground; the three
exiles sat down and drew it about them, huddling in the cold (pbk).

12–13 In Pimlott's production, Touchstone was filled with 'self-righteous indignation at being
dragged along' and the lines 'positively [dripped] with sarcasm' (Tennant, p. 38).

13 SD With a dog (Benson 1905 pbk). Corin and Silvius are spotted through the trees in
the 1978 BBC film, Corin wearing a sheepskin around his shoulders, despite the
summery weather. Edzard's Corin (Roger Hammond, who also plays Le Beau)
leads a sheep on a leash; Silvius, a pale-faced punk, has a heavy rural Scots
accent.

ROSALIND Aye, be so, good Touchstone. Look you who comes here:
      A young man and an old in solemn talk.   15
CORIN That is the way to make her scorn you still.
SILVIUS O Corin, that thou knew'st how I do love her.
CORIN I partly guess, for I have loved ere now.
SILVIUS No, Corin, being old, thou canst not guess,
      Though in thy youth thou wast as true a lover   20
      As ever sighed upon a midnight pillow.
      But if thy love were ever like to mine –
      As sure I think did never man love so –
      How many actions most ridiculous
      Hast thou been drawn to by thy fantasy?   25
CORIN Into a thousand that I have forgotten.
SILVIUS O thou didst then never love so heartily.
      If thou remembrest not the slightest folly
      That ever love did make thee run into,
      Thou hast not loved.   30
      Or if thou hast not sat as I do now,
      Wearing thy hearer in thy mistress' praise,
      Thou hast not loved.
      Or if thou hast not broke from company
      Abruptly as my passion now makes me,   35
      Thou hast not loved.
      O Phoebe, Phoebe, Phoebe!   *Exit*
ROSALIND Alas, poor shepherd, searching of thy wound,
      I have by hard adventure found mine own.

16–37   At Shakespeare's Globe, Jonathan Cecil (who doubled as Le Beau) 'imagined a whole
        sequence of little actions for Corin: drinking, lighting his pipe etc. He subsequently fell
        asleep after Silvius left' (Miller-Schütz, 'Findings').

30   Corin answers 'Mm' to Silvius's plaint, repeating this sound at 33 and 36 (Bridges-Adams
        pbk).

37 SD   Frank Benson reports that Edmund Kean, 'in one of his earliest impersonations in London',
        ranted: 'O, Phoebe, Phoebe, Phoebe! Damn and blast Phoebe!' (Frank Benson, p. 157).
        Silvius exits with outstretched arms; Corin looks after him, laughingly shakes his head, then
        'toddles out after him' (Sothern–Marlowe pbk).

38   Susan Fleetwood's Rosalind, 'as exhausted by sheer erotic frustration as by her journey . . .
        established an immediate rapport' with Silvius, who expressed his own frustration by
        twining his arms around a shepherd's crook across his shoulders (*SS* 34, 1981, pp. 149–50).

38–50   Cut in Czinner's film.

TOUCHSTONE And I mine: I remember when I was in love, I broke my   40
sword upon a stone and bid him take that for coming a-night to Jane
Smile; and I remember the kissing of her batler and the cow's dugs
that her pretty chapped hands had milked; and I remember the
wooing of a peasecod instead of her, from whom I took two cods
and, giving her them again, said with weeping tears, 'Wear these for   45
my sake.' We that are true lovers run into strange capers; but as all
is mortal in Nature, so is all nature in love mortal in folly.
ROSALIND Thou speak'st wiser than thou art ware of.
TOUCHSTONE Nay, I shall ne'er be ware of mine own wit till I break my
shins against it.   50
ROSALIND Jove, Jove, this shepherd's passion
      Is much upon my fashion.
TOUCHSTONE And mine, but it grows something stale with me.
CELIA I pray you, one of you question yond man
      If he for gold will give us any food: 55
      I faint almost to death.
TOUCHSTONE Holla, you, clown!
ROSALIND Peace, fool; he's not thy kinsman.
CORIN Who calls?
TOUCHSTONE Your betters, sir.   60
CORIN Else are they very wretched.
ROSALIND [*To Touchstone*] Peace, I say. – Good even to you, friend.

40–7 At the 1986 Oregon Shakespeare Festival, Larry Paulsen's Touchstone did not play the Jane Smile speech simply for laughs, as a send-up of romantic love. Rather, Paulsen sought to 'convey . . . a sense of the effect of Arden upon outsiders by having his Touchstone . . . remember something from his past that had long been forgotten' (*SQ* 38, 1987, p. 91).

42 'Bucket' replaced 'batler' in Cheek by Jowl.

42a Celia breaks in to question 'Jane Smile?'; Touchstone's response: 'Mm!' (Helpmann pbk).

44b–6 The line about the peasecod has often been cut (Phelps, Benson 1904, Sothern–Marlowe pbks).

51–3 Cut, presumably for decorum, from the eighteenth to the early twentieth centuries. Rosalind kneels (Elliott pbk).

58 Modjeska discreetly whispered the line (pbk).

59 Corin answered from off stage in Asche's production (pbk). Elliott had him sit up from his nap (pbk).

60 Touchstone flourishes his staff over Corin's head (Moore pbk).

62 Edzard's Rosalind approaches Corin confidently, extending her hand.

CORIN And to you, gentle sir, and to you all.
ROSALIND I prithee, shepherd, if that love or gold
    Can in this desert place buy entertainment,   65
    Bring us where we may rest ourselves and feed.
    Here's a young maid with travel much oppressed
    And faints for succour.
CORIN   Fair sir, I pity her
    And wish, for her sake more than for mine own,
    My fortunes were more able to relieve her;   70
    But I am shepherd to another man,
    And do not shear the fleeces that I graze.
    My master is of churlish disposition
    And little recks to find the way to heaven
    By doing deeds of hospitality.   75
    Besides, his cot, his flocks, and bounds of feed
    Are now on sale, and at our sheepcote now
    By reason of his absence there is nothing
    That you will feed on. But what is, come see,
    And in my voice most welcome shall you be.   80
ROSALIND What is he that shall buy his flock and pasture?
CORIN That young swain that you saw here but erewhile,
    That little cares for buying anything.
ROSALIND I pray thee, if it stand with honesty,
    Buy thou the cottage, pasture, and the flock,   85
    And thou shalt have to pay for it of us.
CELIA And we will mend thy wages. I like this place
    And willingly could waste my time in it.
CORIN Assuredly the thing is to be sold.
    Go with me. If you like upon report   90
    The soil, the profit, and this kind of life,

---

63 In Donnellan's production, Corin looked Rosalind up and down questioningly; she moved her feet apart for a more convincing display of masculinity. Corin pointedly paused before 'sir'.

68a Papp had Celia fall back melodramatically, 'caught deftly by Touchstone' (*SQ* 24, 1973, p. 424).

68b–80 Corin, seated by Celia and looking into her eyes, spoke very slowly and deliberately in Cheek by Jowl.

79 In Asche's production, Touchstone groaned several times during the interaction with Corin (pbk).

89 Rosalind and Corin shake hands, spitting (Jones pbk).

I will your very faithful feeder be,
And buy it with your gold right suddenly.

Exeunt

93 SD   Here occurred a traditional bit of business, apparently begun by Phelps, whereby Corin,
Rosalind, and Touchstone exit, leaving Celia to cry out for Touchstone; he returns and assists
her (Phelps, Daly pbks). Modjeska's Rosalind pulled back Touchstone as he was about to exit
alone, enjoining him to help support Celia as the three exited together (pbk). In Benson's
version, Touchstone coughs to Corin, then loads him with his wallet; Rosalind coughs to
Touchstone, then she and Celia both lean on his shoulders, having passed him their spear
and crook; the group exits sighing, preceded by a laughing Corin (1904 pbk). In Dexter's
production, horn music was heard as the scene ended and a tent was erected by the forest
folk (pbk). Edzard has the group exit into the construction hut in which Corin lived.

ACT 2, SCENE 5

Enter AMIENS, JAQUES, *and others* [: *Lords dressed as foresters*]

Song

AMIENS Under the greenwood tree,
           Who loves to lie with me

0 SD   Oxberry describes Jaques's costume as a green, fur-trimmed doublet, pantaloons,
and cap, with buff waistcoat, boots, and gauntlets. In Macready's production, Jaques lay
stretched on a bench, near a table bearing wooden dishes, flagons, and casks (Shattuck,
Macready). Amiens's song 'Under the greenwood tree' followed line 12 in early
productions (Bell's, 1786, Kemble edns; Phelps pbk). Daly combined this scene with 2.1:
Jaques exited during Amiens's song, and Duke Senior entered shortly afterwards (pbk).
Benson sometimes put the opening song at 30, replacing 'Who doth ambition shun' (1904
pbk), and sometimes at the beginning, with the foresters entering severally (1905 pbk). In
the Sothern–Marlowe production, the song began softly as Rosalind was exiting from the
previous scene, then grew louder as Amiens and then other foresters arrived on stage.
Then pages brought on a table and Jaques entered applauding (pbk). Bridges-Adams had
Amiens discovered stirring a pot over a fire, and feeding the flames with twigs (pbk). The
scene is cut from Czinner's film. In the 1963 RSC/BBC version, Amiens sings while
accompanying himself on mandolin. Stephen Oliver composed a 'rudimentary baroque
opera' score for Nunn's production (*Times*, 9 Sept. 1977). Richard Pasco's Jaques, wearing
a worn white suit and 'glasses with cheap frames', 'smoked without evident pleasure' and
'knew that his breath smelt vile' – and 'that no one would dare tell him' (*SS* 27, 1974,
p. 149). Dishevelled and apparently drunk, Pasco's Jaques stood apart from the group,
leaning against a tree, before coming forward aggressively. In Cheek by Jowl's production,
the foresters entered calling 'Mr Jaques'. They found him seated on the stage, head bowed.
In Edzard's film, the scene precedes 1.3; Jaques, comfortable in a wool overcoat, watches
as the Duke's men collect cardboard boxes and Amiens sings. At Shakespeare's Globe,
Amiens sang as the foresters set out the picnic; Jaques came up through the yard, calling
'more' (Miller-Schütz, 'Findings'). Peter Nicholas's Jaques entered 'with a dead stag slung
over his shoulders, which he dumped on the stage and brooded over' (*SS* 54, 2001,
p. 271).

And turn his merry note
Unto the sweet bird's throat:

Come hither, come hither, come hither: 5
   Here shall he see
    No enemy
But winter and rough weather.
JAQUES More, more, I prithee more.
AMIENS It will make you melancholy, Monsieur Jaques.   10
JAQUES I thank it. More, I prithee more: I can suck melancholy out of
  a song as a weasel sucks eggs. More, I prithee more.
AMIENS My voice is ragged: I know I cannot please you.
JAQUES I do not desire you to please me, I do desire you to sing. Come,
  more, another stanzo – call you 'em 'stanzos'?   15
AMIENS What you will, Monsieur Jaques.
JAQUES Nay, I care not for their names; they owe me nothing. Will you
  sing?
AMIENS More at your request than to please myself.
JAQUES Well then, if ever I thank any man, I'll thank you; but that they   20
  call 'compliment' is like th'encounter of two dog-apes. And when a
  man thanks me heartily, methinks I have given him a penny and he
  renders me the beggarly thanks. Come, sing; and you that will not,
  hold your tongues.
AMIENS Well, I'll end the song. – Sirs, cover the while; the Duke will   25
  drink under this tree. – He hath been all this day to look you.
JAQUES And I have been all this day to avoid him: he is too disputable
  for my company: I think of as many matters as he, but I give heaven
  thanks and make no boast of them. Come, warble, come.

Song. All together here

11 After 'I thank it', Kemble inserted lines 3–6 and 13–16 from 4.1 here, with Amiens speaking
the lines assigned to Rosalind. Many nineteenth-century productions included the
interpolated material (Kean, Moore, Modjeska pbks).
12 'Come, warble, warble' (29b) replaced the second half of this line in the rearrangement
initiated in the eighteenth century (Bell's, Kemble edns).
13–51a Cut in early versions, to produce a less joking, more dignified Jaques (Bell's, 1786, Kemble
edns). Macready restored the lines, although he insisted that 'ducdame' be pronounced
'duc-ad-me' (Shattuck, *Macready*). Frequently cut or abridged in later productions.
20–3 Amiens and Jaques sit back-to-back on an industrial spool in Edzard's film.
26–9 Daly cut Jaques's criticism of the Duke.

Who doth ambition shun 30
And loves to live i'th'sun;
Seeking the food he eats
And pleased with what he gets:
Come hither, come hither, come hither:
    Here shall he see 35
     No enemy
But winter and rough weather.

JAQUES I'll give you a verse to this note that I made yesterday in despite
  of my invention.
AMIENS And I'll sing it. 40
JAQUES Thus it goes:
If it do come to pass
That any man turn ass,
Leaving his wealth and ease,
A stubborn will to please, 45

Ducdame, ducdame, ducdame:
    Here shall he see
    Gross fools as he,
And if he will come to me.
AMIENS What's that 'ducdame'? 50

30–7 While Amiens sang, Phelps had attendants bring fruit and wine to the table (pbk). In Doran's production, Amiens sang to accompanying accordion music.

41–9 Alan Howard delivered the lines 'as an attack on the banished Duke' (*New Statesman*, 23 June 1967). In Nunn's production, Amiens sang each line after it was dictated by Jaques. In keeping with 1.1.94, 'gentlemen' including Charles and Le Beau actually 'flock[ed] to' Duke Senior. One such showed up here, so that lines 44–5 'appl[ied] directly to him' (*SS* 31, 1978, p. 147). In the 1978 BBC version, Jaques performs the verse in nasty temper; after he exits, Amiens repeats the lines in a pleasanter tone. In Donnellan's production, Amiens read the written script of Jaques's song, trying out several pronunciations of the key term: 'duck dame?' 'due dame?' 'duke dame?' At Shakespeare's Globe, Jaques 'handed a paper to Amiens', who sang the third stanza (Miller-Schütz, 'Findings').

46 'Beckons lords to him' (Bridges-Adams pbk). The syllables were pronounced slowly and dramatically in Noble's production.

46–9 Toye's foresters froze during the 'ducdame' rhyme (pbk).

50–1 The foresters rise and gather in a semi-circle, then laugh and disperse at Jaques's joke (Benson 1904 pbk) – a traditional staging. Michael Bryant as Jaques made an obscene gesture to the country folk looking on; they retreated to their tent (Dexter pbk).

JAQUES 'Tis a Greek invocation to call fools into a circle. I'll go sleep if
    I can: if I cannot, I'll rail against all the first-born of Egypt.
AMIENS And I'll go seek the Duke: his banquet is prepared.

Exeunt

53   Although it does not necessitate the on stage appearance of the banquet, the line has often
      been cut in production. In the 1990 ACTER production, a loaf of bread was placed on a cloth,
      and remained visible through 2.6, although the starving Adam and Orlando were unable to
      see it (*SQ* 42, 1991, p. 218). At Shakespeare's Globe, 'the foresters who had been preparing
      the Duke's meal remained on stage, one reading, the other sleeping, both by the stage-left
      pillar', as Orlando and Adam entered through the central opening for 2.6 (Miller-Schütz,
      'Findings').
53 SD   Holloway's promptbook indicates 'table-siesta'; evidently Jaques took his nap on stage.

ACT 2, SCENE 6

Enter ORLANDO *and* ADAM

ADAM Dear master, I can go no further. O, I die for food. Here lie I
down and measure out my grave. Farewell, kind master.
ORLANDO Why, how now, Adam, no greater heart in thee? Live a little,
comfort a little, cheer thyself a little. If this uncouth forest yield
anything savage, I will either be food for it or bring it for food to   5
thee. Thy conceit is nearer death than thy powers. For my sake be
comfortable; hold death a while at the arm's end. I will here be with
thee presently, and if I bring thee not something to eat, I will give
thee leave to die; but if thou diest before I come, thou art a mocker
of my labour. Well said, thou look'st cheerly, and I'll be with thee   10
quickly. Yet thou liest in the bleak air. Come, I will bear thee to
some shelter, and thou shalt not die for lack of a dinner if there live
anything in this desert. Cheerly, good Adam.

Exeunt

Julia Arthur's promptbook indicates that music (to the tune of 'Under the greenwood
tree') should begin at the end of 2.4 (2.5 was cut) and continue throughout this scene.
Asche's promptbook indicates that the scene takes place in early morning. Czinner
cut the scene. In the 1963 RSC/BBC version, the wind roars as Orlando crawls over bare
rocks, making Adam's difficulties understandable. In the 1978 BBC version, Adam stops
suddenly, as if he suffers a heart attack or has been struck, and falls on his back among
the ferns. In Noble's production, a threatening wind blew under the silk cloth covering the
stage, so that Adam lay down in the midst of a suggested blizzard. Edzard's Orlando has
Adam sit on a piece of luggage as they cross a muddy field; Adam falls off and has to be
helped up.

7–10a Presumably considered morbid, these lines were cut in early versions (Bell's, 1786 edns).
   11 Toye's Orlando knew how to revive Adam: he pulled out a bottle and offered him a swig
(pbk).
13 SD Phelps specified that Orlando should carry Adam off in his arms (pbk). Benson's Orlando
put the staff in Adam's hand and encouraged him to stand and walk; they exited together
(1904 pbk). Orlando carried Adam on his back in Noble's production. Donnellan's Orlando
kissed Adam tenderly.

ACT 2, SCENE 7

Enter DUKE SENIOR, [AMIENS,] *and Lords like outlaws* [*who set out a banquet*]

DUKE SENIOR I think he be transformed into a beast,
        For I can nowhere find him like a man.
AMIENS My lord, he is but even now gone hence;
        Here was he merry, hearing of a song.
DUKE SENIOR If he, compact of jars, grow musical,   5
        We shall have shortly discord in the spheres.
        Go seek him; tell him I would speak with him.

Enter JAQUES

AMIENS He saves my labour by his own approach.
DUKE SENIOR Why, how now, monsieur, what a life is this
        That your poor friends must woo your company?   10
        What, you look merrily?

0 SD   The rural meal presents an opportunity to establish the degree of hardship suffered by the exiles. A boar's head, apples, bread, flagons, and drinking horns graced the well-stocked table in Modjeska's production (pbk). George Alexander's production featured 'a welcome touch of archaeological correctness . . . in the serving of the wine . . . from a pigskin' (unidentified clipping, 6 Dec. 1896, TM). The 1963 RSC/BBC version features meat roasting on a spit over the camp fire. In Papp's production, 'it was a plush kind of exile where lords lounged about in pink and white satin, drank from gold goblets, and munched grapes' (*SQ* 24, 1973, p. 423). Hirsch's exiles enjoyed a 'picnic sent over by Fortnum and Mason', so 'delectable' it was 'no wonder Orlando would have killed for it' (*SQ* 34, 1983, p. 465). A camp stove on stage evoked the meal for Cheek by Jowl. In Edzard's film, a makeshift table is cluttered with bottles; the exiles huddle round an oil-drum brazier on which one of them cooks. Jaques is handed an umbrella as rain begins to fall. Social hierarchies were firmly intact in Pimlott's production: the Duke drank from a silver goblet, with 'wooden cups for everyone' else (*SS* 50, 1997, p. 204).

1–6   Cut in Asche's production, where this scene followed 2.1 directly (pbk).

JAQUES A fool, a fool: I met a fool i'th'forest,
           A motley fool – a miserable world –
           As I do live by food, I met a fool
           Who laid him down and basked him in the sun   15
           And railed on Lady Fortune in good terms,
           In good set terms, and yet a motley fool.
           'Good morrow, fool', quoth I. 'No, sir', quoth he,
           'Call me not fool till heaven hath sent me fortune'.
           And then he drew a dial from his poke   20
           And looking on it, with lack-lustre eye,
           Says, very wisely, 'It is ten o'clock.
           Thus we may see', quoth he, 'how the world wags:
           'Tis but an hour ago since it was nine,
           And after one hour more 'twill be eleven;   25
           And so, from hour to hour, we ripe and ripe,
           And then, from hour to hour, we rot and rot,
           And thereby hangs a tale'. When I did hear
           The motley fool thus moral on the time,
           My lungs began to crow like Chanticleer   30
           That fools should be so deep-contemplative;
           And I did laugh, sans intermission,
           An hour by his dial. O noble fool,

12–28   As proof against charges of monotony, John Hill cited James Quin's performance: 'there is
         more variety in Mr Quin's speaking this, than any player we are able to remember ever gave
         his audience in barely telling a story' (p. 205). Macready 'came on the scene laughing to
         himself, evidently much diverted with his thoughts; and the interjections of mirth with which
         he broke his reply to the Duke's observation . . . had a due measure of bitterness in them;
         while during his pause between "a motley fool – a miserable world", the expression of his
         countenance gave to the passage its true significance, showing his contemptuous pity for
         humanity which could be so sharply satirized by the common jester' (Pollock, p. 135).
         Sothern's merrier Jaques gave the lines laughingly (Sothern–Marlowe pbk). Richard Pasco
         stumbled drunkenly, evidently giddy with laughter over the fool's words. Cheek by Jowl's
         Jaques was seated, wearing a bulbous red clown nose that he used as a finger puppet to
         mime the fool's words.

13   Noble's Jaques indicated 'motley' by wearing one green and one red glove.

26   In Papp's production, Frederick Coffin's 'sour, snarling Jaques' – 'part leering undertaker
         and part Mississippi riverboat gambler' – gave the line a bawdy turn: 'from whore to whore
         we rot and rot' (*SQ* 24, 1973, p. 424). Michael Bryant used the same pronunciation, and
         added an illustrative gesture, slowly raising, then lowering, and then – at line 28 – dangling
         a stick (Dexter pbk).

    O worthy fool: motley's the only wear.
DUKE SENIOR What fool is this? 35
JAQUES A worthy fool: one that hath been a courtier
    And says, 'If ladies be but young and fair,
    They have the gift to know it'; and in his brain,
    Which is as dry as the remainder biscuit
    After a voyage, he hath strange places crammed 40
    With observation, the which he vents
    In mangled forms. O that I were a fool!
    I am ambitious for a motley coat.
DUKE SENIOR Thou shalt have one.
JAQUES   It is my only suit,
    Provided that you weed your better judgements 45
    Of all opinion that grows rank in them
    That I am wise. I must have liberty
    Withal, as large a charter as the wind,
    To blow on whom I please: for so fools have.
    And they that are most gallèd with my folly, 50
    They most must laugh. And why, sir, must they so?
    The why is plain as way to parish church:
    He that a fool doth very wisely hit,
    Doth very foolishly, although he smart,
    If he seem senseless of the bob. If not, 55
    The wise man's folly is anatomised
    Even by the squand'ring glances of the fool.
    Invest me in my motley; give me leave
    To speak my mind, and I will through and through
    Cleanse the foul body of th'infected world, 60
    If they will patiently receive my medicine.

34 Kean's Jaques removed his gauntlets and handed them with his spear to an attendant before sitting at the table (pbk).

35–87a Cut in most eighteenth- and nineteenth-century productions, rendering a smaller and radically less bitter part for Jaques. The pruning supported the interpretation of Jaques as a kindly philosopher, eliminating much of his cynicism as well as the Duke's description of him as a 'libertine' (65). Kemble restored lines 35–44a but followed the cut otherwise. Macready originally marked the lines for inclusion but then changed his mind (Shattuck, *Macready*). Sothern and Marlowe cut 45–57 and 62–87, as did Asche and later Helpmann (pbks).

43 In Stein's production, Jaques's wish for a motley coat was answered by the lords 'covering him with ribbons and giving him a crown of leaves – an authentic image of the Lord of Misrule' (Patterson, p. 140).

60 Alan Howard 'clutch[ed] his cloak about his lower parts as if to hide "embossed sores" ...

DUKE SENIOR Fie on thee! I can tell what thou wouldst do.
JAQUES What, for a counter, would I do but good?
DUKE SENIOR Most mischievous foul sin in chiding sin:
       For thou thyself hast been a libertine,   65
       As sensual as the brutish sting itself,
       And all th'embossèd sores and headed evils
       That thou with licence of free foot hast caught
       Wouldst thou disgorge into the general world.
JAQUES Why, who cries out on pride   70
       That can therein tax any private party?
       Doth it not flow as hugely as the sea
       Till that the weary very means do ebb?
       What woman in the city do I name
       When that I say the city-woman bears   75
       The cost of princes on unworthy shoulders?
       Who can come in and say that I mean her,
       When such a one as she, such is her neighbour?
       Or what is he of basest function
       That says his bravery is not on my cost,   80
       Thinking that I mean him, but therein suits
       His folly to the mettle of my speech?
       There then! How then? What then? Let me see wherein
       My tongue hath wronged him. If it do him right,
       Then he hath wronged himself; if he be free,   85
       Why then my taxing like a wild goose flies
       Unclaimed of any man. But who come here?

Enter ORLANDO [*with sword drawn*]

His melancholy [was] part guilt at his own excesses' (*SS* 22, 1969, p. 140). Derek Godfrey was described as a 'bisexual hysteric,' threatening to cleanse the world 'by chucking a beer barrel at it' (*Guardian*, 5 Apr. 1980).

65   In Coleman's version, the Duke rises and approaches Jaques authoritatively, forcing him to become more sombre. Donnellan's Duke pretended to wash Jaques's mouth with soap, then marched him around the stage before throwing him to the floor.

70–87   Alan Rickman found these lines 'notoriously difficult': 'it wasn't until I put all its disjointedness and seeming non-sequiturs into the mouth of a wounded and trapped animal that the speech had any real focus' (Rickman, p. 77).

87   In Lester Wallack's promptbook, 'Duke – blesses – repast' before Orlando enters (cited in Sprague, p. 35).

87 SD   Moore indicates that an energetic Orlando should force his way through 'vampire bushes

ORLANDO Forbear, and eat no more!

JAQUES Why, I have eat none yet.

ORLANDO Nor shalt not, till necessity be served.   90

JAQUES Of what kind should this cock come of?

DUKE SENIOR Art thou thus boldened, man, by thy distress,
        Or else a rude despiser of good manners
        That in civility thou seem'st so empty?

ORLANDO You touched my vein at first: the thorny point   95
        Of bare distress hath ta'en from me the show
        Of smooth civility; yet am I inland bred
        And know some nurture. But forbear, I say;
        He dies that touches any of this fruit
        Till I and my affairs are answerèd.   100

JAQUES And you will not be answerèd with reason, I must die.

DUKE SENIOR What would you have? Your gentleness shall force
        More than your force move us to gentleness.

ORLANDO I almost die for food, and let me have it.

on top of bluff' and jump down near the table (pbk). In Modjeska's production, the alert foresters drew their spears upon his entrance and remained locked in position until Amiens gave a signal to lower the weapons (pbk). Jones had Orlando take one of the foresters hostage, threatening him with a knife at his throat (pbk). Noble's production had a 'truly astonishing moment when Orlando leapt upon Duke Senior's woodland dining-table . . . Jaques's response was not a comic aside but a piece of calm bravado. In entire silence he walked steadily from downstage to the table and, on "An you will not be answer'd with reason, I must die", picked up an apple and bit it' (*SS* 39, 1986, p. 202).

92 Daly's Duke rose to his feet, and his men did likewise (pbk). Benson's foresters presented their spears and the bowmen their arrows; the Duke restrained them with a gesture (1904 pbk).

98 Orlando's 'forbear' was evidently directed at Jaques, who was 'about to eat', in Kean's production (pbk).

101 Jaques's aggressive (or self-sacrificing) line has sometimes been cut (1786 edn, Kean, Modjeska, Sothern–Marlowe pbks). More often, he eats an apple here (Asche, Arthur pbks). A critic objected: 'why should he say "I have eat none yet" when he has, as a matter of fact, been talking with his mouth full for the past five minutes?' (W.A., unidentified clipping, TM). In defiance of Orlando's knife, Jaques consumed a grape in Toye's production (pbk), illustrating the apparent pun on 'reason'; likewise, Pasco mockingly eats a raisin in Coleman's production.

DUKE SENIOR Sit down and feed, and welcome to our table.   105
ORLANDO Speak you so gently? Pardon me, I pray you:
    I thought that all things had been savage here
    And therefore put I on the countenance
    Of stern commandment. But whate'er you are
    That in this desert inaccessible,   110
    Under the shade of melancholy boughs,
    Lose and neglect the creeping hours of time –
    If ever you have looked on better days,
    If ever been where bells have knolled to church,
    If ever sat at any goodman's feast,   115
    If ever from your eyelids wiped a tear,
    And know what 'tis to pity and be pitied,
    Let gentleness my strong enforcement be,
    In the which hope, I blush, and hide my sword.
DUKE SENIOR True is it that we have seen better days,   120
    And have with holy bell been knolled to church,
    And sat at goodmen's feasts, and wiped our eyes
    Of drops that sacred pity hath engendered:
    And therefore sit you down in gentleness
    And take upon command what help we have   125
    That to your wanting may be ministered.
ORLANDO Then but forbear your food a little while
    Whiles, like a doe, I go to find my fawn
    And give it food: there is an old poor man
    Who after me hath many a weary step   130
    Limped in pure love. Till he be first sufficed,
    Oppressed with two weak evils, age and hunger,
    I will not touch a bit.
DUKE SENIOR   Go find him out,
    And we will nothing waste till you return.

106   Henry Ainley's Orlando spoke the lines from 'the centre of the stage, within arm's-length of
    the Duke whom he is addressing', rather than bursting more appropriately through the
    bushes (W. A., unidentified clipping, TM).

122–3 Mr Harcourt, playing the Duke at the Queen's Theatre, 'felt constrained to weep, and wipe
    his eye of the identical drops he described'. A critic fulminated: 'How long will it be ere like
    puerilities cease to affront the intelligent spectator, and drive him from the theatre?'
    (*Athenaeum*, 4 Mar. 1871).

126   Donnellan's Duke embraced Orlando.

ORLANDO I thank ye, and be blest for your good comfort. [*Exit*] 135
DUKE SENIOR Thou see'st we are not all alone unhappy:
This wide and universal theatre
Presents more woeful pageants than the scene
Wherein we play in.
JAQUES All the world's a stage
And all the men and women merely players: 140
They have their exits and their entrances
And one man in his time plays many parts,
His acts being seven ages. At first the infant,
Mewling and puking in the nurse's arms;
Then the whining schoolboy with his satchel 145
And shining morning face, creeping like snail
Unwillingly to school; and then the lover,
Sighing like furnace, with a woeful ballad

135 SD Benson directed that Orlando shake hands with the Duke before exiting to fetch Adam (1904 pbk). Arthur's promptbook indicates that the Duke briefly follows Orlando who exits calling out 'Adam! Adam!'

139–66 John Hill on James Quin: 'Whoever remembers his speaking this, remembers one of the greatest things ever executed upon the stage: the masterly manner in which he throws off the measure in these lines has no small merit; but the inimitable beauty with which he delivers the several parts is such as one would think must have sham'd every body out of the charge of monotony against him, and establish'd him as the standard of true and rational variety' (p. 206). The speech was a famous set piece in the nineteenth century, familiar to viewers because frequently anthologised, and typically delivered as an oration intended to edify an appreciative on stage audience. In Macready's production, Jaques stood stage left and spoke with 'spontaneous ease', as if 'giving utterance to thought suggested at the instant by the foregoing remark of the Duke' (Shattuck, *Macready*; *Spectator*, 8 Oct. 1842). At Drury Lane in 1865, Mr Anderson's Jaques spoke without humour or sadness, prompting a reviewer to ask 'was it contempt which made Jaques, in addressing the Duke, look persistently at the pit? Was it his melancholy, or his humour, which made him deliver the celebrated speech of the Seven Ages as if he were repeating a lesson he had learned, and not as if the vivid images were spontaneously rising in his teeming brain?' (*Pall Mall Gazette*, 10 Mar. 1865). Hermann Vezin, considered by many the great Jaques of the era, was praised for a delivery in which 'every line uttered gives evidence of thought . . . That he would desist from any attempt to *act* the personages indicated in the speech was only to be expected from an artist to whom everything like stage-tricks is instinctively abhorrent. But he goes to the height of forgetting his hearers altogether. Sitting at a table with his back

Made to his mistress' eyebrow; then a soldier,
Full of strange oaths and bearded like the pard,   150
Jealous in honour, sudden, and quick in quarrel,
Seeking the bubble 'reputation'
Even in the cannon's mouth; and then the justice,
In fair round belly with good capon lined,
With eyes severe and beard of formal cut,   155

towards them, he reflectively pursues his series of descriptions as if quite alone, all the other persons being reduced to the condition of unobserved listeners' (*Times*, 27 Feb. 1875). Despite the weight of expectation attached to it, Vezin downplayed the speech which was for him 'but an instance that Jacques, like Signior Benedick', 'will always be talking' (*Academy*, 6 Mar. 1880). Disgusted with the speech, Shaw wondered 'how anybody over the age of seven can take any interest in a literary toy so silly in its conceit and common in its ideas' (vol. 2, p. 268). Oscar Asche took up an apple before beginning the speech and munched it throughout (pbk); he pointed the 'pantaloon' lines of the speech at 1 Lord (W.A., unidentified clipping, TM). In Playfair's production, Herbert Marshall 'finished off' the speech with a shudder (Crosse, p. 155). A contemplative Leon Quartermaine munches the traditional apple in Czinner's film; as he finishes speaking, the Duke lays a comforting hand upon his shoulder.

Later in the twentieth century Jaques often delivered the speech more bitterly. Richard Pasco was wry, wandering, and misanthropic, setting viewers to 'wondering about Jaques's past' (*Daily Telegraph*, 13 June 1973). In the 1978 BBC version, Pasco begins the speech abruptly, interrupting the Duke and provoking surprised stares from his men. In Stein's production, the speech became 'a familiar piece of folk wisdom': 'Encouraged by the lords to perform his "party piece", Jaques moved to a raised piece of greenward and, striking a series of rhetorical poses, delivered the speech in its English original, to the delighted applause of the Duke's entourage' (Patterson, pp. 140–1). Alan Rickman acted out each of the seven ages so melodramatically that the courtiers slowly drew away from him. Clifford Rose, doubling the parts of Jaques and Adam in ACTER's 1991 production, concluded the speech by 'transform[ing] himself into Adam on cue, himself becoming the "last scene of all" in his own speech' (Mazer, '*As You Like It*,' p. 23). Joe Dixon in Cheek by Jowl spoke the lines directly to the Duke, as part of their running colloquy on virtue and attitude. He pointed out examples of some of the stages, smoking a cigarette as he spoke. At Shakespeare's Globe, John McEnery's Jaques 'disguised the undue familiarity of the line as he launched into "All the world's a stage" by tossing an apple among the groundlings' (*SS* 52, 1999, p. 223).

Full of wise saws and modern instances –
And so he plays his part; the sixth age shifts
Into the lean and slippered pantaloon,
With spectacles on nose and pouch on side,
His youthful hose well saved – a world too wide   160
For his shrunk shank – and his big manly voice,
Turning again toward childish treble, pipes
And whistles in his sound; last scene of all
That ends this strange eventful history
Is second childishness and mere oblivion,   165
Sans teeth, sans eyes, sans taste, sans everything.

      Enter ORLANDO *with* ADAM [*on his back*]

DUKE SENIOR Welcome. Set down your venerable burden,
    And let him feed.
ORLANDO   I thank you most for him.
ADAM So had you need: I scarce can speak
    To thank you for myself.   170
DUKE SENIOR Welcome; fall to: I will not trouble you
    As yet to question you about your fortunes. –
    Give us some music, and, good cousin, sing.

162   At this point in Edzard's film, Orlando and Adam enter the picture. The Duke's greeting and
     offers of assistance overlap the end of Jaques's speech.

166   In Cheek by Jowl, Jaques poked his fingers into the Duke's chest.

166 SD In 1774 Edward Capell reported 'a traditional story' from an old man in Stratford 'that he saw
     him once brought on the stage upon another man's back', taken to indicate Shakespeare's
     performance as Adam (Chambers, *William Shakespeare*, vol. 2, p. 289). In *Love in a Forest*,
     Orlando promises Adam to 'bear thee to some Shelter' but returns 'leading Adam' rather
     than carrying him. Asche's Adam entered with an arm slung around Orlando's neck.
     Jaques gave up his seat for the old man, who was promptly served soup by the Page (pbk).
     One of the foresters feeds Adam bits of bread in the 1963 RSC/BBC version. Orlando
     carried Adam in Williams's production (pbk). Likewise, Cheek by Jowl's Orlando carried in
     the wheezing Adam; then the foresters gathered around the old man and fed and sang to
     him.

168   Jones had Adam placed in the Duke's chair (pbk). Goodbody had Jaques wrap a rug around
     the old man (pbk).

Song

AMIENS Blow, blow, thou winter wind,
                Thou art not so unkind   175
                As man's ingratitude;
                Thy tooth is not so keen,
                Because thou art not seen,
                Although thy breath be rude.
                        Hey-ho, sing hey-ho   180
                        Unto the green holly,
                        Most friendship is feigning,
                        Most loving mere folly.
                        The hey-ho, the holly,
                        This life is most jolly.   185

                Freeze, freeze, thou bitter sky,
                That dost not bite so nigh
                As benefits forgot;
                Though thou the waters warp,
                Thy sting is not so sharp   190
                As friend remembered not.
                        Hey-ho, sing hey-ho
                        Unto the green holly,
                        Most friendship is feigning,
                        Most loving mere folly.   195
                        The hey-ho, the holly,
                        This life is most jolly.
DUKE SENIOR If that you were the good Sir Roland's son,
                As you have whispered faithfully you were,
                And as mine eye doth his effigies witness   200

174–97   During the song's choruses, the lords at the table 'act[ed] with their drinking horns as
          though participating' (Phelps pbk). Sothern and Marlowe had a curtain on the scene
          after the song's first verse; the second was presented as an encore (pbk). In Asche's
          food-oriented presentation of the scene, the shepherds wiped their pipes and ate rolls
          after the song (pbk). In Dexter's anthropological production, the foresters collected
          holly branches during the song, then lined up to give a chorus accompanied by sweeping
          gestures (pbk).
198–207   Cut by Daly and Sothern–Marlowe (pbks).

Most truly limned and living in your face,
Be truly welcome hither. I am the Duke
That loved your father. The residue of your fortune
Go to my cave and tell me. – Good old man,
Thou art right welcome as thy master is. –   205
[*To Orlando*] Support him by the arm. [*To Ada*m] Give me
    your hand,
And let me all your fortunes understand.

                                                          Exeunt

203   Peter McEnery as Orlando halted, swung about for a closer look, and then fell to his knee
       (*Financial Times*, 9 Sept. 1977).
205   In the 1978 BBC version, Jaques exits here, laughing bitterly, after drinking alone and
       watching in disgust while Adam was cared for.
206   Charles Dickens complained of the production at the Comédie Française, which used
       George Sand's translation: 'Nobody has anything to do but sit upon as many grey stones as
       he can. When Jacques had sat upon seventy-seven stones and forty-two roots of trees
       (which was at the end of the second act) we came away' (letter of 22 Apr. 1856, quoted in
       Edgar Johnson, vol. 2, p. 860). Victorian productions typically ended the second act with a
       warm show of emotion. In Benson's production, the Duke took Adam's hand to help him
       rise; the curtain came down as Orlando took Adam's other hand (1904 pbk). Adam was
       given a goblet in Toye's production, and the scene ended with the second verse of 'Blow,
       blow, thou winter wind', everyone on stage joining in the chorus (pbk). Adam was a realistic
       peasant who 'shook with loyal amazement when . . . he realized that it was his monarch
       who was embracing him' at the end of the scene in Hytner's production (*SS* 40, 1987, p. 174).
          Twentieth-century productions sometimes took a darker turn. Adam died at the climax of
       the wintry banquet scene in the Oregon Shakespeare Festival production in 1986 (*SQ* 38,
       1987, p. 91). Pimlott also had Adam expire in the wintry weather, despite the courtiers' efforts
       to revive him; in the second half of the show, a mound with sprouting daffodils seemed to
       mark his resting place (*SQ* 48, 1997, p. 209; *SS* 50, 1997, p. 204). In Hands's production, the
       'lights faded' for the interval on the 'lonely seated figure' of Jaques (*SS* 34, 1981, p. 149).

ACT 3, SCENE I

Enter DUKE [FREDERICK], *Lords, and* OLIVER

DUKE FREDERICK 'Not see him since'? Sir, sir, that cannot be!
But were I not the better part made mercy,
I should not seek an absent argument
Of my revenge, thou present. But look to it:
Find out thy brother, wheresoe'er he is;   5
Seek him with candle; bring him dead or living
Within this twelvemonth, or turn thou no more
To seek a living in our territory.
Thy lands and all things that thou dost call thine
Worth seizure, do we seize into our hands   10
Till thou canst quit thee by thy brother's mouth
Of what we think against thee.
OLIVER O that your highness knew my heart in this:
I never loved my brother in my life.

The scene has often been cut, because it interrupts the pastoral mood with a nagging
reminder of court unpleasantness. Benson moved it back to follow 2.1, where it replaced 2.2,
and sometimes omitted it altogether (1904 pbk).

0 SD   Duke Frederick paced about through the scene in Macready's production; Oliver was
guarded by attendants (pbk). In the twentieth century, Frederick became more violent.
Elliott opened the scene with Oliver being flung to center stage; he lay prostrate until the
Lords dragged him out at 15 (pbk). In the 1963 RSC/BBC version, Frederick repeatedly
strikes a sweating, bleeding Oliver. A final closeup shot shows a guilty Frederick grimacing
in spiritual agony, a preparation for his eventual conversion. Monette had Oliver 'dragged
out of bed with a mistress who remained onstage for the entire scene' (*SQ* 42, 1991, p. 215).
Donnellan's Oliver was blindfolded. In Pimlott's production, 'Duke Frederick, tetchy,
goggle-eyed, and highly neurotic from the start', had entered 'the last stages of
psychopathic dementia', and was 'having Oliver drowned in a little tin bath as he
interrogated him about his brother' (*SS* 50, 1997, p. 204).

DUKE FREDERICK More villain thou. [*To Lords*] Well, push him out
    of doors   15
  And let my officers of such a nature
  Make an extent upon his house and lands.
  Do this expediently and turn him going.
                      Exeunt [*severally*]

ACT 3, SCENE 2

Enter ORLANDO [*with a paper*]

ORLANDO Hang there, my verse, in witness of my love;
        And thou, thrice-crownèd queen of night, survey
        With thy chaste eye, from thy pale sphere above,
        Thy huntress' name that my full life doth sway.
        O Rosalind, these trees shall be my books,   5
        And in their barks my thoughts I'll character
        That every eye which in this forest looks
        Shall see thy virtue witnessed everywhere.
        Run, run, Orlando, carve on every tree
        The fair, the chaste, and unexpressive she.   *Exit*   10

Macready opened the scene with Sylvius, playing a pipe while seated on a bank; he exited without speaking (Shattuck, *Macready*). Moore's promptbook calls for a 'distant waterfall' on the scenic backdrop. Daly set the scene in 'a clearing in the forest', with lighting to indicate 'morning' (pbk). The 1963 RSC/BBC version used recorded night sounds of crickets and frogs; the previously barren forest had now sprouted leaves and vegetation. The second half of Dexter's production opened with several groups spreading green cloths over the bare stage, before a slender tree with white blossoms rose through the trap door (pbk; *SS* 33, 1980, p. 179). In Noble's production, the white silk cloth was drawn up to form a high canopy. 'Green furniture' maintained 'the original notion of familiar things subtly altered. But a grassy stage-cloth and a large pool of water took us, inevitably, back to the conventionally pastoral image of a context in which the self could be transformed' (*SS* 39, 1986, p. 200). In Czinner's film, Orlando hangs poster-size scrolls on the trees; Jaques wanders on, carrying a bunch of wildflowers, and reads the verses. In the 1978 BBC version, Orlando embraces the trees as he attaches poems to them. Edzard's Orlando spray-paints the poems as graffiti on the quay. Caird had Orlando '[offer] his poems to members of the front row audience' (*SQ* 41, 1989–90, p. 493). Cheek by Jowl's production saw long strips of green paper descend from above, as Orlando, who had been seated on the fore-stage writing verses throughout the previous scene, rose and spoke. Several foresters played musical instruments to add to the festive effect.

10   The 'spring sounds and the bird trills' were interrupted by a 'mischievous "Cuckoo!"' sounding after Orlando's declaration of love in Glen Byam Shaw's 1957 production (*SQ* 8, 1957, p. 479).

ACT 3, SCENE 3

Enter CORIN *and* TOUCHSTONE

CORIN And how like you this shepherd's life, Master Touchstone?

TOUCHSTONE Truly, shepherd, in respect of itself, it is a good life; but
in respect that it is a shepherd's life, it is naught. In respect that it
is solitary, I like it very well; but in respect that it is private, it is a
very vile life. Now in respect it is in the fields, it pleaseth me well; 5
but in respect it is not in the court, it is tedious. As it is a spare life,
look you, it fits my humour well; but as there is no more plenty in

Lady Pollock describes walking through a country meadow with Macready when 'a flock of
startled sheep scrambled over the hedge . . . and the leader's bell tinkling with its delicate
tender tone pleasantly broke the silence. "Listen to that sound", said Macready; "isn't it
delicious? I introduced it in 'As You Like It'"' (Pollock, p. 20). Many later productions
included tinkling sheep bells in this scene. For the 1978 BBC filming at Glamis Castle,
'they had to construct a shepherd's cottage (twice, since cows ate the first one)'
(Willis, p. 190).

0 SD Corin nearly stumbles over Touchstone, napping on the ground, in the 1963 RSC/BBC
version. Touchstone claims the lunch Corin draws from his satchel (Jones pbk). Coleman
has Corin busily tying up sheep skins; Touchstone steps in sheep dung as he approaches.
The effect was funnier because more obviously imaginary when Noble's Touchstone
entered with his extended umbrella and suffered the indignity of soiling his shoe with sheep
droppings. Touchstone arrived with 'a lit, two-candle candelabra and a picnic basket' in a
production by the Grove Repertory Company; 'it was immediately obvious that both men
had been drinking, and the "discussion" ended in a draw' (SQ 33, 1982, p. 389). Ciulei had
Touchstone 'applying white-face to himself' and later to Corin (SQ 34, 1983, p. 232).

1–64 Cut in Czinner's film.

2–9 John Hill's diagnosis of eighteenth-century performances: 'With all the intrinsick merit of this
speech, with all its true humour, it at the utmost only draws from us an indolent smile upon
the stage: And why? because the player who acts the part wants that address [of mimicry]
which we have been recommending . . . It is spoke in a sort of unmeaning, yet affected
tone, and is truly a fool's speech, as we hear it. We will not name any person upon this
occasion, speaking these kind of nothings, with all the solemnity of a philosopher' (p. 274).

it, it goes much against my stomach. Hast any philosophy in thee, shepherd?

CORIN   No more but that I know the more one sickens, the worse at ease 10
he is; and that he that wants money, means, and content is without
three good friends; that the property of rain is to wet and fire to
burn; that good pasture makes fat sheep; and that a great cause of
the night is lack of the sun; that he that hath learned no wit by
nature nor art may complain of good breeding, or comes of a very 15
dull kindred.

TOUCHSTONE   Such a one is a natural philosopher. – Wast ever in court, shepherd?

CORIN   No, truly.

TOUCHSTONE   Then thou art damned. 20

CORIN   Nay, I hope.

TOUCHSTONE   Truly thou art damned: like an ill-roasted egg, all on one side.

CORIN   For not being at court? Your reason.

TOUCHSTONE   Why, if thou never wast at court, thou never saw'st good 25
manners; if thou never saw'st good manners, then thy manners
must be wicked, and wickedness is sin, and sin is damnation. Thou
art in a parlous state, shepherd.

CORIN   Not a whit, Touchstone: those that are good manners at the
court are as ridiculous in the country as the behaviour of the coun- 30
try is most mockable at the court. You told me you salute not at the
court but you kiss your hands: that courtesy would be uncleanly if
courtiers were shepherds.

TOUCHSTONE   Instance, briefly; come, instance.

CORIN   Why, we are still handling our ewes, and their fells, you know, 35
are greasy.

TOUCHSTONE   Why, do not your courtier's hands sweat, and is not the
grease of a mutton as wholesome as the sweat of a man? Shallow,
shallow! A better instance, I say – come.

CORIN   Besides, our hands are hard. 40

TOUCHSTONE   Your lips will feel them the sooner. Shallow again: a
more sounder instance, come.

10–16   In Cheek by Jowl's production, Corin's 'thoughts come so slowly it's like listening to a
partially blind person reading out an optician's chart' (*Independent*, 6 Dec. 1991).

16   Touchstone patronisingly pats Corin on the head (Moore pbk).

19–62   These tedious and/or indecorous lines were cut in Macklin's partbook; more often, the cut
begins at the middle of 31 (Bell's, 1786 edns). Kemble restored 19 to 28 and cut the rest;
likewise others up to Daly and Sothern–Marlowe (pbks).

CORIN And they are often tarred over with the surgery of our sheep, and would you have us kiss tar? The courtiers' hands are perfumed with civet.   45

TOUCHSTONE Most shallow man! Thou worms' meat in respect of a good piece of flesh, indeed! Learn of the wise and perpend: civet is of a baser birth than tar, the very uncleanly flux of a cat. Mend the instance, shepherd.

CORIN You have too courtly a wit for me; I'll rest.   50

TOUCHSTONE Wilt thou rest damned? God help thee, shallow man. God make incision in thee, thou art raw.

CORIN Sir, I am a true labourer: I earn that I eat, get that I wear, owe no man hate, envy no man's happiness, glad of other men's good, content with my harm; and the greatest of my pride is to see my   55
ewes graze and my lambs suck.

TOUCHSTONE That is another simple sin in you: to bring the ewes and the rams together and to offer to get your living by the copulation of cattle; to be bawd to a bell-wether and to betray a she-lamb of a twelvemonth to a crooked-pated old cuckoldly ram out of all rea-   60
sonable match. If thou be'st not damned for this, the devil himself will have no shepherds. I cannot see else how thou shouldst 'scape.

CORIN Here comes young Monsieur Ganymede, my new mistress's brother.

Enter ROSALIND [*as* GANYMEDE]

ROSALIND [*Reading from a paper*]
  'From the East to Western Inde   65
   No jewel is like Rosalind;
  Her worth, being mounted on the wind,
  Through all the world bears Rosalind;

43 Corin makes a castrating gesture with his knife; Touchstone swallows fearfully (Dexter pbk).

53–6 In Pimlott's production, Corin 'wins the battle', remaining 'splendidly stolid and unflappable, arching the occasional eyebrow at Touchstone's excesses' (Tennant, p. 39).

56 Modjeska cut the last part of this line, evidently to avoid the indecorous 'suck' (pbk).

57–62 Francis Gentleman lamented this speech as 'would-be wit, and real indecency: it should be banished the stage', although apparently it was not in the eighteenth century (Bell's edn). Later, directors from Macready to Holloway cut all or part of the passage. Corin releases sheep from a pen in the 1978 BBC version; Touchstone is repulsed.

58–9 Williams had Touchstone blow a whistle at 'copulation of cattle' (pbk).

62 The clown's red nose appeared on Corin here in Cheek by Jowl. Edzard's Corin bleats at Touchstone.

64 SD Mary Anderson entered singing the 'Cuckoo song', conventionally sung by Rosalinds to

All the pictures fairest lined
   Are but black to Rosalind;   70
Let no face be kept in mind
   But the fair of Rosalind.'
TOUCHSTONE I'll rhyme you so eight years together, dinners and sup-
    pers and sleeping-hours excepted. It is the right butter-women's
    rank to market.   75
ROSALIND Out, fool!
TOUCHSTONE For a taste:
If a hart do lack a hind,
   Let him seek out Rosalind;
If the cat will after kind,   80
   So be sure will Rosalind;
Wintered garments must be lined,
   So must slender Rosalind;

tease Orlando in Act 4 but maligned by some critics as vulgar. Anderson 'came on to the stage singing it in an aimless and indifferent mood, her mind being apparently occupied by other thoughts' (*Birmingham Daily Post*, n.d., SCL). Ada Rehan 'dashed through the trees of Arden, snatching the verses of Orlando from their boughs, and cast herself at the foot of a great elm, to read those fond messages' with trembling hands (Winter, *Shadows of the Stage*, Second Series, 1898, p. 251, cited in Sprague, p. 35). Constance Benson entered reading, saw the paper attached to a tree, and dropped one paper to grab the other (Benson 1904 pbk). Vanessa Redgrave drew from her shirt the poem she had previously found. Janet Suzman's Rosalind 'almost tucks Orlando's poem into her bosom before remembering that she's supposed to be a boy and stuffs it into her pocket' (*Financial Times*, 22 May 1968). Edzard's Emma Croft reads the poems painted on the walls. Victoria Hamilton 'could barely reach Orlando's poems off the trees' (*SS* 54, 2001, p. 268).

65–90   There is often considerable jostling as Rosalind, Celia, and Touchstone grab the poems from one another.

72   Benson's production followed Walker's emendation, substituting 'face' for 'fair' (1904 pbk).

75   For clarity and decorum, 'fate' was substituted for 'rank' (Macready pbk).

77–89   Touchstone's song was too bawdy for the eighteenth- and nineteenth-century stages; from Kemble to Daly, lines 82–3 and 88–9 were virtually always cut. Nineteenth-century productions introduced a nonsense rhyme to conclude the verse: 'ti tum ti tum ti tum tind, ti tum ti tum Rosalind' (Moore, Daly pbks). Benson replaced 89 with this interpolation but otherwise allowed Touchstone's parody (1904 pbk). Elliott and Jones cut the 'prick' rhyme (pbk). In the 1978 BBC version, Rosalind turns her back on Touchstone, but the camera catches her giggles.

> They that reap must sheaf and bind,
>> Then to cart with Rosalind; 85
> Sweetest nut hath sourest rind,
>> Such a nut is Rosalind;
> He that sweetest rose will find,
>> Must find love's prick – and Rosalind.
> This is the very false gallop of verses: why do you infect yourself 90
> with them?

ROSALIND Peace, you dull fool. I found them on a tree.

TOUCHSTONE Truly, the tree yields bad fruit.

ROSALIND I'll graft it with you, and then I shall graft it with a medlar;
then it will be the earliest fruit i'th'country, for you'll be rotten ere 95
you be half ripe, and that's the right virtue of the medlar.

TOUCHSTONE You have said – but whether wisely or no, let the forest
judge.

Enter CELIA [*as* ALIENA] *with a writing*

ROSALIND Peace, here comes my sister, reading. Stand aside.

CELIA 'Why should this a desert be? 100
>> For it is unpeopled? No:
> Tongues I'll hang on every tree,
>> That shall civil sayings show:
> Some how brief the life of man
>> Runs his erring pilgrimage 105
> That the stretching of a span
>> Buckles in his sum of age;
> Some of violated vows
>> 'Twixt the souls of friend and friend;
> But upon the fairest boughs 110
>> Or at every sentence end
> Will I "Rosalinda" write,
>> Teaching all that read to know

---

87   Noble's Touchstone grabbed the paper, balled it up, and threw it, prompting Rosalind to
retrieve the cherished item; in the course of doing so, she knocked Touchstone into the
stream.

89   In Czinner's film, Rosalind swats at Touchstone with the rolled-up scroll.

94–8 Frequently cut as obscure from Kemble to Daly.

98 SD In Coleman's version, Rosalind, Corin, and Touchstone hide in the branches of a tree as
Celia approaches.

100–29 Portions of the poem have frequently been cut. Edzard cut the entire passage.

The quintessence of every sprite
   Heaven would in little show.   115
Therefore Heaven Nature charged
   That one body should be filled
With all graces wide-enlarged;
   Nature presently distilled
Helen's cheek but not her heart,   120
   Cleopatra's majesty,
Atalanta's better part,
   Sad Lucretia's modesty.
Thus Rosalind of many parts
   By heavenly synod was devised,   125
Of many faces, eyes, and hearts,
   To have the touches dearest prized.
Heaven would that she these gifts should have,
   And I to live and die her slave.'

ROSALIND [*Coming forward*] O most gentle Jupiter, what tedious   130
homily of love have you wearied your parishioners withal, and never
cried, 'Have patience, good people!'

CELIA How now? Backfriends! – Shepherd, go off a little. – Go with
him, sirrah.

TOUCHSTONE Come, shepherd, let us make an honourable retreat,   135
though not with bag and baggage, yet with scrip and scrippage.
Exeunt Touchstone and Corin

CELIA Didst thou hear these verses?

ROSALIND O yes, I heard them all, and more too, for some of them had
in them more feet than the verses would bear.

129   Ada Rehan as Rosalind advanced while Celia read the verses; they read the last three
words of this line in unison (Daly pbk). In Julia Arthur's production, Rosalind and Touchstone
read the last line together, then laughed (pbk). Asche had Rosalind snatch the verses from
Celia, who grabbed them back, only to have Touchstone snatch them from her (pbk). Fiona
Shaw's Celia read 'slav' with a short vowel sound; Juliet Stevenson's Rosalind corrected
her.

130   Modjeska and Jones used Spedding's emendation of 'Pulpiter' for 'Jupiter' (pbks).

134   When Corin is ordered off, Touchstone waves his hand to dismiss him – then is himself
dismissed (Moore pbk). In Daly's production, Touchstone was ordered off after peering
over Celia's shoulder and reading in dumbshow; as he exited, he continued to mime the act
of reading (pbk). In Cheek by Jowl's production, the joke was Corin's crush on Celia; here
he brought her a flower.

137–210   Edzard moves this scene inside the hut where Celia and Rosalind camp out. Celia boils eggs,
this simple fare contrasting with the opulent party foods at court.

CELIA That's no matter: the feet might bear the verses. 140
ROSALIND Aye, but the feet were lame and could not bear themselves
without the verse, and therefore stood lamely in the verse.
CELIA But didst thou hear without wondering how thy name should be
hanged and carved upon these trees?
ROSALIND I was seven of the nine days out of the wonder before you 145
came, for look here what I found on a palm-tree. I was never so
berhymed since Pythagoras' time that I was an Irish rat – which I
can hardly remember.
CELIA Trow you who hath done this?
ROSALIND Is it a man? 150
CELIA And a chain that you once wore about his neck? Change you
colour?
ROSALIND I prithee, who?
CELIA O Lord, Lord, it is a hard matter for friends to meet, but moun-
tains may be removed with earthquakes and so encounter. 155
ROSALIND Nay, but who is it?
CELIA Is it possible?
ROSALIND Nay, I prithee now, with most petitionary vehemence, tell
me who it is.
CELIA O wonderful, wonderful, and most wonderful wonderful, and yet 160
again wonderful, and after that out of all hooping.
ROSALIND Good my complexion, dost thou think, though I am
caparisoned like a man, I have a doublet and hose in my disposition?
One inch of delay more is a South Sea of discovery. I prithee tell me
who is it – quickly, and speak apace. I would thou couldst stammer 165
that thou might'st pour this concealed man out of thy mouth as
wine comes out of a narrow-mouthed bottle: either too much at
once or none at all. I prithee take the cork out of thy mouth that I
may drink thy tidings.

140–2 Sometimes cut as tedious or obscure.

150 In Cheek by Jowl's production, Rosalind spat with the word 'man', in keeping with her and
Celia's custom.

151 Stein's production: 'Particularly memorable was the delighted mockery of Celia as she
adorned Rosalind with sheet after sheet of love-poems or laughed with unconcealed delight
before the line: "Change you colour?"' (Patterson, p. 142).

159 Rosalind puts her arm around Celia's neck, 'almost stuttering with eagerness' (Moore pbk).

165–8 Cut as taxing or suggestive in many productions. In Noble's production, Juliet Stevenson
chased Fiona Shaw about the stage, then hit her with a cushion.

168–9 Hannah Pritchard received little audience response to her performance in 1740 until she
spoke these lines, but her spirited delivery excited those present and 'Every speech after
this, convinc'd us more and more, that we had been long in possession of a jewel that we

CELIA So you may put a man in your belly.   170
ROSALIND Is he of God's making? What manner of man? Is his head
    worth a hat or his chin worth a beard?
CELIA Nay, he hath but a little beard.
ROSALIND Why, God will send more if the man will be thankful. Let
    me stay the growth of his beard, if thou delay me not the knowledge   175
    of his chin.
CELIA It is young Orlando, that tripped up the wrestler's heels and your
    heart both in an instant.
ROSALIND Nay, but the devil take mocking! Speak sad brow and true
    maid.   180
CELIA I'faith, coz, 'tis he.
ROSALIND Orlando?
CELIA Orlando.
ROSALIND Alas the day, what shall I do with my doublet and hose?

had scandously neglected; till toward the end of the play, her raillery to her lover, who
pretended to be dying for her, shew'd us fully what she was' (Hill, p. 113). The line was often
cut in nineteenth-century editions and performances.

170–2   Considering that eighteenth-century actresses often played Rosalind while visibly pregnant,
        the scrupulous cutting of these suggestive lines is understandable (Bell's, Kemble edns).
        Daly cut up to 171a (pbk).

183   In Edzard's film, Emma Croft jumps up and down childishly, repeating 'Orlando!'

184   Mrs Kendal covered her face with her hands and 'half whispered' the line in Celia's ear
        (*Dramatic Review*, 1 Feb. 1885, cited in Sprague, p. 36). Emphasising their embarrassment
        at being caught in boys' clothing, nineteenth-century actresses called attention to their
        bodies with elaborate displays of modesty. A critic wrote that Adelaide Neilson's 'boyish
        assumption lacks delicacy . . . here are touches – for instance, that in which she endeavours
        to arrange her drapery into something like the form of a skirt – that smack too much of the
        burlesque lady of the French stage' (unidentified clipping, TM). When Mary Anderson
        appeared at Stratford, 'it was the prospect of seeing the new Rosalind's nether limbs that
        was responsible for the excited rush for seats' (*Bat*, 1 Sept. 1885). Anderson obliged with
        'little tricks' such as pulling her cloak about her legs: 'the device is well enough when in the
        first timidity of Orlando's presence in the forest her maiden modesty is shocked at the
        thought of being seen by him in her boy's clothes; but, being constantly repeated, it
        becomes wearisome, and invests the character with an unnecessary suggestion of prudery'
        (*Birmingham Daily Post*, 31 Aug. 1885). Daly's promptbook indicates that Rosalind should
        seize Celia's dress and try to cover herself. One critic asked 'what can Miss Rehan mean by
        pulling down her doublet as she speaks the words, as though she would accomplish the
        impossible feat of hiding her legs under it, – an indelicacy of suggestion at which one can

What did he when thou saw'st him? What said he? How looked he? 185
Wherein went he? What makes he here? Did he ask for me? Where
remains he? How parted he with thee? And when shalt thou see him
again? Answer me in one word.

CELIA You must borrow me Gargantua's mouth first: 'tis a word too
great for any mouth of this age's size. To say 'aye' and 'no' to these 190
particulars is more than to answer in a catechism.

ROSALIND But doth he know that I am in this forest and in man's
apparel? Looks he as freshly as he did the day he wrestled?

CELIA It is as easy to count atomies as to resolve the propositions of a
lover; but take a taste of my finding him and relish it with good 195
observance. I found him under a tree like a dropped acorn.

ROSALIND [*Aside*] It may well be called Jove's tree when it drops forth
such fruit.

CELIA Give me audience, good madam.

ROSALIND Proceed. 200

CELIA There lay he stretched along like a wounded knight.

ROSALIND Though it be pity to see such a sight, it well becomes the
ground.

CELIA Cry 'holla' to thy tongue, I prithee: it curvets unseasonably. He
was furnished like a hunter. 205

ROSALIND O ominous: he comes to kill my heart.

CELIA I would sing my song without a burden; thou bring'st me out of
tune.

only shudder?' (*Blackwood's*, Sept. 1890, cited in Sprague, p. 36). Another wrote that Rehan
'made as much fuss as though she had been Susannah surprised by the Elders' (Walkley,
p. 32). Adrian Lester shrieked and gesticulated wildly. Reviving the exaggerated emphasis,
Anastasia Hille 'started to pull down her trousers' in 'buttock-flashing panic' (*SQ* 50, 1999,
p. 77; *SS* 52, 1999, p. 224).

184–8 Of Edith Evans's 1936 Rosalind: 'at Celia's discovery of Orlando her breathless stream of
interrogation, the words dancing tip-toe in eagerness, had in it the tingling ecstasy of love'
(Williamson, p. 63).

195–6 Cut by Macready (pbk).

198 Adrian Lester drew out 'f-ru-it' suggestively.

201–4 Sometimes cut (1786, Kemble edns, Macready pbk).

203 Helen Mirren as Rosalind tries to embrace the ground in desperate passion.

206 Adrian Lester's Rosalind lay on her back, stamping her feet.

208 Benson introduced a procession of foresters who crossed the stage carrying a deer.
Orlando was among them, and Celia and a disappointed Rosalind gazed after until he
abruptly returned, when they hid behind a tree (1904 pbk).

ROSALIND Do you not know I am a woman? When I think, I must
        speak. Sweet, say on.   210

                 Enter ORLANDO *and* JAQUES

CELIA You bring me out. – Soft, comes he not here?
ROSALIND 'Tis he. Slink by, and note him.
                 [*Rosalind and Celia stand aside*]
JAQUES I thank you for your company, but, good faith, I had as lief have
        been myself alone.
ORLANDO And so had I. But yet, for fashion sake, I thank you too for   215
        your society.
JAQUES God buy you. Let's meet as little as we can.
ORLANDO I do desire we may be better strangers.
JAQUES I pray you mar no more trees with writing love-songs in their
        barks.   220
ORLANDO I pray you mar no mo of my verses with reading them ill-
        favouredly.
JAQUES 'Rosalind' is your love's name?
ORLANDO Yes, just.
JAQUES I do not like her name.   225
ORLANDO There was no thought of pleasing you when she was
        christened.
JAQUES What stature is she of?
ORLANDO Just as high as my heart.
JAQUES You are full of pretty answers: have you not been acquainted   230
        with goldsmiths' wives and conned them out of rings?

210 SD   In Asche's production, Jaques entered with a staff and kerchief, followed by Orlando, who
         hung verses on trees, and climbed the bank to carve 'Ros' on a treetrunk with his dagger
         (pbk). Daly had Orlando enter 'cutting Rosalind's name on a broken branch' (pbk). In
         Noble's production, Jaques looked Orlando over as they entered and stood silently by the
         stream. Orlando and Jaques entered through the audience in Cheek by Jowl's production.
         The response of the girls has often been played as slapstick: in the 1978 BBC version,
         Rosalind, attempting to hide behind Celia, pulls her off the log on which she sits. Fiona
         Shaw's Celia controlled Rosalind by sitting on her.
217   'Heaven be with you' for 'God buy you' (Kemble partbook).
223   Rosalind steps from behind the tree and starts to wave in Czinner's film.
229   Orlando puts the stick he is whittling up to his heart; Rosalind, hiding at the back of the
         stage, expresses her gratification by 'hugging herself' (Arthur pbk). Sothern–Marlowe's
         Celia grabbed Rosalind's cloak to drag her back when she began to run towards Orlando
         (pbk). As Noble's Rosalind cried out, Celia clapped a hand over her mouth.

ORLANDO Not so; but I answer you right painted cloth, from whence you have studied your questions.

JAQUES You have a nimble wit; I think 'twas made of Atalanta's heels. Will you sit down with me, and we two will rail against our mistress the world and all our misery. 235

ORLANDO I will chide no breather in the world but myself, against whom I know most faults.

JAQUES The worst fault you have is to be in love.

ORLANDO 'Tis a fault I will not change for your best virtue: I am weary of you. 240

JAQUES By my troth, I was seeking for a fool, when I found you.

ORLANDO He is drowned in the brook: look but in, and you shall see him.

JAQUES There I shall see mine own figure. 245

ORLANDO Which I take to be either a fool or a cipher.

JAQUES I'll tarry no longer with you. Farewell, good Signor Love.

ORLANDO I am glad of your departure. Adieu, good Monsieur Melancholy.

[*Exit Jaques*]

ROSALIND I will speak to him like a saucy lackey, and under that habit play the knave with him. [*To Orlando*] Do you hear, forester? 250

232–3 Cut in many productions, from Kemble to Daly and Benson.

240 'Throws him a kiss' (Arthur pbk).

245 On Nicholas Pennell's 'intelligent and self-aware' Jaques: 'the repartee that Orlando is apparently allowed to win (the reflection in the pool) was clear to Jaques well in advance, and he allowed the lines to be played out with a full consciousness of their meaning' (*SQ* 34, 1983, p. 465).

249 Orlando exited here in Macready's production, and re-entered upon Ganymede's summons (Macready pbk). Daly had Orlando '[throw] himself on the ground at the foot of a tree', repeating that production's typical action (pbk).

250–357 Edzard's Rosalind approaches Orlando across a wide vacant lot. Shot at middle distance, the scene catches the growing attraction of the two as Emma Croft prances, skips, circles, and stamps, although the sound of aircraft rumbling overhead mars the technical presentation.

251 An account of Helena Faucit's performance: she 'calls after Orlando "Who-whoop-whoop!" and beckons him insolently back with her spear. He returns abruptly. She half recoils but recovers herself and says with bravado "do you hear . . . "' (Moore pbk). Ada Rehan approached the recumbent Orlando and 'rap[ped] him on the shoulder', repeating the gesture when he failed to respond. She became suddenly 'timid' when he did 'start up' (Daly pbk). Julia Marlowe proceeded bravely to centre stage, then paused, straightening up, pulling down her jerkin, and looking back to Celia while swallowing and motioning for Celia

ORLANDO Very well. What would you?

ROSALIND I pray you, what is't o'clock?

ORLANDO You should ask me what time o'day: there's no clock in the
forest.   255

ROSALIND Then there is no true lover in the forest, else sighing every
minute and groaning every hour would detect the lazy foot of Time
as well as a clock.

to join her. Celia shook her head and motioned for Rosalind to proceed, so she braced up,
took a couple of 'brave steps', then paused, clearing her throat, coughing, folding her arms,
and at last called out in a 'commanding manner' (Sothern–Marlowe pbk). In Czinner's film,
Rosalind very hesitantly approaches Orlando, repeatedly running back to the comfort of
Celia's arms. The physical closeness of the two girls strikingly contrasts Rosalind's
skittishness when near Orlando, at least initially; she quickly gains confidence and by 299 is
pushing him back, using the rolled-up scroll as a weapon. Helen Mirren as Rosalind tried to
whistle but failed, so she called out for Orlando instead. Patrick Allen lay face down on the
ground after Jaques's departure; Vanessa Redgrave kicked his foot, then strutted around
him while he watched her from his recumbent position.

Does Orlando recognise Rosalind? In a production at Gelsenkirchen by Otto Falckenberg
in 1958, Orlando 'very soon recognizes the disguised Rosalind and she, too, becomes aware
that she has been discovered, but both conceal their knowledge' (*SS* 13, 1960, p. 128).
Similarly, in Bergen in 1983, 'Orlando knew that his courting game was directed at "her" and
not at "him" from the start' (*SQ* 35, 1984, p. 95). Simon Callow as Orlando did 'an elaborate
double take' (*Spectator*, 11 Aug. 1979). In Cheek by Jowl's production, Rosalind fully
expected Orlando to recognise her. She giggled as she approached him, then prompted him
by fingering the necklace around his neck (her gift to him after the wrestling). Rosalind
became increasingly irritated with his failure to realise who she was.

251–3   Ronald Bryden on Clifford Williams's production: 'Rosalind, lanky in white synthetic leather
trouser suit and Beatle cap, and Celia, moonfaced in nylon curls and granny-glasses, lurk
in a shimmering brake of giant Perspex canes. Orlando, rereading a sonnet to his love,
saunters into a glade of white Formica, dappled with light filtering through two perforated
awnings of milky plastic. The Rosalind starts forward boldly, loses his nerve and stammers:
"I pray you, what is't o'clock?" The audience, startled into hush by the lunar beauty of the
previous moment, breaks up in giggles at this antique gambit of the shy queer' (*Observer*, 8
Oct. 1967).

252   Orlando replies 'half inclined to resent her insolent manner but letting his good nature
predominate'. He pauses briefly as if recalling her features (Moore pbk).

255   Asche's Orlando picked up a handful of the leaves littering the stage and used them to clean
his dagger before replacing it (pbk).

ORLANDO And why not the swift foot of Time? Had not that been as
　　proper?　　　　　　　　　　　　　　　　　　　　　　　　　　　　260
ROSALIND By no means, sir. Time travels in diverse paces with diverse
　　persons. I'll tell you who Time ambles withal, who Time trots
　　withal, who Time gallops withal, and who he stands still withal.
ORLANDO I prithee, who doth he trot withal?
ROSALIND Marry, he trots hard with a young maid between the con-　　265
　　tract of her marriage and the day it is solemnised. If the interim be
　　but a sennight, Time's pace is so hard that it seems the length of
　　seven year.
ORLANDO Who ambles Time withal?
ROSALIND With a priest that lacks Latin, and a rich man that hath not　　270
　　the gout; for the one sleeps easily because he cannot study, and the
　　other lives merrily because he feels no pain; the one lacking the
　　burden of lean and wasteful learning, the other knowing no burden
　　of heavy tedious penury. These Time ambles withal.
ORLANDO Who doth he gallop withal?　　　　　　　　　　　　　　275
ROSALIND With a thief to the gallows; for though he go as softly as foot
　　can fall, he thinks himself too soon there.
ORLANDO Who stays it still withal?
ROSALIND With lawyers in the vacation; for they sleep between term
　　and term, and then they perceive not how Time moves.　　　　280
ORLANDO Where dwell you, pretty youth?
ROSALIND With this shepherdess, my sister, here in the skirts of the
　　forest, like fringe upon a petticoat.

259–80　Cut by Williams (pbk). Anastasia Hille presented 'every single image and conceit physically,
　　almost dancing', to convey a playful sense of two boys 'flirting without really being aware
　　of it' (Miller-Schütz, 'Findings').
272b–4a　Cut by Macready, Phelps, Benson (1904), Jones (pbks).
276–7　With these lines, Helena Faucit's Rosalind turned 'from mirth to solemnity', and 'a shadow
　　[came] over the face that [had] been wreathed with smiles' (*Theatrical Times*, 15 May 1847,
　　pp. 156–57, cited in Carlisle, p. 82).
281　Noble's Orlando slaps Rosalind on the chest.
282–357　In Stein's production, Tina Engel as Celia 'stood at a distance throwing clods of earth at
　　Rosalind', thus 'show[ing] her disapproval' of the love-game (Patterson, p. 142).
283　Lillie Langtry 'put out her hand with a perfectly natural gesture to pick up her own petticoat,
　　and finding none, paused awkwardly for half a second' (Graham Robertson, cited in
　　Shattuck, *American Stage*, p. 116). Constance Benson as Rosalind similarly 'indicate[d]
　　where her own petticoats should be'; on discovering their absence, she sat by Celia and

ORLANDO Are you native of this place?

ROSALIND As the cony that you see dwell where she is kindled.   285

ORLANDO Your accent is something finer than you could purchase in so
removed a dwelling.

ROSALIND I have been told so of many; but indeed an old religious
uncle of mine taught me to speak, who was in his youth an inland
man, one that knew courtship too well, for there he fell in love. I   290
have heard him read many lectures against it, and I thank God I am
not a woman to be touched with so many giddy offences as he hath
generally taxed their whole sex withal.

ORLANDO Can you remember any of the principal evils that he laid to
the charge of women?   295

ROSALIND There were none principal; they were all like one another as
halfpence are, every one fault seeming monstrous till his fellow-
fault came to match it.

ORLANDO I prithee recount some of them.

ROSALIND No. I will not cast away my physic but on those that are sick.   300
There is a man haunts the forest that abuses our young plants with
carving 'Rosalind' on their barks; hangs odes upon hawthorns and
elegies on brambles; all, forsooth, defying the name of Rosalind. If
I could meet that fancy-monger, I would give him some good
counsel, for he seems to have the quotidian of love upon him.   305

ORLANDO I am he that is so love-shaked. I pray you tell me your
remedy.

ROSALIND There is none of my uncle's marks upon you. He taught me
how to know a man in love, in which cage of rushes I am sure
you are not prisoner.   310

ORLANDO What were his marks?

ROSALIND A lean cheek, which you have not; a blue eye and sunken,
which you have not; an unquestionable spirit, which you have not;
a beard neglected, which you have not – but I pardon you for that,

attempted to 'hide her knees with Celia's skirts'. When Celia snatches her skirts away,
Rosalind covered her knees with her hat (Benson 1904 pbk).

284–5   Frequently cut in early productions.

288–9   John Justin slightly raised his hat on mention of the 'religious uncle' (Toye pbk).

295   Patrick Allen grasped Vanessa Redgrave's arm and pulled her towards him.

296   Celia exited at this point in Daly's production (pbk).

301   An abashed Orlando holds the knife and stick behind his back (Moore pbk). In the 1963
RSC/BBC production, the couple leans on a small tree trunk bearing a carving of 'Rosalind'.

308   Rosalind circles around Orlando as she quizzes him (Moore pbk).

314b–5   Cut by Macready (pbk). Helena Faucit included the lines and delivered them acerbically,

for, simply, your having in beard is a younger brother's revenue. 315
Then your hose should be ungartered, your bonnet unbanded, your
sleeve unbuttoned, your shoe untied, and everything about you
demonstrating a careless desolation. But you are no such man; you
are rather point-device in your accoutrements, as loving yourself
than seeming the lover of any other. 320
ORLANDO Fair youth, I would I could make thee believe I love.
ROSALIND Me believe it? You may as soon make her that you love
believe it, which I warrant she is apter to do than to confess she
does. That is one of the points in the which women still give the lie
to their consciences. But, in good sooth, are you he that hangs the 325
verses on the trees wherein Rosalind is so admired?
ORLANDO I swear to thee, youth, by the white hand of Rosalind, I am
that he, that unfortunate he.

'attain[ing] the very quintessence of mock solemnity' (*Manchester Courier*, 16 Apr. 1866,
cited in Carlisle, p. 82). Peggy Ashcroft lightly touched Orlando's check (*SQ* 8, 1957, p. 480).
Edzard's Rosalind swats at Orlando.
318   Demonstrating 'careless desolation', Noble's Orlando almost toppled backwards into the
       stream.
321   'Orlando takes out cross and kisses it' (Modjeska pbk).
324–5 Modjeska cut the misogynistic line about women's consciences; so did Jones (pbks).
325   A critic on Helena Faucit at Drury Lane: she stood 'a little in front of him with her face
       turned from him that her blushes, almost ready to dissolve into tears of happiness, may not
       betray her. Her attitude is that of manly *insouciance*, such as might be chosen by one
       unaccustomed to exchange such confidences as that to which her question leads; but her
       face, which he cannot see, is radiant with content and happiness. In her hand, crumpled up
       and pressed with longing earnestness, is one of the very sonnets of which she speaks so
       cavalierly, and while she waits his answer it is furtively pressed to her lips, and a long and
       rapturous kiss bestowed upon it' (*London Sunday Times*, 18 Mar. 1865). A decade later, a
       reviewer lamented the absence of 'underlying tenderness' in Mrs Kendal's Rosalind, and
       continued: 'One actress in modern times has shown the character as Shakespeare drew it.
       This is Miss Faucit. To the last the rapture of the tenderness she displayed in asking, "In
       good sooth, are you he that hangs the verses on the trees, wherein Rosalind is so much
       admired?" was maintained; and the manner in which the verses themselves were hugged to
       her heart, then furtively pressed to her lips, was one of those masterly touches the memory
       of which never forsakes us. This is the true Rosalind . . .' (*Athenaeum*, 27 Feb. 1875).
328   Orlando sighs; Rosalind mocks him. When he turns away in confusion, 'she gently touches
       his elbow' and delivers the next line 'good naturedly' (Moore pbk). In Julia Arthur's
       production, Orlando looked away from Rosalind as he spoke this line. She reponded to the

ROSALIND But are you so much in love as your rhymes speak?
ORLANDO Neither rhyme nor reason can express how much.   330
ROSALIND Love is merely a madness and, I tell you, deserves as well a
    dark-house and a whip as madmen do; and the reason why they are
    not so punished and cured is that the lunacy is so ordinary that the
    whippers are in love too. Yet I profess curing it by counsel.
ORLANDO Did you ever cure any so?   335
ROSALIND Yes, one, and in this manner. He was to imagine me his love,
    his mistress, and I set him every day to woo me. At which time
    would I, being but a moonish youth, grieve, be effeminate, change-
    able, longing and liking, proud, fantastical, apish, shallow, incon-
    stant, full of tears, full of smiles; for every passion something, and   340
    for no passion truly anything, as boys and women are, for the most
    part, cattle of this colour; would now like him, now loathe him; then
    entertain him, then forswear him; now weep for him, then spit at
    him; that I drave my suitor from his mad humour of love to a living
    humour of madness, which was to forswear the full stream of the   345
    world and to live in a nook, merely monastic. And thus I cured him,

confession by sighing happily, at which he quickly turned, necessitating her rapid
resumption of a boyish manner (Arthur pbk).

330 Cheek by Jowl played this as a moment of deep intensity, with Rosalind and Orlando gazing
     into one another's eyes.

331 Julia Arthur was 'about to impulsively cluck him in her arms', when she suddenly
     remembered her Ganymede disguise and spoke this line abruptly (pbk). Helen Mirren
     similarly cried out in delight at Orlando's profession of love, and used this line to mask her
     outburst. In Hands's production, Celia and Rosalind 'both collapsed on the floor in gales of
     laughter'; but in seconds Rosalind had modulated to a rapt, still 'yet I profess curing it by
     counsel' (SS 34, 1981, p. 150).

334 Cheek by Jowl's Orlando exited on the first half of this line, and Rosalind called him back
     with the second half.

336 Juliet Stevenson removed her bowler hat and pulled the stage cloth around herself to
     suggest a dress.

337 Modjeska decorously cut 'his mistress' (pbk). Arthur as Rosalind retained the word; she and
     Orlando both laughed after it (pbk).

345 Emma Croft spins wildly about on 'humour of madness'.

346 At this point in the 1978 BBC video, a fly is visible buzzing about Helen Mirren's face; she
     swats at it without breaking character.

346–8 Edzard's Rosalind kneels before Orlando to conclude the speech.

and this way will I take upon me to wash your liver as clean as a
sound sheep's heart, that there shall not be one spot of love in't.
ORLANDO I would not be cured, youth.
ROSALIND I would cure you if you would but call me Rosalind and   350
come every day to my cot and woo me.
ORLANDO Now, by the faith of my love, I will. Tell me where it is.
ROSALIND Go with me to it and I'll show it you; and by the way you
shall tell me where in the forest you live. Will you go?
ORLANDO With all my heart, good youth.   355
ROSALIND Nay, you must call me 'Rosalind'. – Come, sister, will you
go?

                                                    Exeunt

348 Vanessa Redgrave thumped Orlando's chest.
349 Laurence Olivier tosses the line off with a shrug in Czinner's film. In the 1963 RSC/BBC
version, Patrick Allen tilts his head back to gaze soberly at Vanessa Redgrave, repeating the
look the two had exchanged when she placed the necklace around his neck in 1.2. Hilton
McRae's Orlando walked away in Noble's production. In Cheek by Jowl, the kneeling couple
gazed into each other's eyes; when Rosalind broke away to put on her spectacles, Orlando
had consented to the game.
350–1 Sinead Cusack's Celia, a 'sexual competitor for Orlando', registered 'mute, horrified
amazement' at the suggested love cure (*Guardian*, 5 Apr. 1980).
354 Orlando holds Rosalind, then slaps her shoulder (Williams pbk). Janet Suzman returned
Orlando's punch (pbk).
356a Helena Faucit 'would linger on the name' when instructing Orlando to call her Rosalind,
her proposal a 'half-urged request, that hesitates with the fear of its being denied' (*The
Scotsman*, 12 Apr. 1845, cited in Carlisle, p. 83). In Benson's production, Orlando repeated
'Rosalind', and she echoed him in return, establishing a pact between them (1904 pbk).
Asche's Rosalind smacked Orlando on the back; he returned the smack as he said her name
and they ran out together, laughing (pbk). Bridges-Adams directed a little dumbshow:
Rosalind holds out one hand and Orlando shakes it; she holds it under his nose, and he
looks to Celia, who nods; he kisses the hand and mouths 'Rosalind' (pbk).
357 They swing their clasped hands and laugh together, momentarily forgetting Celia as they
exit (Moore pbk). Daly had Celia had exit earlier in the scene, thus cutting the address to
her here (pbk). At Stratford in 1957, as 'Ganymede starts to lead the way out . . . Orlando
catches him by the belt, pulls him back with a look as much as to say, Mind your manners,
my lad!, and himself arms Celia out in style, Ganymede following' (*SQ* 8, 1957, p. 480). An
angry Celia exited alone in Cheek by Jowl's version.

ACT 3, SCENE 4

Enter TOUCHSTONE, AUDREY, *with* JAQUES [*behind, watching them*]

TOUCHSTONE Come apace, good Audrey; I will fetch up your goats,
Audrey. And how, Audrey, am I the man yet? Doth my simple
feature content you?

AUDREY Your features, Lord warrant us – what features?

Jaques and Sir Oliver Martext were cut from this scene in the eighteenth century. Macready restored them (pbk), but they often remained absent in later productions (Phelps, Moore, Modjeska, Arthur pbks), as from Czinner's film. Asche placed the scene after 4.1. In the Sothern–Marlowe production, Jaques leaned against a tree watching as Touchstone set Audrey on a stump and stood back to look at her before speaking (pbk). Bridges-Adams specified that Touchstone should drag Audrey on stage, with Jaques following and hiding behind a tree (pbk). Toye had Jaques enter and pull a poem from a tree before moving behind it to watch Touchstone, who was attempting to sketch Audrey (pbk). Jaques's asides are cut in the 1963 RSC/BBC version; he watches the couple silently before stepping forward at line 54.

By tradition, Audrey munches a turnip during this scene. The turnip appeared in a performance in 1825 (Sprague, p. 37), and by 1842, Macready was warning 'no apple or turnip munching – mind, Audrey!' (Shattuck, *Macready*). Audrey continued to munch – or to be instructed to forebear from doing so – for decades. In 1885 at Stratford, the turnip 'had been plucked near Anne Hathaway's cottage' (Sprague, p. 38). Benson provided Audrey with a knife to pare her turnip (1904 pbk). Anthony Hopkins as Audrey carried a bucket which was placed on the ground when she sat with Touchstone (Williams pbk). In Czinner's film, pretty-faced Audrey sports frizzled, unkempt hair; here she sings 'It was a lover and his lass' while milking a cow; she giggles whenever she speaks. In Noble's production, Audrey was 'a leggy clown in torn stockings and apple green miniskirt who lopes about like a dislocated fell-walker and gets vertigo while curtseying to her betters' (*Observer*, 28 Apr. 1985). She pulled an artificial goat by a rope. In the multi-racial Arden of the Nimrod Theatre's production in 1985, 'topsyish-haired Audrey was part Negro or aboriginal' (*SQ* 35, 1984, p. 481). Cheek by Jowl's Audrey, wearing overalls and a tattered sweater, yodelled incessantly. Edzard's plump Audrey tends a snack caravan; this encounter occurs as she 'industriously makes ketchup sandwiches with Wonder Bread' (Lennox, p. 60).

TOUCHSTONE I am here with thee and thy goats as the most capricious   5
    poet honest Ovid was among the Goths.
JAQUES O knowledge ill-inhabited, worse than Jove in a thatched house!
TOUCHSTONE When a man's verses cannot be understood, nor a man's
    good wit seconded with the forward child, understanding, it strikes
    a man more dead than a great reckoning in a little room. Truly, I   10
    would the gods had made thee poetical.
AUDREY I do not know what 'poetical' is. Is it honest in deed and word?
    Is it a true thing?
TOUCHSTONE No, truly; for the truest poetry is the most feigning, and
    lovers are given to poetry; and what they swear in poetry it may be   15
    said, as lovers, they do feign.
AUDREY Do you wish then that the gods had made me poetical?
TOUCHSTONE I do, truly; for thou swear'st to me thou art honest. Now
    if thou wert a poet, I might have some hope thou didst feign.
AUDREY Would you not have me honest?   20
TOUCHSTONE No, truly, unless thou wert hard-favoured: for honesty
    coupled to beauty is to have honey a sauce to sugar.
JAQUES A material fool.
AUDREY Well, I am not fair, and therefore I pray the gods make me
    honest.   25
TOUCHSTONE Truly, and to cast away honesty upon a foul slut were to
    put good meat into an unclean dish.
AUDREY I am not a slut, though I thank the gods I am foul.
TOUCHSTONE Well, praised be the gods for thy foulness: sluttishness

11   Audrey stares at him uncomprehendingly and 'gnaws vigorously at her turnip'. Touchstone 'snatches it from her' and tosses it off stage. She immediately takes an apple from her pocket and 'begins again' (Moore pbk).

12   As Audrey scratched her leg in Noble's production, Touchstone pulled the stage cloth about them to suggest bed clothes.

19   'Business with apple repeated. She takes out another' (Moore pbk).

21–2   'Business with apple repeated' (Moore pbk). In Edzard's film Griff Rhys Jones as Touchstone kisses Audrey's stubby fingers one by one; no glamour-girl, she wears fingerless gloves.

24–5   Noble's Touchstone chased Audrey around the stage; she arranged the silk stage cloth around herself in semblance of a wedding gown.

26–30   Cut by Modjeska, Arthur, Sothern–Marlowe (pbks). Touchstone is tempted to snatch the apple away again, but finally recognises the futility of doing so. Alternatively, he holds down her right hand while she pulls out another apple with her left (Moore pbk). Audrey lies in Touchstone's lap (1963 RSC/BBC), hits Touchstone with a paddle (Williams pbk), kneels (Jones pbk).

may come hereafter. But be it as it may be, I will marry thee, and to   30
that end I have been with Sir Oliver Martext, the vicar of the next
village, who hath promised to meet me in this place of the forest and
to couple us.

JAQUES I would fain see this meeting.

AUDREY Well, the gods give us joy.   35

TOUCHSTONE Amen. A man may, if he were of a fearful heart, stagger
in this attempt; for here we have no temple but the wood, no
assembly but horn-beasts. But what though? Courage! As horns are
odious, they are necessary. It is said, 'Many a man knows no end of
his goods'. Right: many a man has good horns and knows no end of   40
them. Well, that is the dowry of his wife, 'tis none of his own
getting. Horns? Even so. Poor men alone? No, no: the noblest deer
hath them as huge as the rascal. Is the single man therefore blessed?
No: as a walled town is more worthier than a village, so is the
forehead of a married man more honourable than the bare brow of   45
a bachelor. And, by how much defence is better than no skill, by so
much is a horn more precious than to want.

Enter SIR OLIVER MARTEXT

30   Cheek by Jowl's Touchstone presented a wedding veil to Audrey.

34   Macklin as Touchstone appropriated Jaques's line, as 'I had rather he should see' (partbook).

35   Phelps, and many after him, had Audrey dance with joy (pbk). For Kean, the dance is 'a
      Boorish step, almost a hop' (pbk). Holloway's Audrey kissed him – left cheek, right cheek –
      and flopped onto his knee, bursting the balloon Touchstone was carrying (pbk). Toye's
      Audrey offered her face, but Touchstone was repulsed (pbk). Elliott has Touchstone fall to
      the ground with Audrey in a long kiss (1963 RSC/BBC).

38   Toye's Touchstone not only kissed her but ran behind the bush with her (pbk).

38–47 The extended riff on cuckoldry has often been cut or abridged from Macready on.

47   Touchstone, astride Audrey on the floor, spies Sir Oliver and rises to greet him (Jones pbk).

47 SD Martext was cut from many early productions, from Macklin to Daly. Various means have
      been employed to make Martext comical. Toye gave him an umbrella, Elliott a dead rabbit
      (pbks). Goodbody conceived Martext as 'an Irish priest swinging a censer, wheeling a
      perambulator, and proferring a wedding cake' (*SQ* 24, 1973, p. 403); he also supplied 'Just
      Married' signs (*Evening Standard*, 13 June 1973). In Coleman's version, Martext, a buffoon
      with several missing teeth, clutches a prayerbook. Cheek by Jowl had Martext provide a
      recording of choral music. Playing against tradition, Otto Sander 'possessed a quiet dignity'
      in Stein's production. 'Opening a minuscule suitcase, he produced from it a collapsible
      table, a collapsible chalice and a stole which he solemnly kissed before laying it over his
      shoulders' (Patterson, p. 144).

48–83 Early on the passage was cut, retaining only lines 73–4a as Touchstone's exit line. Macready

Here comes Sir Oliver. – Sir Oliver Martext, you are well met. Will
you dispatch us here under this tree, or shall we go with you to your
chapel?   50

MARTEXT Is there none here to give the woman?

TOUCHSTONE I will not take her on gift of any man.

MARTEXT Truly, she must be given, or the marriage is not lawful.

JAQUES [*Coming forward*] Proceed, proceed: I'll give her.

TOUCHSTONE Good-even, good Monsieur What-Ye-Call't. How do   55
you, sir? You are very well met. God'ild you for your last company;
I am very glad to see you. Even a toy in hand here, sir.
                         [*Jaques removes his hat*]
Nay, pray be covered.

JAQUES Will you be married, Motley?

TOUCHSTONE As the ox hath his bow, sir, the horse his curb, and the   60
falcon her bells, so man hath his desires, and as pigeons bill, so
wedlock would be nibbling.

JAQUES And will you, being a man of your breeding, be married under
a bush like a beggar? Get you to church, and have a good priest that
can tell you what marriage is. This fellow will but join you together   65
as they join wainscot; then one of you will prove a shrunk panel and,
like green timber, warp, warp.

TOUCHSTONE I am not in the mind; but I were better to be married of
him than of another, for he is not like to marry me well and, not

restored the passage but eliminated the traditional exit line, with its offensive reference to
'bawdry' (pbk). Daly retained 58–72 and 79–81 (pbk).

48 Asche had Touchstone dodge about in an attempt to shake hands with a stumbling, drunken
Sir Oliver, whose hat fell off in the grappling (pbk). Dexter's Audrey carried the head of a
deer, which terrified Martext; he snatched it from her and threw it down (pbk).

49 Jones had Sir Oliver embrace Audrey – and pat her bottom – in greeting (pbk).

51 Edzard's Martext gestured that he wanted someone to 'give' him money.

53 Sir Oliver sits on a tree stump and dozes (Asche pbk). He turns the page and hiccoughs
(Bridges-Adams pbk).

54 Hugh Ross played Jaques as 'very much the act*or*': 'the whole world seemed a show put on
for his benefit; indeed, at times he took a seat in the front of the stalls to watch the parade of
folly, leaping back onto the stage to help Touchstone get married' (*SS* 44, 1991, pp. 162, 163).

55–6 Touchstone bows after each sentence to Sir Oliver (Sothern–Marlowe pbk).

55–72 Touchstone and Jaques go apart to discuss proper weddings while Audrey speaks in the
background with Martext (1978 BBC).

58 Touchstone himself 'covered' Audrey by pulling the stage cloth over her face in Noble's
production.

being well married, it will be a good excuse for me hereafter to leave   70
    my wife.
JAQUES Go thou with me and let me counsel thee.
TOUCHSTONE Come, sweet Audrey, we must be married or we must
    live in bawdry. – Farewell, good Master Oliver. Not
    [*Sings*]   O sweet Oliver,   75
                 O brave Oliver,
           Leave me not behind thee;
    but [*Sings*]
                 Wind away,
                 Begone, I say,   80
           I will not to wedding with thee.
MARTEXT [*Aside*] 'Tis no matter; ne'er a fantastical knave of them all
    shall flout me out of my calling.

                                                            Exeunt

73   'We must be married *in church*' inserted Touchstone in Cheek by Jowl.
74–81 Cut by Jones, with these lines written in: 'Dearly beloved, we are gathered together in the
       sight of god in the face of this congregation – to satisfy man's carnal lusts and appetites –'
       (pbk).
83 SD Sir Oliver hiccoughs repeatedly (Bridges-Adams pbk); he takes a bottle from his pouch and
       drinks (Payne pbk). At Stratford in 1952, goats brayed as Martext fell backwards into the
       on-stage pool (Shaw pbk). Dexter's Oliver picked up Touchstone's volume of Ovid instead of
       his own prayer book and reacted with horror (pbk). Noble had Touchstone run off with
       Jaques; when Martext followed, Audrey was left shrieking on stage.

ACT 3, SCENE 5

Enter ROSALIND [*as* GANYMEDE] *and* CELIA [*as* ALIENA]

ROSALIND Never talk to me; I will weep.

CELIA Do, I prithee; but yet have the grace to consider that tears do not become a man.

ROSALIND But have I not cause to weep?

CELIA As good cause as one would desire: therefore weep.   5

ROSALIND His very hair is of the dissembling colour.

CELIA Something browner than Judas's: marry, his kisses are Judas's own children.

ROSALIND I'faith, his hair is of a good colour.

CELIA An excellent colour: your chestnut was ever the only colour.   10

ROSALIND And his kissing is as full of sanctity as the touch of holy bread.

CELIA He hath bought a pair of cast lips of Diana. A nun of winter's sisterhood kisses not more religiously: the very ice of chastity is in them.   15

ROSALIND But why did he swear he would come this morning and comes not?

CELIA Nay, certainly, there is no truth in him.

ROSALIND Do you think so?

CELIA Yes, I think he is not a pickpurse nor a horse-stealer but, for his   20
verity in love, I do think him as concave as a covered goblet or a worm-eaten nut.

ROSALIND Not true in love?

CELIA Yes, when he is in; but I think he is not in.

Edzard inserts the scene into 3.6 between lines 73 and 82, and sets it in the hut, where Celia rolls a cigarette.

0 SD   Rosalind leans against the door of the cottage as Celia washes clothes (Bridges-Adams pbk). A sheepdog keeps Rosalind company in Czinner's film.

6–15   Cut in most early productions and sometimes abridged later.

19–22   Cut from the eighteenth century to Daly.

24   Celia gives wet clothes to Rosalind (Bridges-Adams pbk).

ROSALIND You have heard him swear downright he was.   25

CELIA 'Was' is not 'is'; besides, the oath of a lover is no stronger than
the word of a tapster: they are both the confirmers of false reckon-
ings. He attends here in the forest on the Duke your father.

ROSALIND I met the Duke yesterday and had much question with him;
he asked me of what parentage I was. I told him of as good as he: so   30
he laughed and let me go. But what talk we of fathers when there is
such a man as Orlando?

CELIA O that's a brave man: he writes brave verses, speaks brave words,
swears brave oaths, and breaks them bravely, quite traverse, athwart
the heart of his lover as a puny tilter that spurs his horse but on one   35
side, breaks his staff like a noble goose. But all's brave that youth
mounts and folly guides. – Who comes here?

Enter CORIN

CORIN Mistress and master, you have oft enquired
          After the shepherd that complained of love
          Who you saw sitting by me on the turf,   40
          Praising the proud disdainful shepherdess
          That was his mistress.

CELIA   Well, and what of him?

CORIN If you will see a pageant truly played
          Between the pale complexion of true love
          And the red glow of scorn and proud disdain,   45
          Go hence a little, and I shall conduct you
          If you will mark it.

ROSALIND   O come, let us remove,
          The sight of lovers feedeth those in love. –
          Bring us to this sight and you shall say
          I'll prove a busy actor in their play.   50

                                                      Exeunt

26   Rosalind throws washing into tub (Bridges-Adams pbk).

29–32 Adrian Lester as Rosalind seemed genuinely upset by the meeting with her father.

34b–7 Cut from Macready to Benson, also by Williams and Jones (pbks).

35   In Edzard's film, Celia leaps to remove a pan boiling over on the hotplate.

37   In Czinner's film, the Duke's followers march through the forest singing the hunting song
from 4.2.

38–50 Cut by Donnellan, with the action moving directly into the next scene.

Enter SILVIUS *and* PHOEBE

SILVIUS Sweet Phoebe, do not scorn me, do not, Phoebe.
        Say that you love me not, but say not so
        In bitterness. The common executioner,
        Whose heart th'accustomed sight of death makes hard,
        Falls not the axe upon the humbled neck   5
        But first begs pardon. Will you sterner be
        Than he that dies and lives by bloody drops?

        Enter ROSALIND [*as* GANYMEDE], CELIA [*as* ALIENA],
                and CORIN [; *they stand aside*]

PHOEBE I would not be thy executioner;
        I fly thee for I would not injure thee.
        Thou tell'st me there is murder in mine eye: 10
        'Tis pretty, sure, and very probable
        That eyes, that are the frail'st and softest things,

This scene and the previous one usually ran together in early stagings.

0 SD Asche had Phoebe carry a yoke and pails, which she put down to approach Silvius and later
        Ganymede (pbk). Czinner presents Phoebe perched on a log with her back to Silvius.
        Williams had an amorous Silvius give Phoebe flowers and spread a rug for her to lie upon
        (pbk). In Dexter's production, the couple carried bowls of eggs that they hung on the
        branches of the tree of life dominating the stage (pbk). Stein staged the scene on a platform
        above the pool, distancing it from the main action as a 'pageant truly play'd' (Patterson,
        p. 144). Cheek by Jowl's Phoebe was 'a short, stumpy bully with the infuriating
        self-assurance of Charlie Brown's Lucy, who also had the irritating habit of indignantly
        flinging her head back at the smallest provocation. She was preposterously oversexed . . .'
        (Ko, p. 17). Edzard's punk Phoebe struts in a leather jacket, mini-skirt, and fish-net stockings,
        eating a packet of chips as she disdainfully rejects Silvius's advances. At Shakespeare's
        Globe, as Silvius chased Phoebe across the balcony, he called her name 'as if he had never
        stopped doing so since his exit in 2.4' (Miller-Schütz, 'Findings').

11–27 Early productions cut 17–27 (Bell's, 1786, Kemble edns); Macready, Modjeska, and Daly also
        cut 11–14 (pbks).

Who shut their coward gates on atomies,
Should be called tyrants, butchers, murderers!
Now I do frown on thee with all my heart;   15
And if mine eyes can wound, now let them kill thee.
Now counterfeit to swoon, why, now fall down
Or, if thou canst not, O for shame, for shame,
Lie not to say mine eyes are murderers.
Now show the wound mine eye hath made in thee.   20
Scratch thee but with a pin, and there remains
Some scar of it; lean upon a rush,
The cicatrice and capable impressure
Thy palm some moment keeps. But now mine eyes,
Which I have darted at thee, hurt thee not,   25
Nor I am sure there is no force in eyes
That can do hurt.
SILVIUS   O dear Phoebe,
If ever – as that 'ever' may be near –
You meet in some fresh cheek the power of fancy,
Then shall you know the wounds invisible   30
That love's keen arrows make.
PHOEBE   But till that time
Come not thou near me; and, when that time comes,
Afflict me with thy mocks, pity me not,
As till that time I shall not pity thee.
ROSALIND [*Coming forward*] And why, I pray you? Who might be
     your mother   35
That you insult, exult, and all at once

16   Phoebe aggressively backs Silvius into a tree in the 1978 BBC version.
32   Noble's Phoebe beat Silvius with a cushion.
35   Helena Faucit attributed Phoebe's infatuation to Rosalind's 'distinction of . . . bearing – the unconscious imperiousness of . . . the princess' (Faucit Martin, *On Rosalind*, p. 51).
35–63 Mrs Pritchard was a 'judicious actress . . . where she falls in with the luckless shepherd and his cruel mistress, she sees merit enough in the matter she has to deliver without any additional flourishes; she therefore reserves them for future occasions, and seems there proud of shewing us the beauty of speaking plainly and simply: with how perfectly natural an accent does she deliver the speech she has on this occasion, and yet how pleas'd is every body that hears her?' (Hill, p. 280). Mary Anderson's Rosalind 'bantered with Phoebe with the cruelest ease . . . her manner as the mocking censor of the rustic coquette was quite free from the touches of anxiety which she sought – often unsuccessfully – to impart to her raillery of her lover' (*Academy*, 5 Sept. 1885). Later performers have tended to embellish

Over the wretched? What though you have no beauty,
As, by my faith, I see no more in you
Than without candle may go dark to bed,
Must you be therefore proud and pitiless? 40
Why, what means this? Why do you look on me?
I see no more in you than in the ordinary
Of Nature's sale-work – Od's my little life,
I think she means to tangle my eyes too. –
No, faith, proud mistress, hope not after it; 45
'Tis not your inky brows, your black silk hair,
Your bugle eyeballs, nor your cheek of cream
That can entame my spirits to your worship. –
You, foolish shepherd, wherefore do you follow her
Like foggy South, puffing with wind and rain? 50
You are a thousand times a properer man
Than she a woman. 'Tis such fools as you
That makes the world full of ill-favoured children.
'Tis not her glass but you that flatters her,
And out of you she sees herself more proper 55
Than any of her lineaments can show her. –
But, mistress, know yourself. Down on your knees,
      [*Phoebe kneels to Rosalind*]
And thank heaven, fasting, for a good man's love;
For I must tell you friendly in your ear,

the lines heavily. In Czinner's film, Elisabeth Bergner brandishes a branch as a switch, tapping Silvius with it and threatening Phoebe at 'I like you not' (73). At Shakespeare's Globe, Belinda Davidson was a 'strapping' Phoebe, 'capable of inflicting grievous bodily harm and relentlessly energetic in her pursuit of Ganymede, round pillars, up the ladder, almost off the edge of the stage' (*SS* 52, 1999, p. 222).

40 Phoebe 'advances gazing with intense ardour at Rosalind' (Phelps pbk). Lesley Manville vamped in obvious pin-up girl postures in Noble's production. Edzard's Phoebe, munching a packet of chips, offers one to Rosalind.

53 Helen Mirren laid a sympathetic arm on Silvius's shoulder.

57 Edzard's Rosalind shakes Phoebe by the shoulders.

59 Phoebe is urged to come closer, 'expecting to hear something pretty'. Rosalind speaks 'half whispering confidentially in her ear and tapping her shoulder with the tips of her fingers' (Moore pbk). Moore notes: 'the rest of this scene frequently omitted. Better in'. Noble's Phoebe trailed about after Rosalind on her knees. At Shakespeare's Globe Phoebe was also on her knees, facing the audience while Ganymede stood beside her and leaned down to whisper in her ears (Miller-Schütz, 'Findings').

                 Sell when you can: you are not for all markets.　　　　60
                 Cry the man mercy, love him, take his offer,
                 Foul is most foul, being foul to be a scoffer. –
                 So take her to thee, shepherd; fare you well.
PHOEBE　Sweet youth, I pray you chide a year together;
                 I had rather hear you chide than this man woo.　　65
ROSALIND　He's fallen in love with your foulness – [*To Silvius*] and
           she'll fall in love with my anger. If it be so, as fast as she answers
           thee with frowning looks, I'll sauce her with bitter words. – Why
           look you so upon me?
PHOEBE　For no ill will I bear you.　　　　　　　　　70
ROSALIND　I pray you do not fall in love with me
                 For I am falser than vows made in wine;
                 Besides, I like you not. – [*To Silvius*] If you will know my
                    house,
                 'Tis at the tuft of olives, here hard by. –
                 Will you go, sister? – Shepherd, ply her hard. –　　75
                 Come, sister. – Shepherdess, look on him better
                 And be not proud, though all the world could see,
                 None could be so abused in sight as he. –
                 Come, to our flock.
                            Exit [*with Celia and Corin*]
PHOEBE　Dead shepherd, now I find thy saw of might:　　80
                 'Who ever loved that loved not at first sight?'
SILVIUS　Sweet Phoebe, –

  65　Rosalind 'makes a sign to Phoebe to go to Silvius. She shakes her head. She does the same
       to Silvius. He does the same. Rosalind gives Phoebe a little angry push. Then as she starts to
       go, makes signs to Silvius to "push his love"' (Arthur pbk).
66–70　Cut in early productions (Bell's, 1786, Kemble edns; Macready, Modjeska pbks).
 71–9　In the 1978 BBC version, when Rosalind realises Phoebe's attraction, she becomes very
       self-conscious about her gender-bending, and covers her chest with her crossed arms,
       deepens her voice, and backs away as Phoebe follows, trance-like.
  72　A snort from Celia, in Cheek by Jowl's production.
73b–8　Cut in Edzard's film, which here shifts to 3.5.
 80–1　Perhaps considered confusing, these lines have often been cut. In Goodbody's production,
       Phoebe 'was an art student, who found the saw of might . . . by looking it up in a Penguin
       Book of Verse' (*SS* 27, 1974, p. 149). In Noble's production, Lesley Manville reclined
       swooningly, then removed her bodice and rinsed it in the on-stage stream.
80–138　Cut in Czinner's film, which moves directly to 4.1.25.
  82　Macready had Phoebe continue to gaze off after Ganymede (Shattuck, *Macready*).

PHOEBE	Ha, what say'st thou, Silvius?
SILVIUS	Sweet Phoebe, pity me.
PHOEBE	Why I am sorry for thee, gentle Silvius.
SILVIUS	Wherever sorrow is, relief would be.

SILVIUS Wherever sorrow is, relief would be.   85
         If you do sorrow at my grief in love,
         By giving love your sorrow and my grief
         Were both extermined.
PHOEBE Thou hast my love: is not that neighbourly?
SILVIUS I would have you.
PHOEBE   Why, that were covetousness.   90
         Silvius, the time was that I hated thee,
         And yet it is not that I bear thee love;
         But since that thou canst talk of love so well,
         Thy company, which erst was irksome to me,
         I will endure – and I'll employ thee too.   95
         But do not look for further recompense
         Than thine own gladness that thou art employed.
SILVIUS So holy and so perfect is my love,
         And I in such a poverty of grace
         That I shall think it a most plenteous crop   100
         To glean the broken ears after the man
         That the main harvest reaps. Loose now and then
         A scattered smile, and that I'll live upon.
PHOEBE Know'st thou the youth that spoke to me erewhile?
SILVIUS Not very well; but I have met him oft   105
         And he hath bought the cottage and the bounds
         That the old carlot once was master of.
PHOEBE Think not I love him, though I ask for him;
         'Tis but a peevish boy – yet he talks well.

91   In Julia Arthur's production, Silvius made a step towards Phoebe with these seemingly
     encouraging lines, and again at 95 (pbk). In Sothern and Marlowe's production, Silvius knelt
     beside Phoebe (pbk). Holloway had him take her hand, but she snatched it away (pbk).
98–103 Macready cut these lines, as did Phelps, Modjeska, Holloway (pbks). Daly substituted the
     phrase 'that if you only loose' for the prolix 100–2 (pbk).
103 Silvius plays pipe (Goodbody pbk).
109–22 Cut from early productions to eliminate Phoebe's gender-bending admiration for
     Ganymede. Macready and Kemble cut to 125. In the 1990 ACTER production, Miranda
     Foster's Phoebe 'stationed herself downstage and directed' the speech forcefully at the
     audience, while Stephen Jenn's Silvius, up stage of her, 'varied his expression according to
     her comments about Ganymede'. As a result, the 'sequence was as much about Silvius as
     about Phoebe', a useful preparation for 4.3 (*SQ* 42, 1991, p. 218). In Cheek by Jowl's

But what care I for words? Yet words do well   110
When he that speaks them pleases those that hear.
It is a pretty youth – not very pretty;
But sure he's proud – and yet his pride becomes him;
He'll make a proper man. The best thing in him
Is his complexion; and faster than his tongue   115
Did make offence, his eye did heal it up;
He is not very tall, yet for his years he's tall;
His leg is but so-so, and yet 'tis well;
There was a pretty redness in his lip,
A little riper and more lusty red   120
Than that mixed in his cheek: 'twas just the difference
Betwixt the constant red and mingled damask.
There be some women, Silvius, had they marked him
In parcels as I did, would have gone near
To fall in love with him: but, for my part,   125
I love him not nor hate him not – and yet
Have more cause to hate him than to love him.
For what had he to do to chide at me?
He said mine eyes were black, and my hair black,
And, now I am remembered, scorned at me.   130
I marvel why I answered not again;
But that's all one. Omittance is no quittance.
I'll write to him a very taunting letter
And thou shalt bear it – wilt thou, Silvius?
SILVIUS Phoebe, with all my heart.
PHOEBE   I'll write it straight: 135
The matter's in my head and in my heart;
I will be bitter with him and passing short.
Go with me, Silvius.

Exeunt

production, Phoebe caressed Silvius as she fantasised about Ganymede; Silvius swooned at her embraces.

135   Silvius takes out pencil and paper (Goodbody pbk).

138   In Daly's production, hunters' horns sounded as the scene ended, leading directly to 4.2 (pbk). Asche's production featured a brief enactment of dominance and submission: Silvius approached Phoebe, offering his hand; she pointed to her abandoned yoke, turning up her nose, and flounced away; Silvius knelt to take on the yoke and followed her (pbk). Payne had Silvius exit crying 'Phebe, Phebe, Phebe!' (pbk).

ACT 4, SCENE I

Enter ROSALIND [*as* GANYMEDE], *and* CELIA [*as* ALIENA], *and* JAQUES

JAQUES I prithee, pretty youth, let me be better acquainted with thee.
ROSALIND They say you are a melancholy fellow.

0 SD The encounter between Jaques and Rosalind/Ganymede was cut in the eighteenth century. Kemble initiated a fairly major revision of Jaques's part, moving lines 9–16 back to 2.5, where his self-diagnosis was interpolated into dialogue with Amiens. Macready restored the opening dialogue between Jaques and Rosalind (pbk). But nineteenth-century acting editions, such as the 1848 Modern Standard Drama version, omit the lines, and they are absent from Modjeska's, Arthur's, and Sothern–Marlowe's promptbooks. Others restored them (Moore, Asche, Bridges-Adams pbks). The encounter is excised from Czinner's film. In Edzard's film it occurs after Orlando's exit at 161sd, before the continuation of the scene inside the bungalow.

Is Celia present? Not in Benson's production (1904 pbk). Asche had her cross the stage and enter the cottage, leaving Rosalind and Jaques alone (pbk). She sat sewing in Payne's production (pbk), reclined in a hammock in Goodbody's (pbk). At Shakespeare's Globe, Celia walked across the stage playing the recorder, then returned in a playful mood with Rosalind (Miller-Schütz, 'Findings').

1 In Cheek by Jowl's production, this line was addressed to Silvius, still on stage from the previous scene; Silvius refused Jaques's advance but took his cigarette.

1–30 Often Rosalind flirts with Jaques. Benson's Rosalind threw leaves at him, then lay at his feet as they conversed (1904 pbk). Bridges-Adams had her drop stones on the book Jaques tried to read (pbk). In the 1978 BBC version, Rosalind reclines against a tree as Jaques throws darts. The meeting has evoked fears of impropriety, and in Hands's production Derek Godfrey's Jaques approached Rosalind in 'a prolonged pass' or what some took to be 'an attempt at rape' (*Guardian*, 5 Apr. 1980; *Observer*, 13 Apr. 1980). Jaques 'enveloped Rosalind in his cloak as if in huge sinister wings for their casual conversation about travel (pronounced "travail") and appeared to attempt to seduce her, with much stress on "experience" – but Rosalind? or Ganymede? And why?' (*SS* 34, 1981, p. 150).

2 Cheek by Jowl's Adrian Lester approached Jaques with this line.

JAQUES I am so: I do love it better than laughing.

ROSALIND Those that are in extremity of either are abominable
    fellows, and betray themselves to every modern censure worse than   5
    drunkards.

JAQUES Why, 'tis good to be sad and say nothing.

ROSALIND Why then, 'tis good to be a post.

JAQUES I have neither the scholar's melancholy, which is emulation;
    nor the musician's, which is fantastical; nor the courtier's, which is   10
    proud; nor the soldier's, which is ambitious; nor the lawyer's, which
    is politic; nor the lady's, which is nice; nor the lover's, which is all
    these; but it is a melancholy of mine own, compounded of many
    simples, extracted from many objects, and indeed the sundry con-
    templation of my travels, in which my often rumination wraps me   15
    in a most humorous sadness.

ROSALIND A traveller! By my faith, you have great reason to be sad. I
    fear you have sold your own lands to see other men's. Then to have
    seen much and to have nothing is to have rich eyes and poor hands.

JAQUES Yes, I have gained my experience.   20

Enter ORLANDO

ROSALIND And your experience makes you sad. I had rather have a fool
    to make me merry than experience to make me sad – and to travel
    for it too!

ORLANDO Good day, and happiness, dear Rosalind.

JAQUES Nay then, God buy you, and you talk in blank verse!   25

ROSALIND Farewell, Monsieur Traveller. Look you lisp and wear
    strange suits; disable all the benefits of your own country; be out of
    love with your nativity, and almost chide God for making you that

---

9   Celia enters here in the 1978 BBC version, but remains in the background.

17   In Cheek by Jowl a morose Jaques buried his face in Rosalind's lap and sobbed heartily.

20 SD Orlando enters with a handful of bluebells, which he throws at Rosalind (Asche pbk). In
      Noble's production, Orlando dashed on stage, leaping over furniture, his exuberance a
      welcome contrast to Jaques's dreariness.

25   Macready had Jaques exit hastily; Celia followed after nodding at Orlando (pbk). Jaques
      should be 'pouting' and display 'a sulky eye' (Moore pbk).

26–30 Cut by Macready, Phelps, and Bridges-Adams (pbks). Daly cut 28b–29a (pbk). Constance
      Benson shouted the line after a departing Jaques (Benson 1904 pbk). Adrian Lester put Joe
      Dixon's hand on his chest, thus revealing the secret of 'her' sex.

countenance you are, or I will scarce think you have swam in a
gondola.   30

                                             [Exit Jaques]

Why, how now , Orlando, where have you been all this while? You
a lover? And you serve me such another trick, never come in my
sight more.

ORLANDO My fair Rosalind, I come within an hour of my promise.

ROSALIND Break an hour's promise in love? He that will divide a   35
    minute into a thousand parts and break but a part of the thousand
    part of a minute in the affairs of love, it may be said of him that
    Cupid hath clapped him o'th'shoulder; but I'll warrant him heart-
    whole.

ORLANDO Pardon me, dear Rosalind.   40

ROSALIND Nay, and you be so tardy, come no more in my sight – I had
    as lief be wooed of a snail.

ORLANDO Of a snail?

ROSALIND Aye, of a snail; for though he comes slowly, he carries his
    house on his head; a better jointure, I think, than you make a   45
    woman. Besides, he brings his destiny with him.

ORLANDO What's that?

ROSALIND Why, horns; which such as you are fain to be beholden to
    your wives for. But he comes armed in his fortune and prevents the
    slander of his wife.   50

ORLANDO Virtue is no horn-maker, and my Rosalind is virtuous.

ROSALIND And I am your Rosalind.

CELIA It pleases him to call you so, but he hath a Rosalind of a better
    leer than you.

---

30   In Daly's production, Celia exited here, as she had done in 3.3, allowing Orlando and
        Ganymede to pursue their games without a chaperone (pbk).

34   Asche's Celia entered carrying a bowl of apples, which she began to peel (pbk).

35–50 Elisabeth Bergner gestures with her switch, bullying Laurence Olivier's Orlando throughout
        this exchange. Rosalind has often been very physically active in this encounter; Ada Rehan's
        'restless' Rosalind 'cover[ed] a distance that, on a pedometer, would probably tot up to a
        respectable figure' (Arthur B. Walkley, cited in Mullin, pp. 376–7).

41–54 With cuckold jokes no longer as popular as on the Renaissance stage, these lines were cut in
        the eighteenth century (Bell's, 1786 edns). Kemble cut 46–54 as did others up to Payne
        (pbk). Macready cut up to 56b.

48   Helen Mirren indicated 'horns' by holding her fingers above her head.

51   Cheek by Jowl's Orlando slapped Rosalind's face.

53   Edzard's Celia picks wildflowers in the distance.

ROSALIND Come, woo me, woo me; for now I am in a holiday humour   55
and like enough to consent. What would you say to me now and I
were your very, very Rosalind?
ORLANDO I would kiss before I spoke.
ROSALIND Nay, you were better speak first, and when you were grav-
elled for lack of matter you might take occasion to kiss. Very good   60
orators when they are out, they will spit, and for lovers, lacking –
God warrant us – matter, the cleanliest shift is to kiss.
ORLANDO How if the kiss be denied?
ROSALIND Then she puts you to entreaty, and there begins new matter.
ORLANDO Who could be out, being before his beloved mistress?   65
ROSALIND Marry, that should you if I were your mistress, or I should
think my honesty ranker than my wit.
ORLANDO What, of my suit?

55-7 Charles Wingate on Adelaide Neilson's Rosalind: 'Her utterance of the simple words, "woo
me! woo me!" to Orlando, as her cheek was laid upon his shoulder and her arm stole coyly
about his neck, was sweet as a blackbird's call to its mate' (Wingate, p. 146). Juliet Stevenson
arranged the stage cloth about herself like a dress. Adrian Lester's Rosalind borrowed
Celia's apron.
　　Ian McEwan notes that 'Orlando has the difficult task of persuading us to believe, with
him, in Rosalind's Ganymede.' In Dexter's production, 'Simon Callow managed this by
appearing unconsciously to have recognized his lover in the boy, and by being alternately
drawn and then startled by the implications of his attraction. It was a neat balancing act,
carried off with precision and humour' (*New Statesman*, 10 Aug. 1979). Not every Orlando
has been up to the challenge. Of Forbes Robertson's Orlando, a critic wrote: 'what can we
make of an Orlando who accepts his mistress's challenge to woo her in her disguise as a
Girton graduate might accept a proposal to analyse a case of modern witchcraft; who
declines, until compelled, to kiss the small gloved hand; and who in all her saucy ways finds
nothing that piques or stimulates him, or leaves him other than anxious to quit her to go on
the Duke's behest?' (*Athenaeum*, 27 Oct. 1888).
58 Kean's confident Orlando here put his arm around Rosalind's waist (pbk). In the 1978 BBC
video, Orlando 'has been looking admiringly at her bosom' and here 'teasingly tries to steal
a kiss' (Bulman, p. 177).
60-2 The lines referring to spitting were cut by Macready, although a later hand marks them as
restored (Shattuck, *Macready*). Daly substituted 'cough' for 'spit' and cut 'God warrant us'
(pbk). Arthur's promptbook has 'God warn us' restored by hand.
65-9 These lines were cut in decorous times to avoid the reference to 'mistress'.

ROSALIND Not out of your apparel, and yet out of your suit. Am not I
  your Rosalind?   70
ORLANDO I take some joy to say you are, because I would be talking of
  her.
ROSALIND Well, in her person, I say I will not have you.
ORLANDO Then, in mine own person, I die.
ROSALIND No, faith, die by attorney. The poor world is almost six   75
  thousand years old and in all this time there was not any man died
  in his own person, videlicet, in a love-cause. Troilus had his brains
  dashed out with a Grecian club, yet he did what he could to die
  before, and he is one of the patterns of love; Leander, he would have
  lived many a fair year though Hero had turned nun, if it had not   80
  been for a hot midsummer night, for, good youth, he went but forth
  to wash him in the Hellespont and, being taken with the cramp, was
  drowned, and the foolish chroniclers of that age found it was Hero
  of Sestos. But these are all lies: men have died from time to time –
  and worms have eaten them – but not for love.   85
ORLANDO I would not have my right Rosalind of this mind, for I
  protest her frown might kill me.
ROSALIND By this hand, it will not kill a fly. But come, now I will be
  your Rosalind in a more coming-on disposition and, ask me what
  you will, I will grant it.   90

69–74 Both lovers lost their tempers and shouted angrily in Cheek by Jowl's production, in which
       Rosalind had difficulty controlling Orlando in the love game.

73   Moore indicated that Rosalind should speak the first part of the line 'slowly and kindly',
       inviting Orlando to lean closer, then conclude 'flippantly' (pbk).

74   Orlando 'lies full length on ground' (Asche pbk), draws his dagger (Bridges-Adams pbk,
       Czinner).

75   In Edzard's film, the lovers, with Celia following, crawl into Orlando's tent of loose plastic
       sheeting.

77b–84a Macready cut 'Troilus . . . lies' (pbk).

84–5   'Orlando's head was in Rosalind's lap' in Hands's production (*SS* 34, 1981, p. 150).

88   Kean had Celia enter here, rather than at the start of the scene (pbk). A reviewer admired
       the way Mrs Rousby's Rosalind 'withdrew her hand from her lover when, in her disguise of
       Ganymede, she sees it regarded too curiously by him' (*Athenaeum*, 4 Mar. 1871). At
       Stratford in 1980, 'Rosalind's hand hovered in pent-up desire above Orlando's head', and
       then 'she *did* kill a fly against [his] chest, thus shattering the sweet-sad moment' (*SS* 34,
       1981, p. 150). Adrian Lester kissed Orlando's hand, then playfully punched him in the arm.

89   Constance Benson curtseyed to indicate her 'coming-on disposition' (Benson 1904 pbk).

ORLANDO Then love me, Rosalind.

ROSALIND Yes, faith, will I, Fridays and Saturdays and all.

ORLANDO And wilt thou have me?

ROSALIND Aye, and twenty such.

ORLANDO What sayest thou?   95

ROSALIND Are you not good?

ORLANDO I hope so.

ROSALIND Why then, can one desire too much of a good thing? –
    Come, sister, you shall be the priest and marry us. – Give me your
    hand, Orlando. – What do you say, sister?   100

ORLANDO Pray thee, marry us.

CELIA I cannot say the words.

ROSALIND You must begin: 'Will you, Orlando –'

CELIA Go to. – Will you, Orlando, have to wife this Rosalind?

ORLANDO I will.   105

91   As the lovers rolled around together on the ground in Noble's production, Celia hid her face in a book.

96   Rosalind pointedly looked at Orlando's crotch in Cheek by Jowl's production.

99   Macready indicates that Rosalind runs to the cottage and calls for Celia, who re-enters (pbk).

99–116   Helena Faucit wrote of the mock marriage that she 'could never speak these words without a trembling of the voice, and the involuntary rushing of happy tears to the eyes, which made it necesary for me to turn my head away from Orlando' (Faucit Martin, *On Rosalind*, p. 56). A reviewer noted 'the way in which . . . she uttered her own share of the vows in an aside of solemn tone and deep feeling' as evidence of Faucit's maintaining her feminine persona (*Observer*, 12 Mar. 1865); another reported that Faucit 'invested the scene with almost tragic impressiveness' (*Edinburgh Evening Courant*, 2 Dec. 1869, cited in Carlisle, p. 87). By contrast, Stein presented the mock wedding 'like a children's game, with Celia assuming a priest-like voice and striking the couple with her butterfly net to prompt them. The disadvantage in rendering the relationship between Orlando and his substitute beloved so innocent, childlike and flirtatious, was that the dangers of the situation never became apparent. What if Orlando came to love the pretty boy more than his absent sweetheart? How much was his love already a homosexual passion?' (Patterson, p. 144).

101   Orlando rises, crosses, and takes Rosalind's hand, a staging that partially mitigates her forwardness (Payne pbk).

102   'Celia is *appalled*' notes Juliet Stevenson, and 'rendered speechless by the loss of [her] friend' (Rutter, p. 116).

103   Rosalind speaks in a deep, mock-solemn voice in Czinner's film.

ROSALIND Aye, but when?

ORLANDO Why, now, as fast as she can marry us.

ROSALIND Then you must say, 'I take thee, Rosalind, for wife.'

ORLANDO I take thee, Rosalind, for wife.

ROSALIND I might ask you for your commission, but I do take thee,   110
Orlando, for my husband. There's a girl goes before the priest, and
certainly a woman's thought runs before her actions.

ORLANDO So do all thoughts: they are winged.

ROSALIND Now, tell me how long you would have her after you have
possessed her?   115

ORLANDO For ever and a day.

ROSALIND Say a day without the 'ever'. No, no, Orlando: men are April
when they woo, December when they wed; maids are May when
they are maids, but the sky changes when they are wives. I will be
more jealous of thee than a Barbary cock-pigeon over his hen; more   120
clamorous than a parrot against rain, more new-fangled than an ape;
more giddy in my desires than a monkey. I will weep for nothing,
like Diana in the fountain, and I will do that when you are disposed
to be merry. I will laugh like a hyena, and that when thou art
inclined to sleep.   125

ORLANDO But will my Rosalind do so?

ROSALIND By my life, she will do as I do.

ORLANDO O, but she is wise.

ROSALIND Or else she could not have the wit to do this: the wiser, the
waywarder. Make the doors upon a woman's wit, and it will out at   130
the casement; shut that, and 'twill out at the keyhole; stop that,
'twill fly with the smoke out at the chimney.

110a   Assigned to Celia in Benson's production (1904 pbk).

110–13   Frequently cut from the eighteenth century to Daly and Asche. The mood became so
charged in Hands's production that both Rosalind and Orlando 'had to break away for a
moment' (*SS* 34, 1981, p. 150). Juliet Stevenson as Rosalind fell towards Orlando. In Pimlott's
production, Rosalind gave Orlando 'a quick little kiss' (*SS* 50, 1997, p. 205). At Shakespeare's
Globe, 'the mock-wedding ended with a prolonged kiss that left Orlando gasping for
breath'; he was 'too conventional and unsophisticated not to react with a "yuck" after he
and his new pal let themselves get carried away' (*SS* 52, 1999, p. 224; *SQ* 50, 1999, p. 77).

115   Modjeska substituted the more proper 'married her' for the suggestive 'possessed her' (pbk).

117   Susan Fleetwood's Rosalind was 'strident rather than wry' (*SS* 34, 1981, p. 150).

121   Modjeska cut the slangy 'more new-fangled than an ape' (pbk).

132   A trumpet (Benson 1904 pbk) or horn (Asche pbk) sounds in the distance.

ORLANDO A man that had a wife with such a wit, he might say, 'Wit, whither wilt?'

ROSALIND Nay, you might keep that check for it till you met your   135
wife's wit going to your neighbour's bed.

ORLANDO And what wit could wit have to excuse that?

ROSALIND Marry, to say she came to seek you there: you shall never
take her without her answer unless you take her without her tongue.
O, that woman that cannot make her fault her husband's occasion,   140
let her never nurse her child herself for she will breed it like a fool.

ORLANDO For these two hours, Rosalind, I will leave thee.

ROSALIND Alas, dear love, I cannot lack thee two hours.

ORLANDO I must attend the Duke at dinner; by two o'clock I will be
with thee again.   145

ROSALIND Aye, go your ways, go your ways. I knew what you would

133–8   Cut by Helena Faucit (Moore pbk). Modjeska kept the lines but substituted 'house' for 'bed' in line 136 (pbk). Many others cut or abridged to 142.

141   Celia was assigned the song 'When daisies pied' from *Love's Labour's Lost*, with a new setting by Thomas Arne, in the 1740 production at Drury Lane. Depending on the vocal ability of the performers, in subsequent productions Rosalind sometimes performed the song. William Robson remembered Dora Jordan as Rosalind, 'with her two fingers saucily held up over the head of Orlando, while she warbled and laughed "Cuckoo" in his ear' (Robson, p. 142). Hazlitt recalled Miss Boyle's Rosalind at Covent Garden in 1816: 'We must not forget her Cuckoo-song; indeed we could not, if we would . . . The tone and manner in which she repeated the word Cuckoo, was as arch and provoking as possible, and seemed to grow more saucy every time by the repetition, but still, though it hovered very near them, it was restrained from passing the limits of delicacy and propriety' (Hazlitt, pp. 363–4). In 1842 Macready eliminated the 'Cuckoo song' because of moralists' and literary purists' objections (Shattuck, *Macready*). According to Moore's promptbook, Helena Faucit insisted it be cut. Mary Anderson's solution was to hum or sing the song when she entered in 3.3, rather than mocking Orlando with it here. Daly won praise from a reviewer (presumably William Winter) for 'reject[ing] the ancient and vulgar interpolation of "The Cuckoo Song" . . . long ago put into the mouth of the stage Rosalind, in order, apparently, to degrade her' (*The New York Daily Tribune*, 18 Dec. 1889).

142   Vanessa Redgrave, seated on the ground, grabbed Patrick Allen's leg and tugged him back as he began to depart. Cheek by Jowl's Orlando rose, shrieking, as he remembered his appointment.

146–9   Furness quotes a newspaper clipping describing Helena Faucit: 'Rosalind goes off in a fit of pouting and tears, the counterfeiting was so admirably done as to induce the momentary fancy that her character had broken down under the strain of self-denying deception. But in

prove – my friends told me as much, and I thought no less. That
flattering tongue of yours won me. 'Tis but one cast away, and so
come, Death! Two o'clock is your hour?

ORLANDO Aye, sweet Rosalind.　　　　　　　　　　　　　　　　150

ROSALIND By my troth, and in good earnest, and so God mend me,
　　and by all pretty oaths that are not dangerous, if you break one jot of
　　your promise or come one minute behind your hour, I will think
　　you the most pathetical break-promise, and the most hollow lover,
　　and the most unworthy of her you call Rosalind that may be chosen　　155
　　out of the gross band of the unfaithful. Therefore beware my cen-
　　sure, and keep your promise.

ORLANDO With no less religion than if thou wert indeed my Rosalind.
　　So adieu.

ROSALIND Well, Time is the old justice that examines all such offend-　　160
　　ers, and let Time try. Adieu.

　　　　　　　　　　　　　　　　　　　　　　Exit [Orlando]

---

an instant a radiant smile, growing to a half-railing laugh, altered the whole current, and
gave us back the arch yet earnest woman who overflows with gayety' (Furness edn.,
p. 428). Adelaide Neilson's 'low, thrilling cadences filled the house with such mournful
music, such despairing sweetness, as were never heard there. The effect upon the audience
was almost miraculous; for a stillness fell upon it, broken only by some sobbing women in
the boxes, who, in the next moment, were startled from their delicious tears by the actress's
sudden change to the most jubilant laughter, evoked by her triumphant befooling of her
lover' (Wingate, pp. 146–7). Cheek by Jowl's Orlando literally applauded Rosalind's
melodramatic performance of these lines.

149　Rosalind 'sinks her head on his shoulder as if about to faint. He bends forward anxiously to
　　look into her face. She bursts into a laugh "Two o'clock!"' (Moore pbk). Noble directed
　　Rosalind to fall and lie prone until Orlando approached; then she rose threateningly. In
　　Kahn's 1992 production, 'she pretended to kill herself by miming a plunge into a lake.
　　Orlando, entering into the spirit of the game, threw himself on top of her and began
　　playfully to administer CPR and mouth-to-mouth resuscitation. They both began to laugh,
　　and, forgetting that she is supposedly a boy, Rosalind put her arms around Orlando and
　　kissed him passionately before he pulled back in sudden confusion and Celia looked on,
　　appalled' (*SQ* 43, 1992, p. 471).

151–4　Edzard's Rosalind runs shouting after Orlando.

158　In Pimlott's production, the pair exchanged a long and passionate kiss 'which worried
　　Orlando deeply' (*SS* 50, 1997, p. 205).

161　Benson's Rosalind hooked Orlando's leg with her shepherd's crook and called him back.
　　Schooling him, she removed her cap and threw it on the ground; he did likewise. But when

CELIA You have simply misused our sex in your love-prate. We must have your doublet and hose plucked over your head, and show the world what the bird hath done to her own nest.

ROSALIND O coz, coz, coz, my pretty little coz, that thou didst know   165
how many fathom deep I am in love! But it cannot be sounded: my affection hath an unknown bottom like the Bay of Portugal.

CELIA Or rather bottomless, that as fast as you pour affection in, it runs out.

ROSALIND No, that same wicked bastard of Venus that was begot of   170
thought, conceived of spleen, and born of madness, that blind rascally boy that abuses everyone's eyes because his own are out, let him be judge how deep I am in love. I'll tell thee, Aliena, I cannot be out of the sight of Orlando. I'll go find a shadow and sigh till he come.   175

CELIA And I'll sleep.

Exeunt

she extended her hand for him to kiss, he merely shook it, and when she made 'kissing noises with her mouth', he playfully slapped her hand and exited. Left sitting on the bank, Rosalind kissed her own hand (Benson 1904 pbk). In Czinner's film, a weeping Rosalind calls 'at two o'clock', prompting Orlando to repeat the phrase and inspiring her to hug and kiss the tree beside her. In the 1978 BBC version, Rosalind reclines swooningly against a tree.

162–4   Bergner's Rosalind hugs Celia euphorically, despite being reprimanded. Celia appears reflective rather than angry in the 1978 BBC video.

162b–4   Frequently cut as indecorous, from Kemble to Daly and later in Elliott.

167   Elisabeth Bergner executes her notorious somersault with 'Bay of Portugal' in Czinner's film.

170–3   These lines were traditionally cut; Macready restored them but substituted 'child' for 'bastard' (Shattuck, *Macready*).

173–4   Susan Fleetwood's Rosalind 'verged on despair' (*SS* 34, 1981, p. 150).

176   Celia's closing line was cut when the action moved directly to 4.3 (Kemble edn, Daly pbk). Noble's Celia stayed sleeping on stage, and the hunt was staged as her nightmare/erotic dream.

ACT 4, SCENE 2

Enter JAQUES *and* LORDS, FORESTERS [*bearing the antlers and skin of a deer*]

JAQUES Which is he that killed the deer?
I LORD Sir, it was I.
JAQUES Let's present him to the Duke like a Roman conqueror – and it
    would do well to set the deer's horns upon his head for a branch of
    victory. – Have you no song, forester, for this purpose?   5
I FORESTER Yes, sir.
JAQUES Sing it. 'Tis no matter how it be in tune, so it make noise
    enough.

This scene appeared in Johnson's *Love in a Forest* but was cut from many early productions (Bell's, 1786, Kemble edns; Kean pbk). Macready restored it in 1842 for a pageant of forest lords and hunters who carried weapons and a slain deer on a pole; they were accompanied by dogs (Shattuck, *Macready*). Phelps put the deer carcass on a litter carried by the foresters; during the song, one of the huntsmen climbed astride the litter and was borne away triumphantly (pbk). In Arthur's promptbook, the scene is restored by hand as a pageant without dialogue. Three couples bearing garlanded shepherd's crooks entered, singing 'What shall he have that killed the deer', followed by more singing foresters, some hoisting a deer on their shoulders, others carrying boar spears. Modjeska moved the scene to Act 5, where it replaced 5.3 (pbk). Daly cut all the dialogue and made the scene a musical interlude preceding 4.1, with the hunters carrying a slain deer (pbk). Of the Pastoral Players' performance at Coombe house, a reviewer carped: 'when he who killed the deer was rewarded by being hoisted on to two poles and carried in the direction of a hidden fire the blue smoke of which drifted picturesquely across the scene, it seemed as if his reward were to be that of the hero of the Fifth of November [Guy Fawkes Day]' (*Bat*, 2 June 1885). In the 1963 RSC/BBC version, hunters with bows and arrows pursue deer; they shout jubilantly when a hit is scored and lift the deer on a pole, then the victorious hunter on their shoulders. Jaques approaches in a threatening, disapproving manner. In Stein's production, 'the slaughtered hart was skinned whereupon the men fell into a wild hunting dance' (Hortmann, p. 199). Dexter turned the scene into a pagan sacrifice. The gutted stag's entrails, 'formalised as a red garland', were draped in the on-stage tree, and 'the victorious

Music
Song

LORDS   What shall he have that killed the deer?
His leather skin and horns to wear.
Then sing him home,   10
The rest shall bear this burden:

Take thou no scorn to wear the horn,
It was a crest ere thou wast born;
    Thy father's father wore it,
    And thy father bore it;   15
The horn, the horn, the lusty horn,
Is not a thing to laugh to scorn.

Exeunt

William was smeared' with blood and crowned with the deer's antlers (*SS* 33, 1980,
pp. 179–80). Noble interpreted the scene as a disturbingly erotic dream by the sleeping
Celia. Jaques and the courtiers draped a bloody cloth around her and pursued her as the
prey. Ciulei offered a stylised staging, with 'a beautiful young woman as a "deer", from
whose neck streamed long red ribbons, as though of blood' (*SQ* 34, 1983, p. 233). In Cheek
by Jowl's production, several shirtless foresters washed up following their bloody sport.
Jaques struck the victorious killer of the deer with his gloves, and the others, singing, shoved
him. Edzard omits the scene. At Shakespeare's Globe, all the male characters wore Morris
bells for a ritual dance in which Amiens, wearing horns, played the part of the deer who was
'killed' (Miller-Schütz, 'Findings').

ACT 4, SCENE 3

Enter ROSALIND [*as* GANYMEDE] *and* CELIA [*as* ALIENA]

ROSALIND How say you now, is it not past two o'clock? And here much
 Orlando!

CELIA I warrant you, with pure love and troubled brain he hath ta'en his
 bow and arrows and is gone forth – to sleep. Look who comes here.

Enter SILVIUS [*with a letter*]

SILVIUS My errand is to you, fair youth;   5
                  My gentle Phoebe did bid me give you this:
                  I know not the contents but, as I guess
                  By the stern brow and waspish action
                  Which she did use as she was writing of it,
                  It bears an angry tenor. Pardon me,   10
                  I am but as a guiltless messenger.

ROSALIND [*After reading the letter*] Patience herself would startle at
                  this letter
                  And play the swaggerer: bear this, bear all.
                  She says I am not fair, that I lack manners;
                  She calls me proud, and that she could not love me   15
                  Were man as rare as phoenix. Od's my will,
                  Her love is not the hare that I do hunt –
                  Why writes she so to me? Well, shepherd, well?
                  This is a letter of your own device.

---

0 SD   In Czinner's film, Celia sings while Rosalind sleeps inside the cottage. Rosalind awakens
            angry about Orlando's absence; she shoves Celia at line 4. The two sit outside their cabin in
            Edzard's version, Rosalind playing with a yoyo, Celia working a crossword puzzle.

1–4   Cut when the action followed directly from the end of 4.1, as it frequently did from the
            eighteenth to the early twentieth century.

5–69   Cut in Czinner's film and the 1963 RSC/BBC version. Edzard cut 1–69.

11   The 'guiltless messenger' Silvius backs away in the 1978 BBC version, smiling slightly as
            Rosalind reads the letter.

11–29   Cut in Benson's 1904 promptbook.

12   Rosalind put on spectacles to read the letter in Cheek by Jowl's production.

SILVIUS No, I protest, I know not the contents;   20
          Phoebe did write it.
ROSALIND   Come, come, you are a fool
          And turned into the extremity of love.
          I saw her hand, she has a leathern hand,
          A freestone-coloured hand. (I verily did think
          That her old gloves were on, but 'twas her hands.)   25
          She has a hussif's hand – but that's no matter.
          I say she never did invent this letter:
          This is a man's invention and his hand.
SILVIUS Sure, it is hers.
ROSALIND Why, 'tis a boisterous and a cruel style,   30
          A style for challengers. Why, she defies me
          Like Turk to Christian. Woman's gentle brain
          Could not drop forth such giant-rude invention,
          Such Ethiop words, blacker in their effect
          Than in their countenance. Will you hear the letter?   35
SILVIUS So please you, for I never heard it yet,
          Yet heard too much of Phoebe's cruelty.
ROSALIND She Phoebes me. Mark how the tyrant writes:
          Reads 'Art thou god to shepherd turned,
                  That a maiden's heart hath burned?'   40
          Can a woman rail thus?
SILVIUS   Call you this railing?
ROSALIND *Reads* 'Why, thy godhead laid apart,
                  Warr'st thou with a woman's heart?' –
          Did you ever hear such railing? –
                  'Whiles the eye of man did woo me,   45
                  That could do no vengeance to me.' –
          Meaning me a beast!
                  'If the scorn of your bright eyne
                  Have power to raise such love in mine,
                  Alack, in me what strange effect   50
                  Would they work in mild aspect?

23–6   Sometimes cut, presumably as uncouth (1786 edn, Daly, Jones pbks). Kemble, Macready,
        Bridges-Adams, Holloway cut to line 30.

30–5a   Sometimes cut or abridged.

38–61   Cheek by Jowl's Rosalind gave the letter to illiterate Silvius, who held it upside down.
        Wearing her spectacles, Rosalind looked over his shoulder to read it, teaching him to
        recognize the word 'love'.

48–53   Cut or abridged by Daly, Benson (1904), Holloway, Williams (pbks).

> Whiles you chid me, I did love;
> How then might your prayers move?
> He that brings this love to thee
> Little knows this love in me;   55
> And by him seal up thy mind,
> Whether that thy youth and kind
> Will the faithful offer take
> Of me and all that I can make,
> Or else by him my love deny,   60
> And then I'll study how to die.'

SILVIUS Call you this chiding?

CELIA   Alas, poor shepherd.

ROSALIND Do you pity him? No, he deserves no pity. – Wilt thou love
such a woman? What, to make thee an instrument and play false
strains upon thee? Not to be endured! Well, go your way to her – for   65
I see love hath made thee a tame snake – and say this to her: that if
she love me, I charge her to love thee; if she will not, I will never
have her, unless thou entreat for her. If you be a true lover, hence,
and not a word; for here comes more company.

> *Exit Silvius*

> *Enter* OLIVER

61 Moore's and Daly's promptbooks have Rosalind repeat Touchstone's joking verse addition
from 3.3; she reads the last two lines in singsong tone and adds 'ti tum ti tum'.

63 Cheek by Jowl's Celia was especially sympathetic with the distraught Silvius.

65 'When Silvius continued his devotion in spite of the evidence of Phoebe's letter, Rosalind
spontaneously hugged him, giving her blessing to this tested and proven true lover' at the
Birmingham Repertory Theatre's production in 1981 (*SQ* 33, 1982, p. 191).

69 SD.2 Oliver's appearance creates a puzzle: is he ragged and hairy, as he describes himself in line
101? Or has he donned the 'fresh array' mentioned in line 138? Is he even recognisable? In
the early nineteenth century, Oxberry describes a brown, fur-trimmed doublet and
pantaloons for Oliver here, replacing the earlier, more ornate, outfit decorated with silver
embroidery. Moore's promptbook indicates that Oliver should be dressed less richly than in
his previous appearances and that Rosalind should seem briefly to recognise him. In
Czinner's film, Oliver sports boots, a short tunic, and a cape; his demeanour is strikingly
more free and lively than previously. Edzard's Oliver wears the same suit and dress coat as
before, now tattered and dirty as a result of his descent into the urban underworld. A
peculiarly modern solution to the problem was staged in a production at Oslo's National
Theatre in 1982: in the opening acts, a nasty Oliver was 'ungainly and fat'; his miraculous
transformation involved slimming down and becoming more cheerful (*SQ* 34, 1983, p. 241).

OLIVER Good morrow, fair ones. Pray you, if you know   70
    Where in the purlieus of this forest stands
    A sheepcote fenced about with olive-trees.
CELIA West of this place, down in the neighbour bottom;
    The rank of osiers by the murmuring stream,
    Left on your right hand, brings you to the place.   75
    But at this hour the house doth keep itself:
    There's none within.
OLIVER If that an eye may profit by a tongue,
    Then should I know you by description:
    Such garments, and such years. 'The boy is fair,   80
    Of female favour, and bestows himself
    Like a ripe sister; the woman low
    And browner than her brother.' Are not you
    The owners of the house I did enquire for?
CELIA It is no boast, being asked, to say we are.   85
OLIVER Orlando doth commend him to you both,
    And to that youth he calls his Rosalind
    He sends this bloody napkin. Are you he?
ROSALIND I am. What must we understand by this?
OLIVER Some of my shame, if you will know of me   90
    What man I am, and how, and why, and where
    This handkerchief was stained.
CELIA   I pray you tell it.
OLIVER When last the young Orlando parted from you,
    He left a promise to return again
    Within an hour and, pacing through the forest,   95
    Chewing the food of sweet and bitter fancy,
    Lo what befell. He threw his eye aside
    And mark what object did present itself.

80–3 Macready cut the quoted description (pbk).

86 In Macready's production, as Oliver advanced to tell his story, Celia put her arm around
    Rosalind's neck and drew back to listen (pbk).

88 Sometimes 'kerchief' has been substituted for 'napkin', here and throughout the scene
    (Arthur, Benson 1904 pbks).

98–115 The encounter is shown in the 1912 Vitagraph film: after a brief glimpse of the lion, Orlando
    disappears behind a bush and re-emerges with his arm bloodied, then Oliver rises to reveal
    himself. Czinner's film features a similar, though more suspenseful, scene: a snake slithers
    around the sleeping Oliver's neck, then a lioness approaches; the camera pans away as
    Orlando watches. The scene occurs before 4.3, leaving the outcome of the encounter
    temporarily unknown to viewers. In Edzard's film, a flashback shows Oliver sleeping in an

Under an old oak whose boughs were mossed with age,
And high top bald with dry antiquity,   100
A wretched ragged man, o'ergrown with hair,
Lay sleeping on his back; about his neck
A green and gilded snake had wreathed itself,
Who, with her head, nimble in threats, approached
The opening of his mouth. But suddenly   105
Seeing Orlando, it unlinked itself
And with indented glides did slip away
Into a bush; under which bush's shade
A lioness, with udders all drawn dry,
Lay couching head on ground, with cat-like watch   110
When that the sleeping man should stir – for 'tis
The royal disposition of that beast
To prey on nothing that doth seem as dead.
This seen, Orlando did approach the man
And found it was his brother, his elder brother.   115
CELIA O I have heard him speak of that same brother,
And he did render him the most unnatural
That lived amongst men.
OLIVER   And well he might so do,
For well I know he was unnatural.
ROSALIND But to Orlando – did he leave him there,   120
Food to the sucked and hungry lioness?
OLIVER Twice did he turn his back and purposed so.
But kindness, nobler ever than revenge,
And nature, stronger than his just occasion,
Made him give battle to the lioness,   125
Who quickly fell before him; in which hurtling
From miserable slumber I awaked.

underpass as a thief approaches and Orlando does battle with the human predator. The action is more difficult to stage in the theatre, but the huge space of the CCC Film Studio allowed multiple platforms of action in Stein's production: Orlando could be seen 'wrestl[ing] for his very life with a wild beast' as Oliver narrated the action (Patterson, p. 135). Noble had Oliver 'paint' the scene with outstretched arm. As he gazed into the distance, Celia and Rosalind seemed to share his vision. In Geraldine McEwan's production, Oliver took Celia 'confidentially by the arm and [told] his story very much for her benefit' (*SS* 42, 1989, p. 129). Cheek by Jowl's Oliver spoke exclusively to Celia, kneeling beside her. Rosalind stood behind the pair, horrified at Oliver's words.

116–18 Rosalind spoke these lines in Kean's production, eliminating the problem of Celia criticising the person with whom she is about to fall in love (pbk).

CELIA Are you his brother?
ROSALIND   Was't you he rescued?
CELIA Was't you that did so oft contrive to kill him?
OLIVER 'Twas I, but 'tis not I. I do not shame   130
          To tell you what I was, since my conversion
          So sweetly tastes, being the thing I am.
ROSALIND But for the bloody napkin?
OLIVER   By and by.
          When from the first to last betwixt us two,
          Tears our recountments had most kindly bathed –   135
          As how I came into that desert place –
          In brief, he led me to the gentle Duke
          Who gave me fresh array and entertainment,
          Committing me unto my brother's love,
          Who led me instantly unto his cave;   140
          There stripped himself and here, upon his arm,
          The lioness had torn some flesh away,
          Which all this while had bled; and now he fainted,
          And cried in fainting upon Rosalind.
          Brief, I recovered him, bound up his wound,   145
          And, after some small space, being strong at heart,
          He sent me hither, stranger as I am,
          To tell this story that you might excuse
          His broken promise, and to give this napkin,
          Dyed in this blood, unto the shepherd youth   150
          That he in sport doth call his Rosalind.
                    [*Rosalind faints*]

128–9, 133 Kean assigned Celia's speeches to Rosalind, and Rosalind's to Celia (pbk).

     133 In Cheek by Jowl's staging, Oliver and Celia gestured for Rosalind to move away.

   140–5 Helena Faucit believed Rosalind's faint should result from the 'strain upon her feelings',
          rather than the mere sight of the bloody napkin (Faucit Martin, *On Rosalind*, p. 63).

  140–51 In Edzard's film, Emma Croft as Rosalind hypnotically follows the napkin in Oliver's hand;
          her eyes roll back as she faints.

  151 SD In Macready's version, Ganymede was caught by Oliver and Celia as she fell backward
          (Shattuck, *Macready*). Daly directed Oliver to move quickly forward and support the
          collapsing Rosalind (pbk). A reviewer called Ada Rehan's response to the bloody kerchief
          'incomparably beautiful': 'in an instant the face alters – gaiety is dismissed for a look of
          horror. It has become prematurely old. The masquerading boy has gone, and the veritable
          woman has come back again' (*Daily Telegraph*, 16 July 1890). Julia Neilson 'positively
          seemed to turn pale, the totter and fall had not the appearance of a stage trick at all' (*Daily*

CELIA Why, how now? Ganymede, sweet Ganymede!
OLIVER Many will swoon when they do look on blood.
CELIA There is more in it. – Cousin! Ganymede!
OLIVER [*Raising Rosalind*] Look, he recovers.   155
ROSALIND I would I were at home.
CELIA We'll lead you thither. – I pray you, will you take him by the arm.
OLIVER Be of good cheer, youth. You a man? You lack a man's heart.
ROSALIND I do so, I confess it. Ah, sirrah, a body would think this was
    well counterfeited. I pray you tell your brother how well I counter-   160
    feited. Heigh-ho!
OLIVER This was not counterfeit: there is too great testimony in your
    complexion that it was a passion of earnest.
ROSALIND Counterfeit, I assure you.
OLIVER Well then, take a good heart, and counterfeit to be a man.   165

Telegraph, 3 Dec. 1896). Julia Arthur's promptbook: 'as Rosalind holds out her right hand
to take the handkerchief from Oliver, she falls forward'. Supported by Oliver and Celia, her
'head falls back on Celia's shoulder. Rosalind is not the kind of woman to faint *dead away*
at the sight of a little blood. So she does not fall to stage. During this business, Celia drops
flowers.' Julia Marlowe, asked if she powdered her face to make Rosalind turn pale, denied
ever having done so: 'though I do at that point turn my back to the audience, I do it for so
very brief a moment that I have no opportunity to powder my face . . . [But if] I act Rosalind
skilfully enough, the idea of her pallor will so take its place in the minds of the spectators
that they will not concern themselves too much with the actual color of my face' (Russell,
p. 455). Vanessa Redgrave's Rosalind approached to take the cloth, tottered, and fell to the
ground. Juliet Stevenson fell on her back at the feet of Celia and Oliver, but the smitten
couple gazed at one another for several long moments before Celia broke off to attend to
Ganymede. At Shakespeare's Globe in 1998, Celia 'seized and kissed [Oliver] intently over
the body of the fainting Ganymede' (*SS* 52, 1999, p. 224).

154 At Stratford in 1968, Celia was 'clearly suggesting that there is more in the shirt rather than
    more in the argument' (*Financial Times*, 22 May 1968). Similarly in the 1978 BBC version,
    when 'Oliver stoops to undo Ganymede's doublet, Aliena stops his hand' (Bulman, p. 177).

157 Julia Marlowe stood 'swaying meekly' (Sothern–Marlowe pbk). Fiona Shaw as Celia
    pointedly removed Oliver's hands from Rosalind's chest, and emphasised 'take him by the
    arm'.

159–60 'Ah, sirrah . . . counterfeited' was cut in early productions (Bell's, 1786 edns; Macready pbk).

161 'Heigh ho' is cut in Benson's 1904 promptbook, damping Rosalind's spirits a bit.

165 Oliver often slaps or punches Rosalind with this line. Moore's promptbook has him 'slapping
    her gently on the shoulder' so that she 'winces' but recovers herself with an arch glance at
    Celia. Julia Marlowe's Rosalind cried out and nearly fell when Oliver slapped her on the

ROSALIND So I do. But, i'faith, I should have been a woman by right.
CELIA Come, you look paler and paler: pray you, draw homewards. –
     Good sir, go with us.
OLIVER That will I. For I must bear answer back how you excuse my
     brother, Rosalind.   170
ROSALIND I shall devise something. But I pray you commend my
     counterfeiting to him. Will you go?

Exeunt

back (Sothern–Marlowe pbk). Jones's politer Oliver put his arm around Rosalind's shoulder, and she 'curled into him' with the second semi-faint (pbk). In Ciulei's 1982 production, Oliver 'clapped a hand to her breast and recoiled in understandable astonishment turning to amusement, with "counterfeit to be a man!" taking a literal turn' (SQ 34, 1983, p. 233).

167–72   Cut in Kean's production (pbk).

168   Celia's line to Oliver is 'her last in the play, and the two women never speak to each other again' (Shaw and Stevenson, p. 70).

172   Rosalind sometimes has suffered a second faint or semi-collapse at this point, if not sooner. At Stratford in 1885, Mary Anderson 'fainted first this way, then that, ostensibly posing all the while for effect' (*Stage*, 4 Sept. 1885). Constance Benson's Rosalind cried out 'Celia' in place of 'will you go', and collapsed into her cousin's arms (Benson 1904 pbk). Edith Evans gave a 'half-challenging, half-pitiful cry, that her "counterfeiting" should be commended' (unidentified clipping, Mar. 1926, TM). Juliet Stevenson as Rosalind managed to walk off but Celia and Oliver remained behind staring at one another until Rosalind prompted them to go.

172 SD   At Wallack's in 1898–99, a bit of business showed the alliance between Oliver and Celia. As Rosalind turned to exit, Oliver knelt and picked up the flowers Celia had dropped. He pulled one flower from the bunch and returned the balance to a blushing Celia, both 'show[ing] love in this business'. When Rosalind turned and observed, 'astonished', Oliver shook his finger at Rosalind, who looked 'frowningly' on Oliver 'as a brother who found his sister flirting might do'. But when Oliver pantomimed 'I'll tell on you', Rosalind laughed and held out her hand to the couple, and all exited laughing (Arthur pbk).

ACT 5, SCENE I

Enter TOUCHSTONE *and* AUDREY

TOUCHSTONE We shall find a time, Audrey; patience, gentle Audrey.
AUDREY Faith, the priest was good enough, for all the old gentleman's
　　saying.
TOUCHSTONE A most wicked Sir Oliver, Audrey, a most vile Martext.
　　But, Audrey, there is a youth here in the forest lays claim to you.　　　5
AUDREY Aye, I know who 'tis. He hath no interest in me in the world.

Enter WILLIAM
　　Here comes the man you mean.

O SD The order of this scene and 5.2 has sometimes been reversed. Edzard cut the scene. Audrey is usually unhappy and sometimes desperate. At Wallack's in 1898–9, Audrey tried to embrace Touchstone as the scene began, but he stopped her (Arthur pbk). Bridges-Adams indicates that Audrey should enter weeping, Touchstone following her (pbk). In Czinner's film, Audrey hangs laundry while conversing with Touchstone, who is now dressed in a goatskin tunic. Audrey sits on the branch of a tree in the 1963 RSC/BBC version. In Noble's production she stuck her fingers in her ears, impatient with Touchstone's excuses.

6 SD Slow-witted William helps to confirm the class differences between Arden's countryfolk and their loftier visitors. Westland Marston recalled the 'air of peasant wonder and panic' conveyed by Robert Keeley as William in 1842 (Marston, vol. 2, p. 108). At Stratford, Ontario, in 1972, Colin Bernhardt played William as as 'a gorgeous placid rustic' who 'watched Touchstone's ferocious attempts to vanquish him like a large, amiable dog puzzled by the antics of a busy bug' (SQ 4, 1972, p. 393). In Papp's production, William was 'so deep in a fog that his blank smile never changed from entrance to exit' (SQ 24, 1973, p. 424). Dexter rehabilitated William: he was 'a local country boy who had killed the deer, who was clearly employed by the Duke as a page (and so sang "It was a lover and his lass") and by Rosalind to play Hymen, and who was at the heart' of the rituals opening the play (SS 33, 1980, p. 179). Noble's production featured a gigantic William who hefted a log on his shoulder. Cheek by Jowl's William was not only dressed like Audrey in overalls and tattered sweater, but yodelled as much and as loudly.

TOUCHSTONE It is meat and drink to me to see a clown. By my troth,
we that have good wits have much to answer for. We shall be
flouting; we cannot hold.   10
WILLIAM Good ev'n, Audrey.
AUDREY God ye good ev'n, William.
WILLIAM [*Taking off his hat*] And good ev'n to you, sir.
TOUCHSTONE Good ev'n, gentle friend. Cover thy head, cover thy
head. Nay prithee, be covered. How old are you, friend?   15
WILLIAM Five and twenty, sir.
TOUCHSTONE A ripe age. Is thy name William?
WILLIAM William, sir.
TOUCHSTONE A fair name. Wast born i'th'forest here?
WILLIAM Aye, sir, I thank God.   20
TOUCHSTONE 'Thank God': a good answer. Art rich?
WILLIAM Faith, sir, so-so.
TOUCHSTONE 'So-so' is good, very good, very excellent good – and
yet it is not: it is but so-so. Art thou wise?
WILLIAM Aye, sir, I have a pretty wit.   25
TOUCHSTONE Why, thou say'st well. I do now remember a saying:
'The fool doth think he is wise, but the wise man knows himself to
be a fool.'
                        [*William gapes*]
The heathen philosopher, when he had a desire to eat a grape,
would open his lips when he put it into his mouth, meaning thereby   30
that grapes were made to eat and lips to open. You do love this
maid?
WILLIAM I do, sir.
TOUCHSTONE Give me your hand. Art thou learned?

13–19 William repeatedly lifts his hat and returns it to his head, laughing foolishly
(Sothern–Marlowe pbk).
14 Cheek by Jowl's William covered his head with his hands, giving his hat to Audrey.
18 Pronounced 'Will-um' in Cheek by Jowl's production.
34 Touchstone must invent some sort of business to account for taking William's hand. In
Arthur's promptbook, Touchstone takes Audrey's hand as well as William's and is 'about to
join them together' when he 'stops suddenly'. Benson indicates that when William offers his
hand, Touchstone slaps it away, then wipes his own hand on his clothes; Touchstone
proceeds to take William's left hand, touching the palm in a way that causes William to
laugh as if tickled (1904 pbk). Touchstone tickled William's hand with his bauble in
Bridges-Adams's version (pbk). In Noble's production, the strength of William's grip forced
Touchstone to his knees.

WILLIAM No, sir.   35

TOUCHSTONE Then learn this of me: to have is to have. For it is a figure
    in rhetoric that drink, being poured out of a cup into a glass, by
    filling the one doth empty the other. For all your writers do consent
    that '*ipse*' is he. Now you are not *ipse*, for I am he.

WILLIAM Which he, sir?   40

TOUCHSTONE He, sir, that must marry this woman. Therefore, you
    clown, abandon, which is in the vulgar 'leave', the society, which in
    the boorish is 'company', of this female, which in the common is
    'woman': which together is 'abandon the society of this female'; or,
    clown, thou perishest or, to thy better understanding, 'diest', or, to   45
    wit, 'I kill thee', 'make thee away', 'translate thy life into death, thy
    liberty into bondage'! I will deal in poison with thee, or in bastinado,
    or in steel! I will bandy with thee in faction, I will o'errun thee with
    policy – I will kill thee a hundred and fifty ways! Therefore, tremble
    and depart.   50

AUDREY Do, good William.

WILLIAM God rest you merry, sir.   *Exit*

Enter CORIN

CORIN Our master and mistress seeks you. Come away, away.

TOUCHSTONE Trip, Audrey, trip, Audrey. – I attend, I attend.

Exeunt

41–50 Macready had William retreat 'in fright and bewilderment', only to be chased around the
    stage by Touchstone (Shattuck, *Macready*). The chase became traditional. David Tennant,
    who played Touchstone at Stratford in 1996, recalled how William (Simeon Defoe) watched
    'impassively as Touchstone's mania mounted so that by "I will o'errun thee with policy; I will
    kill thee a hundred and fifty ways" . . . I was dancing around him, shrieking and threatening
    him with my walking stick, and with "therefore tremble and depart" I was screaming in his
    face. Simeon coolly grabbed me by the shoulder and floored me with a headbutt . . .'
    (Tennant, p. 41).

50 Czinner's William knocks down the line of drying laundry. Jones indicates that William raises
    his hand to hit Touchstone, but upon Audrey's request, he offers instead to shake it (pbk).

51 Cheek by Jowl's Audrey kissed William.

52 SD In Noble's production, Touchstone strove to stay out of William's way but was knocked into
    the stream by the log carried on the yokel's shoulder.

53 Corin's line was cut in the eighteenth century and frequently thereafter. Daly inserted the
    bulk of 5.3 here (pbk).

54 Touchstone's line became 'drip, drip' in Noble's production, in which the clown was twice
    dunked in a large pool on stage (*SQ* 37, 1986, p. 116).

ACT 5, SCENE 2

Enter ORLANDO *and* OLIVER

ORLANDO Is't possible that on so little acquaintance you should like
her, that, but seeing, you should love her, and, loving, woo, and,
wooing, she should grant? And will you persevere to enjoy her?
OLIVER Neither call the giddiness of it in question, the poverty of her,
the small acquaintance, my sudden wooing, nor her sudden con-   5
senting. But say with me I love Aliena; say with her that she loves
me; consent with both that we may enjoy each other. It shall be to
your good, for my father's house and all the revenue that was old Sir
Roland's will I estate upon you, and here live and die a shepherd.

Enter ROSALIND [*as* GANYMEDE]

ORLANDO You have my consent. Let your wedding be tomorrow;   10
thither will I invite the Duke and all's contented followers. Go you,
and prepare Aliena, for look you, here comes my 'Rosalind'.
ROSALIND God save you, brother.

Asche presented this scene after 5.3, which followed directly from 5.1 (pbk).

0 SD   Frequently Orlando's arm is in a sling. Benson opened the scene with Orlando seated on a
bank, Oliver kneeling beside him (1904 pbk). In Czinner's film, a shot of Orlando and Oliver
walking through the forest is followed by one of Celia singing to Rosalind ('Tell me where is
fancy bred' from *The Merchant of Venice*) within the cottage; the camera then returns to the
two brothers.

1–14   Cut in 1963 RSC/BBC, where the scene opens with Rosalind kneeling pityingly beside a
recumbent Orlando. In Edzard's film, where the scene takes place inside Orlando's tent, this
passage is cut.

3, 7   Benson substituted 'marry' for 'enjoy' in these lines (1904 pbk).

9   Orlando looked sceptical until Oliver offered his estate in Cheek by Jowl's production.

9 SD   Asche had Celia enter with Rosalind, and exit with Oliver after 14 (pbk). Emma Croft as
Rosalind brings a packet of grapes to Orlando, who writes a letter by flashlight within his
tent.

OLIVER And you, fair 'sister'.   [*Exit*]
ROSALIND O, my dear Orlando, how it grieves me to see thee wear thy   15
    heart in a scarf.
ORLANDO It is my arm.
ROSALIND I thought thy heart had been wounded with the claws of a
    lion.
ORLANDO Wounded it is, but with the eyes of a lady.   20
ROSALIND Did your brother tell you how I counterfeited to swoon
    when he showed me your handkerchief?
ORLANDO Aye, and greater wonders than that.
ROSALIND O, I know where you are. Nay, 'tis true, there was never
    anything so sudden but the fight of two rams, and Caesar's   25
    thrasonical brag of 'I came, saw, and overcame.' For your brother
    and my sister no sooner met but they looked; no sooner looked, but
    they loved; no sooner loved, but they sighed; no sooner sighed,
    but they asked one another the reason; no sooner knew the reason,
    but they sought the remedy; and in these degrees have they made a   30
    pair of stairs to marriage, which they will climb incontinent – or else
    be incontinent before marriage. They are in the very wrath of love,
    and they will together – clubs cannot part them.
ORLANDO They shall be married tomorrow and I will bid the Duke to
    the nuptial. But O, how bitter a thing it is to look into happiness   35
    through another man's eyes. By so much the more shall I tomorrow
    be at the height of heart-heaviness, by how much I shall think my
    brother happy in having what he wishes for.
ROSALIND Why then, tomorrow, I cannot serve your turn for Rosalind?

14 Oliver slaps Rosalind on the back, causing her to stumble, in the 1978 BBC version. Cheek
    by Jowl's Oliver showed considerable irritation, even anger, with Rosalind.
21 Helpmann cut 'to swoon' (pbk).
23 In Noble's production, Orlando stared at Rosalind's body (which Oliver had touched after
    her swoon in 4.3).
31–2 Macready cut 'which . . . marriage' (pbk), as did others up to Daly and Benson. Modjeska
    substituted 'which they must climb together' for the line about marriage and incontinence
    (pbk). Arthur restored 'which they will climb incontinent' but not the rest (pbk). Obviously
    Freud was not the first to think climbing stairs a metaphor for sexual intercourse.
39–40 Copeau's direction: 'She goes toward him and, from behind, puts her hand on his shoulder.
    These are vows that they are about to exchange, strangely formulated: "Why then tomorrow
    I cannot serve your turn for Rosalind?" "I can live no longer by thinking." He has bowed his
    head and shaken it. She is behind him; tender and mysterious' (quoted in Speaight, p. 193).

ORLANDO I can live no longer by thinking.   40
ROSALIND I will weary you then no longer with idle talking. Know of
    me, then – for now I speak to some purpose – that I know you are
    a gentleman of good conceit. I speak not this that you should bear a
    good opinion of my knowledge, insomuch, I say, I know you are;
    neither do I labour for a greater esteem than may in some little   45
    measure draw a belief from you to do yourself good, and not to
    grace me. Believe then, if you please, that I can do strange things. I
    have, since I was three year old, conversed with a magician, most
    profound in his art, and yet not damnable. If you do love Rosalind
    so near the heart as your gesture cries it out, when your brother   50
    marries Aliena shall you marry her. I know into what straits of
    fortune she is driven, and it is not impossible to me, if it appear not
    inconvenient to you, to set her before your eyes tomorrow, human
    as she is, and without any danger.
ORLANDO Speak'st thou in sober meanings?   55
ROSALIND By my life, I do, which I tender dearly, though I say I am a
    magician. Therefore put you in your best array, bid your friends.
    For if you will be married tomorrow, you shall, and to Rosalind, if
    you will.

Enter SILVIUS *and* PHOEBE

    Look, here comes a lover of mine and a lover of hers.   60
PHOEBE Youth, you have done me much ungentleness
    To show the letter that I writ to you.

40   Roger Warren on Andrew Gillies's 'firm but gentle' Orlando: 'Other Orlandos have made "I
     can live no longer by thinking" a frustrated outburst, or merely dismissive; Mr Gillies spoke
     the line quietly, reasonably, almost unwilling to spoil Ganymede's fun' (*SS* 39, 1986, p. 181).
     Juliet Stevenson as Rosalind stood behind Orlando, who was seated by the stream, 'so what
     he gazed upon was Ganymede's reflection in the water. And as he looked, Ganymede
     began to look more and more like Rosalind' (Rutter, pp. 117–18). Orlando 'pushed
     Ganymede roughly away in frustration' in Kahn's staging (*SQ* 43, 1992, p. 469).
42–7 Rosalind's prolixity was corrected on eighteenth- and nineteenth-century stages, and
     sometimes later, by omission of these lines.
47   In 1973, Papp's Orlando 'backed off warily' – and homophobically – 'when [Ganymede] said
     with a knowing smile that he could "do strange things"' (*SQ* 24, 1973, p. 424). Adrian Lester
     paused suggestively before claiming the ability to 'do strange things'.
48   In apparent deference to developmental psychology, Modjeska substituted 'five' for 'three'
     (pbk).
60–7 As Cheek by Jowl's Rosalind sat beside Orlando with a blanket over their legs, first Phoebe,
     then Silvius, joined them.

ROSALIND I care not if I have. It is my study
    To seem despiteful and ungentle to you.
    You are there followed by a faithful shepherd;   65
    Look upon him, love him: he worships you.
PHOEBE Good shepherd, tell this youth what 'tis to love.
SILVIUS It is to be all made of sighs and tears,
    And so am I for Phoebe.
PHOEBE And I for Ganymede.   70
ORLANDO And I for Rosalind.
ROSALIND And I for no woman.
SILVIUS It is to be all made of faith and service,
    And so am I for Phoebe.
PHOEBE And I for Ganymede.   75
ORLANDO And I for Rosalind.
ROSALIND And I for no woman.
SILVIUS It is to be all made of fantasy,
    All made of passion, and all made of wishes,
    All adoration, duty, and observance,   80
    All humbleness, all patience, and impatience,
    All purity, all trial, all obedience.
    And so am I for Phoebe.
PHOEBE And so am I for Ganymede.
ORLANDO And so am I for Rosalind.   85
ROSALIND And so am I for no woman.
PHOEBE [*To Rosalind*] If this be so, why blame you me to love you?
SILVIUS [*To Phoebe*] If this be so, why blame you me to love you?
ORLANDO If this be so, why blame you me to love you?
ROSALIND Who do you speak to 'Why blame you me to love you'?   90
ORLANDO To her that is not here nor doth not hear.

72 Rosalind made a 'just-in-time correction of a confession that was going to end "for
  Orlando"' in a performance by the Birmingham Repertory Theatre; the repetitions of the
  line were 'a mournful reminder to herself that her love still could not be expressed openly'
  (*SQ* 33, 1982, p. 191).

73–91 The lovers' chorus can be tediously ritualistic; it was cut in the eighteenth century (Bell's
  edn) and has sometimes been abridged. Macready restored all but the last three lines (pbk).
  In Nunn's production, the chorus was sung, with overlapping musical repetitions (*SS* 31,
  1978, p. 147). At Stratford in 1980, the 'formal litany . . . became the verbal release of
  pent-up frustration which – just – managed to stave off mocking laughter' (*SS* 34, 1981,
  p. 150). In Edzard's film, the four lovers' faces are barely seen as they stand apart in the fog;
  the confusion of lines 89–90 results in part from the obscuring of vision.

ROSALIND Pray you no more of this: 'tis like the howling of Irish wolves
against the moon. [*To Silvius*] I will help you, if I can. [*To Phoebe*]
I would love you, if I could. – Tomorrow meet me all together. –
[*To Phoebe*] I will marry you, if ever I marry woman, and I'll be   95
married tomorrow. [*To Orlando*] I will satisfy you, if ever I satisfy
man, and you shall be married tomorrow. [*To Silvius*] I will content you, if what pleases you contents you, and you shall be married
tomorrow. [*To Orlando*] As you love Rosalind, meet; [*To Silvius*]
as you love Phoebe, meet – and as I love no woman, I'll meet. So   100
fare you well: I have left you commands.
SILVIUS I'll not fail, if I live.
PHOEBE Nor I.
ORLANDO Nor I.

                                            Exeunt

92   Silvius, Phoebe, and Orlando were all bawling in Cheek by Jowl's version.
101–4 Kean had the lovers exit seriatim as Rosalind addressed them (pbk).

ACT 5, SCENE 3

Enter TOUCHSTONE *and* AUDREY

TOUCHSTONE Tomorrow is the joyful day, Audrey; tomorrow will we
be married.
AUDREY I do desire it with all my heart, and I hope it is no dishonest
desire to desire to be a woman of the world?

Enter two PAGES

Here come two of the banished Duke's pages.   5
1 PAGE Well met, honest gentleman.
TOUCHSTONE By my troth, well met. Come, sit, sit, and a song.
2 PAGE We are for you; sit i'th'middle.
1 PAGE Shall we clap into't roundly, without hawking, or spitting, or
saying we are hoarse, which are the only prologues to a bad voice?   10

The scene was frequently cut early on, reducing Touchstone and Audrey's potentially
offensive romance but also eliminating the song 'It was a lover and his lass.' Macready
restored the scene and the song. Daly combined the scene with 5.1 (pbk); a reviewer
commented: 'probably for the first time in modern memory Touchstone sits between the
pages [who] . . . sing that most delicious poem in all the Shakespearean anthology' (*Daily
Telegraph*, 16 July 1890). Sothern and Marlowe sometimes cut the scene; or staged it with
the song presented as a round, the second and third pages joining in separately. Cheek by
Jowl's Touchstone and Audrey played a cassette tape of the traditional wedding march. In
Edzard's film, the scene takes place in the now abandoned office foyer where the court
scenes were played earlier.

1–2   Toye substituted 'today' for 'tomorrow' in each instance (pbk). Derek Jacobi's Touchstone
was 'thrown back' in an 'embrace' by Anthony Hopkins' Audrey (Williams pbk). Noble's
Touchstone pronounced the words mournfully.

4 SD   The two nervous young singers in Coleman's BBC version take up posts on either side of
Touchstone, as Audrey moves apart. In Edzard's film they are a pair of sweet-voiced
derelicts drinking in the abandoned building.

5   'Followers' for 'pages' (Bridge-Adams pbk).

2 PAGE Aye, faith, i'faith, and both in a tune like two gipsies on a horse.

1 AND 2 PAGE It was a lover and his lass,

    With a hey, and a ho, and a hey nonny-no,

    That o'er the green cornfield did pass,

        In spring-time, 15

        The only pretty ring-time,

           When birds do sing;

        Hey ding-a-ding, ding,

           Sweet lovers love the spring.

    Between the acres of the rye, 20

    With a hey, and a ho, and a hey nonny-no,

    These pretty country folks would lie,

        In spring-time,

        The only pretty ring-time,

           When birds do sing; 25

        Hey ding-a-ding, ding,

           Sweet lovers love the spring.

    This carol they began that hour,

    With a hey, and a ho, and a hey nonny-no,

    How that a life was but a flower; 30

        In spring-time,

        The only pretty ring-time,

           When birds do sing;

        Hey ding-a-ding, ding,

           Sweet lovers love the spring. 35

12–43   Audrey joins in the song, out of tune, while Touchstone dozes; at its conclusion he wakes up, sees the pages with Audrey and pulls her away (Bridges-Adams pbk). Toye choreographed an elaborate ballet between Touchstone and Audrey, ending with their exit (pbk). Touchstone plays the pipe for the 'hey nonny nonnies' in the 1963 RSC/BBC version. In the 1978 BBC video, the pages punch Touchstone and eventually he sends them rolling down the hillside. Noble staged the song as a comically gymnastic dance routine, featuring coloured sashes that added visual variety to the black and white costuming. Kenneth Branagh's Touchstone 'appropriated' the song, 'singing it with hand-clapping gusto to Corin's banjo accompaniment' (*SS* 42, 1989, p. 130). It was 'a show-stopping chorus as Touchstone tried to keep Audrey away from the adult pages, while the four sat and cuddled under a blanket with their eight feet dancing to the tune' in Cheek by Jowl (*SS* 44, 1991, p. 130). At Shakespeare's Globe, the song included a 'farcical striptease' (*SS* 52, 1999, 222).

And therefore take the present time; 35
With a hey, and a ho, and a hey nonny-no,
For love is crownèd with the prime,
    In spring-time,
    The only pretty ring-time,
        When birds do sing; 40
    Hey ding-a-ding, ding,
        Sweet lovers love the spring.

TOUCHSTONE Truly, young gentlemen, though there was no great
    matter in the ditty, yet the note was very untunable.

I PAGE You are deceived, sir: we kept time; we lost not our time. 45

TOUCHSTONE By my troth, yes. I count it but time lost to hear such a
    foolish song. God buy you, and God mend your voices. – Come,
    Audrey.

Exeunt

47   One of the two small singers in Goodbody's production retorted 'same to you' to
     Touchstone's rebuke (*Financial Times*, 13 June 1973).

ACT 5, SCENE 4

Enter DUKE SENIOR, AMIENS, JAQUES, ORLANDO, OLIVER,
CELIA [*as* ALIENA]

DUKE SENIOR Dost thou believe, Orlando, that the boy
    Can do all this that he hath promisèd?
ORLANDO I sometimes do believe and sometimes do not,
    As those that fear they hope and know they fear.

Enter ROSALIND [*as* GANYMEDE], SILVIUS, *and* PHOEBE

ROSALIND Patience once more whiles our compact is urged. –   5
    You say, if I bring in your Rosalind,
    You will bestow her on Orlando here?
DUKE SENIOR That would I, had I kingdoms to give with her.
ROSALIND And you say you will have her, when I bring her?
ORLANDO That would I, were I of all kingdoms king.   10
ROSALIND You say you'll marry me, if I be willing.
PHOEBE That will I, should I die the hour after.
ROSALIND But if you do refuse to marry me,
    You'll give yourself to this most faithful shepherd.
PHOEBE So is the bargain.   15
ROSALIND You say that you'll have Phoebe if she will.

0 SD   The scene has frequently been abridged. Benson opened it with a pageant that took the place of Hymen's appearance: a chorus of foresters, maids, and children arranged their assorted crooks, spades, hoes, and pitchforks to form an arch under which the bridal couples passed (1904 pbk). Czinner sets the scene in a courtyard, less grand than that at Frederick's castle but far from rustic. Shepherds with herds of sheep, followed by bands of young women, enter through the gates to be received by Duke Senior and his men. In Cheek by Jowl's staging, choral music played as an altar was set up. Celia was greeted by her admirer Corin, who offered a newspaper-wrapped packet – evidently a gift of freshly killed meat.

4–92   Omitted in Czinner's film.

5–25   Rosalind's pre-wedding appearance in this scene has often been cut. Cheek by Jowl's Adrian Lester spoke very rapidly, as if ticking items from a check-list.

SILVIUS Though to have her and death were both one thing.
ROSALIND I have promised to make all this matter even. –
      Keep you your word, O Duke, to give your daughter. –
      You yours, Orlando, to receive his daughter. –   20
      Keep your word, Phoebe, that you'll marry me
      Or else, refusing me, to wed this shepherd. –
      Keep your word, Silvius, that you'll marry her
      If she refuse me – and from hence I go
      To make these doubts all even.   25
                    Exeunt Rosalind and Celia
DUKE SENIOR I do remember in this shepherd boy
      Some lively touches of my daughter's favour.
ORLANDO My lord, the first time that I ever saw him,
      Methought he was a brother to your daughter;
      But, my good lord, this boy is forest-born   30
      And hath been tutored in the rudiments
      Of many desperate studies by his uncle
      Whom he reports to be a great magician,
      Obscurèd in the circle of this forest.

      Enter TOUCHSTONE *and* AUDREY

JAQUES There is sure another flood toward, and these couples are com-   35
    ing to the ark. Here comes a pair of very strange beasts which, in all
    tongues, are called fools.
TOUCHSTONE Salutation and greeting to you all.
JAQUES Good my lord, bid him welcome. This is the motley-minded
    gentleman that I have so often met in the forest: he hath been a   40
    courtier, he swears.
TOUCHSTONE If any man doubt that, let him put me to my purgation.
    I have trod a measure; I have flattered a lady; I have been politic
    with my friend, smooth with mine enemy; I have undone three
    tailors; I have had four quarrels, and like to have fought one.   45
JAQUES And how was that ta'en up?
TOUCHSTONE Faith, we met and found the quarrel was upon the
    seventh cause.
JAQUES How, 'seventh cause'? – Good my lord, like this fellow.

---

35 Touchstone carried Audrey up the ramp to the stage 'pick-a-back' (Jones pbk).
38 Robson's Touchstone 'strutted, he crowed, and to continue the simile, he flapped his wings
    with the triumphant satisfaction of a barnyard rooster' (Frederick Warde, *The Fools of*
    Shakespeare, pp. 67, 68, cited in Sprague, p. 39).

DUKE SENIOR I like him very well.   50

TOUCHSTONE God'ild you, sir; I desire you of the like. I press in here,
    sir, amongst the rest of the country copulatives, to swear and to
    forswear according as marriage binds and blood breaks. A poor
    virgin, sir, an ill-favoured thing, sir, but mine own. A poor humour
    of mine, sir, to take that that no man else will. Rich honesty dwells   55
    like a miser, sir, in a poor house, as your pearl in your foul oyster.

DUKE SENIOR By my faith, he is very swift and sententious.

TOUCHSTONE According to 'the fool's bolt', sir, and such dulcet
    diseases.

JAQUES But, for 'the seventh cause': how did you find the quarrel on   60
    'the seventh cause'?

TOUCHSTONE Upon a lie seven times removed. – Bear your body more
    seeming, Audrey. – As thus, sir: I did dislike the cut of a certain
    courtier's beard. He sent me word, if I said his beard was not cut

---

51   Macklin's Touchstone substituted 'I thank you' for 'God'ild you' (partbook). Arthur's
     promptbook has Silvius and Phebe enter slowly from up stage at this point.

52   Benson substituted 'folk' for 'copulatives' (1904 pbk).

54   Asche's Audrey laughed after 'virgin' (pbk). Helpmann's Touchstone inserted 'bear your
     body more seeming, Audrey' mid-line (pbk).

62   Ways to embarrass your lover: 'Audrey is stooping looking at her feet' (Phelps pbk).
     'Audrey goes to sleep on Touchstone's shoulder' (Arthur pbk). She leans against
     Touchstone, he steps away and she nearly falls. She 'starts crying after his rebuke' (Asche
     pbk). She scratches her leg (Holloway pbk). 'Audrey scratch bottom' (Elliott pbk). Noble's
     Audrey curtseyed compulsively and increasingly flamboyantly. As Cheek by Jowl's Phoebe
     knelt in her skimpy skirt, Touchstone covered her rear with his hat. In Edzard's film she
     adjusts her bosom.

62–88   Wiles believes the lines were written with Robert Armin's physique and talents in mind: 'the
     pompous or parodic utterances of a man with total vocal control are counterpointed by a
     deformed body' (p. 150). They have sometimes been cut, as in the 1963 RSC/BBC version.
     Professional comedian Roy Kinnear, playing Touchstone at Stratford in 1967, 'either lost
     track, or pretended to lose track, of "the degrees of the lie", with the result that Jaques's line
     had the effect of a challenge from one actor to another and Kinnear's successful repetition
     of the list got audience applause' (*SS* 42, 1989, p. 92). At Sydney's Nimrod Theatre in 1983,
     Tony Taylor's Touchstone 'stunned' his audience with 'dialogue with his penis. This
     squeaky-voiced organ, whose high-pitched impertinence Touchstone echoed each time he
     said "if" . . . responded to one [word] only: "horn"' (*SQ* 35, 1984, p. 480). Noble had
     Touchstone lead the entire company in pantomime gestures to accompany each degree.
     Cheek by Jowl's Audrey spoke the parts attributed to the offended 'courtier'.

well, he was in the mind it was: this is called 'the retort courteous'.   65
If I sent him word again it was not well cut, he would send me word
he cut it to please himself: this is called 'the quip modest'. If again
it was not well cut, he disabled my judgement: this is called 'the
reply churlish'. If again it was not well cut, he would answer I spake
not true: this is called 'the reproof valiant'. If again it was not well   70
cut, he would say I lied: this is called 'the countercheck quarrelsome'. And so to 'the lie circumstantial' and 'the lie direct'.

JAQUES And how oft did you say his beard was not well cut?

TOUCHSTONE I durst go no further than the lie circumstantial, nor he
durst not give me the lie direct; and so we measured swords, and   75
parted.

JAQUES Can you nominate, in order now, the degrees of the lie?

TOUCHSTONE O, sir, we quarrel in print, by the book – as you have
books for good manners. I will name you the degrees: the first, the
retort courteous; the second, the quip modest; the third, the reply   80
churlish; the fourth, the reproof valiant; the fifth, the countercheck quarrelsome; the sixth, the lie with circumstance; the
seventh, the lie direct. All these you may avoid but the lie direct,
and you may avoid that too with an 'if'. I knew when seven justices
could not take up a quarrel but, when the parties were met   85
themselves, one of them thought but of an 'if': as, 'If you said so,
then I said so.' And they shook hands and swore brothers. Your
'if' is the only peacemaker: much virtue in 'if'.

JAQUES Is not this a rare fellow, my lord? He's as good at anything, and
yet a fool.   90

DUKE SENIOR He uses his folly like a stalking-horse, and under the
presentation of that he shoots his wit.

     Still music. Enter HYMEN, [*with*] ROSALIND *and* CELIA
             [*as themselves*]

65 At Stratford in 1985, Nicky Henson's 'hectic' Touchstone had 'the whole company making
rude barnyard noises during the Retort Courteous speech' (*Guardian*, 26 Apr. 1985).

70 Griff Rhys Jones pauses to consult a small notebook for the term 'reproof valiant' in Edzard's
film.

88 During the applause following Touchstone's speech on the virtues of 'if', he crossed up stage
to join Pages who dressed him as Hymen (Toye pbk).

92 In the eighteenth century, the Duke continued, 'But let us think no more of him, and drown
his remembrance, in a song' (Bell's edn). Some nineteenth- and early twentieth-century
productions had Jacques de Boys enter here and speak lines 135–50a (Kemble, Daly,
Benson), making for a less spectacular *deus ex machina*, especially when Hymen's
appearance was omitted, as it often was.

92 SD   'Shakespeare did not make this god fly' in the original Globe staging, despite the probable existence there of a descent machine, although 'it is unlikely that such a magical figure would make an entrance from one of the flanking doors. The central opening is more appropriate for this special entrance made by the god of marriage accompanied by the two brides' (Gurr and Ichikawa, p. 109).

Hymen has frequently been eliminated in production. Kemble restored Hymen, who appeared with 'two Cupids, waving on eight Masquers' who danced before Hymen's song (Kemble edn). Macready's production featured a demystified Hymen in an elaborate masque involving a crowd of flower-laden shepherds and shepherdesses. They 'erect[ed] a kind of rural temple', placed an altar within it, and attired one of the pages as 'Hymen'. Music commenced and the wedding party processed down stage, and after the song Hymen led Rosalind to the Duke (Shattuck, *Macready*). Phelps had Hymen appear from a temple on a pageant wagon, drawn on stage by villagers carrying wands and garlands (pbk). 'The fanciful and poetical side of the conception of the play' were emphasised when Miss Litton played Hymen at the Imperial (*Academy*, 24 Apr. 1880). A priest replaced Hymen at Wallack's in 1898–9, and some of the accompanying shepherds and shepherdesses were dressed as monks (Arthur pbk). George Alexander staged an elaborate masque with music composed by Edward German. A contemporary described the spectacle of piping shepherds and dancing shepherdesses, flower-children, maidens crowned with white wood-anemones, and dancing Cupids, preparing the way for 'Hymen (Miss Julie Opp), a radiant figure in draperies of deepest orange shading into red, and with a scarf of brilliant yellow silk caught round the arm' (*Sketch*, 9 Dec. 1896). In Czinner's film, Hymen is represented by a Cupid-like young boy, half-naked and wearing wings. He does not speak. Rosalind pronounced lines 96–100; the rest was cut. Nunn had Hymen and his cherub attendants descend on a 'cloud which opened and shut'; Hymen sang not only his own lines with 'sheepdoggy wobble' but stole some of Rosalind's lines as well (*SS* 31, 1978, p. 146; *Financial Times*, 9 Sept. 1977). In the 1978 BBC version, the scene of the Duke and company dissolves into a vision of Hymen – 'a fey figure dressed in gossamer . . . a laurel wreath about his temples' (Bulman, p. 177) – leading Rosalind and Celia, dressed in white togas. At Washington, DC's, Arena Stage in 1983, Hymen arrived 'in a royal blue hot-air balloon, leaning out of his golden gondola to sprinkle silver dust over the couples and then depart' (*SQ* 35, 1984, p. 226).

The part of Hymen has often been taken by other characters, or doubled by the actors presenting them. Corin played Hymen in the 1963 RSC/BBC version and in Hands's Stratford production. William Hutt 'dispensed with Hymen and brought Corin on, bedecked with flowers and looking like some minor woodland god, sweetened by years' (*SQ* 4, 1972, 393). Sometimes Hymen's lines have been given to old Adam, as in a production by the Champlain Shakespeare Festival in 1981 (*SQ* 32, 1981, p. 185). William, the victorious deer hunter in Dexter's production, appeared as 'an antlered Hymen, naked except for fronds of leaves'. The final scene was heavy in its fertility symbolism, with the on-stage tree

HYMEN Then is there mirth in heaven,
When earthly things made even
Atone together.   95

transformed into a Maypole amid bountiful flowers (*SS* 33, 1980, p. 180; *Guardian*,
3 Aug. 1979). In Caird's production, Hymen was played by the same actor who played
William and Charles the Wrestler; he '[strode] downstage in a bright green suit . . . meant
to suggest pajamas, with a winged Cupid on his shoulder' (*SQ* 44, 1993, p. 493). Amiens
played Hymen in Cheek by Jowl's production, appearing in a short tunic and gold face
mask. Judith Greenwood's lighting design created a stage dappled with purple, green,
and blue to create a beautifully celebratory effect (*Evening Standard*, 5 Dec. 1991).
Touchstone took the part in Toye's production, a choice that implicitly recognised the
contingency of the final couplings. At Shakespeare's Globe, Leader Hawkins, who had
played Adam and appeared as old Sir Roland in the invented prologue, returned as Hymen,
'horned like a stag and clad in a crown and jockstrap of straw and thorny twigs' (*SS* 52, 1999,
p. 222).

There is also been presented in less conventional ways. In Stein's production, when
Hymen 'entered all in gold' atop a pageant wagon, 'the forest-dwellers threw off their rough
cloaks to reveal their Elizabethan garments underneath, as if they had been playing at exile
all along' (Kennedy, p. 262). In Noble's production, Hymen was 'represented as a flickering
silhouette on a lighted screen, placed upstage'. When the production moved to London,
'Hymen became a mere beam of light whose source was *behind* the audience, so that the
actors beheld him facing out front', and the audience focused 'on the faces of those whose
futures he is deciding' (Shaw and Stevenson, p. 70). In voiceover, Hymen spoke in deep
male tones. Perhaps most unusually, Hymen was represented in Pimlott's production 'by a
robust, motherly figure, a lady of mature years in a pantsuit and a permanent wave who
emerged from the front stalls to set the odds all even like the *commère* of some daytime
television show' (*SQ* 48, 1997, p. 210).

There is no Hymen in Edzard's film. The two brides appear in dresses fashioned of plastic
wrapping material, as the two pages/derelicts from 5.3 continue their chorus. After lines
101–8, the credits begin to roll, and the Second Brother's speech (135–49) is heard in
voiceover during offtakes of the bridal couples. Jaques gives his farewell speech (168–77)
and walks away over a bridge as a final chorus of 'It was a lover and his lass' concludes the
film.

93–100 In the eighteenth century, this song was performed by the stage ensemble (Bell's edn).
Daly's Hymen, who sang these lines, was accompanied by shepherds and shepherdesses
(pbk).

Good Duke, receive thy daughter;
Hymen from heaven brought her,
     Yea, brought her hither
That thou might'st join her hand with his,
Whose heart within his bosom is.   100
ROSALIND [*To the Duke*] To you I give myself, for I am yours.
     [*To Orlando*] To you I give myself, for I am yours.
DUKE SENIOR If there be truth in sight, you are my daughter.
ORLANDO If there be truth in sight, you are my Rosalind.
PHOEBE If sight and shape be true, why then, my love, adieu.   105
ROSALIND [*To the Duke*] I'll have no father, if you be not he.
     [*To Orlando*] I'll have no husband, if you be not he.
     [*To Phoebe*] Nor ne'er wed woman, if you be not she.
HYMEN Peace, ho: I bar confusion,
     'Tis I must make conclusion   110
Of these most strange events.
Here's eight that must take hands
To join in Hymen's bands,
If truth holds true contents.

101–2   Sarah Siddons, 'mistress of the passions', spoke the first line on bended knee to her father,
the second while falling into Orlando's arms in 'enamoured transport' (Anna Seward, Letter
to Miss Weston, 1786, cited in Salgado, p. 163). Vanessa Redgrave 'relished the formality of
the final scene, caressing every word, slowly sighing out "To you I give myself, for I am
yours": she could risk this delivery because she had laid the emotional foundations so
firmly in her earlier scenes with Orlando' (*SS* 39, 1986, p. 181).

In Czinner's film, Laurence Olivier as Orlando appears amazed but not unhappy at the
sight of Rosalind. By contrast, when Adrian Lester as Rosalind 'lifted her bridal veil and
offered herself to Orlando, Orlando turned on his heel and stormed to the back of the stage,
shocked at the trick and shamed at his failure to have recognized her' (*SS* 45, 1992, p. 130).
Rosalind collapsed in dejected tears on the Duke's shoulder. Eventually Orlando
'reconsider[ed] and return[ed]'. This Orlando 'had doubts and self-doubts all along, but
now he accepts the scope and contradictions of his sexuality' (*Times*, 5 Dec. 1991), and the
lovers shared a passionate long kiss.

105   Czinner's Phoebe seems happy rather than resigned to be marrying Silvius. Phoebe appears
sickened by the sight of Rosalind in the 1978 BBC version and willingly gives herself to
Silvius. Cheek by Jowl's Phoebe fainted as she recognized the truth.

109–30   Cut with the excision of Hymen. Kemble restored Hymen's first song but cut these lines.
Daly rearranged Hymen's lines, so that part of the material (lines 125–30) was sung by the
ensemble and other parts spoken by Hymen (pbk).

    [*To Orlando and Rosalind*] You and you no cross
        shall part.   115
    [*To Oliver and Celia*] You and you are heart in heart.
    [*To Phoebe*] You to his love must accord,
    Or have a woman to your lord.
    [*To Touchstone and Audrey*] You and you are sure together
    As the winter to foul weather. –   120
    Whiles a wedlock hymn we sing,
    Feed yourselves with questioning,
    That reason, wonder may diminish
    How thus we met and these things finish.

                    Song

    Wedding is great Juno's crown,   125
      O blessed bond of board and bed.
    'Tis Hymen peoples every town,
      High wedlock then be honourèd.
    Honour, high honour, and renown
    To Hymen, god of every town.   130
DUKE SENIOR O my dear niece: welcome thou art to me
    Even daughter; welcome in no less degree.
PHOEBE I will not eat my word now thou art mine:
    Thy faith my fancy to thee doth combine.

     Enter [JACQUES DE BOYS, *the*] *second brother*

JACQUES DE BOYS Let me have audience for a word or two.   135

119–20   Audrey scratches her rear as she processes toward Hymen in the 1963 RSC/BBC version.

133–4   To deflect attention from Phoebe, some productions cut her lines here.

134 SD   In Czinner's film, a trumpet announces the approach of an armoured knight on horseback, who does not identify himself as Jacques de Boys. The second brother likewise arrives on horseback in the 1978 BBC version. In Noble's production, the second brother entered through the magical mirror frame into which the melancholy Jaques soon disappeared.

135–50   The assembled foresters registered changing responses to Jacques de Boys in Kean's production, advancing towards him when he announced his identity (136), making another movement with his reference to his brother's sword (142), and offering gestures of congratulation with his conclusion (Kean pbk). J. C. Trewin notes that 'For an actor it is a tormenting entrance: the Bensonians, calling it "the Shilling Speech", would give a shilling to any young player who, in the day's theatrical jargon, was "dead-letter-perfect". The prize was seldom won' (Trewin, p. 144). When his brother appeared, Orlando shouted 'Jacques!' in Cheek by Jowl.

I am the second son of old Sir Roland,
That bring these tidings to this fair assembly.
Duke Frederick, hearing how that every day
Men of great worth resorted to this forest,
Addressed a mighty power which were on foot   140
In his own conduct, purposely to take
His brother here and put him to the sword;
And to the skirts of this wild wood he came,
Where, meeting with an old religious man,
After some question with him, was converted   145
Both from his enterprise and from the world,
His crown bequeathing to his banished brother,
And all their lands restored to them again
That were with him exiled. This to be true,
I do engage my life.
DUKE SENIOR   Welcome, young man.   150
Thou offer'st fairly to thy brother's wedding:
To one his lands withheld, and to the other
A land itself at large, a potent dukedom. –
First, in this forest, let us do those ends
That here were well begun and well begot;   155
And, after, every of this happy number
That have endured shrewd days and nights with us
Shall share the good of our returnèd fortune
According to the measure of their states.
Meantime forget this new-fall'n dignity   160
And fall into our rustic revelry. –

138–49   At Sydney's Nimrod Theatre in 1983, 'news' of Frederick's conversion came as 'an announcement from Touchstone's wireless, in the definitively humane-astringent tones of the Australian Broadcasting Commission . . . Ever the busybody, Jaques turned this on. Fanning himself with his straw panama, peripatetic, fastidious' (*SQ* 135, 1984, p. 481).

147   'It was Duke Frederick himself who placed the crown on the head of his brother, and wrapped the ducal cloak round his shoulders' in Copeau's 1934 production. The exiled Duke had appeared 'in the same frayed costume throughout until, in the final scene, Rosalind and Celia adorned it with flowers' (Speaight, p. 191). In the 1963 RSC/BBC production, Jacques de Boys presents the Duke with a crown perched atop a pillow. The entire company kneels in respect as the Duke places the crown on his head. Cheek by Jowl's Second Brother brought Frederick's medal and presented it to Duke Senior, who passed it to Orlando, who bestowed it on Rosalind – an emblem of the production's sliding lines of affiliation and affection.

Play, music – and, you brides and bridegrooms all,
With measure heaped in joy to th'measures fall.
JAQUES Sir, by your patience. [*To Jacques de Boys*] If I heard you rightly,
The Duke hath put on a religious life   165
And thrown into neglect the pompous court.
JACQUES DE BOYS He hath.
JAQUES To him will I: out of these convertites
There is much matter to be heard and learned.
[*To the Duke*] You to your former honour I bequeath: 170
Your patience and your virtue well deserves it.
[*To Orlando*] You to a love that your true faith doth merit.
[*To Oliver*] You to your land and love and great allies.
[*To Silvius*] You to a long and well-deservèd bed.
[*To Touchstone*] And you to wrangling, for thy loving voyage   175
Is but for two months victualled. – So to your pleasures;
I am for other than for dancing measures.
DUKE SENIOR Stay, Jaques, stay.
JAQUES To see no pastime, I. What you would have
I'll stay to know at your abandoned cave.   *Exit*   180

168–77 In Czinner's film, Jaques's departure lines – and his exit – are omitted, contributing to the
general frivolity of the conclusion. By contrast, at Bergen in 1983, Hymen, the 'rustic
revelry', and Rosalind's epilogue were all cut; Jaques's farewell speech was 'a parting wet
blanket' that closed the play (*SQ* 35, 1984, p. 96).

172–4 As Jaques addressed him, each male character was joined by his female partner
(Sothern–Marlowe pbk).

176 In the interest of class decorum, nineteenth-century stagings regularly eliminated
Touchstone, Audrey, Silvius, and Phoebe from the final tableau. Moore has Touchstone
and Audrey exit in a 'crestfallen and sneaking manner' (pbk). Benson's Touchstone
coughs and brings Audrey forward, attracting Jaques's attention and thus his address
(1904 pbk). Jaques concludes his speech in a disgusted tone in the 1978 BBC
video.

180 SD The other characters waved farewell to Jaques in Ciulei's production (*SQ* 34, 1983, p. 230).
'Abandoning cynicism for a curiosity about the religious life', Noble's Jaques 'stepped back
through the looking-glass. And then the grandfather clock started ticking. "Real" time
reasserted itself' (*SS* 40, 1987, p. 199; Rutter, p. 120). In Caird's production, Jaques
'withdrew upstage to the rear wall to push open' a hidden door and disappear into another
space of existence, 'suggesting a close encounter of the third kind' (*SQ* 41, 1989–90, p. 492;
SS 44, 1991, p. 163). In Monette's 1990 production at Stratford, Ontario, David Williams's
Jaques was 'almost willing to be a part of the rejuvenated society': he paused before exiting

DUKE SENIOR Proceed, proceed. – We will begin these rites
   As we do trust they'll end, in true delights.
                                         [*They dance.*] *Exeunt all but Rosalind*

'as if he were waiting for another call from the duke to return, a call that did not come' (*SQ* 42, 1991, p. 216). Rather than exiting, Jaques embraced Amiens/Hymen in Cheek by Jowl's production, and the pair joined in the final dance. At Stratford in 1996, 'as Jaques stalked haughtily from the marriage scene, Touchstone . . . presented him with a skull' (*SS* 50, 1997, p. 207).

182 SD   Phelps specified a folk dance to rustic music, with couples lining up and linking hands to form an archway for others to pass beneath (pbk). Goodbody's production featured a 'dancing epithalamium' with rock-and-roll music by Guy Woolfenden; coloured paper hearts rained from the ceiling and streamers were thrown in the audience's direction (*Financial Times*, 13 June 1973). In the 1978 BBC version, the company forms a circle and dances; Rosalind steps out of line to come forward as the rest dance away. In Stein's production, 'the wedding dance continued' atop a pageant wagon that rolled towards a door through which the court was glimpsed. 'But the wagon wouldn't fit through the door, stopped with a bump and knocked off the actors, who stumbled back on foot to the world of politics and intrigue.' Meanwhile Duke Frederick and his men actually arrived in Arden, but inexplicably laid down their arms (Kennedy, p. 265). Noble's production featured a 'rather formal' dance, 'ritualising the segregation of the sexes'. When the production transferred to London, the dance became 'a more informal and spontaneous expression, in a folk tradition'. At its culmination the characters 'exited, through a moon-shaped hole in the backdrop', emphasising Arden's fantasy aspect, and leaving Rosalind alone on stage for the epilogue (Shaw and Stevenson, pp. 70, 71). In Cheek by Jowl's production, each couple was featured for a turn in the final tango.

[EPILOGUE]

The cast may remain on stage for the epilogue; so it was in early performances (Bell's edn). In Macready's production, the curtain did not fall until after Rosalind had stepped forward to speak, with the other principal characters arranged in a crescent behind her (Shattuck, *Macready*). Moore's promptbook has the Duke and Orlando lead Rosalind forward, then advance after the epilogue to escort her back to the company; a closing chorus of 'What shall he have that killed the deer?' followed. At Stratford in 1885, 'a dance ending the play was so briskly engaged in . . . that it was feared Miss Anderson would be too much out of breath to speak the epilogue' (*Daily Chronicle*, 31 Aug. 1885). Julia Neilson delivered the speech with 'refinement and charm . . . [she] did not turn the pretty and graceful Epilogue into a coarse winking farce as many of our Rosalinds have done before her' (*Daily Telegraph*, 3 Dec. 1896). Juliet Stevenson stepped forward after the lights had come up in the theatre; the other characters remained sitting on stage watching her. In a production by the Birmingham Repertory Theatre, 'just before the epilogue Rosalind handed her bridal bouquet to Orlando, who tossed it to Silvius, who formally presented it to Phebe' (*SQ* 33, 1982, p. 191). Caird's 'Orlando stepped forward to speak . . . but lost his nerve at the last moment and gratefully handed over to Rosalind' (*SS* 41, 1989–90, p. 492). In Kahn's production, Rosalind came down stage at the conclusion of the dance, wearing a company ('Shakespeare Free For All') tank top; suddenly the scenic panels disappeared, 'revealing the skeletal structure of the set and the backstage area', against which 'denuded backdrop she delivered her epilogue' (*SQ* 43, 1992, p. 471).

Fineman supposes that the actor on the Renaissance stage here 'shows himself a boy' (p. 92), although how this was done remains in question. Helena Faucit began the epilogue with her 'veil down' (Faucit pbk). William Archer criticised Mary Anderson's presentation, because 'instead of summoning up all the femininity she could muster, she rather reverted to the tone and manner of the "saucy lackey". The speech was written to be spoken by a boy, but a modern Rosalind should be all woman' (*The World*, 2 Sept. 1885). In Czinner's film, Rosalind appears dressed in her wedding gown, but through cinematic 'conjuring', her image is temporarily replaced by that of Ganymede for the lines (8–10) directed towards women. J. C. Trewin recalled 'how Edith Evans burnished the speech by turning Rosalind, without pretence, into a Restoration belle and ending the night in a quick blaze of Millamantine sophistication' (Trewin, p. 145).

In place of the epilogue, Stein substituted a poem by Francis Ponge on the patterns of nature, read by Frederick. Afterwards 'Corin began to clean up the mess left by these

ROSALIND It is not the fashion to see the lady the Epilogue, but it is no
more unhandsome than to see the lord the Prologue. If it be true
that good wine needs no bush, 'tis true that a good play needs no
Epilogue. Yet to good wine they do use good bushes, and good plays
prove the better by the help of good Epilogues. What a case am I in,   5
then, that am neither a good Epilogue nor cannot insinuate with you
in the behalf of a good play? I am not furnished like a beggar,
therefore to beg will not become me. My way is to conjure you, and
I'll begin with the women. I charge you, O women, for the love you
bear to men, to like as much of this play as please you. – And I   10
charge you, O men, for the love you bear to women – as I perceive
by your simpering none of you hates them – that between you and
the women the play may please. If I were a woman, I would kiss as
many of you as had beards that pleased me, complexions that liked
me, and breaths that I defied not. And I am sure as many as have   15
good beards, or good faces, or sweet breaths will, for my kind offer,
when I make curtsey, bid me farewell.   *Exit*

FINIS

over-civilized *pastores:* a powerful memorandum that the work of the working class goes
on' (Kennedy, p. 265). The epilogue is cut from the 1963 RSC/BBC version, the production
ending instead with the dance.

1–2 After it became fashionable to see ladies as the Epilogue, these lines were often cut (Kemble
to Daly).

13 With a female performer, 'among you' typically replaces 'a woman' (Kemble to Daly). Helen
Mirren delivered the line intact, raising an eyebrow pointedly at 'if I were a woman'. Adrian
Lester removed his earrings and headband to reveal his male identity.

13–14 In 1757, Peg Woffington spoke these lines before faltering, 'then in a voice of tremor
screamed O God! O God! tottered to the stage door speechless, where she was caught'.
'Stricken with paralysis', Woffington survived for a few years but never returned to the stage
(Tate Wilkinson, *Memoirs*, 1790, cited in Salgado, p. 162; Robins, p. 112).

13–15 Cut at Shakespeare's Globe, since Anastasia Hille's Rosalind 'was *all* woman' (*SS* 52, 1999,
p. 224).

15, 16 The references to breath have often been cut.

17 SD At the epilogue's conclusion, a 'merry rollicking dance' concluded the Sothern–Marlowe
production (pbk). In Toye's production, Rosalind and Orlando bowed together (pbk). Janet
Suzman curtseyed and then went up stage with Orlando (Jones pbk).

BIBLIOGRAPHY

Anderson, Mary. *A Few Memories*. 2nd edn. London, 1896.

Appleton, William. *Charles Macklin: An Actor's Life*. Cambridge, MA: Harvard University Press, 1960.

Arthur, Julia. Promptbook, 1898–9. Folger Shakespeare Library. (Shattuck, *AYLI*, 72.)

As You Like It. Dir. Basil Coleman. Prod. Cedric Messina. Col. TV. BBC, 1978.

As You Like It. Dir. Paul Czinner. B/w film. Inter-Allied, 1936.

As You Like It. Dir. Declan Donnelan. Cheek by Jowl. Albery Theatre, 11 Feb. 1995. Col. videotape. National Video Archive of Stage Performances. Theatre Museum and Federation of Entertainment Unions.

As You Like It. Dir. Michael Elliott. Prod. Richard Eyre. B/w TV. RSC/BBC, 1963.

As You Like It. Dir. Christine Edzard. Col. film. Sands Film, 1992.

As You Like It. Dir. Charles Kent. B/w silent film. Vitagraph, 1912.

As You Like It. Dir. Adrian Noble. RSC, 1985. Col. videotape. Shakespeare Centre Library.

As You Like It: a comedy, by Shakespeare, as performed at the Theatre Royal, Drury-lane. London: John Bell, 1774.

As You Like It: a comedy, by William Shakespeare, marked with the variations in the manager's book, at the Theatre-Royal in Covent-Garden. London, 1786.

Asche, Oscar. *Oscar Asche: His Life*. London: Hurst & Blackett, 1929. Promptbook, 1907. Shakespeare Centre Library. (Shattuck, *AYLI*, 86.)

Barber, C. L. *Shakespeare's Festive Comedy: A Study of Dramatic Form and Its Relation to Social Custom*. Princeton University Press, 1959.

Barton, Anne. '*As You Like It* and *Twelfth Night*: Shakespeare's Sense of an Ending'. *Shakespearian Comedy*. Ed. David Palmer and Malcolm Bradbury. London: Edward Arnold, 1972. Pp. 160–80.

Bate, Jonathan, and Russell Jackson, eds. *Shakespeare: An Illustrated Stage History*. Oxford University Press, 1996.

Beauman, Sally. *The Royal Shakespeare Company: A History of Ten Decades*. Oxford University Press, 1982.

247

Benson, Lady [Constance]. *Mainly Players.* London: Thornton
    Butterworth, 1926.
Benson, Sir Frank. *My Memoirs.* London: Ernest Benn, 1930.
    Promptbook, c. 1904. Shakespeare Centre Library. (Shattuck, *AYLI*,
        76.)
    Promptbook, c. 1905. Shakespeare Centre Library. (Shattuck, *AYLI*, 77.)
Blumenfeld, Odette-Irenne. 'Shakespeare in Post-revolutionary Romania:
    the Great Directors are Back Home'. *Shakespeare in the New Europe.*
    Ed. Michael Hattaway, Boika Sokolova, and Derek Roper. Sheffield
    Academic Press, 1994. Pp. 230–46.
Boaden, James. *The Life of Mrs Jordan.* 2 vols. London, 1831.
Booth, Michael R. 'The Social and Literary Context'. *The Revels History
    of Drama in English.* Vol. 6: 1750–1880. By Michael R. Booth,
    Richard Southern, Frederick and Lise-Lone Marker, and Robertson
    Davies. London: Methuen, 1975.
Boquet, Guy. 'Shakespeare on the French Stage: a Historical Survey'.
    Trans. Carol Boquet, Yves Boquet, and Holger Klein. *Shakespeare
    and France.* Ed. Holger Klein and Jean-Marie Maguin. Shakespeare
    Yearbook 5. Lewiston: Mellen, 1995.
Bridges-Adams, W. Promptbook, 1933. Shakespeare Centre Library.
    (Shattuck, *AYLI*, 97.)
Bulman, J. C. '*As You Like It* and the Perils of Pastoral'. *Shakespeare on
    Television: An Anthology of Essays and Reviews.* Ed. J. C. Bulman and
    H. R. Coursen. Hanover and London: University Press of New
    England, 1988. Pp. 174–9.
Campbell, Thomas. *Life of Mrs Siddons.* London, 1839. Rpt New York:
    Benjamin Blom, 1972.
Carlisle, Carol J. 'Helen Faucit's Rosalind'. *Shakespeare Studies* 12 (1979):
    65–94.
Chambers, E. K. *Shakespearean Gleanings.* London: Oxford University
    Press, 1944.
    William Shakespeare: A Study of Facts and Problems. 2 vols. Oxford:
    Clarendon Press, 1930.
Child, Harold. 'The Stage History of *As You Like It*'. *As You Like It.*
    Ed. Sir Arthur Quiller-Couch and John Dover Wilson. Cambridge
    University Press, 1968. Pp. 167–71.
Clarke, Charles Cowden. *Shakespearean Characters; Chiefly Those
    Subordinate.* London, 1863.
Clement, Clara Erskine. *Charlotte Cushman.* Boston, 1882.
Cole, John William. *The Life and Theatrical Times of Charles Kean, F.S.A.*
    2nd edn. 2 vols. London: Richard Bentley, 1860.

Coleman, John. *Players and Playwrights I Have Known: A Review of the English Stage from 1840 to 1880.* 2nd edn. 2 vols. Philadelphia: Gebbie, 1890.

Coleman, Marion Moore. *Fair Rosalind: The American Career of Helena Modjeska.* Cheshire, CN: Cherry Hill Books, 1969.

Cooke, William. *Memoirs of Charles Macklin, Comedian.* 2nd edn. London, 1806.

Crosse, Gordon. *Shakespearean Playgoing 1890–1952.* London: A. R. Mowbray, 1953.

Cunningham, Peter. *Extracts from the Accounts of the Revels at Court, in the Reigns of Queen Elizabeth and King James I.* London: The Shakespeare Society, 1842.

Daly, Augustin. Promptbook, 1889. Daly's souvenir album. Folger Shakespeare Library. (Shattuck, *AYLI*, 60.)

Daly, Joseph Francis. *The Life of Augustin Daly.* New York: Macmillan, 1917.

Davies, Thomas. *Memoirs of the Life of David Garrick Esq.* 1780. Ed. Stephen Jones. 2 vols. London, 1808.

Derrick, Patty S. 'Rosalind and the Nineteenth-century Woman: Four Stage Interpretations'. *Theatre Survey* 26 (1985): 143–62.

Dexter, John. Promptbook, 1979. National Theatre Archive. (Not in Shattuck.)

Dobbs, Brian. *Drury Lane: Three Centuries of the Theatre Royal, 1663–1971.* London: Cassell, 1972.

Dobson, Michael. *The Making of the National Poet: Shakespeare, Adaptation and Authorship, 1660–1769.* Oxford: Clarendon Press, 1992.

Dunbar, Janet. *Peg Woffington and her World.* London: Heinemann, 1968.

Dusinberre, Juliet. 'As *Who* Liked It?' *SS* 46 (1994): 9–21.

Elliott, Michael. Promptbook, 1962. Shakespeare Centre Library. (Shattuck, *AYLI*, 109.)

Empson, William. *Some Versions of Pastoral.* 1935. New Directions: [1950].

Faucit, Helena. Rehearsal copy, 1839. Folger Shakespeare Library. (Shattuck, *AYLI*, 15.)

Faucit Martin, Helena. *On Rosalind.* [Edinburgh: 1884?]. *On Some of Shakespeare's Female Characters.* London, 1887.

Fineman, Joel. 'Fratricide and Cuckoldry: Shakespeare's Doubles'. *The Psychoanalytic Review* 64 (Fall 1977). Rpt in *Representing Shakespeare: New Psychoanalytic Essays.* Ed. Murray M. Schwartz and Coppélia Kahn. Baltimore: Johns Hopkins University Press, 1980. Pp. 70–109.

Fletcher, George. *Studies of Shakespeare.* London, 1847.

Forbes, Bryan. *Dame Edith Evans: Ned's Girl*. Boston: Little, Brown, 1977.

Freedman, Barbara. 'Critical Junctures in Shakespeare Screen History: the Case of *Richard III*'. *The Cambridge Companion to Shakespeare on Film*. Ed. Russell Jackson. Cambridge University Press, 2000. Pp. 47–71.

Furness, Horace Howard, edn. *As You Like It*. A New Variorum Edition. 1890. Rpt New York: American Scholar, 1965.

Gentleman, Francis. *The Dramatic Censor; or, Critical Companion*. 2 vols. London, 1770.

Gifford, Terry. *Pastoral*. London: Routledge, 1999.

Goodbody, Buzz. Promptbook, 1973. Shakespeare Centre Library. (Not in Shattuck.)

Gosson, Stephen. *School of Abuse*. 1579. London: Shakespeare Society, 1841.

Gurr, Andrew. *The Shakespearian Playing Companies*. Oxford: Clarendon Press, 1996.

   The Shakespearean Stage 1574–1642. 2nd edn. Cambridge University Press, 1980.

   and Mariko Ichikawa. *Staging in Shakespeare's Theatres*. Oxford University Press, 2000.

Hamer, Mary. 'Shakespeare's Rosalind and Her Public Image'. *Theatre Research International* 2.2 (1986): 105–18.

Hankey, Julie. 'Helen Faucit and Shakespeare: Womanly Theater'. *Cross-Cultural Performances: Differences in Women's Re-Visions of Shakespeare*. Ed. Marianne Novy. Urbana and Chicago: University of Illinois Press, 1993. Pp. 50–69.

Harbage, Alfred. 'Shakespeare's Technique'. *The Complete Pelican Shakespeare*. Ed. Alfred Harbage. Baltimore, MD: Penguin, 1969.

Hattaway, Michael. 'The Comedies on Film'. *The Cambridge Companion to Shakespeare on Film*. Ed. Russell Jackson. Cambridge University Press, 2000. Pp. 85–98.

Hattaway, Michael, ed. *As You Like It*. The New Cambridge Shakespeare. Cambridge University Press, 2000.

Hazlitt, William. *A View of the English Stage*. London, 1818.

Helpmann, Robert. Promptbook, 1955. University of Bristol Theatre Collection. (Shattuck, *AYLI*, 104.)

Hill, John. *The Actor: or, a Treatise on the Art of Playing*. London, 1750.

Holding, Edith. '*As You Like It* Adapted: Charles Johnson's *Love in a Forest*'. *SS* 32 (1979): 37–48.

Holloway, Baliol. Promptbook, 1942. Shakespeare Centre Library.
(Shattuck, *AYLI*, 99.)

Hortmann, Wilhelm. *Shakespeare on the German Stage: The Twentieth Century*. Cambridge University Press, 1998.

Hudson, Rev. H. N. *Shakespeare: His Life, Art, and Characters*. 4th edn.
2 vols. Boston, 1895.

Hunt, Leigh. *The Autobiography of Leigh Hunt*. Ed. Roger Ingpen. 2 vols.
London: Constable, 1903.

Isaac, Winifred F. E. C. *Ben Greet and the Old Vic: A Biography of Sir Philip Ben Greet*. London: Greenbank Press, [1964?].

Jackson, Russell. '"Perfect Types of Womanhood": Rosalind, Beatrice and Viola in Victorian Criticism and Performance'. *SS* 32 (1979): 15–26.

'Shakespeare's Comedies on Film'. *Shakespeare and the Moving Image: The Plays on Film and Television*. Ed. Anthony Davies and Stanley Wells. Cambridge University Press, 1994. Pp. 99–120.

Jamieson, Michael. '*As You Like It* – Performance and Reception'. As You Like It *from 1600 to the Present: Critical Essays*. Ed. Edward Tomarken. New York: Garland, 1997. Pp. 623–46.

Jardine, Lisa. *Still Harping on Daughters: Women and Drama in the Age of Shakespeare*. 2nd edn. New York: Columbia University Press, 1989.

Jenkins, Harold. '*As You Like It*'. *SS* 8 (1955): 40–51.

Johnson, Charles. *Love in a Forest: A Comedy*. London: W. Chetwood and Thomas Edlin, 1723.

Johnson, Edgar. *Charles Dickens: His Tragedy and Triumph*. 2 vols. New York: Simon and Schuster, 1953.

Johnson, Samuel. *Johnson on Shakespeare*. Ed. Arthur Sherbo. *The Yale Edition of the Works of Samuel Johnson*. Vol. 7. New Haven and London: Yale University Press, 1968.

Jones, David. Promptbook, 1968. Shakespeare Centre Library. (Not in Shattuck.)

Kean, Charles. Promptbook, 1851. Folger Shakespeare Library. (Shattuck, *AYLI*, 31.)

Kelly, Linda. *The Kemble Era: John Philip Kemble, Sarah Siddons and the London Stage*. New York: Random House, 1980.

Kemble, Frances Ann. *Records of Later Life*. New York: Henry Holt, 1882.

Kemble, John Philip. Partbook, 1799, 1805. Folger Shakespeare Library.
(Shattuck, *AYLI*, 8.)

Kemp, T. C. and J. C. Trewin. *The Stratford Festival: A History of the Shakespeare Memorial Theatre*. Birmingham: Cornish Brothers, 1953.

Kennedy, Dennis. *Looking at Shakespeare: A Visual History of Twentieth-Century Performance*. Cambridge University Press, 1993.

Knowles, Richard, ed. *A New Variorum Edition of 'As You Like It'*. New York: Modern Language Association, 1977.

Ko, Yu Jin. 'Straining Sexual Identity: Cheek by Jowl's All-Male *As You Like It*'. *Shakespeare Bulletin* (Summer 1995): 16–17.

Kott, Jan. *Shakespeare our Contemporary*. Trans. Boleslaw Taborski. 2nd edn. London: Methuen, 1972.

Lamb, Charles. *Critical Essays*. Vol. 3 of *The Works of Charles Lamb*. Ed. William MacDonald. 12 vols. London: Dent, 1903.

Latham, Agnes, ed. *As You Like It*. The Arden Shakespeare. London: Methuen, 1975.

Lazarovich-Hrebelianovich, Princess [Eleanor Calhoun]. *Pleasures and Palaces: The Memoirs*. New York: Century, 1915.

Lee, Sidney. *A Life of William Shakespeare*. London: Smith, Elder, 1898.

Leiter, Samuel L., ed. *Shakespeare Around the Globe: A Guide to Notable Postwar Revivals*. New York: Greenwood, 1986.

Lennox, Patricia. 'A Girl's Got to Eat: Christine Edzard's Film of *As You Like It*'. *Transforming Shakespeare: Contemporary Women's Re-Visions in Literature and Performance*. Ed. Marianne Novy. New York: St Martin's Press, 1999. Pp. 51–65.

Levine, Laura. *Men in Women's Clothing: Anti-theatricality and Effeminization 1579–1642*. Cambridge University Press, 1994.

Lewes, George Henry. *On Actors and the Art of Acting*. Leipzig, 1875.

The London Stage 1660–1800. Ed. W. Van Lennep, Emmett L. Avery, Arthur H. Scouten, George W. Stone, Charles B. Hogan. 5 pts in 11 vols. Carbondale: Southern Illinois University Press, 1960–8.

Lunacharsky, Anatoli. 'Bacon and the Characters of Shakespeare's Plays'. *Shakespeare in the Soviet Union*. Comp. Roman Samarin and Alexander Nikolyukin. Trans. Avril Pyman. [Moscow: Progress, 1966.] Pp. 25–50.

Macklin, Charles. Partbook, 1741. Folger Shakespeare Library. (Shattuck, *AYLI*, 2.)

Macready, William Charles. *Macready's Reminiscences*. Ed. Frederick Pollock. New York, 1875.

Promptbook, 1842. Folger Shakespeare Library. (Shattuck, *AYLI*, 18.)

Marriette, Amelia. 'Urban Dystopias: Reapproaching Christine Edzard's *As You Like It*'. *Shakespeare, Film, Fin de Siècle*. Ed. Mark Thornton Burnett and Ramona Wray. London: Macmillan; New York: St Martin's, 2000. Pp. 73–88.

Marston, Westland. *Our Recent Actors*. 2 vols. London, 1888.

Mazer, Cary M. '*As You Like It*'. *Shakespeare Bulletin* (Summer 1991): 22–3.

Shakespeare Refashioned: Elizabethan Plays on Edwardian Stages. Ann
  Arbor: UMI Research Press, 1981.
Miller-Schütz, Chantal. 'Findings from the 1998 Season: *As You Like It*'.
  Shakespeare's Globe, Research Bulletin, Issue 10 (July 1999).
  'Interview of the Red Company cast members (1998)'. Shakespeare's
  Globe, Research Bulletin, Annex to Issues 10 and 11 (July
  1999).
Modjeska, Helena. Promptbook, 1882. Folger Shakespeare Library.
  (Shattuck, *AYLI*, 54.)
Moore, John. Record of productions, 1855–76. Folger Shakespeare
  Library. (Shattuck, *AYLI*, 37.)
Morley, Henry. *Journal of a London Playgoer.* 1866. Leicester University
  Press, 1974.
Morozov, Mikhail M. *Shakespeare on the Soviet Stage.* Trans. David
  Magarshack. London: Soviet News, 1947.
Mullin, Donald, ed. *Victorian Actors and Actresses in Review.* Westport, CN
  and London: Greenwood, 1983.
Odell, George C. D. *Annals of the New York Stage.* 15 vols. New York:
  Columbia University Press, 1927–49.
  Shakespeare From Betterton to Irving. 2 vols. New York: Charles
  Scribner's Sons, 1920.
Orgel, Stephen. *Impersonations: The Performance of Gender in
  Shakespeare's England.* Cambridge University Press, 1996.
Oxberry, W., ed. *As You Like It. A Comedy; by W. Shakespeare.* London,
  1819.
Oxberry, William. *Oxberry's Dramatic Biography and Histrionic Anecdotes.*
  Ed. Catherine Oxberry. 9 vols. London, 1825–7.
  Oxberry's Dramatic Mirror. Ed. Catherine Oxberry. London, 1827.
Patterson, Michael. *Peter Stein: Germany's Leading Theatre Director.*
  Cambridge University Press, 1981.
Payne, Ben Iden. Promptbook, 1935. Shakespeare Centre Library.
  (Shattuck, *AYLI*, 98.)
Phelps, Samuel. Promptbook, 1847. Folger Shakespeare Library.
  (Shattuck, *AYLI*, 26.)
Playfair, Nigel. *The Story of the Lyric Theatre Hammersmith.* London:
  Chatto & Windus, 1925.
Pollock, [Lady] Juliet. *Macready As I Knew Him.* London, 1884.
  Poet and the Stage, n.p, n.p., [1875?].
Powell, Jocelyn. *Restoration Theatre Production.* London: Routledge &
  Kegan Paul, 1984.
Praz, Mario. 'Italy: Surrealist "Rosalind"'. *SS* 3 (1950): 117–18.

Rickman, Alan. 'Jaques in *As You Like It*'. *Players of Shakespeare 2*. Ed. Russell Jackson and Robert Smallwood. Cambridge University Press, 1988. Pp. 73–80.

Robins, Edward. *Twelve Great Actresses*. London: G. P. Putnam's Sons, 1900.

Robinson, Henry Crabb. *The London Theatre 1811–1866*. Ed. Eluned Brown. London: Society for Theatre Research, 1966.

Robson, William. *The Old Play-goer*. London, 1854.

Rothwell, Kenneth S. *A History of Shakespeare on Screen: A Century of Film and Television*. Cambridge University Press, 1999.

Rowell, George. *Queen Victoria Goes to the Theatre*. London: Paul Elek, 1978.

Russell, Charles Edward. *Julia Marlowe: Her Life and Art*. New York and London: D. Appleton, 1926.

Rutter, Carol. *Clamorous Voices: Shakespeare's Women Today*. Ed. Faith Evans. London: Women's Press, 1989.

Salgado, Gamini. *Eyewitnesses of Shakespeare: First Hand Accounts of Performances 1590–1890*. Sussex University Press, 1975.

Sand, George. *A Letter to M. Regnier, of the Théâtre Français*. Trans. Theodosia Lady Monson. London, 1856.

Scheil, Katherine West. 'Early Georgian Politics and Shakespeare: the Black Act and Charles Johnson's *Love in a Forest* (1723)'. *SS* 51 (1998): 45–56.

Shattuck, Charles. *Mr Macready Produces 'As You Like It.'* Urbana, IL: Beta Phi Mu, 1962.

Shakespeare on the American Stage. 2 vols. Washington: Folger Shakespeare Library, 1976 (Vol. 1); Washington: Folger Shakespeare Library & Associated University Presses, 1987 (Vol. 2.)

Shattuck, Charles, ed. *John Philip Kemble Promptbooks*. Charlottesville: University Press of Virginia for The Folger Shakespeare Library, 1974.

Shaw, Fiona and Juliet Stevenson. 'Celia and Rosalind in *As You Like It*'. *Players of Shakespeare 2*. Ed. Russell Jackson and Robert Smallwood. Cambridge University Press, 1988. Pp. 55–72.

Shaw, George Bernard. *Our Theatres in the Nineties*. 3 vols. London: Constable, 1932; originally published in *The Saturday Review*, Jan. 1895–May 1898.

Shaw, Glen Byam. Promptbook, 1952. Shakespeare Centre Library. (Shattuck, *AYLI*, 102.)

Sothern, E. H. and Julia Marlowe. Promptbook, 1907. Folger Shakespeare Library. (Shattuck, *AYLI*, 83.)

Southern, Richard. 'Theatres and Actors'. *The Revels History of Drama in English*. Vol. 6: 1750–1880. By Michael R. Booth, Richard Southern, Frederick and Lise-Lone Marker, and Robertson Davies. London: Methuen, 1975.

Speaight, Robert. *Shakespeare on the Stage*. Boston: Little, Brown, 1973.

Sprague, Arthur Colby. *Shakespeare and the Actors: The Stage Business in His Plays (1660–1905)*. Cambridge, MA: Harvard University Press, 1945.

Straub, Kristina. *Sexual Suspects: Eighteenth-Century Players and Sexual Ideology*. Princeton University Press, 1992.

Stríbrny, Zdenek. *Shakespeare and Eastern Europe*. Oxford University Press, 2000.

Symons, Arthur. 'Great Acting in English'. *Monthly Review* (June 1907): 12–17.

Taylor, George. *Players and Performances in the Victorian Theatre*. Manchester University Press, 1989.

Taylor, John Russell. 'Shakespeare in Film, Radio, and Television'. *Shakespeare on Television: An Anthology of Essays and Reviews*. Ed. J. C. Bulman and H. R. Coursen. Hanover and London: University Press of New England, 1988.

Tennant, David. 'Touchstone in *As You Like It*'. *Players of Shakespeare* 4. Ed. Robert Smallwood. Cambridge University Press, 1998. Pp. 30–44.

Terry, Ellen. *The Story of My Life: Recollections and Reflections*. New York: McClure Company, 1908.

Tomalin, Claire. *Mrs Jordan's Profession: The Actress and the Prince*. New York: Knopf, 1995.

Toye, Wendy. Promptbook, 1959. University of Bristol Theatre Collection. (Shattuck, *AYLI*, 107.)

Trewin, J. C. *Shakespeare on the English Stage 1900–1964*. London: Barrie and Rockliff, 1964.

Vaughan, Anthony. *Born to Please: Hannah Pritchard, Actress, 1711–1768*. London: Society for Theatre Research, 1979.

Walkley, A. B. *Playhouse Impressions*. London: T. Fisher Unwin, 1892.

Wayne, Valerie. 'A Denaturalized Performance: Gender and Body Construction in Thailand's *As You Like It*'. *Gender and Culture in Literature and Film East and West: Issues of Perception and Interpretation*. Ed. Nitaya Masavisut, George Simson, and Larry E. Smith. Honolulu: College of Languages, Linguistics, and Literature, University of Hawaii, 1994. Pp. 197–204.

Westwood, Doris. *These Players: A Diary of the 'Old Vic'*. London: Heath Cranton, 1926.

White, Richard Grant. *Studies in Shakespeare.* 1885. 9th edn. Boston: Houghton, Mifflin, 1896.

Wiles, David. *Shakespeare's Clown: Actor and Text in the Elizabethan Playhouse.* Cambridge University Press, 1987.

Williams, Clifford. Promptbook, 1967. National Theatre Archive. (Not in Shattuck.)

Williamson, Audrey. *Old Vic Drama: A Twelve Years' Study of Plays and Players.* London: Rockliff, 1948.

Willis, Susan. *The BBC Shakespeare Plays: Making the Television Canon.* Chapel Hill and London: University of North Carolina Press, 1991.

Wingate, Charles E. L. *Shakespeare's Heroines on the Stage.* New York: Crowell, 1895.

Winter, William. *Ada Rehan: A Study.* New York: Privately printed for Augustin Daly, 1898.

  Shakespeare on the Stage. 2nd series. New York: Moffat, Yard, 1915.

INDEX